Fodors 90
Washington, D.C.

Fodor's Travel Publications, Inc.
New York • Toronto • London • Sydney • Auckland

Fodor's Washington, D.C.

Editor: Anastasia Redmond Mills

Contributors: Rob Andrews, Bob Blake, Mary Case, Michael Dolan, John F. Kelly, Laura M. Kidder, Deborah Papier, Betty Ross, Mary Ellen Schultz, Dinah Spritzer, M. T. Schwartzman, Bruce Walker, Jan Ziegler

Creative Director: Fabrizio La Rocca

Cartographer: David Lindroth

Cover Photograph: Steve Weber

Text Design: Between the Covers

Copyright

Special Sales

Fodor's Travel Publications are available at special discounts for bulk purchases for sales promotions or premiums. Special editions, including personalized covers, excerpts of existing guides, and corporate imprints, can be created in large quantities for special needs. For more information, contact your local bookseller or write to Special Markets, Fodor's Travel Publications, 201 East 50th Street, New York, NY 10022. Inquiries from Canada should be directed to your local Canadian bookseller or sent to Random House of Canada, Ltd., Marketing Dept., 1265 Aerowood Drive, Mississauga, Ontario L4W 1B9. Inquiries from the United Kingdom should be sent to Fodor's Travel Publications, 20 Vauxhall Bridge Road, London SW1V 2SA.

MANUFACTURED IN THE UNITED STATES OF AMERICA

10 9 8 7 6 5 4 3 2 1

CONTENTS

ON THE ROAD WITH FODOR'S

A GOOD TRAVEL GUIDE IS LIKE A wonderful traveling companion. It's charming, it's brimming with sound recommendations and solid ideas, it pulls no punches in describing lodging and dining establishments, and it's consistently full of fascinating facts that make you view what you've traveled to see in a rich new light. In the creation of *Washington, D.C. '96*, we at Fodor's have gone to great lengths to provide you with the very best of all possible traveling companions—and to make your trip the best of all possible vacations.

About Our Writers

The information in these pages is a collaboration of several extraordinary writers.

John F. Kelly, who originally wrote most of this guide, is the editor of *The Washington Post's* "Weekend" section. A new dad, Kelly passed the updating torch to his *Post* colleague, **Bruce Walker.** A D.C.-area resident for most of his life, Walker has perfect credentials for a Fodor's revisor: He's old enough to be a seasoned journalist with an eagle eye for detail, yet hip enough to be up on the latest trends and hot spots about town. Walker, who has been with the *Post* since 1981, updated The Gold Guide and chapters 5 through 10.

Mary Case, who updated chapters two through four, is valuable to this guide for her knowledge of museums—edifices D.C. is not short on. After seven years of managing the Smithsonian Institution's collections of 140 million objects and specimens, Case began an independent consulting firm dedicated to improving the ways museums achieve their missions. She lives on Capitol Hill with her husband and two Basinji mixed breeds that she walks daily at the Congressional Cemetery.

A Manhattanite, editor **Anastasia Mills** visited D.C. three times while working on this guide, and found each attraction more impressive than the next. She believes that a tour of Washington will leave Americans in a patriotic frenzy, no matter what their political leanings or policy beefs.

What's New

New Takes on History

We've added a list of U.S. presidents and a historical time line to this edition—a welcome refresher for those whose memories of American history classes are hazy. While researching presidents, the editor learned a fun fact she'd like to share: The S. in Harry S. Truman doesn't stand for anything.

A New Design

If this is not the first Fodor's guide you've purchased, you'll immediately notice our new look. More readable and easier to use than ever? We think so—and we hope you do, too.

Let Us Do Your Booking

Our writers have scoured Washington, D.C., to come up with an extensive and well-balanced list of the best B&Bs, inns, and hotels, both small and large, new and old. But you don't have to beat the bushes to come up with a reservation. Now we've teamed up with an established hotel-booking service to make it easy for you to secure a room at the property of your choice. It's fast, it's free, and confirmation is guaranteed. If your first choice is booked, the operators can line up your second right away. Just call 800/FODORS–1 or (800/363–6771 (0800/89–1030 when in Great Britain; 0014/800–12–8271 when in Australia; 1800/55–9109 when in Ireland).

Travel Updates

In addition, just before your trip, you may want to order a Fodor's Worldview Travel Update. From local publications all over Washington, D.C., the lively, cosmopolitan editors at Worldview gather information on concerts, plays, opera, dance performances, gallery and museum shows, sports competitions, and other special events that coincide with your visit. See the order blank at the back of this book, call 800/799–9609, or fax 800/799–9619.

And in Washington, D.C.

The **White House Visitor Center** opened in the Commerce Department's Baldrige Hall in March 1995. Run by the Department of Parks, the center disperses timed-entry tickets March through September. (They are often gone by 9 AM.) It is open from Memorial Day to Labor Day, Tuesday through Saturday from 7 to 7; the remainder of the year, its hours are 8 to 5. The center also has historical exhibitions on the architecture, furnishings, and inhabitants of this famous dwelling. In other White House news, **Pennsylvania Avenue** is now closed to vehicular traffic from 15th to 17th streets NW for security reasons. The two-block stretch in front of the executive mansion remains open to pedestrians, bicyclists, and skaters.

1996 is the **150th anniversary of the Smithsonian Institution** and on August 10 there will be a birthday party on the National Mall. Smithsonian museums are trying to outdo one another: the **National Museum of African Art** and the **Arthur M. Sackler Gallery** team to present "Dar-Al-Islam: Art, Life and Cultures of the Islamic World" (late Apr.–late Oct.); "Cosmic Voyage," a new IMAX film, can be seen at the **National Air and Space Museum;** the newly refurbished gem hall has reopened at the **National Museum of Natural History;** and the **National Portrait Gallery** will have two rebel-themed exhibits: "East Coast/West Coast: Poet Rebels of the 1950s" (late Jan.–early May) and "Rebel Painters: The New York School, 1945–1960" (late Jan.–early Jun.).

The **Phillips Collection** celebrates its most famous painting, Renoir's *Luncheon of the Boating Party,* with an exhibit of Impressionist artists such as Monet, Manet, and Pissaro (late Sept.–early Feb. 1997).

The highlight of Washington's bustling restaurant scene continues to be the **Pennsylvania Quarter,** roughly the area from 6th to 13th Streets NW between Pennsylvania Avenue and H Street. This slowly gentrifying neighborhood offers a growing number of fine dining establishments in an area that for years was only inhabited during the day. Southern cooking and South American and Spanish cuisines, with bite-size portions, continue to be popular, although steaks are coming back in vogue.

Clubs and restaurants—catering to punk, jazz, and sports aficionados—continue to pop up on U Street NW between 13th and 16th streets. Manute Bol, the 7-foot, 7-inch basketball star, opened his sports bar and grill, **Spotlight,** last year. Adams-Morgan has some new clubs, among them **Rancho Deluxe,** whose decor is Maya Day of the Dead, with an assortment of bones, masks, and fetishes. For something unusual elsewhere in town, try the Elvis happy hour at **Las Cruces** or the weekly drag bingo night at **Planet Fred.**

Although no new hotels have been built in Washington recently, the trend of multimillion-dollar renovations continues. The city's largest hotel, the 1,505-room **Sheraton Washington,** completed an $8 million renovation of 1,000 of its rooms in 1995, with further renovations planned for 1996. The **Phoenix Park** last year built a new wing on the site of a former fast-food restaurant, adding 61 rooms and suites, three meeting rooms, and a ballroom.

As for politics, last year was a year of big change on both the national and the local levels. The national electorate threw out the Democratic rascals in favor of Republican rascals. Former mayor Marion S. Barry Jr., voted out of office four years ago after a widely publicized drug sting landed him in jail, made an amazing comeback and was re-elected mayor of Washington. It happened just as the city's financial troubles were prompting talk in Congress of returning control of the city to the federal government. Ah, Washington . . .

How to Use this Guide

Organization

Up front is the **Gold Guide,** comprising two sections on gold paper that are chock-full of information about traveling within your destination and traveling in general. Both are in alphabetical order by topic. **Important Contacts A to Z** gives addresses and telephone numbers of organizations and companies that offer destination-related services and detailed information or publications. Here's where you'll find information about how to get to Washington, D.C., from wherever you are. **Smart Travel Tips A to Z,** the Gold Guide's second section, gives specific tips on how to get the most out of your travels, as well as information on how to accomplish what you need to in Washington, D.C.

At the end of the book you'll find Portraits: a historical timeline—a chronology of Washington's history; a list of U.S. presidents; quotes about the nation's capitol from famous Washingtonians, past and present; anecdotes about Washington's many inscriptions; and a description of how our government works. These are followed by suggestions for pretrip reading, both fiction and nonfiction. Here we also recommend movies you can rent on videotape to get you in the mood for your travels.

Stars

Stars in the margin are used to denote highly recommended sights, attractions, hotels, and restaurants.

Restaurant and Hotel Criteria and Price Categories

Restaurants and lodging places are chosen with a view to giving you the cream of the crop in each location and in each price range.

Hotel Facilities

Note that, in general, you incur charges when you use many hotel facilities. We wanted to let you know what facilities a hotel has to offer, but we don't always specify whether or not there's a charge, so when planning a vacation that entails a stay of several days, it's wise to ask what's included in the rate.

Hotel Meal Plans

Assume that hotels operate on the **European Plan** (EP, with no meals) unless we note that they use the **American Plan** (AP, with all meals), the **Modified American Plan** (MAP, with breakfast and dinner daily), or the **Continental Plan** (CP, with a Continental breakfast daily).

Credit Cards

The following abbreviations are used: **AE,** American Express; **D,** Discover; **DC,** Diners Club; **MC,** MasterCard; and **V,** Visa.

Please Write to Us

Everyone who has contributed to *Washington, D.C. '96* has worked hard to make the text accurate. All prices and opening times are based on information supplied to us at press time, and the publisher cannot accept responsibility for any errors that may have occurred. The passage of time will bring changes, so it's always a good idea to call ahead and confirm information when it matters—particularly if you're making a detour to visit specific sights or attractions. When making reservations at a hotel or inn, be sure to mention if you have a disability or are traveling with children, if you prefer a private bath or a certain type of bed, or if you have specific dietary needs or any other concerns.

Were the restaurants we recommended as described? Did our hotel picks exceed your expectations? Did you find a museum we recommended a waste of time? We would love your feedback, positive and negative. If you have complaints, we'll look into them and revise our entries when the facts warrant it. If you've happened upon a special place that we haven't included, we'll pass the information along to the writers so they can check it out. So please send us a letter or postcard (we're at 201 East 50th Street, New York, New York 10022.) We'll look forward to hearing from you. And in the meantime, have a wonderful trip!

Karen Cure
Editorial Director

Washington, D.C. Area

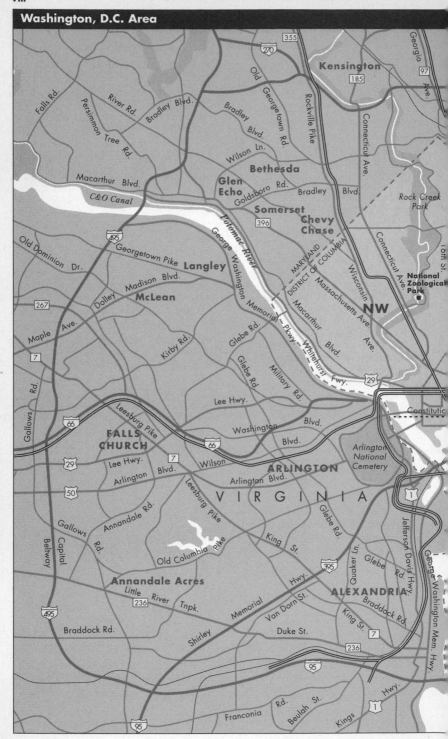

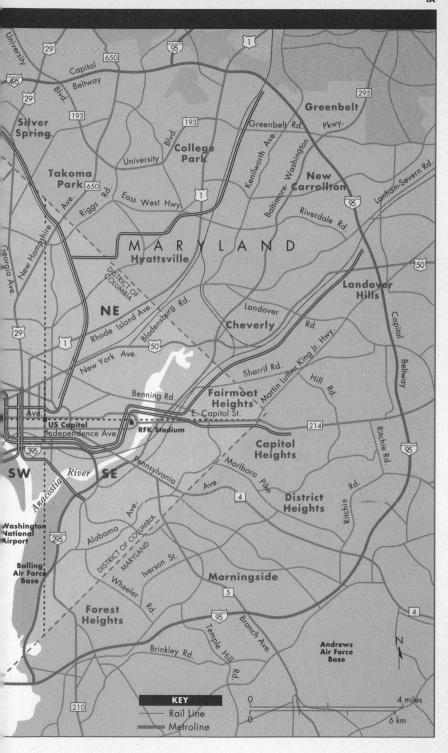

Washington, D.C.

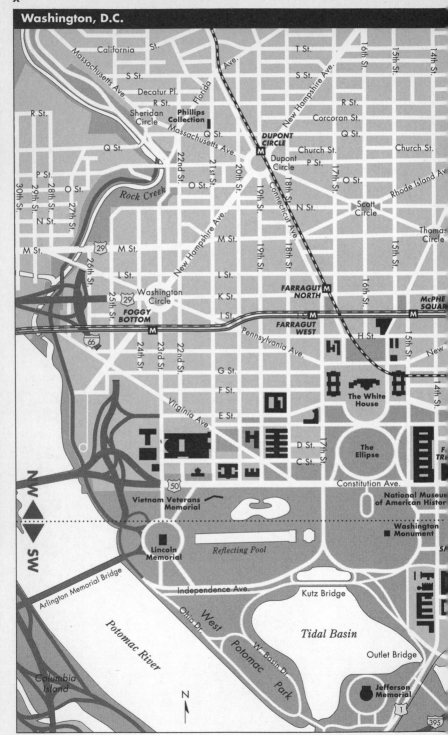

California St.

Massachusetts Ave.

S St.

Decatur Pl.

R St.

Sheridan
Circle

R St.

Q St.

P St.

O St.

M St.

L St.

Washington
Circle

FOGGY
BOTTOM

I-66

Florida Ave.

Phillips
Collection

Massachusetts Ave.

Q St.

O St.

New Hampshire Ave.

M St.

L St.

K St.

I St.

30th St.
29th St.
28th St.
27th St.
26th St.
25th St.
24th St.
23rd St.
22nd St.
21st St.
20th St.
19th St.

Rock Creek

US 29

US 29

T St.

S St.

Corcoran St.

Q St.

DUPONT
CIRCLE

Dupont
Circle

Church St.

P St.

N St.

FARRAGUT
NORTH

FARRAGUT
WEST

Pennsylvania Ave.

18th St.

Connecticut Ave.

19th St.

18th St.

16th St.

15th St.

14th St.

R St.

Church St.

O St.

Rhode Island Av

Scott
Circle

Thomas
Circle

17th St.

16th St.

15th St.

McPHE
SQUAR

New

Virginia Ave.

US 50

G St.

F St.

E St.

D St.

C St.

17th St.

The White
House

The
Ellipse

H St.

Constitution Ave.

14th St.

F.
TR

Vietnam Veterans
Memorial

Lincoln
Memorial

Reflecting Pool

Washington
Monument

National Museum
of American Histor

NW

SW

N

Arlington Memorial Bridge

Independence Ave.

Kutz Bridge

S

Columbia
Island

Potomac River

Ohio Dr.

West Potomac Park

W. Basin Dr.

Tidal Basin

Outlet Bridge

Jefferson
Memorial

US 1

I-395

T St.
S St.
Rhode Island Ave.
R St.
Q St.
Florida Ave.
S St.
Lincoln Rd.
R St.
Q St.
Logan Circle
O St.
New Jersey Ave.
3rd St.
P St.
1st St.
O St.
Vermont Ave.
9th St.
8th St.
7th St.
6th St.
5th St.
4th St.
N St.
N St.
M St.
1st St.
13th St.
12th St.
11th St.
10th St.
Massachusetts Ave.
New York Ave.
M St.
L St.
North Capitol St.
MT. VERNON
Mt. Vernon Square
Washington Convention Center
I St.
H St.
Massachusetts Ave.
New Jersey Ave.
2nd St.
National Postal Museum
G St.
METRO CENTER
F St.
GALLERY PLACE/ CHINATOWN
National Building Museum
JUDICIARY SQUARE
UNION STATION
Columbus Memorial Fountain
E St.
D St.
ARCHIVES/ NAVY MEMORIAL
395
Louisiana Ave.
NE
 madison Dr.
National Museum of Natural History
Pennsylvania Ave.
National Gallery of Art
Smithsonian Institution
THE MALL
National Air and Space Museum
Jefferson Dr.
US Capitol
E. Capitol St.
SONIAN
Independence Ave.
Maryland Ave.
Canal St.
SE
C St.
L'ENFANT PLAZA
D St.
D St.
CAPITOL SOUTH
E St.
FEDERAL CENTER SW
395
Southwest Fwy.
New Jersey Ave.
Virginia Ave.
G St.
0   500 yards
0   500 meters
Francis Case Memorial Bridge
SW   SE
395
Ave.

NW   NE

Washington, D.C. Metro System

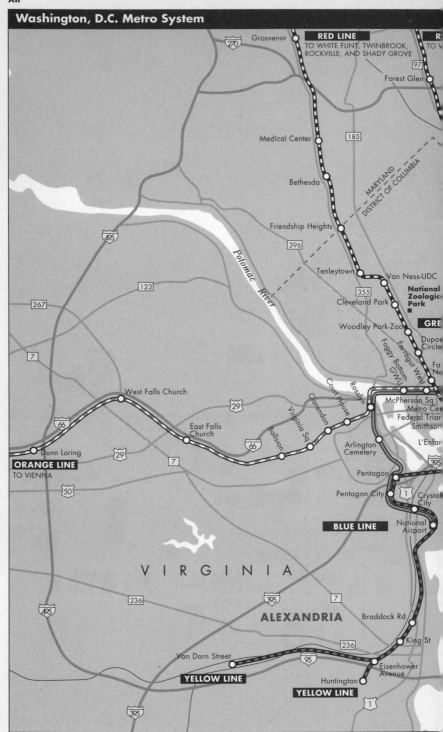

270
Grosvenor

RED LINE
TO WHITE FLINT, TWINBROOK,
ROCKVILLE, AND SHADY GROVE

R
TO

97
Forest Glen

185
Medical Center

MARYLAND
DISTRICT OF COLUMBIA

Bethesda

495
Friendship Heights

396

Potomac River

123
Tenleytown
Van Ness-UDC

267
355
**National
Zoologic
Park**
Cleveland Park

7
Woodley Park-Zoo
GRE

Dupo
Circle

West Falls Church
Court House
Rosslyn
Farragut West
GWU
Fa
Ne

29
Clarendon
McPherson Sq
Metro Ce

East Falls
Church
Virginia Sq
Federal Triar
Smithson

66
66
Ballston
Arlington
Cemetery
L'Enfar

Dunn Loring
29
7
Pentagon
395

ORANGE LINE
TO VIENNA
50

Pentagon City
1
Crystal
City

BLUE LINE
National
Airport

V I R G I N I A

495
236
395
7
Braddock Rd

ALEXANDRIA

236
King St

Van Dorn Street
95
Eisenhower
Avenue

YELLOW LINE
Huntington
YELLOW LINE
1

395

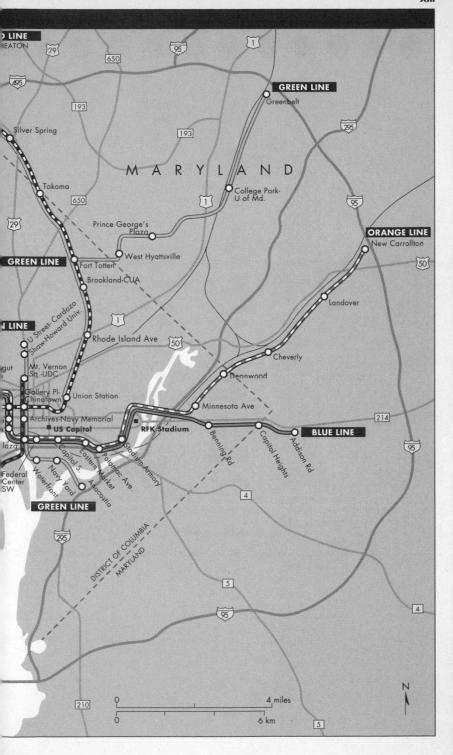

GREEN LINE
WHEATON

GREEN LINE
Greenbelt

M A R Y L A N D

Silver Spring

Takoma

College Park-
U of Md.

Prince George's
Plaza

GREEN LINE

ORANGE LINE
New Carrollton

West Hyattsville

Fort Totten

Brookland-CUA

Landover

N LINE

U Street-Cardozo
Shaw-Howard Univ.

Rhode Island Ave

Cheverly

Mt. Vernon
Sq.-UDC

Deanwood

Gallery Pl-
Chinatown

Union Station

Minnesota Ave

Archives-Navy Memorial

US Capitol

RFK Stadium

BLUE LINE

laza

Stadium-Armory

Eastern Market

Benning Rd

Capitol Heights

Addison Rd

Federal
Center
SW

Waterfront

Navy Yard

Capitol S.

Potomac Ave

Anacostia

GREEN LINE

DISTRICT OF COLUMBIA
MARYLAND

0   4 miles
0   6 km

N

World Time Zones

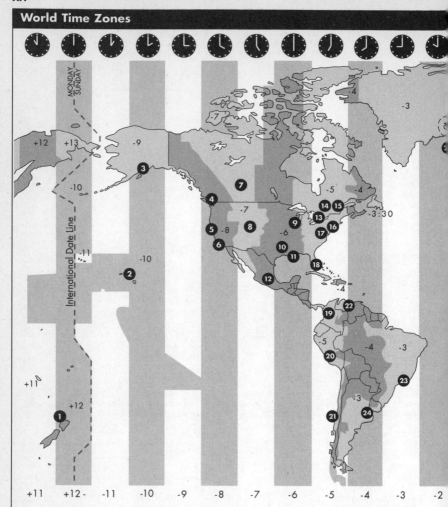

Numbers below vertical bands relate each zone to Greenwich Mean Time (0 hrs.).
Local times frequently differ from these general indications,
as indicated by light-face numbers on map.

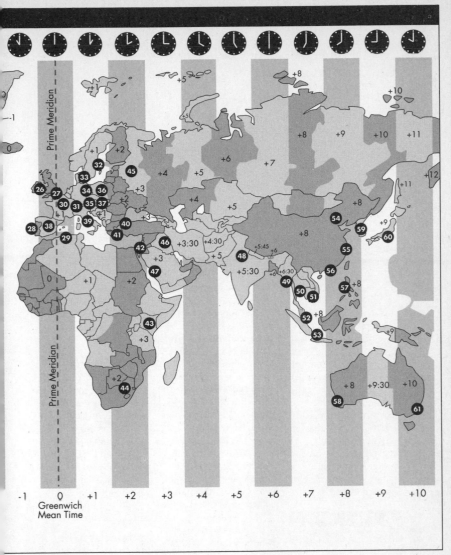

THE GOLD GUIDE / IMPORTANT CONTACTS

IMPORTANT CONTACTS A TO Z

An Alphabetical Listing of Publications and Organizations, and Companies That Will Help You Before, During, and After Your Trip

No single travel resource can give you every detail about every topic that might interest or concern you at the various stages of your journey—when you're planning your trip, while you're on the road, and after you get back home. The following organizations, books, and brochures will supplement the information in *Washington, D.C. '96*. For related information, including both basic tips on visiting Washington, D.C., and background information on many of the topics below, study Smart Travel Tips A to Z, the section that follows Important Contacts A to Z.

A

AIR TRAVEL

The major gateways to Washington, D.C., include **National Airport** (☎ 703/419–8000), in Virginia, 4 miles south of downtown Washington; **Dulles International Airport** (☎ 703/661–2700), 26 miles west of Washington; and **Baltimore-Washington International (BWI) Airport** (☎ 410/859–7100), in Maryland, about 25 miles northeast of Washington. Flying time is one hour from New York, two hours from

Chicago, and five hours, 40 minutes from Los Angeles.

CARRIERS

Major air carriers serving the three airports include **Air Canada** (☎ 800/776–3000), **Air France** (☎ 800/237–2747), **All Nippon Airways** (☎ 800/235–9262), **America West** (☎ 800/235–9292), **American Airlines** (☎ 800/433–7300), **British Airways** (☎ 800/247–9297), **Business Express** (☎ 800/345–3400), **Continental** (☎ 800/525–0280), **Delta** (☎ 800/221–1212), **El Al** (☎ 800/223–6700), **Icelandair** (☎ 800/223–5500), **Japan Air Lines** (☎ 800/525–3663), **KLM Royal Dutch** (☎ 800/374–7747), **Lufthansa** (☎ 800/645–3880), **Northwest** (☎ 800/225–2525), **Saudi Arabian Airlines** (☎ 800/472–8342), **Swissair** (☎ 800/221–4750), **TWA** (☎ 800/221–2000), **United** (☎ 800/241–6522), and **USAir** (☎ 800/428–4322).

For inexpensive, no-frills flights, contact **MarkAir** (☎ 800/627–5247), **Midwest Express** (☎ 800/452–2022), **Private Jet** (☎ 404/231–7571, 800/546–7571, or 800/949–9400), and **ValuJet**

(☎ 404/994–8258 or 800/825-8538).

COMPLAINTS

To register complaints about charter and scheduled airlines, contact the U.S. Department of Transportation's **Office of Consumer Affairs** (400 7th St. NW, Washington, DC 20590, ☎ 202/366–2220 or 800/322–7873).

CONSOLIDATORS

Established consolidators selling to the public include **Euram Tours** (1522 K St. NW, Suite 430, Washington DC, 20005, ☎ 800/848–6789) and **TFI Tours International** (34 W. 32nd St., New York, NY 10001, ☎ 212/736–1140 or 800/745–8000).

PUBLICATIONS

For general information about charter carriers, ask for the Office of Consumer Affairs' brochure **"Plane Talk: Public Charter Flights."** The Department of Transportation also publishes a 58-page booklet, **"Fly Rights"** (Consumer Information Center, Dept. 133-B, Pueblo, CO 81009; $1.75).

For other tips and hints, consult the Consumers Union's monthly **"Consumer Reports Travel**

Letter" (Box 53629, Boulder CO 80322, ☎ 800/234–1970; $39 a year) and the newsletter *"Travel Smart"* (40 Beechdale Rd., Dobbs Ferry, NY 10522, ☎ 800/327–3633; $37 a year); *The Official Frequent Flyer Guidebook,* by Randy Petersen (4715-C Town Center Dr., Colorado Springs, CO 80916, ☎ 719/597–8899 or 800/487–8893; $14.99 plus $3 shipping); *Airfare Secrets Exposed,* by Sharon Tyler and Matthew Wonder (Universal Information Publishing; $16.95 plus $3.75 shipping from Sandcastle Publishing, Box 3070-A, South Pasadena, CA 91031, ☎ 213/255–3616 or 800/655–0053); and *202 Tips Even the Best Business Travelers May Not Know,* by Christopher McGinnis (Irwin Professional Publishing, Box 52927, Atlanta, GA 30355, ☎ 708/789–4000 or 800/634–3966; $10 plus $3 shipping).

AIRPORT TRANSFERS

BY BUS

National and Dulles airports are served continuously by **Washington Flyer** (☎ 703/685–1400). The ride from National to downtown takes 20 minutes and costs $8 ($14 round-trip); from Dulles, the 45-minute ride costs $16 ($26 round-trip). The bus takes you to 1517 K Street NW, where you can board a free shuttle bus that serves downtown hotels. The shuttle bus will also transport you from your hotel to the K Street address to catch the main airport bus on your return journey. Washington Flyer also provides service to Maryland and Virginia suburbs. Fares may be paid in cash or with Visa or MasterCard; children under age six ride free.

BWI SuperShuttle buses (☎ 800/809–7080) leave BWI every hour for 1517 K Street NW. The 65-minute ride costs $15 ($25 round-trip); drivers accept traveler's checks and major credit cards in addition to cash.

Some hotels provide van service to and from the airports; check with your hotel.

BY LIMOUSINE

Call at least a day ahead and **Diplomat Limousine** (☎ 703/461–6800) will have a limousine waiting for you at the airport. The ride downtown from National or Dulles is about $75; it's $90 from BWI. **Private Car** (☎ 800/685–0888) has a counter at BWI Airport and charges $62 from there to downtown; or call ahead to have a car waiting for you at National ($45) or Dulles ($75).

BY SUBWAY

If you are coming into Washington National Airport, have little to carry, and are staying at a hotel near a subway stop, it makes sense to take the Metro downtown. The station is within walking distance of the baggage claim area, but a free airport shuttle stops outside each terminal and brings you to the National Airport station. The Metro ride downtown takes about 20 minutes and costs either $1.10 or $1.40, depending on the time of day.

BY TAXI

Expect to pay about $13 to get from National Airport to downtown, $45 from Dulles, and $50 from BWI. Unscrupulous cabbies prey on out-of-towners, so if the fare strikes you as astronomical, get the driver's name and cab number and threaten to call the **D.C. Taxicab Commission** (☎ 202/645–6018). A $1.25 airport surcharge is added to the total at National.

BY TRAIN

Free shuttle buses carry passengers between airline terminals and the train station at BWI Airport. **Amtrak** (☎ 800/872–7245) and **Maryland Rail Commuter Service** (MARC, ☎ 800/325–7245) trains run between BWI and Washington's Union Station from around 6 AM to midnight. The cost of the 40-minute ride is $10 on an Amtrak train, $4.50 on a MARC train (weekdays only).

B BETTER BUSINESS BUREAUS

Contact the **Better Business Bureau of Washington, D.C.** (1012 14th Street NW, 9th Floor, Washington, DC 20005, ☎ 202/393-8000). For other local contacts, consult the

THE GOLD GUIDE / IMPORTANT CONTACTS

Council of Better Business Bureaus (4200 Wilson Blvd., Arlington, VA 22203, ☎ 703/276–0100).

BUS TRAVEL

Washington is a major terminal for **Greyhound Bus Lines** (1005 1st St. NE, ☎ 202/289–5160 or 800/231–2222). The company also has stations in nearby Silver Spring and Laurel, Maryland, and in Arlington and Springfield, Virginia. Check with your local Greyhound ticket office for prices and schedules.

WITHIN WASHINGTON

For schedule and route information, contact the **Washington Metropolitan Area Transit Authority** (WMATA, ☎ 202/637–7000, TTY 202/638–3780; open daily 6 AM–11:30 PM).

C

CAR RENTAL

Major car-rental companies represented in Washington include **Alamo** (☎ 800/327–9633, 0800/272–2000 in the United Kingdom); **Avis** (☎ 800/331–1212, 800/879–2847 in Canada); **Budget** (☎ 800/527–0700, 0800/181–181 in the United Kingdom); **Hertz** (☎ 800/654–3131, 800/263–0600 in Canada, 0181/679–1799 in the United Kingdom); and **National** (☎ 800/227–7368, 0181/950–5050 in the United Kingdom, where it is known as Europcar). In Washington, D.C., rates begin at $42 a day and $150 a week for an economy car

with unlimited mileage. This does not include tax, which is 8% on car rentals.

CHILDREN AND TRAVEL

FLYING

Look into **"Flying with Baby"** (Third Street Press, Box 261250, Littleton, CO 80126, ☎ 303/595–5959; $5.95 plus $1 shipping), cowritten by a flight attendant. **"Kids and Teens in Flight,"** free from the U.S. Department of Transportation's Office of Consumer Affairs, offers tips for children flying alone. Every two years the February issue of *Family Travel Times* (*see* Know-How, *below*) details children's services on three dozen airlines.

KNOW-HOW

Family Travel Times, published 10 times a year by Travel with Your Children (TWYCH, 45 W. 18th St., New York, NY 10011, ☎ 212/206–0688; annual subscription $55), covers destinations, types of vacations, and modes of travel.

The *Family Travel Guides* catalogue (☎ 510/527–5849; $1 postage) lists about 200 books and articles on family travel. *Where Should We Take the Kids? The Northeast,* straight talk by parents for parents, is loaded with great ideas and family-friendly places to stay and eat (Random House, ☎ 800/733–3000; $16). *Great Vacations with Your*

Kids, by Dorothy Jordon and Marjorie Cohen (Penguin USA, 120 Woodbine St., Bergenfield, NJ 07621, ☎ 201/387–0600 or 800/253–6476; $13) and *Traveling with Children—And Enjoying It,* by Arlene K. Butler (Globe Pequot Press, Box 833, 6 Business Park Rd., Old Saybrook, CT 06475, ☎ 203/395–0440 or 800/243–0495, 800/962–0973 in CT; $11.95 plus $3 shipping) help you to plan your trip with children, from toddlers to teens. Also check *Take Your Baby and Go! A Guide for Traveling with Babies, Toddlers and Young Children,* by Sheri Andrews, Judy Bordeaux, and Vivian Vasquez (Bear Creek Publications, 2507 Minor Ave., Seattle, WA 98102, ☎ 206/322–7604 or 800/326–6566; $5.95 plus $1.50 shipping).

LOCAL INFO

A Kid's Guide to Washington, D.C. (Gulliver Books/Harcourt Brace Jovanovich, 111 5th Ave., New York, NY 10003; $6.95) includes games, photographs, maps, and a travel diary. *Kidding Around Washington, D.C., A Young Person's Guide to the City,* by Anne Pedersen (John Muir Publications, Box 613, Santa Fe, NM 87504, ☎ 800/888–7504; $9.95) highlights the sights in each neighborhood that are of most interest to children; it includes maps of the major sectors of the city.

TOUR OPERATORS

Contact **Grandtravel** (6900 Wisconsin Ave., Suite 706, Chevy Chase, MD 20815, ☎ 301/986–0790 or 800/247–7651), which has tours for people traveling with grandchildren ages 7 to 17.

CUSTOMS

CANADIANS

Contact **Revenue Canada** (2265 St. Laurent Blvd. S, Ottawa, Ontario, K1G 4K3, ☎ 613/993–0534) for a copy of the free brochure **"I Declare/Je Déclare"** and for details on duties that exceed the standard duty-free limit.

U.K. CITIZENS

HM Customs and Excise (Dorset House, Stamford St., London SE1 9NG, ☎ 0171/202–4227) can answer questions about U.K. customs regulations and publishes **"A Guide for Travellers,"** which details standard procedures and import rules.

D
FOR TRAVELERS
WITH DISABILITIES

COMPLAINTS

To register complaints under the provisions of the Americans with Disabilities Act, contact the U.S. Department of Justice's **Public Access Section** (Box 66738, Washington, DC 20035, ☎ 202/514–0301, FAX 202/307–1198, TTY 202/514–0383).

ORGANIZATIONS

FOR TRAVELERS WITH HEARING IMPAIRMENTS➤ Contact the **American Academy of Otolaryn-**

gology (1 Prince St., Alexandria, VA 22314, ☎ 703/836–4444, FAX 703/683–5100, TTY 703/519–1585).

FOR TRAVELERS WITH MOBILITY PROBLEMS➤ Contact the **Information Center for Individuals with Disabilities** (Fort Point Pl., 27–43 Wormwood St., Boston, MA 02210, ☎ 617/727–5540, 800/462–5015 in MA, TTY 617/345–9743); **Mobility International USA** (Box 10767, Eugene, OR 97440, ☎ and TTY 503/343–1284; FAX 503/343–6812), the U.S. branch of an international organization based in Belgium (*see below*) that has affiliates in 30 countries; **MossRehab Hospital Travel Information Service** (1200 W. Tabor Rd., Philadelphia, PA 19141, ☎ 215/456–9603, TTY 215/456–9602); the **Society for the Advancement of Travel for the Handicapped** (347 5th Ave., Suite 610, New York, NY 10016, ☎ 212/447–7284, FAX 212/725–8253); the **Travel Industry and Disabled Exchange** (TIDE, 5435 Donna Ave., Tarzana, CA 91356, ☎ 818/344–3640, FAX 818/344–0078); and **Travelin' Talk** (Box 3534, Clarksville, TN 37043, ☎ 615/552–6670, FAX 615/552–1182).

FOR TRAVELERS WITH VISION IMPAIRMENTS➤ Contact the **American Council of the Blind** (1155 15th St. NW, Suite 720, Washington, DC 20005, ☎ 202/467–5081, FAX 202/467–5085) or the **American Foundation**

for the Blind (15 W. 16th St., New York, NY 10011, ☎ 212/620–2000, TTY 212/620–2158).

In the United Kingdom, contact the **Royal Association for Disability and Rehabilitation** (RADAR, 12 City Forum, 250 City Rd., London EC1V 8AF, ☎ 0171/250–3222) or **Mobility International** (Rue de Manchester 25, B1070 Brussels, Belgium, ☎ 00–322–410–6297), an international clearinghouse of travel information for people with disabilities.

PUBLICATIONS

Several free publications are available from the U.S. Information Center (Box 100, Pueblo, CO 81009, ☎ 719/948–3334): **"New Horizons for the Air Traveler with a Disability"** (address to Dept. 355A), describing legally mandated changes; the pocket-size **"Fly Smart"** (Dept. 575B), good on flight safety; and the Airport Operators Council's worldwide **"Access Travel: Airports"** (Dept. 575A).

Fodor's **Great American Vacations for Travelers with Disabilities** (available in bookstores or call 800/533–6478; $18) details accessible attractions, restaurants, and hotels in U.S. destinations. The 500-page **Travelin' Talk Directory** (☎ 615/552–6670; $35) lists people and organizations who help travelers with disabilities. For specialist travel agents worldwide, consult the **Directory of Travel Agencies for the Dis-**

THE GOLD GUIDE / IMPORTANT CONTACTS

abled by Helen Hecker (Twin Peaks Press; Disability Bookshop, Box 129, Vancouver, WA 98666, ☎ 206/694–2462 or 800/637–2256; $19.95 plus $3.50 shipping and handling).

The **Information, Protection and Advocacy Center for People with Disabilities** (4455 Connecticut Ave. NW, Suite B100, 20008, ☎ 202/966–8081, TTY 202/966–2500) publishes "Access Washington: A Guide to Metropolitan Washington for the Physically Disabled" for $4. The Smithsonian Institution (☎ 202/786–2942, TTY 202/357–1729) offers the booklet "Smithsonian Institution: A Guide for Disabled Visitors." Neither of these guides is up to date. Baltimore/Washington International Airport (Marketing and Development Office, Box 8766, BWI Airport, MD 21240, ☎ 410/859–7100) publishes the free brochure "BWI Special Services & Access Guide."

TRAVEL AGENCIES AND TOUR OPERATORS

The Americans with Disabilities Act requires that travel firms serve the needs of all travelers. However, some agencies and operators specialize in making group and individual arrangements for travelers with disabilities, among them is **Access Adventures** (206 Chestnut Ridge Rd., Rochester, NY 14624, ☎ 716/889–9096), run by a former physi-

cal-rehab counselor. In addition, many of the operators and agencies listed below can also arrange vacations for travelers with disabilities.

FOR TRAVELERS WITH MOBILITY IMPAIRMENTS➤ A number of operators specialize in working with travelers with mobility impairments. Two are: **Hinsdale Travel Service** (201 E. Ogden Ave., Suite 100, Hinsdale, IL 60521, ☎ 708/325–1335 or 800/303–5521), a travel agency that will give you access to the services of wheelchair traveler Janice Perkins; and **Wheelchair Journeys** (16979 Redmond Way, Redmond, WA 98052, ☎ 206/885–2210), which can handle arrangements worldwide.

FOR TRAVELERS WITH DEVELOPMENTAL DISABILITIES➤ Such travelers and their families can contact the nonprofit **New Directions** (5276 Hollister Ave., Suite 207, Santa Barbara, CA 93111, ☎ 805/967–2841) as well as the general-interest operations above.

DISCOUNT CLUBS

Options include **Entertainment Travel Editions** (Box 1068, Trumbull, CT 06611, ☎ 800/445–4137; fee $25–$48 depending on destination); **Great American Traveler** (Box 27965, Salt Lake City, UT 84127, ☎ 800/548–2812; $49.95 annually); **Moment's Notice Discount Travel Club** (425 Madison Ave., New York, NY 10017, ☎ 212/486–0503; $25

annually, single or family); **Privilege Card** (3391 Peachtree Rd. NE, Suite 110, Atlanta GA 30326, ☎ 404/262–0222 or 800/236–9732; $74.95 annually); **Travelers Advantage** (CUC Travel Service, 49 Music Sq. W, Nashville, TN 37203, ☎ 800/548–1116 or 800/648–4037; $49 annually, single or family); and **Worldwide Discount Travel Club** (1674 Meridian Ave., Miami Beach, FL 33139, ☎ 305/534–2082; $50 annually for family, $40 single).

DRIVING

I–95 skirts Washington as part of the Beltway, the six- to eight-lane highway that encircles the city. The eastern half of the Beltway is labeled both I–95 and I–495; the western half is just I–495. If you are coming from the south, take I–95 to I–395 and cross the 14th Street Bridge to 14th Street in the District. From the north, stay on I–95 south before heading west on Route 50, the John Hanson Highway, which turns into New York Avenue.

I–66 approaches the city from the southwest, but you may not be able to use it during weekday rush hours, when high-occupancy vehicle (HOV) restrictions apply: Cars must carry at least three people from 6:30 AM to 9 AM traveling eastbound inside the Beltway (I–495) and 4 PM to 6:30 PM traveling westbound. If you're traveling at off-peak hours or have enough people in your car to satisfy the rules, you can get downtown by taking I–66 across the Theodore Roosevelt Bridge to Constitution Avenue.

I–270 approaches Washington from the northwest before hitting I–495. To get downtown, take I–495 east to Connecticut Avenue south, toward Chevy Chase.

E
EMERGENCIES

Dial 911 for **police, fire,** or **ambulance** in an emergency.

DOCTOR

Prologue (☎ 202/362–8677) is a referral service that locates doctors, dentists, and urgent-care clinics in the greater Washington area. The hospital closest to downtown is **George Washington University Hospital** (901 23rd St. NW, ☎ 202/994–3211, emergencies only).

DENTIST

The **D.C. Dental Society** (☎ 202/547–7615) operates a referral line weekdays 8–4.

24-HOUR PHARMACY

CVS Pharmacy operates 24-hour pharmacies at 14th Street and Thomas Circle NW (☎ 202/628–0720) and at 7 Dupont Circle NW (☎ 202/785–1466).

G
GAY AND
LESBIAN TRAVEL

ORGANIZATIONS

The **International Gay Travel Association** (Box 4974, Key West, FL

33041, ☎ 800/448–8550), a consortium of 800 businesses, can supply names of travel agents and tour operators.

PUBLICATIONS

The premiere international travel magazine for gays and lesbians is *Our World* (1104 N. Nova Rd., Suite 251, Daytona Beach, FL 32117, ☎ 904/441–5367; $35 for 10 issues). The 16-page monthly *"Out & About"* (☎ 203/789–8518 or 800/929–2268; $49 for 10 issues), covers gay-friendly resorts, hotels, cruise lines, and airlines.

TOUR OPERATORS

Toto Tours (1326 W. Albion, Suite 3W, Chicago, IL 60626, ☎ 312/274–8686 or 800/565–1241) has group tours worldwide.

TRAVEL AGENCIES

The largest agencies serving gay travelers are **Advance Travel** (10700 Northwest Freeway, Suite 160, Houston, TX 77092, ☎ 713/682–2002 or 800/695–0880); **Islanders/Kennedy Travel** (183 W. 10th St., New York, NY 10014, ☎ 212/242–3222 or 800/988–1181); **Now Voyager** (4406 18th St., San Francisco, CA 94114, ☎ 415/626–1169 or 800/255–6951); and **Yellowbrick Road** (1500 W. Balmoral Ave., Chicago, IL 60640, ☎ 312/561–1800 or 800/642–2488). **Skylink Women's Travel** (746 Ashland Ave., Santa Monica, CA 90405, ☎ 310/452–0506 or 800/225–5759) works with lesbians.

I
INSURANCE

Travel insurance covering baggage, health, and trip cancellation or interruptions is available from **Access America** (Box 90315, Richmond, VA 23286, ☎ 804/285–3300 or 800/284–8300); **Carefree Travel Insurance** (Box 9366, 100 Garden City Plaza, Garden City, NY 11530, ☎ 516/294–0220 or 800/323–3149); **Near Travel Services** (Box 1339, Calumet City, IL 60409, ☎ 708/868–6700 or 800/654–6700); **Tele-Trip** (Mutual of Omaha Plaza, Box 31716, Omaha, NE 68131, ☎ 800/228–9792); **Travel Insured International** (Box 280568, East Hartford, CT 06128-0568, ☎ 203/528–7663 or 800/243–3174); **Travel Guard International** (1145 Clark St., Stevens Point, WI 54481, ☎ 715/345–0505 or 800/826–1300); and **Wallach & Company** (107 W. Federal St., Box 480, Middleburg, VA 22117, ☎ 703/687–3166 or 800/237–6615).

IN THE U.K.

The **Association of British Insurers** (51 Gresham St., London EC2V 7HQ, ☎ 0171/600–3333; 30 Gordon St., Glasgow G1 3PU, ☎ 0141/226–3905; Scottish Provident Bldg., Donegall Sq. W, Belfast BT1 6JE, ☎ 01232/249176; and other locations) gives advice by phone and publishes the free *"Holiday Insurance,"* which

THE GOLD GUIDE / IMPORTANT CONTACTS

sets out typical policy provisions and costs.

L
LODGING

APARTMENT AND VILLA RENTAL

Among the companies to contact are **Hometours International** (Box 11503, Knoxville, TN 37939, ☎ 615/588–8722 or 800/367–4668) and **Rent-a-Home International** (7200 34th Ave. NW, Seattle, WA 98117, ☎ 206/789–9377 or 800/488–7368).

M
MONEY MATTERS

ATMS

For specific **Cirrus** locations in the United States and Canada, call 800/424–7787. For **Plus** locations in the United States, call 800/843–7587 and enter the area code and first three digits of the number you're calling from (or of the calling area where you want an ATM).

WIRING FUNDS

Funds can be wired via **American Express MoneyGram℠** (☎ 800/926–9400 from the United States and Canada for locations and information) or **Western Union** (☎ 800/325–6000 for agent locations or to send using MasterCard or Visa, 800/321–2923 in Canada).

P
PASSPORTS
AND VISAS

U.K. CITIZENS

For fees, documentation requirements, and to get

an emergency passport, call the **London Passport Office** (☎ 0171/271–3000). For visa information, call the **U.S. Embassy Visa Information Line** (☎ 0891/200–290; calls cost 49p per minute or 39p per minute cheap rate) or write the **U.S. Embassy Visa Branch** (5 Upper Grosvenor St., London W1A 2JB). If you live in Northern Ireland, write the **U.S. Consulate General** (Queen's House, Queen St., Belfast BTI 6EO).

PHOTO HELP

The **Kodak Information Center** (☎ 800/242–2424) answers consumer questions about film and photography. Pick up the *Kodak Guide to Shooting Great Travel Pictures* (Random House, ☎ 800/733–3000; $16.50), which gives you tips on how to take travel pictures like a pro.

R
RAIL TRAVEL

More than 80 trains a day arrive at Washington, D.C.'s **Union Station** on Capitol Hill (50 Massachusetts Ave. NE, ☎ 202/484–7540 or 800/872–7245). Also *see* Airport Transfers, *above.*

S
SENIOR CITIZENS

EDUCATIONAL TRAVEL

The nonprofit **Elderhostel** (75 Federal St., 3rd Floor, Boston, MA 02110, ☎ 617/426–7788), for people 60 and older, has offered inexpensive study programs since 1975.

The nearly 2,000 courses cover everything from marine science to Greek myths and cowboy poetry. Fees for programs in the United States and Canada, which usually last one week, run about $300, not including transportation.

ORGANIZATIONS

Contact the **American Association of Retired Persons** (AARP, 601 E St. NW, Washington, DC 20049, ☎ 202/434–2277; $8 per person or couple annually). Its Purchase Privilege Program gets members discounts on lodging, car rentals, and sightseeing, and the AARP Motoring Plan furnishes domestic trip-routing information and emergency road-service aid for an annual fee of $39.95 per person or couple ($59.95 for a premium version).

For other discounts on lodgings, car rentals, and other travel products, along with magazines and newsletters, contact the **National Council of Senior Citizens** (1331 F St. NW, Washington, DC 20004, ☎ 202/347–8800; membership $12 annually) and *Mature Outlook* (6001 N. Clark St., Chicago, IL 60660, ☎ 312/465–6466 or 800/336–6330; subscription $9.95 annually).

PUBLICATIONS

The 50+ Traveler's Guidebook: Where to Go, Where to Stay, What to Do, by Anita Williams and Merrimac Dillon (St. Martin's

Press, 175 5th Ave., New York, NY 10010, ☎ 212/674–5151 or 800/288–2131; $12.95), offers many useful tips. **"The Mature Traveler"** (Box 50820, Reno, NV 89513; $29.95), a monthly newsletter, covers travel deals.

SIGHTSEEING

ORIENTATION TOURS

Tourmobile buses (☎ 202/554–7950 or 202/554–5100), authorized by the National Park Service, stop at 18 historic sights between the Capitol and Arlington National Cemetery; the route includes the White House and the museums on the Mall. Tickets are $10 for adults, $5 for children 3–11.

Old Town Trolley Tours (☎ 301/985–3021), orange-and-green motorized trolleys, take in the main downtown sights and also foray into Georgetown and the upper northwest, stopping at out of the way attractions such as Washington National Cathedral. Tickets are $16 for adults, $8 for children 3–12, free for children under three.

BOAT TOURS

D.C. Ducks (1323 Pennsylvania Ave. NW, ☎ 202/966–3825) offers 90-minute tours in their converted World War II amphibious vehicles. After an hour-long road tour of prominent sights, the tour moves from land to water, as the vehicle is piloted into the waters of the Potomac for a 30-minute boat's-eye view

of the city. Tours run continuously from 10 AM to 4 PM from March through November. Prices are $16 adults, $14 senior citizens, $8 ages 12 and younger.

The enclosed boat **The Dandy** (Prince St., between Duke and King Sts., Alexandria, VA, ☎ 703/683–6076 or 703/683–6090) cruises up the Potomac past the Lincoln Memorial to the Kennedy Center and Georgetown. Lunch cruises board weekdays starting at 10:30 AM and weekends starting at 11:30 AM. Dinner cruises board Monday–Thursday at 6 PM, Friday at 7:30 PM, and Sunday at 7:15 PM. A $21 "midnight cruise" boards at 11:30 PM April–October at Washington Harbour in Georgetown or in Alexandria. Prices are $26–$30 for lunch and $48–$56 for dinner.

The **Spirit of Washington** (Pier 4, 6th and Water Sts. SW, ☎ 202/554–8000), offers lunch cruises Tuesday–Saturday at 11:30 AM and a Sunday brunch cruise at 1. Evening cruises board at 6:30 PM and include dinner and a floor show. Adult "Moonlight Party" cruises board Friday and Saturday at 11:15 PM. Prices range from $21 per person for the moonlight cruise to $55 for dinner on Friday or Saturday night. A sister ship, the **Potomac Spirit,** sails to Mount Vernon, mid-March–October, Tuesday–Sunday. During peak tourist season (mid-June–August), boats depart at 9 AM

and 2 PM. From mid-March through mid-June and September through October, boats leave at 9 AM only. Prices are $22 adults, $19.75 senior citizens, $13.25 children 6–12.

BUS TOURS

All About Town, Inc. (519 6th St. NW, ☎ 202/393–3696) has half-day, all-day, two-day, and twilight bus tours that drive by some sights (e.g., memorials, museums, government buildings) and stop at others. Tours leave from the company's office at 7:45 AM March–September and at 8:15 AM October–February. An all-day tour costs $30 for adults, $15 for children.

Gray Line Tours (☎ 301/386–8300) has a four-hour tour of Washington, Embassy Row, and Arlington National Cemetery that leaves Union Station at 8:30 AM and 2 PM (at 2 PM only November–March; adults $22, children 3–11 $11); tours of Mount Vernon and Alexandria depart at 8:30 AM (adults $20, children, $10). An all-day trip combining both tours leaves at 8:30 AM (adults $36, children $18).

PERSONAL GUIDES

Personal tour services include **Guide Service of Washington** (733 15th St NW, Woodward Bldg., Suite 1040, Washington, DC 20005, ☎ 202/628–2842); **A Tour de Force** (Box 2782, Washington, DC 20013, ☎ 703/525–2948), and **Guide Post, Inc.** (11141 Georgia Ave., Suite A-8, Wheaton, MD 20902, ☎ 301/946–7949). **Sunny Odem** (2530D South Walter Reed Dr., Arlington, VA 22206, ☎ 703/379–1633) offers custom photography tours.

SPECIAL-INTEREST TOURS

Special tours of government buildings—including the Archives, the Capitol, the FBI Building, the Supreme Court, and the White House—can be arranged through your representative's or senator's office. Limited numbers of these so-called VIP tickets are available, so plan up to six months in advance of your trip. With these special passes, your tour will often take you through rooms not normally open to the public.

Government buildings and offices that have regularly scheduled tours include: The **Government Printing Office** (H and North Capitol Sts. NW, ☎ 202/512–1995), which offers free tours Tuesday–Thursday at 10 AM; the **Old Executive Office Building** (Pennsylvania Ave. and 17th St. NW, ☎ 202/395–5895), which is open for tours Saturday 9–noon; and the **Naval Observatory** (34th St. and Massachusetts Ave. NW, ☎ 202/653–1507 or 202/653–1541 for group reservations), which offers tours every Monday night, except on Federal holidays. In addition, tours of the opulent 18th-and early-19th-century **State Department Diplomatic**

Reception Rooms (23rd and C Sts. NW, ☎ 202/647–3241) are given weekdays at 9:30, 10:30, and 2:45; the **Voice of America** (330 Independence Ave. SW, ☎ 202/619–3919) offers free 45-minute tours Tuesday–Thursday at 10:40, 1:40, and 2:40; and the **Washington, D.C., Post Office** (Brentwood Rd. NE between Rhode Island and New York Aves., ☎ 202/636–1200) has free tours weekdays between 9 and 4, and does not admit children under 7.

Reservations are required for tours of all of these sites except the Naval Observatory, which admits the first 90 people in line at the observatory's south gate across from the New Zealand Embassy. It's wise to make your reservations a few weeks before your visit.

The Washington Post (1150 15th St. NW, ☎ 202/334–7969) offers free 50-minute guided tours for ages 11 and up on Monday from 10 to 3. Make reservations well in advance of your trip.

Every second Saturday in May, a half-dozen embassies in Washington open their doors as stops on a self-guided **Goodwill Embassy Tour** (☎ 202/636–4225). The cost is $25, which includes refreshments, a tour booklet, and free shuttle bus transportation between embassies.

Scandal Tours (☎ 202/783–7212) offers a 90-minute tour of Washington's seamier locales. Tours leave

from the Pavilion at the Old Post Office Building on Saturday at 1. The cost is $27 per person, and reservations are required.

WALKING TOURS

The **Black History National Recreation Trail** links a group of sights within historic neighborhoods illustrating aspects of African-American history in Washington, from slavery days to the New Deal. A brochure outlining the trail is available from the National Park Service (1100 Ohio Dr. SW, Washington, DC 20242, ☎ 202/619–7222).

The National Building Museum (☎ 202/272–2448) sponsors several architecture tours including the **"Construction Watch Tour"** ($7), which accompanies architects and construction-project managers to buildings in various stages of completion, and **"Site Seeing"** tours ($60 including bus transportation and a boxed lunch), which are led by architectural historians and visit various Washington neighborhoods and well-known monuments, public buildings, and houses.

The **Smithsonian Resident Associate Program** (☎ 202/357–3030) routinely offers guided walks and bus tours of neighborhoods in Washington and communities outside the city. Many tours are themed and include sights that illustrate such things as Art Deco influences, African-

American architecture, or railroad history.

The **D.C. Foot Tour** (Box 9001, Alexandria, VA 22304, ☎ 703/461–7364) is a walking tour of major historic sites.

Capital Entertainment Services (3629 18th St. NE, Washington, DC 20018, ☎ 202/636–9203) offers African-American history tours.

STUDENTS

GROUPS

A major tour operator is **Contiki Holidays** (300 Plaza Alicante, Suite 900, Garden Grove, CA 92640, ☎ 714/740–0808 or 800/466–0610).

HOSTELING

Contact **Hostelling International–American Youth Hostels** (733 15th St. NW, Suite 840, Washington, DC 20005, ☎ 202/783–6161) in the United States; **Hostelling International–Canada** (205 Catherine St., Suite 400, Ottawa, Ontario K2P 1C3, ☎ 613/748–5638) in Canada; and the **Youth Hostel Association of England and Wales** (Trevelyan House, 8 St. Stephen's Hill, St. Albans, Hertfordshire AL1 2DY, ☎ 01727/855215 and 01727/845047) in the United Kingdom. Membership ($25 in the United States, C$26.75 in Canada, and £9 in the United Kingdom) gets you access to 5,000 hostels worldwide that charge $7–$20 nightly per person.

ID CARDS

To be eligible for discounts on transportation and admissions, get the **International Student Identity Card** (ISIC) if you're a bona fide student or the **International Youth Card** (IYC) if you're under 26. In the United States, the ISIC and IYC cards cost $16 each and include basic travel-accident and illness coverage, plus a toll-free travel hot line. Apply through the Council on International Educational Exchange (*see* Organizations, *below*). Cards are available for $15 each in Canada from **Travel Cuts** (187 College St., Toronto, Ontario M5T 1P7, ☎ 416/979–2406 or 800/667–2887) and in the United Kingdom for £5 each at student unions and student travel companies.

ORGANIZATIONS

A major contact is the **Council on International Educational Exchange** (CIEE, 205 E. 42nd St., 16th Floor, New York, NY 10017, ☎ 212/661–1450) with locations in Boston (729 Boylston St., 02116, ☎ 617/266–1926); Miami (9100 S. Dadeland Blvd., 33156, ☎ 305/670–9261); Los Angeles (1093 Broxton Ave., 90024, ☎ 310/208–3551); 43 other college towns nationwide; and the United Kingdom (28A Poland St., London W1V 3DB, ☎ 0171/437–7767). Twice a year, it publishes *Student Travels* magazine. The CIEE's Council Travel Service offers domestic air passes for bargain travel within the United States and is the exclusive U.S. agent for several student-discount cards.

Campus Connections (325 Chestnut St., Suite 1101, Philadelphia, PA 19106, ☎ 215/625–8585 or 800/428–3235) specializes in discounted accommodations and airfares for students. The **Educational Travel Centre** (438 N. Frances St., Madison, WI 53703, ☎ 608/256–5551) offers rail passes and low-cost airline tickets, mostly for flights departing from Chicago.

In Canada, also contact **Travel Cuts** (*see* above).

SUBWAY TRAVEL

For schedule and route information, contact the **Washington Metropolitan Area Transit Authority** (WMATA; ☎ 202/637–7000, TTY 202/638–3780; open daily 6 AM–11:30 PM).

T

TAXIS

Two major companies serving the District are **Capitol Cab** (☎ 202/546–2400) and **Diamond Cab** (☎ 202/387–6200). See Taxis in Smart Travel Tips A to Z for information on rates.

TOUR OPERATORS

Among the companies selling tours and packages to Washington, D.C., the following have a proven reputation, are nationally known, and offer plenty of options.

GROUP TOURS

For deluxe escorted tours of Washington, D.C., contact **Maupintour** (Box 807, Lawrence KS 66044, ☎ 913/843–1211 or 800/255–4266) and **Tauck Tours** (11 Wilton Rd., Westport, CT 06880, ☎ 203/226–6911 or 800/468–2825). Another operator falling between deluxe and first-class is **Globus** (5301 S. Federal Circle, Littleton, CO 80123, ☎ 303/797–2800 or 800/221–0090). In the first-class and tourist range, try **Collette Tours** (162 Middle St., Pawtucket, RI 02860, ☎ 401/728–3805 or 800/832–4656); **Domenico Tours** (750 Broadway, Bayonne, NJ 07002, ☎ 201/823–8687 or 800/554–8687); and **Mayflower Tours** (1225 Warren Ave., Downers Grove, IL 60515, ☎ 708/960–3430 or 800/323–7604). For budget and tourist class programs, contact **Cosmos** (*see* Globus, *above*).

ORGANIZATIONS

The **National Tour Association** (546 E. Main St., Lexington, KY 40508, ☎ 606/226–4444 or 800/682–8886) and **United States Tour Operators Association** (USTOA, 211 E. 51st St., Suite 12B, New York, NY 10022, ☎ 212/750–7371) can provide lists of member operators and information on booking tours.

PACKAGES

Independent packages are available from major tour operators and airlines. Contact **American Airlines Fly AAway Vacations** (☎ 800/321–2121); **SuperCities** (139 Main St., Cambridge, MA 02142, ☎ 617/621–0099 or 800/333–1234); **Continental Airlines, Grand Destina-**tions (☎ 800/634–5555); **Delta Dream Vacations** (☎ 800/872–7786); **Certified Vacations** (Box 1525, Fort Lauderdale, FL 33302, ☎ 305/522–1414 or 800/233–7260); **United Vacations** (☎ 800/328–6877); and **USAir Vacations** (☎ 800/455–0123). **Funjet Vacations,** based in Milwaukee, Wisconsin, and **Gogo Tours,** based in Ramsey, New Jersey, sell packages to Washington, D.C., only through travel agents. For rail packages, try **Amtrak** (☎ 800/872–7245).

FROM THE U.K.➤ Tour operators offering packages to Washington, D.C., include **British Airways Holidays** (Astral Towers, Betts Way, London Rd., Crawley, West Sussex RH10 2XA, ☎ 01293/518–022); **Key to America** (1–3 Station Rd., Ashford, Middlesex TW15 2UW, ☎ 01784/248–777); **Kuoni Travel** (Kuoni House, Dorking, Surrey RH5 4AZ, ☎ 0306/742222); and **Premier Holidays** (Premier Travel Center, Westbrook, Milton Rd., Cambridge CB4 1YQ, ☎ 01223/516–688).

Travel agencies that offer cheap fares to Washington include **Trailfinders** (42–50 Earl's Court Rd., London W8 6FT, ☎ 0171/937–5400); **Travel Cuts** (295a Regent St., London W1R 7YA, ☎ 0171/637–3161; *see* Students, above); and **Flightfile** (49 Tottenham Court Rd., London W1P 9RE, ☎ 0171/700–2722).

PUBLICATIONS

Consult the brochure **"Worldwide Tour & Vacation Package Finder"** from the National Tour Association (*see above*) and the Better Business Bureau's **"Tips on Travel Packages"** (Publication No. 24-195, 4200 Wilson Blvd., Arlington, VA 22203; $2).

THEME TRIPS

PERFORMING ARTS➤ **Dailey-Thorp Travel** (330 W. 58th St., New York, NY 10019, ☎ 212/307–1555; book through travel agents) specializes in classical music and opera programs; its packages include tickets that are otherwise very hard to get. Also try **Keith Prowse Tours** (234 W. 34th St., Suite 1000, New York, NY 10036, ☎ 212/398–1430 or 800/669–8687).

TRAVEL AGENCIES

For names of reputable agencies in your area, contact the **American Society of Travel Agents** (1101 King St., Suite 200, Alexandria, VA 22314, ☎ 703/739–2782).

V

VISITOR INFO

Contact the **Washington, D.C., Convention and Visitors Association** (1212 New York Ave. NW, 6th Floor, Washington, DC 20005, ☎ 202/789–7000, FAX 202/789–7037); the **D.C. Committee to Promote Washington** (1212 New York Ave. NW, 2nd Floor, Washington, DC 20005, ☎ 800/422–8644); and the **National**

Park Service (Office of Public Affairs, National Capital Region, 1100 Ohio Dr. SW, Washington, DC 20242, ☎ 202/619–7222, FAX 202/619–7302).

The **White House Visitor Center** (☎ 202/208–1631), in Baldrige Hall in the Department of Commerce Building at 1450 Pennsylvania Avenue NW, has information on White House tours and special events. **National Park Service information kiosks** on the Mall, near the White House, next to the Vietnam Veterans Memorial, and at several other locations throughout the city can provide helpful information. **Dial-A-Park** (☎ 202/619–7275) is a recording of events at Park Service attractions in and around Washing-

ton. **Dial-A-Museum** (☎ 202/357–2020) is a recording of exhibits and special offerings at Smithsonian Institution museums.

If you're planning to visit sights in the surrounding areas, contact the **Maryland Department of Economic and Employment/Tourism Development** (Office of Tourist Development, 217 E. Redwood St., 9th Floor, Baltimore, MD 21202, ☎ 410/333–6611) and the **Virginia Division of Tourism** (901 E. Byrd St., Richmond, VA 23219, ☎ 804/786–4484 or 804/847–4882). The **Virginia-Maryland Travel Center** (1629 K St. NW, ☎ 202/659–5523) can book accommodations at Virginia B&Bs (☎ 800/934–9184).

U.K. VISITORS

In the United Kingdom, also contact the **United States Travel and Tourism Administration** (Box 1EN, London W1A 1EN, ☎ 0171/495–4466; for a free USA pack, write the USTTA at Box 170, Ashford, Kent TN24 0ZX; enclose stamps worth £1.50).

W

WEATHER

For current conditions and forecasts, plus the local time and helpful travel tips, call the **Weather Channel Connection** (☎ 900/932–8437; 95¢ per minute) from a Touch-Tone phone. See Climate in Smart Travel Tips A to Z for what weather to expect on your visit.

SMART TRAVEL TIPS A TO Z

Basic Information on Traveling in Washington, D.C., and Savvy Tips to Make Your Trip a Breeze

The more you travel, the more you know about how to make trips run like clockwork. To help make your travels hassle-free, Fodor's editors have rounded up dozens of tips from our contributors and travel experts all over the world, as well as basic information on visiting Washington, D.C. For names of organizations to contact and publications that can give you more information, *see* Important Contacts A to Z, *above.*

A

AIR TRAVEL

If time is an issue, **always look for nonstop flights,** which require no change of plane. If possible, **avoid connecting flights,** which stop at least once and can involve a change of plane, although the flight number remains the same; if the first leg is late, the second waits.

ALOFT

AIRLINE FOOD➤ If you hate airline food, **ask for special meals when booking.** These can be vegetarian, low-cholesterol, or kosher, for example; commonly prepared to order in smaller quantities than standard catered fare, they can be tastier.

SMOKING➤ Smoking is banned on all flights of less than six hours within the United States; the ban also applies to domestic segments of international flights aboard U.S. and foreign carriers. Delta has banned smoking system-wide.

CUTTING COSTS

The Sunday travel section of most newspapers is a good source of deals.

CONSOLIDATORS➤ Consolidators, who buy tickets at reduced rates from scheduled airlines, sell them at prices below the lowest available from the airlines directly—usually without advance restrictions. Sometimes you can even get your money back if you need to return the ticket. Carefully read the fine print detailing penalties for changes and cancellations. If you doubt the reliability of a consolidator, confirm your reservation with the airline.

MAJOR AIRLINES➤ The least-expensive airfares from the major airlines are priced for round-trip travel and are subject to restrictions. You must usually **book in advance and buy the ticket within 24 hours** to get cheaper fares, and

you may have to **stay over a Saturday night.** The lowest fare is subject to availability, and only a small percentage of the plane's total seats are sold at that price. It's good to **call a number of airlines,** and **when you are quoted a good price, book it on the spot**—the same fare on the same flight may not be available the next day. Airlines generally allow you to change your return date for a $25 to $50 fee, but most low-fare tickets are nonrefundable. However, if you don't use your ticket, you can apply the cost toward the purchase price of a one, again for a small charge.

B

BUS TRAVEL

WMATA's red, white, and blue **Metrobuses** crisscross the city and nearby suburbs, with some routes running 24 hours a day. All bus rides within the District are $1.10. Free transfers, good for 1½ to 2 hours, are available on buses and in Metro stations. Bus-to-bus transfers are accepted at designated Metrobus transfer points. Rail-to-bus transfers must be picked up before boarding the train. There may be a transfer charge when boarding the bus. There are no bus-to-rail transfers.

BUSINESS HOURS

Banks are generally open weekdays 9–3. On Friday many stay open until 5 or close at 2 and open again from 4 to 6. Very few banks have lobby hours on Saturday.

Museums are usually open daily 10–5:30; some have extended hours on Thursday. Many private museums are closed Monday or Tuesday, and some museums in government office buildings are closed weekends. The Smithsonian often sets extended spring and summer hours for some of its museums (☎ 202/357–2700 for details).

Stores are generally open Monday–Saturday 10–7 (or 8). Some have extended hours on Thursday and many—especially those in shopping or tourist areas such as Georgetown—open Sunday anywhere from 10 to noon and close at 5 or 6.

C

CAMERAS, CAMCORDERS, AND COMPUTERS

LAPTOPS

Before you depart, **check your portable computer's battery,** because you may be asked at security to turn on the computer to prove that it is what it appears to be. At the airport, you may prefer to **request a manual**

inspection, although security X-rays do not harm hard-disk or floppy-disk storage.

PHOTOGRAPHY

If your camera is new or if you haven't used it for a while, **shoot and develop a few rolls of film** before you leave. Always **store film in a cool, dry place**—never in the car's glove compartment or on the shelf under the rear window.

Every pass of film through an X-ray machine increases the chance of clouding. To protect it, carry it in a clear plastic bag and **ask for hand inspection at security.** Such requests are virtually always honored at U.S. airports. Don't depend on a lead-lined bag to protect film in checked luggage—the airline may increase the radiation to see what's inside.

VIDEO

Before your trip, **test your camcorder, invest in a skylight filter to protect the lens, and charge the batteries.** (Airport security personnel may ask you to turn on the camcorder to prove that it's what it appears to be).

Videotape is not damaged by X-rays, but it may be harmed by the magnetic field of a walk-through metal detector, **so ask that videotapes be hand-checked.**

CHILDREN AND TRAVEL

For advice on what to see and do and where to stay and eat, *see*

Chapter 3, Washington for Children.

BABY-SITTING

For recommended local sitters, **check with your hotel desk.**

DRIVING

If you are renting a car, **arrange for a car seat when you reserve.** Sometimes they're free.

FLYING

On domestic flights, children under two not occupying a seat travel free, and older children currently travel on the lowest applicable adult fare.

BAGGAGE➢ In general, the adult baggage allowance applies for children paying half or more of the adult fare.

SAFETY SEATS➢ According to the Federal Aviation Administration (FAA), it's a good idea to **use safety seats aloft.** Airline policy varies. U.S. carriers allow FAA-approved models, but airlines usually require that you buy a ticket, even if your child would otherwise ride free, because the seats must be strapped into regular passenger seats.

FACILITIES➢ When making your reservation, **ask for children's meals or freestanding bassinets** if you need them; the latter are available only to those with seats at the bulkhead, where there's enough legroom. If you don't need a bassinet, **think twice before requesting bulkhead seats**—the only storage for in-flight necessities is in the inconveniently distant overhead bins.

LODGING

Most hotels allow children under a certain age to stay in their parents' room at no extra charge, while others charge them as extra adults; be sure to **ask about the cutoff age.**

CUSTOMS
AND DUTIES

IN WASHINGTON, D.C.

U.K. CITIZENS➤ British visitors age 21 or over may import the following into the United States: 200 cigarettes or 50 cigars or 2 kilograms of tobacco; 1 U.S. liter of alcohol; gifts with a total value of $100. Restricted items include meat products, seeds, plants, and fruits. Never carry illegal drugs.

BACK HOME

IN CANADA➤ Once per calendar year, when you've been out of Canada for at least seven days, you may bring in C$300 worth of goods duty-free. If you've been away less than seven days but more than 48 hours, the duty-free exemption drops to C$100 but can be claimed any number of times (as can a C$20 duty-free exemption for absences of 24 hours or more). You cannot combine the yearly and 48-hour exemptions, use the C$300 exemption only partially (to save the balance for a later trip), or pool exemptions with family members. Goods claimed under the C$300 exemption may follow you by mail; those claimed under the lesser exemptions must accompany you.

Alcohol and tobacco products may be included in the yearly and 48-hour exemptions but not in the 24-hour exemption. If you meet the age requirements of the province through which you reenter Canada, you may bring in, duty-free, 1.14 liters (40 imperial ounces) of wine or liquor *or* 24 12-ounce cans or bottles of beer or ale. If you are 16 or older, you may bring in, duty-free, 200 cigarettes, 50 cigars or cigarillos, and 400 tobacco sticks or 400 grams of manufactured tobacco. Alcohol and tobacco must accompany you on your return.

An unlimited number of gifts valued up to C$60 each may be mailed to Canada duty-free. These do not count as part of your exemption. Label the package "Unsolicited Gift—Value Under $60." Alcohol and tobacco are excluded.

IN THE U.K.➤ From countries outside the European Union, including the United States, you may import duty-free 200 cigarettes, 100 cigarillos, 50 cigars or 250 grams of tobacco; 1 liter of spirits or 2 liters of fortified or sparkling wine; 2 liters of still table wine; 60 milliliters of perfume; 250 milliliters of toilet water; plus £136 worth of other goods, including gifts and souvenirs.

D
FOR TRAVELERS
WITH DISABILITIES

Every day Washington becomes more and more every American's city as **accessibility continues to improve.** The Metro has excellent facilities for visitors with vision and hearing impairments or mobility problems. Virtually all **streets have wide, level sidewalks with curb cuts,** though in Georgetown the brick-paved terrain can be bumpy. Most museums and monuments are accessible to visitors using wheelchairs.

When discussing accessibility with an operator or reservationist, **ask hard questions.** Are there any stairs, inside *or* out? Are there grab bars next to the toilet *and* in the shower/tub? How wide is the doorway to the room? To the bathroom? For the most extensive facilities, meeting the latest legal specifications, **opt for newer accommodations,** which more often have been designed with access in mind. Older properties or ships must usually be retrofitted and may offer more limited facilities as a result. Be sure to **discuss your needs before booking.**

DISCOUNT CLUBS

Travel clubs offer members unsold space on airplanes, cruise ships, and package tours at as much as 50% below regular prices. Membership may include a regular bulletin or access to a toll-free hot line giving details of available trips departing from three or four months to several months in the future. Most also offer 50% discounts off hotel rack rates. Before booking with a club, **make sure the hotel or other supplier isn't offering a better deal.**

DRIVING

A car can be a drawback in Washington. Traffic is horrendous, especially at rush hours, and **driving is often confusing,** with many lanes and some entire streets changing direction suddenly at certain times of day.

The traffic lights in Washington sometimes stymie visitors. Most of the lights don't hang down over the middle of the streets but stand at the sides of intersections. Radar detectors are illegal in Virginia and the District.

PARKING

Parking in Washington is an adventure; the **police are quick to tow** away or immobilize with a "boot" any vehicle parked illegally. (If you find you've been towed from a city street, call 202/727–5000.) Since the city's most popular sights are within a short walk of a Metro station anyway, **it's best to leave your car at the hotel.** Touring by car is a good idea only if you're considering visiting sights in suburban Maryland or Virginia.

Most of the outlying, suburban Metro stations have parking lots, though these fill quickly with city-bound commuters. If you plan to park in one of these lots, arrive early, armed with lots of quarters. Private **parking lots downtown are expensive,** charging as much

as $4 an hour and $13 a day. There is free, two-hour parking around the Mall on Jefferson Drive and Madison Drive, though these spots always seem to be filled. You can park free—in some spots all day—in parking areas off of Ohio Drive near the Jefferson Memorial and south of the Lincoln Memorial on Ohio Drive and West Basin Drive in West Potomac Park.

I

INSURANCE

Travel insurance can protect your investment, replace your luggage and its contents, or provide for medical coverage should you fall ill during your trip. Most tour operators, travel agents, and insurance agents sell specialized health-and-accident, flight, trip-cancellation, and luggage insurance as well as comprehensive policies with some or all of these features. Before you make any purchase, **review your existing health and homeowner's policies** to find out whether they cover expenses incurred while traveling.

BAGGAGE

Airline liability for your baggage is limited by the terms of your ticket (*see* Packing for Washington, *below*). Insurance for losses exceeding the terms of your airline ticket can be bought directly from the airline at check-in for about $10 per $1,000 of coverage; note that it excludes a rather exten-

sive list of items, shown on your airline ticket.

FLIGHT

You should **think twice before buying flight insurance.** Often purchased as a last-minute impulse at the airport, it pays a lump sum when a plane crashes, either to a beneficiary if the insured dies or sometimes to a surviving passenger who loses eyesight or a limb. Supplementing the airlines' coverage described in the limits-of-liability paragraphs on your ticket, it's expensive and basically unnecessary. Charging an airline ticket to a major credit card often automatically entitles you to coverage and may also embrace travel by bus, train, and ship.

TRIP

Without insurance, you will lose all or most of your money if you must cancel your trip due to illness or any other reason. Especially if your airline ticket, cruise, or package tour is nonrefundable and cannot be changed, it's essential that you **buy trip-cancellation-and-interruption insurance.** When considering how much coverage you need, look for a policy that will cover the cost of your trip plus the nondiscounted price of a one-way airline ticket should you need to return home early. Read the fine print carefully, especially sections defining "family member" and "preexisting medical conditions." Also **consider default or bankruptcy insurance,** which protects you against a supplier's failure to deliver. However, such policies often do not cover default by a travel agency, tour operator, airline, or cruise line if you bought your tour and the coverage directly from the firm in question.

FOR U.K. TRAVELERS

According to the Association of British Insurers, a trade association representing 450 insurance companies, it's wise to **buy extra medical coverage when you visit the United States.** You can buy an annual travel-insurance policy valid for most vacations during the year in which it's purchased. If you go this route, make sure it covers you if you have a preexisting medical condition or are pregnant.

L
LODGING

APARTMENT AND VILLA RENTALS

If you want a home base that's roomy enough for a family and comes with cooking facilities, **consider a furnished rental.** It's generally cost-wise, too, although not always—some rentals are luxury properties (economical only when your party is large). Home-exchange directories do list rentals—often second homes owned by prospective house swappers—and some services search for a house or apartment for you (even a castle if that's your fancy) and handle the paperwork. Some send an illustrated catalogue and others

send photographs of specific properties, sometimes at a charge; up-front registration fees may apply.

M
MONEY AND EXPENSES

ATMS

Chances are that you can **use your bank card at ATMs** to withdraw money from an account and get cash advances on a credit-card account if your card has been programmed with a personal identification number, or PIN. Before leaving home, **check on frequency limits** for withdrawals and cash advances.

On cash advances you are charged interest from the day you receive the money, whether from an ATM or a teller. Transaction fees for ATM withdrawals outside your home turf may be higher than for withdrawals at home.

TRAVELER'S CHECKS

Whether or not to buy traveler's checks depends on where you are headed; **take cash to rural areas and small towns, traveler's checks to cities.** The most widely recognized are American Express, Citicorp, Thomas Cook, and Visa, which are sold by major commercial banks for 1% to 3% of the checks' face value— it pays to **shop around.** Both American Express and Thomas Cook issue checks that can be countersigned and used by you or your traveling companion. Record the

numbers of the checks, cross them off as you spend them, and keep this information separate from your checks.

WIRING MONEY

You don't have to be a cardholder to send or receive funds through MoneyGram^{SM} from American Express. Just go to a MoneyGram agent, located in retail and convenience stores and in American Express Travel Offices. Pay up to $1,000 with cash or a credit card, anything over that in cash. The **money can be picked up within 10 minutes** in cash or check at the nearest Money-Gram agent. There's no limit, and the recipient need only present photo identification. The cost, which includes a free long-distance phone call, runs from 3% to 10%, depending on the amount sent, the destination, and how you pay.

You can also send money using Western Union. Money sent from the United States or Canada will be available for pickup at agent locations in 100 countries within 15 minutes. Once the money is in the system, it can be picked up at any one of 25,000 locations. Fees range from 4% to 10%, depending on the amount you send.

P
PACKAGES AND TOURS

A package or tour to Washington, D.C., can make your vacation less expensive and more convenient. Firms that sell tours and packages purchase airline seats, hotel rooms, and rental cars in bulk and pass some of the savings on to you. In addition, the best operators have local representatives to help you out at your destination.

A GOOD DEAL?

The more your package or tour includes, the better you can predict the ultimate cost of your vacation. Make sure you know exactly what is included, and **beware of hidden costs.** Are taxes, tips, and service charges included? Transfers and baggage handling? Entertainment and excursions? These can add up.

Most packages and tours are rated deluxe, first-class superior, first class, tourist, or budget. The key difference is usually accommodations. If the package or tour you are considering is priced lower than in your wildest dreams, **be skeptical.** Also, **make sure your travel agent knows the hotels** and other services. Ask about location, room size, beds, and whether the facility has a pool, room service, or programs for children, if you care about these. Has your agent been there or sent others you can contact?

BIG VS. SMALL

An operator that handles several hundred thousand travelers annually can use its purchasing power to give you a good price. Its high volume may also indicate financial stability. But some small companies provide more personalized service; because they tend to specialize, they may also be experts on an area.

BUYER BEWARE

Each year consumers are stranded or lose their money when operators go out of business—even very large ones with excellent reputations. If you can't afford a loss, take the time to **check out the operator**—find out how long the company has been in business, and ask several agents about its reputation. Next, **don't book unless the firm has a consumer-protection program.** Members of the United States Tour Operators Association and the National Tour Association are required to set aside funds exclusively to cover your payments and travel arrangements in case of default. Nonmember operators may instead carry insurance; look for the details in the operator's brochure— and the name of an underwriter with a solid reputation. Note: When it comes to tour operators, **don't trust escrow accounts.** Although there are laws governing those of charter-flight operators, no governmental body prevents tour operators from raiding the till.

Next, **contact your local Better Business Bureau and the attorney general's office** in both your own state and the operator's; have any complaints been filed? Last, **pay with a major credit card.** Then you can cancel payment, provided that you can document your complaint. Always **consider trip-cancellation insurance** (*see* Insurance, *above*).

SINGLE TRAVELERS

Prices are usually quoted per person, based on two sharing a room. If traveling solo, you may be required to pay the full double-occupancy rate. Some operators eliminate this surcharge if you agree to be matched up with a roommate of the same sex, even if one is not found by departure time.

USING AN AGENT

Travel agents are an excellent resource. In fact, large operators accept bookings only through travel agents. But it's good to **collect brochures from several agencies,** because some agents' suggestions may be skewed by promotional relationships with tour and package firms that reward them for volume sales. If you have a special interest, **find an agent with expertise in that area;** the American Society of Travel Agents can give you leads in the United States. (Don't rely solely on your agent, though; agents may be unaware of small-niche operators, and some special-interest travel companies only sell direct).

PACKING FOR WASHINGTON

Washington is basically informal, although **many restaurants require a jacket and tie.**

Area theaters and nightclubs range from the slightly dressy (John F. Kennedy Center) to extremely casual (Wolf Trap Farm Park). For sightseeing and casual dining, jeans and sneakers are acceptable just about anywhere. In summer, you'll want shorts and light shirts. Even in August, though, you might still want to have a shawl or light jacket for air-conditioned restaurants. Good walking shoes are a must. In January and February, you'll need a heavy coat and snow boots.

Bring an extra pair of eyeglasses or contact lenses in your carry-on luggage, and if you have a health problem, **pack enough medication** to last the trip. **Don't put prescription drugs or valuables in luggage to be checked,** for it could go astray.

LUGGAGE

Free airline baggage allowances depend on the airline, the route, and the class of your ticket; ask in advance. In general, on domestic flights you are entitled to check two bags—neither exceeding 62 inches or 158 centimeters (length + width + height) or weighing more than 70 pounds (32 kilograms). A third piece may be brought aboard; its total dimensions are generally limited to less than 45 inches (114 centimeters), so it will fit easily under the seat in front of you or in the overhead compartment. In the United States, the FAA gives airlines

broad latitude to limit carry-on allowances and tailor them to different aircraft and operational conditions. Charges for excess, oversize, or overweight pieces vary.

SAFEGUARDING YOUR LUGGAGE➣ Before leaving home, **itemize your bags' contents and** their worth, and label them with your name, address, and phone number. (If you use your home address, cover it so that potential thieves can't see it.) Inside your bag, **pack a copy of your itinerary.** At check-in, **make sure that your bag is correctly tagged** with the airport's three-letter destination code. If your bags arrive damaged or not at all, file a written report with the airline before leaving the airport.

PASSPORTS
AND VISAS

CANADIANS

No passport is necessary to enter the United States.

U.K. CITIZENS

British citizens need a valid passport. If you are staying fewer than 90 days and traveling on a vacation, with a return or onward ticket, you will probably not need a visa. However, you will need to fill out the Visa Waiver Form, 1-94W, supplied by the airline. While traveling, **keep one photocopy of the data page** separate from your wallet and leave another copy with someone at home. If you lose your passport, promptly call the near-

est embassy or consulate and the local police; having the data page can speed replacement.

R
RENTING A CAR

CUTTING COSTS

To get the best deal, **book through a travel agent and shop around.** When pricing cars, **ask where the rental lot is located.** Some off-airport locations offer lower rates—even though their lots are only minutes away from the terminal via complimentary shuttle. You may also want to **price local car-rental companies,** whose rates may be lower still, although service and maintenance standards may not be up to those of a national firm. Also **ask your travel agent about a company's customer-service record.** How has it responded to late plane arrivals and vehicle mishaps? Are there often lines at the rental counter, and, if you're traveling during a holiday period, does a confirmed reservation guarantee you a car?

INSURANCE

When you drive a rented car, you are generally responsible for any damage or personal injury that you cause as well as damage to the vehicle. Before you rent, **see what coverage you already have** under the terms of your personal auto-insurance policy and credit cards. For about $14 a day, rental companies sell insurance, known as a collision damage waiver (CDW), that eliminates your liability for damage to the car; it's always optional and should never be automatically added to your bill.

SURCHARGES

Before picking up the car in one city and leaving it in another, **ask about drop-off charges or one-way service fees,** which can be substantial. Note, too, that some rental agencies charge extra if you return the car before the time specified on your contract. To avoid a hefty refueling fee, **fill the tank just before you turn in the car.**

FOR U.K. CITIZENS

In the United States you must be 21 to rent a car; rates may be higher for those under 25. Extra costs cover child seats, compulsory for children under 5 (about $3 per day), and additional drivers (about $1.50 per day). To pick up your reserved car you will need the reservation voucher, a passport, a U.K. driver's license, and a travel policy covering each driver.

S

SENIOR-CITIZEN
DISCOUNTS

To qualify for age-related discounts, **mention your senior-citizen status up front** when booking hotel reservations, not when checking out, and before you're seated in restaurants, not when paying your bill. Note that discounts may be limited to certain menus, days, or hours. When renting a car, **ask**

about promotional car-rental discounts—they can net lower costs than your senior-citizen discount.

STUDENTS
ON THE ROAD

To save money, **look into deals available through student-oriented travel agencies.** To qualify, you'll need to have a bona fide student ID card. Members of international student groups also are eligible. *See* Students *in* Important Contacts A to Z, *above.*

SUBWAY TRAVEL

The WMATA provides bus and subway service in the District and in the Maryland and Virginia suburbs. The Metro, opened in 1976, is one of the country's cleanest and safest subway systems. Trains run weekdays 5:30 AM–midnight, weekends 8 AM–midnight. During the weekday rush hours (5:30–9:30 AM and 3–8 PM), trains come along every six minutes. At other times and on weekends and holidays, trains run about every 12–15 minutes. The base fare is $1.10; the actual price you pay depends on the time of day and the distance traveled. Children under age five ride free when accompanied by a paying passenger, but there is a maximum of two children per paying adult.

Buy your ticket at the Farecard machines; they accept coins and crisp $1, $5, $10, or $20 bills. If the machine spits your bill back out at you, try folding and unfolding it before

asking a native for help. The Farecard should be inserted into the turnstile to enter the platform. **Make sure you hang onto the card—you'll need it to exit at your destination.**

Some Washingtonians report that the Farecard's magnetic strip interferes with the strips on ATM cards and credit cards, so **keep the cards separated in your pocket or wallet.**

DISCOUNT PASSES

For $5 you can **buy a pass that allows unlimited trips for one day.** It's good all day on weekends, on holidays, and after 9:30 AM on weekdays. Passes are available at Metro Sales Outlets (including the Metro Center station) and at many hotels, banks, and Safeway and Giant grocery stores.

T

TAXIS

Taxis in the District are not metered; they operate instead on a curious zone system. **Before you set off, ask your cab driver how much the fare will be.** The basic single rate for traveling within one zone is $3.20. There is an extra $1.25 charge for each additional passenger and a $1 surcharge during the 4–6:30 PM rush hour. Bulky suitcases are charged at a higher rate, and a $1.50 surcharge is tacked on when you phone for a cab. Maryland and Virginia taxis are metered but are not allowed to take passengers between points in Washington.

THE GOLD GUIDE / SMART TRAVEL TIPS

Also *see* Airport Transfers *and* Taxis *in* Important Contacts A to Z, *above.*

TELEPHONES

LONG DISTANCE

The long-distance services of AT&T, MCI, and Sprint make calling home relatively convenient and let you avoid hotel surcharges; typically, you dial an 800 number.

W
WHEN TO GO

Washington has **two delightful seasons:** **spring and autumn.** In spring, the city's ornamental fruit trees are budding, and its many gardens are in bloom. By autumn, most of the summer crowds have left and visitors can enjoy the museums, galleries, and timeless monuments in peace. Summers can be uncomfortably hot and humid (local legend has it that Washington was considered a "tropical hardship post" by some European diplomats). Winter witnesses the lighting of the National Christmas Tree and countless historic-house tours, but the weather is often bitter, with a handful of modest snowstorms that somehow bring this Southern city to a standstill. If you're interested in government, visit when Congress is in session. When lawmakers break for recess (at Christmas, Easter, July 4, and other holiday periods), the city seems a little less vibrant.

Climate in Washington, D.C.

What follows are the average daily maximum and minimum temperatures for Washington.

Jan.	47F	8C	May	76F	24C	Sept.	79F	26C
	34	– 1		58	14		61	16
Feb.	47F	8C	June	85F	29C	Oct.	70F	21C
	31	– 1		65	18		52	11
Mar.	56F	13C	July	88F	31C	Nov.	56F	13C
	38	3		70	21		41	5
Apr.	67F	19C	Aug.	86F	30C	Dec.	47F	8C
	47	8		68	20		32	0

1 Destination: Washington, D.C.

AMERICA'S HOMETOWN

TO A SURPRISING DEGREE, LIFE in Washington is not that different from life elsewhere in the country. People are born here, grow up here, get jobs here—by no means invariably with the federal government—and go on to have children, who repeat the cycle. Very often, they live out their lives without ever testifying before Congress, being indicted for influence peddling, or attending a state dinner at the White House.

Which is not to say that the federal government does not cast a long shadow over the city. Among Washington's 570,000 inhabitants are an awful lot of lawyers, journalists, and people who include the word "policy" in their job titles. It's just that D.C. is much more of a hometown than most tourists realize.

Just a few blocks away from the monuments and museums on the Mall are residential and business districts whose scale is very human. The houses are a crazy quilt of architectural styles, kept in linear formation by rows of lush trees. On the commercial streets, bookstores and ethnic groceries abound.

Redevelopment has left its mark. Fourteenth Street was once the capital's red-light district. The city was determined to clean up the strip, and to everyone's surprise it succeeded. Nor is much left of the tacky commercial district around Ninth and F streets. Washington's original downtown, it deteriorated when the city's center shifted to the west, to the "new" downtown of Connecticut Avenue and K Street. But the "old" downtown is being rejuvenated. The department stores that once drew crowds with their window displays have been renovated; there are new hotels and office buildings; and as the construction dust clears, the area is looking pretty good.

Many people who come here are worried about crime. Crime is certainly a major problem, as it is in other big cities, but Washington is not nearly as dangerous as its well-publicized homicide rate

might lead you to believe. Most visitors have relatively little to fear. The drug-related shootings that have in the past made Washington a murder capital generally take place in remote sections of the city. Unless you go seeking out the drug markets, there isn't much chance you'll get caught in the cross fire of rival drug gangs. Crimes against property are more widespread, but still far from ubiquitous. Unlike New York, Washington is not full of expert pickpockets; nor is it plagued by gold-chain snatchers.

The city's Metro is generally safe, even at night. However, if you have to walk from your stop in a neighborhood that isn't well lit and trafficked, you probably should invest in a taxi. Of course, even exercising normal prudence, it is still possible that you will have an encounter with someone who believes that what's yours ought to be his. If that happens, don't argue.

Your attachment to the contents of your wallet is certain to be tested in another way, however. Panhandlers are now a fixture of the cityscape, and there is no avoiding their importunities. How you respond to them is a matter only your conscience can advise you on. Wealth and poverty have always coexisted in America's hometown; but poverty is now omnipresent, wearing a very human face.

—By Deborah Papier
A native of Washington, Deborah Papier has worked as an editor and writer for numerous local newspapers and magazines.

WHAT'S WHERE

It is often said that Washington does not have any "real" neighborhoods, the way nearby Baltimore does. Although it's true that Washingtonians are not given to huddling together on their front stoops, each area of the city does have a clearly defined personality.

The Mall

With nearly a dozen diverse museums ringing an expanse of green, **the Mall** is the closest thing the capital has to a theme park—but here, almost everything is free. Lindbergh's *Spirit of St. Louis,* the Hope Diamond, the Fonz's leather jacket, dinosaurs galore, and myriad modern and classical masterpieces await you. Of course, the Mall is more than just a front yard for all these museums: It's a picnicking park and a jogging path, an outdoor stage for festivals and fireworks, and America's town green.

The Monuments

Punctuating the capital like a huge exclamation point is the **Washington Monument**—at 555 feet 5 inches the world's tallest masonry structure. Directly south of the White House, the **Jefferson Memorial's** rotunda rises alongside the Tidal Basin, where you can rent paddleboats and admire over 200 cherry trees, gifts from Japan and focus of a festival each spring. The **Lincoln Memorial** has a somber statue of the seated president gazing out over the Reflecting Pool. The **Vietnam Veterans Memorial** is one of the most visited sights in Washington, its black granite panels reflecting the sky, the trees, and the faces of those looking for the names of loved ones.

The White House Area

In a city full of immediately recognizable images, perhaps none is more familiar than the **White House.** In the neighborhood are some of the oldest houses in the city and two important art galleries: the Renwick Gallery—the Smithsonian's museum of American decorative arts—and the Corcoran Gallery of Art, known for its collections of photography, European Impressionist paintings, and portraits by American artists.

Capitol Hill

Anchoring the neighborhood is the Capitol Building, where the Senate and the House have met since 1800. But **Capitol Hill** is more than just the center of government. There are charming residential blocks here, lined with Victorian row houses and a fine assortment of restaurants, bars, and shops. Union Station, Washington's train depot, has vaulted, gilded ceilings, arched colonnades, statues of Roman legionnaires, and a modern mall-movie complex with food for every palate

and pocketbook. Also in this area are the Supreme Court, the Library of Congress, and the Folger Shakespeare Library.

Old Downtown and Federal Triangle

In **Old Downtown**—the area within the diamond formed by Massachusetts, Louisiana, Pennsylvania, and New York avenues—are Chinatown, Ford's Theatre, and several important museums. The Pension Building, which has the largest columns in the world, houses the National Building Museum, devoted to architecture. Other museums include the National Museum of Women in the Arts, the National Portrait Gallery, and the National Museum of American Art. The National Aquarium is in the **Federal Triangle,** a mass of government buildings. And the Old Post Office Pavilion has shops, restaurants, and an indoor miniature golf course. You can tour the J. Edgar Hoover Federal Bureau of Investigation Building, with its exhibits illustrating famous past FBI cases. And at the National Archives, the original Declaration of Independence, Constitution, and Bill of Rights are on display.

Georgetown

Georgetown, the capital's wealthiest neighborhood (and a haven for architecture buffs) is also its most hopping: Restaurants, bars, nightclubs, and trendy boutiques line the narrow, crowded streets. Originally used for shipping, the C&O Canal today is a part of the National Park system: Walkers follow the towpath and canoeists paddle the calm waters; you can also go on a leisurely, mule-drawn trip aboard a canal barge. Washington Harbour is a postmodern riverfront development that includes restaurants, offices, apartments, and upscale shops; Georgetown Park is a multilevel shopping extravaganza; and Georgetown University is the oldest Jesuit school in the country. Dumbarton Oaks's 10 acres of formal gardens make it one of the loveliest spots in all of Washington.

Dupont Circle

One of the most fashionable and vibrant neighborhoods in Washington, **Dupont Circle** has a cosmopolitan air with its many restaurants, offbeat shops, and specialty bookstores; it is also home to the most visible segment of Washington's gay community. The exclusive Kalorama neighborhood (Greek for "beautiful view") is a peaceful, tree-lined enclave filled with embassies and luxurious homes. For a taste of the beautiful view, look down over Rock Creek Park, 1,800 acres of green, which has a planetarium, an 18-hole golf course, and equestrian and bicycle trails. The Phillips Collection is also here; its best known paintings include Renoir's *Luncheon of the Boating Party,* Degas's *Dancers at the Bar,* and a Cézanne self-portrait. At the National Geographic Society's Explorer's Hall, you can learn about the world in an interactive way.

Foggy Bottom

Foggy Bottom—an appellation earned years ago when smoke from factories combined with swampy air to produce a permanent fog along the waterfront—has three main claims to fame: the State Department, the Kennedy Center, and George Washington University. Watergate, one of the world's most legendary apartment-office complexes, is notorious for the events that took place here on June 17, 1972. As Nixon aides sat in a motel across the street, five men were caught trying to bug the headquarters of the Democratic National Committee.

Cleveland Park and the National Zoo

Tree-shaded **Cleveland Park,** in northwest Washington, has attractive houses and a suburban character, and is popular with professionals. Its Cineplex Odeon Uptown is a marvelous vintage-1936 Art Deco movie house. **The National Zoological Park,** part of the Smithsonian Institution, is one of the foremost zoos in the world. Star denizens include Komodo dragons and a giant panda.

Adams-Morgan

Close to Greenwich Village in spirit, **Adams-Morgan** is one of Washington's most ethnically diverse and interesting neighborhoods, home to a veritable United Nations of cuisines, offbeat shops, and funky bars and clubs. The neighborhood's grand 19th-century apartment buildings and row houses and its bohemian atmosphere have attracted young urban professionals, the businesses that cater to them, and the attendant parking and crowd problems.

Arlington, Virginia

The three attractions here—each linked to the military and accessible by Metro—make **Arlington** a part of any complete visit to the nation's capital: John F. Kennedy, Jacqueline Kennedy Onassis, and Robert Kennedy are buried in Arlington National Cemetery along with 200,000 veterans; the U.S. Marine Corps War Memorial is a 78-foot-high statue based on the Pulitzer-prize-winning photograph of five marines and a Navy corpsman raising a flag atop Mt. Suribachi on Iwo Jima; and the **Pentagon,** the headquarters of the Department of Defense, is an immense five-sided building where 23,000 people work.

Alexandria, Virginia

Alexandria's history is linked to the most significant events and personages of the Colonial, Revolutionary, and Civil War periods. This colorful past is still alive on the cobbled streets; on the revitalized waterfront, where clipper ships dock and artisans display their wares; and in restored 18th- and 19th-century homes, churches, and taverns. The history of African Americans in Alexandria and Virginia from 1749, when the city was founded, to the present is recounted at the Alexandria Black History Resource Center, near Robert E. Lee's boyhood home.

C&O Canal and Great Falls

The **C&O Canal** (*see* Georgetown, *above*) and the twin parks of **Great Falls**—on either side of the Potomac River 13 miles northwest of Georgetown—are part of the National Park system. The steep, jagged falls roar into a narrow gorge, providing one of the most spectacular scenic attractions in the East. Canoeing, bicycling, and fishing are popular. Glen Echo is a charming village of Victorian houses; Glen Echo Park is noted for its whimsical architecture and its splendid 1921 Dentzel carousel.

Annapolis, Maryland

Annapolis, Maryland's capital, is a popular destination for oyster catchers and yachting aficionados, and on warm sunny days at the City Dock, white sails billow against a redbrick background of waterfront shops and restaurants. Annapolis's enduring nautical reputation derives largely from the presence of the United States Naval

Academy, whose handsomely uniformed students can often be seen on the city streets. One of the country's largest assemblages of 18th-century architecture, with no fewer than 50 pre-Revolutionary buildings, recalls the city's days as a major port.

Potomac Plantations

Three splendid examples of plantation architecture remain on the Virginia side of the Potomac just 15 miles or so south of the District. Easily visited in a day, these riverfront mansions offer a look into a way of life long gone: **Mount Vernon,** one of the most popular sights in the area, was the home of George Washington; **Woodlawn** was the estate of Washington's granddaughter; and **Gunston Hall** was the residence of George Mason—patriot and author of the document on which the Bill of Rights was based.

Fredericksburg, Virginia

This compact city 50 miles south of Washington near the falls of the Rappahannock River figured prominently at crucial points in the nation's history, particularly during the Revolutionary and Civil wars. Fredericksburg, a popular day-trip destination for history buffs and antiques collectors, has a 40-block National Historic District containing more than 350 18th- and 19th-century buildings.

PLEASURES AND PASTIMES

Government and Politics in Action

C-SPAN buffs will want to visit **Capitol Hill,** where they can observe the House and the Senate in action; the **Supreme Court's** hearings are also open to visitors. Washington also has many government buildings that can be toured without watching its denizens at work: These include the **Pentagon,** the **FBI Building,** the **Treasury,** and the **Federal Reserve.** And let's not forget the **White House.**

Military Memorials, Pageants, and Museums

Washington is a fitting spot to honor those who served and fell in defense of our country. More than 200,000 veterans are buried in **Arlington National Cemetery,** a place where visitors can trace America's history through the aftermath of its battles; the guard at the **Tomb of the Unknowns** is changed frequently with a precise ceremony. Near the cemetery is the **United States Marine Corps War Memorial,** where there is a sunset parade in summer. The **Vietnam Veteran's Memorial** has more than 58,000 names etched in black granite; the **Korean War Veteran's Memorial** consists of a statue and a reflecting pool. Next to the statue that serves as the **Navy Memorial** is a visitor center and a theater that continuously shows the 30-minute, 70-millimeter film *At Sea,* a visually stunning look at life aboard a modern aircraft carrier. Moored in the Anacostia River nearby and on permanent display is the **Barry,** a decommissioned U.S. Navy destroyer open for tours.

The **Firearms Museum** has hundreds of guns, from those used in the Revolutionary War to high-tech pistols used by Olympic shooting teams. The **National Museum of American Jewish Military History** displays weapons, uniforms, medals, recruitment posters, and other memorabilia from every war in which this country has fought. Inscribed granite slabs in **Pershing Park** recount battles of World War I. The **National Cryptologic Museum** tells the story of military intelligence from 1526 to the present.

The **Marine Corps Museum** follows the corps from its inception in 1775 to its role in Desert Storm. The **Washington Navy Yard** has two military museums and a destroyer you can tour. The **Navy Museum** chronicles the U.S. Navy's history from the Revolution to the present. Exhibits include the foremast of the U.S.S. *Constitution* and a fighter plane that dangles from the ceiling. Children especially enjoy peering through the operating periscopes and pretending to launch torpedoes. In front of the museum is a collection of guns, cannons, and missiles. An annex is full of unusual submarines.

From June through August the Navy and the Marine Corps put on a multimedia **Summer Pageant** at an amphitheater across from the Navy Museum.

In Annapolis, you can tour the **United States Naval Academy** and visit the **museum in Preble Hall,** which tells the story of the U.S. Navy with displays of miniature ships and flags from the original vessels. Periodic **full-dress parades** and (in warmer months) daily noontime midshipmen's musters take place at various spots around campus.

When the Civil War broke out in 1861, **Fredericksburg, Virginia,** became the linchpin of the Confederate defense of Richmond and, as such, the inevitable target of Union assaults. In December 1862, Union forces attacked Fredericksburg in what was to be the first of four major battles fought in and around the town; you can tour its **battlefields and cemeteries.**

Architecture and the Decorative Arts

Washington National Cathedral, the sixth-largest cathedral in the world, will impress even the most hardened cathedral viewer with its Gothic arches, flying buttresses, and imaginative stonework.

Washington has many buildings of architectural interest and filled with exquisite period furniture, draperies, and china. The **White House**—with its watered silk–covered walls, its Empire settees, and personalized china—is the most obvious example of such a building. Others include the **DAR Museum,** with its 33 period rooms decorated in styles representative of various U.S. states and its 50,000-item collection of Colonial and Federal silver, china, porcelain, and glass; and the **Hillwood Museum,** a Georgian mansion that contains a large collection of 18th- and 19th-century French and Russian decorative art such as gold and silver work, icons, lace, tapestries, china, and Fabergé eggs.

The **Renwick Gallery,** the Smithsonian's museum of American decorative arts, has exquisitely designed and crafted utilitarian items, as well as objects created out of such traditional craft materials as fiber and glass. Displays include Shaker furniture, enamel jewelry, and the opulently furnished Victorian-style Grand Salon.

The open interior of the massive redbrick **Pension Building,** one of the city's great spaces, has been the site of inaugural balls for more than 100 years. The eight central Corinthian columns are the largest in the world, rising to a height of 75 feet. This enormous edifice houses the **National Building Museum,** devoted to architecture and the building arts. It outlines the capital's architectural history, from its monuments to its residential neighborhoods.

Many neighborhoods explored in our walking tours cover historic homes and other—formerly commercial—edifices that are open for tours. See especially **Georgetown, Dupont Circle, Annapolis, and Fredericksburg.**

Gardens

The paths of the **Constitution Gardens** wind through groves of trees, around a lake—a memorial to signers of the Declaration of Independence, and past the sobering Vietnam Veterans Memorial. **Dumbarton Oaks'** 10 acres of formal gardens, in a variety of styles, are some of the loveliest in the city. The grounds of Marjorie Merriweather Post's Georgian-style **Hillwood House** have a French-style parterre, a rose garden, a Japanese garden, paths through azaleas and rhododendrons, and a greenhouse containing 5,000 orchids. Exotic water lilies, lotuses, hyacinths, and other water-loving plants thrive at the **Kenilworth Aquatic Gardens,** a sanctuary of quiet pools and marshy flats. The gardens are home to a variety of wetland animals, including turtles, frogs, muskrats, and some 40 species of birds. The **United States Botanic Gardens** house all manner of plants, from cacti to orchids. In spring, the **United States National Arboretum** is a blaze of color. Summer at this 444-acre oasis brings blooms of clematis, peonies, rhododendrons, and roses. Also popular are the National Herb Garden and the National Bonsai Collection.

Parks

C&O Canal National Historical Park has one end in Georgetown and the other in Cumberland, Maryland. Canoeists paddle the canal's "watered" sections, while hikers and bikers use the 12-foot-wide towpath that runs alongside it. In warmer months you can hop a mule-drawn canal boat for a brief trip. You can also walk over a series of bridges to Olmsted Island in the middle of the Potomac for a spectacular view of the falls.

There are playgrounds and picnic tables at the 328-acre **East Potomac Park** as well as opportunities for tennis, swimming, golf, and miniature golf. Double-blossoming cherry trees line Ohio Drive; they bloom about two weeks after the single-blossoming variety that attracts throngs to the Tidal Basin each spring.

The waters of the Potomac River cascade dramatically over a steep, jagged gorge, creating the spectacle that gives the 800-acre **Great Falls Park** its name. Hikers follow trails, climbers scale the rock faces leading down to the water, and experienced kayakers shoot the rapids. There are also mule-drawn boat rides.

Huntley Meadows, a 1,200-acre refuge in Alexandria, Virginia, is known as a birder's delight. More than 200 species of fowl—from ospreys to owls, egrets to ibis—can be spotted here. Since much of the park is wetlands, it is a favorite of aquatic species.

The 1,800 acres of **Rock Creek Park** have bicycle routes and hiking and equestrian trails, a planetarium, and an 18-hole golf course.

FODOR'S CHOICE

Buildings and Monuments

★ **White House.** If you think about it, it really is rather extraordinary that our president opens his house most mornings to throngs of visitors who peer past ropes at his family's dining and living rooms.

★ **East Building of the National Gallery of Art.** The atrium of this angular marble I. M. Pei-designed wing is dominated by an Alexander Calder mobile and a huge wall-hanging by Joan Miró. The galleries here generally display modern art.

★ **Jefferson Memorial.** It faces the Tidal Basin, where you can rent paddleboats, and where cherry trees blossom in spring.

★ **Vietnam Veterans Memorial.** It's a moving tribute to those who died in this war.

★ **Washington National Cathedral.** Although built in modern times, it's soaring medieval Gothic in style.

Activities

★ **Strolling the streets of Georgetown early on a weekend morning** before the narrow sidewalks fill with shoppers, brunchers, and browsers.

★ **Visiting the aviary at the National Zoo.** At this top-ranked zoo, innovative compounds show many animals in naturalistic settings: The Great Flight Cage is a walk-in aviary in which birds fly unrestricted.

★ **Taking a boat ride to Mount Vernon.** The leisurely 4½ hour ride on the Potomac is a cool respite on sweltering days.

★ **Exploring the city with Scandal Tours** (*See* Important Contacts A to Z *in* the Gold Guide). This outrageous tour bypasses the monuments and takes you straight into the gutter. Costumed look-alikes dramatize scandals as you tour such sights as Gary Hart's town house and Watergate.

Museums

★ **United States Holocaust Memorial Museum.** In a clear and often graphic fashion, the museum tells the stories of the 11 million Jews, Gypsies, Jehovah's Witnesses, homosexuals, political prisoners, and others killed by the Nazis between 1933 and 1945.

★ **Phillips Collection.** It is as beloved for its well-known paintings as for its relaxed atmosphere and knowledgeable, art-student guards.

★ **National Air and Space Museum** is the most visited museum in the world. It displays the actual air- and spacecraft that have made history; the flight-simulating IMAX movies are not to be missed.

★ **Corcoran Gallery of Art.** On exhibit are paintings by French Impressionists and the first great American portraitists as well as photography by modern American artists.

★ **National Museum of American History.** Exploring America's cultural, political, technical, and scientific past, it shows off a steam locomotive, Muhammad Ali's boxing glove, and Nancy Reagan's inaugural gown.

Restaurants

★ **Jean-Louis at the Watergate.** This small restaurant, with contemporary French fare drawing on regional American ingredients, is often cited as one of the best in the United States. *$$$$*

★ **Bombay Club.** This elegant Indian restaurant creates unusual seafood and vegetarian dishes, but the real standouts are the breads and the piscine appetizers. *$$$*

★ **Red Sage.** The barbed-wire-and-lizard decor sets the stage for tasty Southwestern cuisine chock-full of chilis. *$$$*

★ **Meskerem.** Spicy Ethiopian food is served in a bright dining room or on a balcony where you can sit on the floor on leather cushions, with large woven baskets for tables. *$*

Hotels

Hay-Adams Hotel, part Italian Renaissance, part English Tudor, has some brightly decorated rooms with picture-postcard views of the White House; the afternoon tea is renowned, and the staff is dignified and friendly. *$$$$*

Willard Inter-Continental, an opulent beaux-arts hotel with a fascinating history, has hosted innumerable U.S. presidents and foreign heads of state. *$$$$*

Hotel Washington is Edwardian in character: Rooms have antique reproductions and windows festooned with swags, heavy draperies, and lace. Washingtonians bring visitors to the rooftop bar for cocktails and a view of the White House grounds and the Washington Monument. *$$*

Morrison-Clark Inn Hotel. Victorian with an airy, modern twist, this small and unusual historic inn has marble fireplaces and antiques-filled rooms. *$$*

Kalorama Guest House. Housed in five separate turn-of-the-century town houses, the Kalorama is eminently comfortable, with its dark wood walls, calico curtains, and antique oak furniture with traditional, slightly worn upholstery. The coffeepot is always on, and the staff is knowledgeable and friendly. *$*

FESTIVALS AND SEASONAL EVENTS

Washington has a lively calendar of special events; listed below are some of the most important or unusual.

DEC.➤ **Christmas celebrations** start early in the month. Major events are listed below.

EARLY DEC.➤ The **Washington National Cathedral's Open House** celebrates the season's holidays with bagpipers, choral sing-alongs, and seasonal decorations in the Gothic-style cathedral. (Call 202/537–6200.)

DEC. 7➤ The **25th Annual Scottish Christmas Walk** salutes Alexandria's Scottish heritage with a parade, bagpipers, house tours, crafts, and children's events. (Call 703/838–4200.)

DEC. 14–15➤ **Old Town Christmas Candlelight Tours** visit historic Ramsay House, Gadsby's Tavern Museum, the Lee-Fendall House, and the Carlyle House in Old Town Alexandria. Included in the tour are music, colonial dancing, and light refreshments. (Call 703/838–4200.)

DEC. 14–JAN. 12, 1997➤ **U.S. Botanic Gardens' Annual Winter Flower Show** bursts forth with more than 1,000 of the traditional holiday red, white, and pink poinsettias as well as a display of Christmas wreaths and trees. (Call 202/225–7099.)

MID-DEC.➤ The **People's Christmas Tree Lighting** on the west side of the U.S. Capitol celebrates its 33rd anniversary this year. Military bands perform. (Call 202/224–6645.)

MID-DEC.–JAN. 1➤ The **National Christmas Tree Lighting/Pageant of Peace** is accompanied by seasonal music and caroling. In mid-December (usually the second Thursday) the president lights the National Christmas Tree (on the Ellipse just south of the White House) at dusk. For the next few weeks the Ellipse grounds are the site of nightly choral performances, a Nativity scene, a burning Yule log, and a display of lighted Christmas trees representing each of the country's states and territories. (Call 202/619–7222.)

MID-LATE DEC.➤ **The Nutcracker** is performed by the Washington Ballet at Warner Theatre. (Call 202/362–3606)

DEC. 24–25➤ The **Washington National Cathedral Christmas Celebration and Services** include Christmas carols, pageants, and seasonal choral performances. (Call 202/537–6200.)

JAN. 4–7➤ **Washington Antiques Show** at the Omni Shoreham Hotel is an established, high-quality presentation for buyers and browsers. (Call 202/234–0700.)

JAN. 15➤ **Martin Luther King, Jr.'s birthday** is celebrated with speeches, dance, choral performances, and special readings. For more information, contact the Martin Luther King, Jr. Memorial Library (call 202/727–1186); the National Park Service (call 202/619–7222); or the Smithsonian (call 202/357–2700).

MID-JAN.➤ The **Chinese New Year Festival** explodes in Chinatown, amid a cacophony of firecrackers and a dragon-led parade. (Call 202/638–1041 or 202/724–4091.)

JAN. 19➤ **Robert E. Lee's birthday** is marked with 19th-century music and period food at Arlington House, the Custis-Lee mansion in Arlington Cemetery. (Call 703/557–0613.)

FEB.➤ **African-American History Month** features special events, museum exhibits, and cultural programs. (Call 202/789–2403 or 202/727–1186.)

FEB. 12➤ **Lincoln's Birthday** celebrations include a wreath-laying ceremony and a reading of the Gettysburg Address at the Lincoln Memorial. (Call 202/619–7222.)

FEB. 14➤ **Frederick Douglass's birthday** is celebrated with a wreath-laying ceremony at the Frederick Douglass National Historic Site in Anacostia. (Call 202/619–7222 or 202/426–5961.)

FEB. 22➤ **George Washington's birthday** is celebrated with a parade down Washington Street in Old Town Alexandria, a historic-homes tour, and Revolutionary War reenactments. (Call 703/838–4200 or 703/838–5005.)

SPRING

MAR. 1–3➤ The **Spring Antiques Show,** at the Armory (call 301/738–1966 or 202/547–9215 during show) hosts more than 185 dealers from 20 states, Canada, and Europe.

MID-MAR.➤ **St. Patrick's Day and Festival** begins with a parade down Constitution Avenue at 1 PM on March 17. The following days feature theater, folk music, and dance concerts (call 202/637–2474). For information on Old Town Alexandria's March 16 parade festivities, call 703/838–4200. Arlington House in Arlington National Cemetery goes green as well (call 703/557–0613).

MAR. 21➤ The **Annual Bach Marathon** honors Johann Sebastian's birthday. Ten organists each play the massive pipe organ at Chevy Chase Presbyterian Church (1 Chevy Chase Circle NW; call 202/363–2202) from 1 to 6.

MAR. 30➤ The **Smithsonian Kite Festival,** for kite makers and kite fliers of all ages, is held on the Washington Monument grounds (call 202/357–3030).

MAR. 30–APR. 13➤ The **National Cherry Blossom Festival** opens with the traditional Japanese Lantern Lighting ceremony on the 30th. (Call 202/728–1137 for the parade, 202/646–0366, or 202/619–7222.)

APR.➤ **Imagination Celebration,** an annual month-long festival for young people at the John F. Kennedy Center for the Performing Arts, draws some of the nation's best children's theater companies. (Call 202/467–4600.)

APR. 8➤ The **White House Easter Egg Roll** brings children ages eight and under, with an accompanying adult, to the White House lawn. (Call 202/456–7041.)

APR. 13➤ The anniversary of **Thomas Jefferson's birthday** is marked by military drills and a wreath-laying at his memorial. (Call 202/619–7222.)

MID-APR.➤ The **White House Spring Garden Tours** are walks around the Jacqueline Kennedy Rose Garden and the West Lawn; public rooms within the White House can also be visited. (Call 202/456–7041.)

APR. 20–21➤ The **Georgetown House Tour,** now in its 69th year, offers the opportunity to view private homes. Admission includes high tea at historic St. John's Georgetown Parish Church. (Call 202/338–1796.)

LATE APR.➤ The **Smithsonian's Washington Craft Show** exhibits one-of-a-kind, handcrafted objects by 100 of the country's best artisans. (Call 202/357–2700.)

APR. 27➤ The **Alexandria Garden Tour** finds six private gardens and another half-dozen historical sights open to the public, with afternoon tea at the historic Athenaeum. (Call 703/838–4200.)

APR. 30–MAY 12➤ The **D.C. International Film Festival** is where dozens of foreign and American films premiere. Tickets are required. (Call 202/274–6810.)

MAY 3–4➤ The **Washington National Cathedral Flower Mart** salutes a different country each year, with flower booths, crafts, and demonstrations. (Call 202/537–6200.)

MAY 11➤ The **Georgetown Garden Tour** shows off more than a dozen private gardens in one of the city's loveliest and most historic neighborhoods. (Call 202/333–6896.)

MID-MAY➤ The **Joint Services Open House** at Andrews Air Force Base in suburban Maryland features two days' worth of static aircraft and weapons displays, precision parachute jumps, and either the Navy's Blue Angels or Air Force Thunderbirds aerobatic team. (Call 301/568–5995.)

MID-MAY➤ **Malcolm X Day** pays tribute to the slain civil-rights leader. A week of workshops and films culminates in a commemoration on May 19, when concerts and speeches are held in Anacostia Park. (Call 202/396–1021 or 202/678–8352.)

MAY 26➤ The **Memorial Day Weekend Concert,** performed by the National Symphony Orchestra at 7:30 PM on the West Lawn of the U.S. Capitol, officially welcomes the summer to Washington. (Call 202/619–7222.)

MAY 27➢ **Memorial Day** is celebrated with a wreath-laying ceremony at the Vietnam Veterans Memorial and a concert by the National Symphony. (Call 202/619–7222.)

MAY 27➢ This is the 17th annual **Memorial Day Jazz Festival** in Old Town Alexandria, with big-band music performed by local artists. (Call 703/883–4686.)

LATE MAY–EARLY SEPT.➢ The **Military Band Summer Concert Series,** featuring the bands of the different branches of the armed forces, runs from Memorial Day to Labor Day. Every August the Army Band performs the *1812 Overture,* complete with real cannons. (Call 202/433–2525, 703/696–3718, 202/433–4011, or 202/767–5658.)

SUMMER

JUNE➢ **Shakespeare Free for All** is a series of free, nightly performances at the open-air Carter Barron Amphitheater by the Washington Shakespeare Theatre. (Call 202/628–5770 or 202/619–7222.)

JUNE 7–9➢ The family-oriented **Alexandria Waterfront Festival** promotes the American Red Cross and recognizes Alexandria's rich maritime heritage. Tall ships are open for visits, and there are arts and crafts displays, a 10K run, and a blessing of the fleet. (Call 703/549–8300.)

MID-JUNE–MID-JULY➢ **Washington National Cathedral's Summer Festival of Music** features everything from Renaissance choral music to contemporary instrumental fare. (Call 202/537–6200.)

JUNE 26–30 AND JULY 3–JULY 7➢ The **Festival of American Folklife,** sponsored by the Smithsonian and held on the Mall, celebrates the music, arts, crafts, and foods of various nations' cultures. (Call 202/357–2700.)

EARLY JULY➢ The **D.C. Free Jazz Festival** showcases some of the world's most accomplished and innovative musicians in free concerts—many of them held outdoors. (Call 202/783–0360.)

JULY 4➢ The **Independence Day Celebration** includes a grand parade that marches past many of the capital's historic monuments. In the evening, the National Symphony Orchestra performs for free on the steps of the Capitol; this is followed by a fireworks display over the Washington Monument. (Call 202/619–7222.)

MID-JULY–LATE AUG.➢ During the **Twilight Tattoo Series,** the 3rd U.S. Infantry, the U.S. Army Band, the Drill Team, and the Old Guard Fife and Drum Corps play on the Ellipse grounds, between the White House and the Washington Monument, every Wednesday evening at 7. (Call 703/696–3718.)

JULY 27–28➢ The **Virginia Scottish Games,** one of the largest Scottish festivals in the United States, includes traditional Highland dance, bagpipes, a national professional heptathlon, animal events, and fiddling competitions on the Episcopal High School grounds (3901 W. Braddock Rd., Alexandria; call 703/838–4200).

JULY 27–28➢ The **Hispanic Festival** spotlights Washington's large Latino community, with activities on the Mall and in the Adams–Morgan and Mount Pleasant neighborhoods. (Call 202/822–9293.)

AUG. 31➢ The **National Frisbee Festival** is the nation's largest noncompetitive assembly of Frisbee lovers. The disc-catching canines almost steal the show from the two-legged pros. (National Mall near the Smithsonian's National Air and Space Museum; call 301/645–5043.)

AUTUMN

SEPT. 1➢ The **Labor Day Weekend Concert** features the National Symphony Orchestra on the West Lawn of the U.S. Capitol. (Call 202/467–4600.)

SEPT. 7–8➢ At the **John F. Kennedy Center's Open House** there are jugglers, musicians, dancers, and other performers on all five stages. Thousands throng to this free event every year. (Call 202/467–4600.)

EARLY SEPT.➢ **Adams-Morgan Day** celebrates the African American and Latin American character of this unique neighborhood with live music, crafts, and cuisine. (Call 202/332–3292 or 202/789–7000.)

SEPT. 16➤ The **Constitution Day Commemoration** observes the anniversary of the signing of the U.S. Constitution. Events include a naturalization ceremony, speakers, and band concerts. (National Archives; call 202/501–5000.)

LATE SEPT.➤ The **Washington National Cathedral Open House** is a chance to share in cathedral-related crafts, music, and activities, including a climb up the central tower. (Call 202/537–6200.)

LATE SEPT.➤ **Rock Creek Park Day** celebrates the park's 106th birthday, with music, children's

activities, foods, and arts and crafts. The party runs from noon to dusk. (Call 202/426–6829.)

MID-OCT.➤ The **White House Fall Garden Tours** provide an opportunity to see the splendid gardens of the White House, including the famous Rose Gardens and the South Lawn. (Call 202/456–7041.)

OCT. 20–27➤ The **Washington International Horse Show** is D.C.'s major equestrian event. (Call 301/840–0281.)

OCT. 20➤ The **Marine Corps Marathon** attracts thousands of world-class runners. It begins at the Iwo Jima Marine Corps Memorial in Arlington,

Virginia. (Call 703/690–3431.)

OCT. 22➤ **Theodore Roosevelt's birthday** is celebrated on Roosevelt Island in the Potomac, with tours of the island, exhibits, and family activities. (Call 202/619–7222.)

NOV. 11➤ **Veteran's Day** activities include a service at Arlington National Cemetery and an 11 AM wreath-laying ceremony at the Tomb of the Unknowns, led by the president or another ranking official. (Call 202/475–0843.)

MID-NOV.–LATE DEC.➤ **A Christmas Carol** returns year after year to historic Ford's Theatre (call 202/347–4833.)

2 Exploring Washington

By John F. Kelly

Updated by
Mary Case

THE BYZANTINE WORKINGS of the federal government; the nonsensical, sound-bite-ready oratory of the well-groomed politician; murky foreign policy pronouncements issued from Foggy Bottom; and $600 toilet seats ordered by the Pentagon cause many Americans to cast a skeptical eye on anything that happens "inside the Beltway." Washingtonians take it all in stride, though, reminding themselves that, after all, those responsible for political hijinks don't come *from* Washington, they come *to* Washington. Besides, such ribbing is a small price to pay for living in a city whose charms extend far beyond the bureaucratic. World-class museums and art galleries (nearly all of them free), tree-shaded and flower-filled parks and gardens, bars and restaurants that benefit from a large and creative immigrant community, and nightlife that seems to get better with every passing year are as much a part of Washington as floor debates or filibusters.

The location of the city that calls to mind politicking, back scratching, and delicate diplomacy is itself the result of a compromise. Tired of its nomadic existence after having set up shop in eight different locations, Congress voted in 1785 to establish a permanent "Federal town." Northern lawmakers wanted the capital on the Delaware River, in the north, southerners wanted it on the Potomac, in the south. A deal was struck when Virginia's Thomas Jefferson agreed to support the proposal that the federal government assume the war debts of the colonies if New York's Alexander Hamilton and other northern legislators would agree to locate the capital on the banks of the Potomac. George Washington himself selected the exact site of the capital, a diamond-shape, 100-square-mile plot that encompassed the confluence of the Potomac and Anacostia rivers, not far from the president's estate at Mount Vernon. To give the young city a bit of a head start, Washington included the already thriving tobacco ports of Alexandria, Virginia, and Georgetown, Maryland, in the District of Columbia.

Pierre-Charles L'Enfant, a young French engineer who had fought in the Revolution, offered his services in creating a capital "magnificent enough to grace a great nation." His 1791 plan owes much to Versailles, with ceremonial circles and squares, a grid pattern of streets, and broad, diagonal avenues. It was these grand streets that sparked the first debates over L'Enfant's design and its execution. The families that owned the estates and tobacco farms that would be transformed into Washington had agreed to sell the sites needed for public buildings at $66.66 an acre, with the understanding that profits could be made by selling the remaining land to those who wanted to be near the federal government. They also agreed to turn over for free the land to be used for streets and highways. When they discovered that L'Enfant's streets were 100 feet wide and that one thoroughfare—the Mall—would be 400 feet across, they were horrified. Half the land on the site would be turned over to the government for free for roads.

L'Enfant won the battle of the roads but he couldn't control his obstinate ways and fought often with the three city commissioners Washington had appointed. When the nephew of one of the commissioners started to build a manor house where L'Enfant had planned a street, the Frenchman ordered it torn down. The overzealous L'Enfant was fired and offered $2,500 and a lot near the White House in pay. He refused, thinking it poor compensation for the services he had performed. (A visionary who was a little too headstrong for his own good, L'Enfant spent his later years petitioning Congress with long, rambling missives demanding satisfaction. He died penniless in 1825.)

L'Enfant had written that his plan would "leave room for that aggrandizement and embellishment which the increase in the wealth of the nation will permit it to pursue at any period, however remote." At times it must have seemed remote indeed, for the town grew so slowly that when Charles Dickens visited Washington in 1842 what he saw were "spacious avenues that begin in nothing and lead nowhere; streets a mile long that only want houses, roads, and inhabitants; public buildings that need but a public to be complete and ornaments of great thoroughfares which need only great thoroughfares to ornament."

It took the Civil War—and every war thereafter—to energize the city, by attracting thousands of new residents and spurring building booms that extended the capital in all directions. Streets in the once-backward town were paved in the 1870s and the first streetcars ran in the 1880s. Memorials to famous Americans like Lincoln and Jefferson were built in the first decades of the 20th century, along with the massive Federal Triangle, a monument to thousands of less-famous government workers.

Despite the growth and despite the fact that blacks have always played an important role in the city's history (black mathematician Benjamin Banneker surveyed the land with Pierre L'Enfant in the 18th century), Washington today remains essentially segregated. Whites—who account for about 30% of the population—reside mostly in northwest Washington. Blacks live largely east of Rock Creek Park and south of the Anacostia River.

It's a city of other unfortunate contrasts: Citizens of the capital of the free world couldn't vote in a presidential election until 1964, weren't granted limited home rule until 1974, and are represented in Congress by a single nonvoting delegate (though in 1990 residents elected two "shadow" senators, one of whom is political gadfly Jesse Jackson). Homeless people sleep on steam grates next to multimillion-dollar government buildings, and a flourishing drug trade has earned Washington the dubious distinction of murder capital of the United States. Though it's little consolation to those affected, most crime is restricted to neighborhoods far from the areas visited by tourists.

Still, there's no denying that Washington, the world's first planned capital city, is also one of its most beautiful. And though the federal government dominates the city psychologically as much as the Washington Monument dominates it physically, there are parts of the capital where you can leave politics behind. The tours that follow will take you through the monumental city, the governmental city, and the residential city. As you walk, look for evidence of L'Enfant's hand, still present despite growing pains and frequent deviations from his plan. His Washington was to be a city of vistas—pleasant views that would shift and change from block to block, a marriage of geometry and art. It remains this way today. Like its main industry, politics, Washington's design is a constantly changing kaleidoscope that invites contemplation from all angles.

TOUR 1: THE MALL

Numbers in the margin correspond to points of interest on the Tour 1: The Mall map.

The Mall is the heart of nearly every visitor's trip to Washington. With nearly a dozen diverse museums ringing the expanse of green, it's the closest thing the capital has to a theme park (unless you count the federal government itself, which has uncharitably been called "Disneyland on the Potomac"). As at a theme park, you may have to stand in an occasional line, but unlike the amusements at Disneyland almost everything you'll see here is free. (You may, however, need free, timed-entry tickets to some of the more popular traveling exhibitions. These are usually available at the museum information desk or by phone, for a service charge, from TicketMaster, ☎ 202/432–7328.)

Don't expect to see it all in one day, though. The holdings of the museums and art galleries of the Smithsonian Institution—the largest museum complex in the world—total more than 135 million objects. Only 1% are on public display at any one time, but that's still over a million different objects vying for your attention. If you can, devote at least two days to the Mall. Do the north side one day and the south the next. Or split your sightseeing on the Mall into museums the first day, art galleries the second. Of course, the Mall is more than just a front yard for all these museums. It's a picnicking park and a jogging path, an outdoor stage for festivals and fireworks, and America's town green.

The Mall is bounded on the north and south by Constitution and Independence avenues, and on the east and west by 3rd and 14th streets. Nearly all of the Smithsonian museums lie within these boundaries. (The nearest Metro stops are Smithsonian, Archives/Navy Memorial, and L'Enfant Plaza).

In this space west of the "Congress House," Pierre L'Enfant had envisioned a "Grand Avenue, 400 feet in breadth, and about a mile in length, bordered with gardens, ending in a slope from the houses on each side." In the middle of the 19th century, horticulturalist Andrew Jackson Downing took a stab at converting the Mall into a large, English-style garden, with carriageways curving through groves of trees and bushes. This was far from the "vast esplanade" L'Enfant had in mind, and by the dawn of the 20th century the Mall had become an eyesore. It was dotted with sheds and bisected by railroad tracks. There was even a railroad station at its eastern end.

In 1900 Senator James McMillan, chairman of the Committee on the District of Columbia, asked a distinguished group of architects and artists to study ways of improving Washington's park system. The McMillan Commission, which included architects Daniel Burnham and Charles McKim, landscape architect Frederick Law Olmsted, Jr., and sculptor Augustus Saint-Gaudens, didn't confine its recommendations just to parks; its 1902 report would shape the way the capital looked for decades. The Mall received much of the group's attention and is its most stunning accomplishment. L'Enfant's plan was rediscovered, the sheds, railroad tracks, and carriageways were removed, and Washington finally had the monumental core it had been denied for so long.

❶ The best place to start an exploration of the museums on the Mall is in front of the first one constructed, the **Smithsonian Institution Building.** British scientist and founder James Smithson had never visited America. Yet his will stipulated that, should his nephew, Henry James Hungerford, die without an heir, Smithson's entire fortune would go to the United States, "to found at Washington, under the name of the Smithsonian Institution, an establishment for the increase and diffusion of knowledge among men."

Smithson died in 1829, Hungerford in 1835, and in 1838 the United States received $515,169 worth of gold sovereigns. After eight years of congressional debate over the propriety of accepting funds from a private citizen, the Smithsonian Institution was finally established in 1846. The red sandstone, Norman-style headquarters building on Jefferson Drive was completed in 1855 and originally housed all of the Smithsonian's operations, including the science and art collections, research laboratories, and living quarters for the institution's secretary and his family. Known as "the Castle," the building was designed by James Renwick, the architect of St. Patrick's Cathedral in New York City. The statue in front of the Castle's entrance is not of Smithson but of Joseph Henry, the scientist who served as the institution's first secretary. Smithson's body was brought to America in 1904 and is entombed in a small room to the left of the Castle's Mall entrance.

The museums on the Mall are the Smithsonian's most visible presence, but the organization also sponsors traveling exhibitions and maintains research posts in such places as the Chesapeake Bay and the tropics of Panama.

Today the Castle houses Smithsonian administrative offices and is home to the Woodrow Wilson International School for Scholars. To get your bearings or to get help deciding which Mall attractions you want to devote your time to, visit the **Smithsonian Information Center** in the Castle. An orientation film provides an overview of the various Smithsonian museums, and monitors display information on the day's events. The Information Center opens at 9 AM, an hour before the other museums open, so you can plan your day on the Mall without wasting valuable sightseeing time. *1000 Jefferson Dr. SW, ☎ 202/357–2700, TTY 202/357–1729. ☛ Free. ☼ Daily 9–5:30; closed Dec. 25.*

Entry to all Smithsonian museums and federal attractions is free, as are most guided tours of them. Prices for films, special events, etc., are noted.

To the right of the Castle is the pagodalike entrance to the **S. Dillon Ripley Center,** an underground collection of classrooms and offices named after a past Smithsonian secretary. Works from around the world are periodically shown in the center's International Gallery.

This tour circles the Mall counterclockwise. Start by walking east on Jefferson Drive to the **Arts and Industries Building,** the second Smithsonian museum to be constructed. In 1876 Philadelphia hosted the United States International Exposition in honor of the nation's Centennial. After the festivities, scores of exhibitors donated their displays to the federal government. In order to house the objects that had suddenly come its way, the Smithsonian commissioned this redbrick and sandstone building. Designed by Adolph Cluss, the building was originally called the United States National Museum, the name that is still engraved in stone above the doorway. It was finished in 1881, just in time to host President James Garfield's inaugural ball.

The Arts and Industries Building housed a variety of artifacts that were eventually moved to other museums as the Smithsonian grew. It was restored to its original appearance and reopened during Bicentennial celebrations in 1976. Today the museum exhibits an extensive collection of American Victoriana; many of the objects on display—which include carriages, tools, furnishings, printing presses, even a steam locomotive—are from the original Philadelphia Centennial. The Smithsonian hopes to open the National African American Museum here by

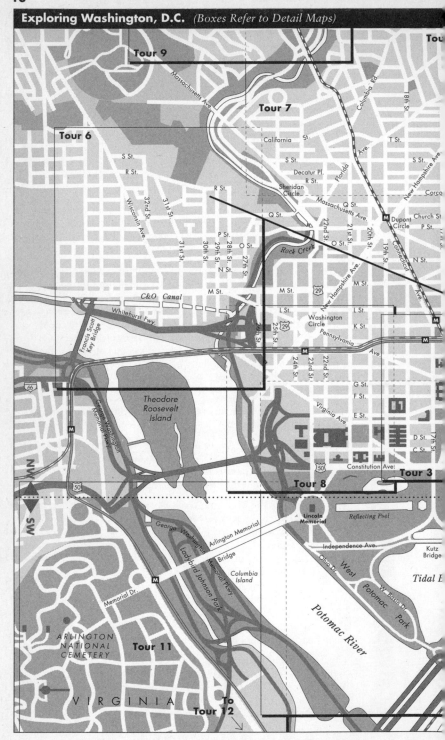

Tour 9

Tour 7

Tou

Tour 6

Massachusetts Ave.

Columbia Rd.

18th St.

California St.

T St.

S St.

New Hampshire Ave.

S St.

R St.

S St.

Decatur Pl.

Florida Ave.

Corco

Wisconsin Ave.

32nd St.

31st St.

R St.

Sheridan Circle

Massachusetts Ave.

Q St.

M Dupont Circle

Church St.

P St.

31st St.

Q St.

22nd St.

21st St.

20th St.

19th St.

Connecticut Ave.

P St.

31st St.

30th St.

29th St.

28th St.

27th St.

P St.

O St.

O St.

N St.

N St.

C&O Canal

M St.

M St.

29

M St.

M St.

Whitehurst Fwy.

26th St.

25th St.

L St.

L St.

L St.

Washington Circle

K St.

Francis Scott Key Bridge

29

Pennsylvania Ave.

M

Theodore Roosevelt Island

24th St.

23rd St.

22nd St.

G St.

F St.

E St.

Virginia Ave.

D St.

C St.

66

Constitution Ave.

Tour 3

M

George Washington Memorial Pkwy.

50

50

Tour 8

NW

SW

George Washington Memorial Pkwy.

Lincoln Memorial

Reflecting Pool

Kutz Bridge

Arlington Memorial Bridge

Independence Ave.

Ohio Dr.

West Potomac Park

Tidal E

M

Memorial Dr.

Ladybird Johnson Park

Columbia Island

W. Basin Dr.

Potomac River

ARLINGTON NATIONAL CEMETERY

Tour 11

VIRGINIA

To Tour 12

10

NW ◀▶ NE

Florida Ave.

16th St.
15th St.
14th St.
U St. M
T St.
S St.
S St.
Rhode Island Ave.
Florida Ave.
S St.
Lincoln Rd.
R St.
3rd St.

St.
St.
St.
Vermont Ave.
R St.
Q St.
New Jersey Ave.
P St.
3rd St.
1st St.
O St.
Q St.
M St.

Church St.
Logan Circle
O St.
9th St.
New York Ave.

St.
Rhode Island Ave.
13th St.
12th St.
11th St.
10th St.
N St.
8th St.
7th St.
6th St.
5th St.
4th St.
N St.
New York Ave.
M St.

Scott Circle
M St.

Thomas Circle
Massachusetts Ave.
L St.
1st St.

15th St.
Mt. Vernon Square M
50

16th St.
New York Ave.
14th St.
T St.
H St.
G St. M
Massachusetts
2nd St.
Ave.
Tour 5
395
Tour 4

H St. M
G St. M
Union Station
Columbus Memorial Fountain

The White House
F St.
E St.
D St.
New Jersey
Louisiana Ave.
Stanton Park

The Ellipse
Pennsylvania Ave.
NE ◀▶ SE

Constitution Ave.
US Capitol
E. Capitol St.

Madison Dr.
National Gallery of Art
Folger Park

Washington Monument
Smithsonian Institution
THE MALL
Jefferson Dr.
National Air and Space Museum
Tour 1

Independence Ave.
Maryland Ave.
C St.
Canal St.

Outlet Bridge
D St.
E St.

Jefferson Memorial
Southwest Fwy.
G St.
Virginia Ave.
395

Francis Case Memorial Bridge
395
I St.

Water St.
Maine Ave.

0 500 yards
0 500 meters

Tour 2
N ↑
Washington Canal
M

SW ◀▶ SE

the year 2000. *900 Jefferson Dr. SW,* ☎ *202/357–2700, TTY 202/357–1729.* ☛ *Free.* ⊙ *Daily 10–5:30; closed Dec. 25.*

In front of the Arts and Industries Building is a **carousel** that is popular with young and old alike. It operates year-round, weather permitting, weekdays 11–5, weekends 10–6 ($1 a ride).

❸ The **Hirshhorn Museum** is the next building to the east on Jefferson Drive, and you would be hard-pressed to find a piece of architecture that contrasts more with the gay Victoriana of the Arts and Industries Building. Dubbed "the Doughnut on the Mall," the reinforced-concrete building designed by Gordon Bunshaft is a fitting home for contemporary art. Opened in 1974, the museum manages a collection that includes 4,000 paintings and drawings and 2,000 sculptures donated by Joseph H. Hirshhorn, a Latvian-born immigrant who made his fortune in this country running uranium mines. American artists such as Eakins, Pollock, Rothko, and Stella are represented, as are modern European and Latin masters, including Francis Bacon, Fernando Botero, Magritte, Miró, and Victor Vasarely.

The Hirshhorn's impressive sculpture collection is arranged in the open spaces between the museum's concrete piers and across Jefferson Drive in the sunken **Sculpture Garden.** The display in the Sculpture Garden includes one of the largest public American collections of works by Henry Moore, as well as works by Honoré Daumier, Max Ernst, Alberto Giacometti, Pablo Picasso, and Man Ray. Auguste Rodin's *Burghers of Calais* is a highlight. The severe exterior lines of the museum were softened a bit in 1993 when its plaza was relandscaped by James Urban. Grass and trees provide a counterpoint to the concrete, and a granite walkway rings the museum and its outside sculpture. The museum's gift shop is known for its contemporary jewelry. *Independence Ave. at 7th St. SW,* ☎ *202/357–2700, TTY 202/357–1729.* ☛ *Free.* ⊙ *Daily 10–5:30; closed Dec. 25. Sculpture garden open daily 7:30–dusk.*

★ ❹ Cross 7th Street to get to the **National Air and Space Museum.** Opened in 1976, Air and Space is the most visited museum in the world, attracting 12 million people each year. (It's thought to be the most-visited building on earth.) Twenty-three galleries tell the story of aviation, from man's earliest attempts at flight. Suspended from the ceiling like plastic models in a child's room are dozens of aircraft, including the actual "Wright Flyer" that Wilbur Wright piloted over the sands of Kitty Hawk, North Carolina; Charles Lindbergh's "Spirit of St. Louis"; the X-1 rocket plane in which Chuck Yeager broke the sound barrier; and the X-15, the fastest plane ever built.

Other highlights include a backup model of the Skylab orbital workshop that visitors can walk through; the Voyager airplane that Dick Rutan and Jeana Yeager flew nonstop around the world; and the U.S.S. *Enterprise* model used in the "Star Trek" TV show. Visitors can also touch a piece of the moon: a 4-billion-year-old slice of rock collected by Apollo 17 astronauts. (Moon rock is one of the rarest substances on earth and, soon after the museum opened, a few zealous tourists tried to add the rock to their collections. The display is now wired with a motion alarm and watched by a uniformed guard.)

Don't let long lines deter you from seeing a show in the museum's **Samuel P. Langley Theater.** IMAX films shown on the five-story-high screen—including *The Dream Is Alive, To Fly!* and *The Blue Planet*—usually feature swooping aerial scenes that will convince you you've left the ground. Buy your tickets ($3.25 adults; $2 children, students, and senior citizens; sometimes higher for special films) as soon as you arrive, then look around the museum. (Or, if you prefer, you can buy tickets up to two weeks in advance.) Upstairs, the **Albert Einstein Planetarium** projects images of celestial bodies on a domed ceiling. *Jefferson Dr. at 6th St. SW,* ☎ *202/357–2700, TTY 202/357–1729.* ☞ *Free.* ☉ *Daily 10–5:30; closed Dec. 25. Extended summer hrs determined annually. Double features are often shown in Langley Theater after museum has closed. For information, call 202/357–1686.*

TIME OUT   Two restaurants are at the eastern end of the National Air and Space Museum: **The Wright Place** is a table-service restaurant that takes reservations (☎ 202/371–8777); the **Flight Line** is a self-service cafeteria. They each have a large selection of foods, but at peak times lines can be long.

After touring the Air and Space Museum, walk east on Jefferson Drive toward the Capitol. What has been called the last open space left for a museum on the periphery of the Mall is bounded by 3rd and 4th streets and Independence Avenue and Jefferson Drive SW. The Smithsonian's **National Museum of the American Indian** is scheduled to open here in 2001.

★   Cross Madison Drive to get to the two buildings of the **National Gallery of Art,** one of the world's foremost collections of paintings, sculptures, and graphics. If you want to view the museum's holdings in (more or less) chronological order, it's best to start your exploration of this mag-

5   nificent gallery in the **West Building.** Opened in 1941, the domed building was a gift to the nation from financier Andrew Mellon. (The dome was one of architect John Russell Pope's favorite devices. He designed the domed Jefferson Memorial and, though it's difficult to see from outside, there's a dome on his National Archives, too.)

A wealthy banker and oil company executive, Andrew Mellon served as secretary of the treasury under three presidents and as ambassador to the United Kingdom. He first came to Washington in 1921, and lived for many years in a luxurious apartment near Dupont Circle, in a building that today houses the National Trust for Historic Preservation (*see* Tour 7, *below*). Mellon had long collected great works of art, acquiring them on his frequent trips to Europe. In 1931, when the Soviet government was short on cash and selling off many of its art treasures, Mellon stepped in and bought $6 million worth of old masters, including *The Alba Madonna* by Raphael and Botticelli's *Adoration of the Magi.* Mellon promised his collection to America in 1937, the year of his death. He also donated the funds for the construction of the huge gallery and resisted suggestions it be named after him.

The West Building's **Great Rotunda,** with its 16 marble columns surrounding a fountain topped with a statue of Mercury, sets the stage for the masterpieces on display in the more than 100 separate galleries. You'll probably want to wander the rooms at your own pace, taking in the wealth of art. A tape-recorded tour of the building's better-known holdings is available for a $3.50 rental fee ($2.75 for senior citizens) at the ground floor sales area. If you'd rather explore on your own, get a map at one of the two information desks; one is just inside the Mall entrance (off Madison Drive), the other is near the Constitution Avenue entrance on the ground floor.

The National Gallery's permanent collection includes works from the 13th to the 20th century. A comprehensive survey of Italian paintings

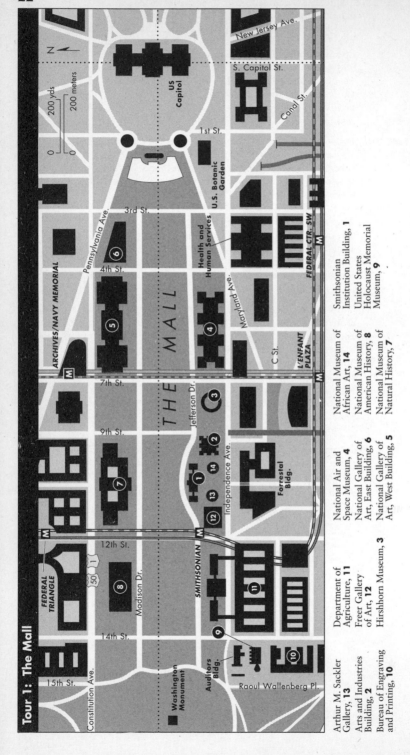

Tour 1: The Mall

US Capitol

New Jersey Ave.

S. Capitol St.

Canal St.

N

200 yds
200 meters

1st St.

U.S. Botanic Garden

Pennsylvania Ave.

3rd St.

Health and Human Services

4th St.

Maryland Ave.

ARCHIVES/NAVY MEMORIAL

THE MALL

C St.

L'ENFANT PLAZA

FEDERAL CTR. SW

7th St.

Jefferson Dr.

9th St.

Independence Ave.

Forrestal Bldg.

12th St.

Madison Dr.

SMITHSONIAN

FEDERAL TRIANGLE

14th St.

Washington Monument

Auditors Bldg.

Raoul Wallenberg Pl.

15th St.

Constitution Ave.

Arthur M. Sackler Gallery, **13**
Arts and Industries Building, **2**
Bureau of Engraving and Printing, **10**

Department of Agriculture, **11**
Freer Gallery of Art, **12**
Hirshhorn Museum, **3**

National Air and Space Museum, **4**
National Gallery of Art, East Building, **6**
National Gallery of Art, West Building, **5**

National Museum of African Art, **14**
National Museum of American History, **8**
National Museum of Natural History, **7**

Smithsonian Institution Building, **1**
United States Holocaust Memorial Museum, **9**

and sculpture includes *The Adoration of the Magi* by Fra Angelico and Fra Filippo Lippi and *Ginevra de'Benci,* the only painting by da Vinci in the western hemisphere. Flemish and Dutch works, displayed in a series of attractive paneled rooms, include *Daniel in the Lions' Den,* by Rubens, and a self-portrait by Rembrandt. The Chester Dale Collection comprises works by Impressionist painters such as Degas, Monet, Renoir, and Mary Cassatt.

❻ To get to the **National Gallery of Art's East Building** you can take a moving walkway that travels below ground between the two buildings. But to appreciate architect I. M. Pei's impressive, angular East Building, enter it from outside rather than from underground. Exit the West Building through its eastern doors, and cross 4th Street. (As you cross, look to the north: Seeming to float above the Doric columns and pediment of the D.C. Superior Court is the green roof and redbrick pediment of the Pension Building, four blocks away.)

The East Building opened in 1978 in response to the changing needs of the National Gallery. The awkward trapezoidal shape of the building site, which had been taken up by tennis courts and rose bushes planted during Lady Bird Johnson's spruce-up campaign, prompted Pei's dramatic approach: Two interlocking spaces shaped like triangles provide room for galleries, auditoriums, and administrative offices. While the East Building's triangles contrast sharply with the symmetrical classical facade and gentle dome of the West Building, both buildings are constructed of pink marble from the same Tennessee quarries. Despite its severe angularity, Pei's building is inviting. The axe-blade-like southwest corner has been darkened and polished smooth by thousands of hands irresistibly drawn to it.

The atrium of the East Building is dominated by two massive works of art: Alexander Calder's mobile *Untitled* (recently refurbished to make it rotate more easily) and *Woman,* a huge wall-hanging by Joan Miró. The galleries here generally display modern art, though the East Building serves as a home for major temporary exhibitions that span years and artistic styles. *Madison Dr. and 4th St. NW, ☎ 202/737–4215, TTY 202/842–6176.* ☛ *Free.* ☉ *Mon.–Sat. 10–5, Sun. 11–6; closed Dec. 25. Extended spring and summer hrs determined annually.*

TIME OUT Two restaurants on the concourse level between the East and West buildings of the National Gallery offer bleary-eyed and foot-sore museum goers the chance to recharge. The **buffet** serves a wide variety of soups, sandwiches, salads, hot entrées, and desserts. The **Cascade Café** has a smaller selection, but customers enjoy the soothing effect of the gentle waterfall that splashes against the glass-covered wall.

Between 7th and 9th streets is the **National Sculpture Garden Ice Rink** (☎ 202/371–5340). In the winter, skates are rented out for use on the circular rink. Ice cream and other refreshments are available at the green building during the summer.

★ ❼ The **National Museum of Natural History** houses the majority of the Smithsonian's collection of objects, a total of some 118 million specimens. It was constructed in 1910, and two wings were added in the '60s. It is a museum's museum, filled with bones, fossils, stuffed animals, and other natural delights. Exhibits also explore the exploits of humans, the world's most adaptive inhabitants.

The first-floor hall under the rotunda is dominated by a stuffed, 8-ton, 13-foot African bull elephant, one of the largest specimens ever found. (The tusks are fiberglass; the original ivory ones were apparently far too heavy for the stuffed elephant to support.) Off to the right is the popular **Dinosaur Hall.** Fossilized skeletons on display range from a 90-foot-long diplodocus to a tiny thesalosaurus neglectus (a small dinosaur so named because its disconnected bones sat forgotten for years in a college drawer before being reassembled).

In the west wing are displays on birds, mammals, and sea life. Many of the preserved specimens are from the collection of animals bagged by Teddy Roosevelt on his trips to Africa. Not everything in the museum is dead, though. The sea-life display features a living coral reef, complete with fish, plants, and simulated waves. The halls north of the rotunda contain tools, clothing, and other artifacts from many cultures, including those of Native America and of Asia, the Pacific, and Africa.

The highlight of the second floor is the **mineral and gem collection.** Objects include the largest sapphire on public display in the country (the Logan Sapphire, 423 carats), the largest uncut diamond (the Oppenheimer Diamond, 253.7 carats), and, of course, the Hope Diamond, a blue gem found in India and reputed to carry a curse (though Smithsonian guides are quick to pooh-pooh this notion). The amazing gem collection is second in value only to the crown jewels of Great Britain. (The Hall of Gems was closed for renovations at press time and is expected to reopen in summer 1996; however, its more spectacular objects will remain on display.)

Also on the second floor is the renovated **O. Orkin Insect Zoo.** Visitors can view all manner of creepy crawlies, from bees to tarantulas, and even go on hands and knees through a termite mound. (And, yes, it's named after the pest control magnate; he donated money for the zoo's renovation.)

If you've always wished you could get your hands on the objects behind the glass, stop by the **Discovery Room,** in the northwest corner of the second floor. Here elephant tusks, petrified wood, seashells, rocks, feathers, and other items from the natural world can be handled by children and their parents. *Madison Dr. between 9th and 12th Sts. NW,* ☎ *202/357–2700, TTY 202/357–1729.* ☛ *Free.* ⊙ *Daily 10–5:30; closed Dec. 25. Discovery Room open weekdays noon–2:30, weekends 10:30–3:30; in spring and summer free passes are distributed starting at 11:45 weekdays, 10:15 weekends. Naturalist Center open Mon.–Sat. 10:30–4. Extended spring and summer hrs determined annually.*

❽ The **National Museum of American History**—the next building to the west, toward the Washington Monument—explores America's cultural, political, technical, and scientific past. It opened in 1964 as the National Museum of History and Technology and was renamed in 1980. The incredible diversity of artifacts here helps the Smithsonian live up to its nickname as "the Nation's attic." This is the museum that displayed Muhammad Ali's boxing gloves, the Fonz's leather jacket, and the Bunkers' living room furniture from "All in the Family." Visitors can wander for hours on the museum's three floors. The exhibits on the first floor emphasize the history of science and technology and include such items as farm machines, antique automobiles, early phonographs, and a 280-ton steam locomotive. The permanent "Science in American Life" exhibit—opened in 1994 and covering a whopping 12,000 square feet—shows how science has shaped American life through such breakthroughs as the mass production of penicillin, the development of plastics, and the birth of the environmental movement. The second floor is devoted to U.S. social and political history and features an exhibit on everyday American life just after the Revolution.

After a 4½-year conservation project, the gowns of the First Ladies are on display again. This new permanent exhibit, "First Ladies: Political Role and Public Image," goes beyond fashion to explore the women behind the satin, lace, and brocade. The third floor has installations on ceramics, money, graphic arts, musical instruments, photography, and news reporting.

Be sure to check out Horatio Greenough's statue of the first president (by the west-wing escalators on the second floor). Commissioned by Congress in 1832, the statue was intended to grace the Capitol Rotunda. It was there for only a short while, however, since the toga-clad likeness proved shocking to legislators who grumbled that it looked as if the father of our country had just emerged from a bath. The statue was first banished to the east grounds of the Capitol, then given to the Smithsonian in 1908. Those who want a more interactive visit should stop at two places: In the **Hands On History Room** visitors can ride a high-wheeler bike, harness a mule, or sort mail as it was done on the railroads in the 1870s. In the **Hands On Science Room** you can do one of 25 experiments, including testing a water sample and exploring DNA fingerprinting. *Madison Ave. between 12th and 14th Sts. NW,* ☎ *202/ 357–2700, TTY 202/357–1729.* ☛ *Free.* ⊙ *Daily 10–5:30; closed Dec. 25. Hands On History and Hands On Science rooms open Tues.–Sat. noon–3. Extended spring and summer hrs determined annually.*

To continue the loop of the Mall, head south on 14th Street. From here you'll be able to view the length of the Mall from its western end, this time seeing the Capitol from afar. Instead of turning east on Jefferson Drive, continue south on 14th Street. On the right you'll pass a turreted, castlelike structure called the **Auditor's Building.** Built in 1879, it was the first building dedicated exclusively to the work of printing America's money. It was renovated in 1991 and is now home to the Forest Service.

★ ⑨ Next door is the new **United States Holocaust Memorial Museum,** designed by James Ingo Freed. It is an atypical museum, since it doesn't celebrate the best that humanity can achieve, but instead illustrates the worst. The museum tells the story of the 11 million Jews, Gypsies, Jehovah's Witnesses, homosexuals, political prisoners, and others killed by the Nazis between 1933 and 1945. The museum's graphic presentation is as atypical as its subject matter: Upon arrival, each visitor is issued an "identity card" containing biographical information on a real person from the Holocaust. As visitors move through the museum, they read sequential updates on their cards. The museum recounts the Holocaust in almost cinematic fashion, with documentary films, videotaped oral histories, and a collection that includes such items as a German freight car, used to transport Jews from Warsaw to the Treblinka death camp, and the Star of David patches that Jewish prisoners were made to wear. Like the history it covers, the museum can be profoundly disturbing; it is not recommended for visitors under 11. Plan to spend at least four hours here. After this powerful—even wrenching—experience, the adjacent **Hall of Remembrance** provides a space for quiet reflection. *100 Raoul Wallenberg Pl. SW (enter from either Raoul Wallenberg Pl. or 14th St. SW),* ☎ *202/488–0400.* ☛ *Free, though same-day timed-entry passes necessary (often not available after 11 AM); tickets also available through TicketMaster,* ☎ *202/432–7328.* ⊙ *Daily 10–5:30. Closed Yom Kippur and Dec. 25.*

⑩ In 1914 the country's money-making operation moved from the Auditor's Building to the **Bureau of Engraving and Printing.** All the paper currency in the United States, as well as stamps, military certificates, and presidential invitations, is printed in this huge building. Despite the fact that there are no free samples, the 20-minute, self-guided tour of the bureau—which takes visitors past presses that turn out some $22.5 million a day—is one of the city's most popular. *14th and C Sts. SW,* ☎ *202/874–3019.* ⊙ *Weekdays 9–2; closed Dec. 25. During peak tourist season, same-day timed-entry passes are issued starting at 8:30* AM.

Return to 14th Street and turn east onto Independence Avenue. Continuing toward the Capitol, you'll walk between the two buildings of the **Department of Agriculture.** The older building, on your left, was started in 1905 and was the first to be constructed by order of the McMillan Commission on the south side of the Mall. The cornices on the north side of this white-marble building feature depictions of forests and of grains, flowers, and fruits—some of the plants the department keeps an eye on. The newer building south of Independence Avenue, to your right, covers three city blocks (an example, perhaps, of big government).

A few steps farther up Independence Avenue, across 12th Street, is the **Freer Gallery of Art,** a gift from Detroit industrialist Charles L. Freer, who retired in 1900 and devoted the rest of his life to collecting Asian treasures. The Freer opened in 1923, four years after its benefactor's death. Its collection includes more than 26,000 works of art from the Far and Near East, including Asian porcelains, Japanese screens, Chinese paintings and bronzes, Korean stoneware, and examples of Islamic art. Freer's friend James McNeill Whistler introduced him to Asian art, and the American painter is represented in the vast collection. On display in Gallery 12 is the "Peacock Room," a blue-and-gold dining room decorated with painted leather, wood, and canvas and designed by Whistler for a British shipping magnate. Freer paid $30,000 for the entire room and moved it from London to the United States in 1904. The works of other American artists Freer felt were influenced by the Orient also are on display. The Freer reopened in 1993 after a $26-million renovation. Additions include three floors of underground space, more storage space, a gift shop, and an auditorium. The spectacular Peacock Room also received a sprucing up. *12th St. and Jefferson Dr. SW,* ☎ *202/357–2700, TTY 202/357–1729.* ☛ *Free.* ⊙ *Daily 10–5:30.*

Just beyond the Freer turn left off of Independence Avenue into the **Enid Haupt Memorial Garden.** This 4-acre Victorian-style garden is built largely on the rooftops of two Smithsonian museums, the Arthur M. Sackler Gallery and the National Museum of African Art, both of which opened in 1987 and sit underground like inverted pyramids.

When Charles Freer endowed the gallery that bears his name, he insisted on a few conditions: Objects in the collection could not be loaned out, nor could objects from outside the collections be put on display. Because of these restrictions it was necessary to build a second, complementary, Oriental art museum. The result was the **Arthur M. Sackler Gallery.** A wealthy medical researcher and publisher who began collecting Asian art as a student, Sackler allowed Smithsonian curators to select 1,000 items from his ample collection and pledged $4 million toward the construction of the museum. The collection includes works from China, the Indian subcontinent, Persia, Thailand, and Indonesia. Articles in the permanent collection include Chinese ritual bronzes, jade ornaments from the 3rd millennium BC, Persian manuscripts, and Indian paintings in gold, silver, lapis lazuli, and malachite. *1050 Independence Ave. SW,* ☎ *202/357–2700, TTY 202/357–1729.* ☛ *Free.* ⊙ *Daily 10–5:30; closed Dec. 25.*

The other half of the Smithsonian's underground museum complex is

⑭ the **National Museum of African Art.** Founded in 1964 as a private educational institution, the museum became part of the Smithsonian in
1979. Dedicated to the collection, exhibition, and study of the traditional arts of sub-Saharan Africa, the museum has a permanent collection of more than 6,000 objects representative of hundreds of
African cultures. Objects on display include masks, carvings, textiles,
and jewelry, all made from materials such as wood, fiber, bronze,
ivory, and fired clay. A new permanent exhibit explores the personal
objects—chairs, pipes, cups, snuff containers—that were a part of
daily life in 19th- and early 20th-century Africa. These items show how
aesthetics are integrated with utility to create works of peculiar beauty.
Because many pieces of African art are made of organic materials, the
museum also runs a conservation laboratory, where curators work to
arrest the decay of the valuable collection. *950 Independence Ave. SW,*
☎ *202/357–4600, TTY 202/357–4814.* ☛ *Free.* ۞ *Daily 10–5:30;
closed Dec. 25.*

You'll find the nearest Metro station, Smithsonian, on Jefferson Drive
in front of the Freer Gallery.

TOUR 2: THE MONUMENTS

*Numbers in the margin correspond to points of interest on the Tour
2: The Monuments map.*

Washington is a city of monuments. In the middle of traffic circles, on
tiny slivers of park, and at street corners and intersections, statues,
plaques, and simple blocks of marble honor the generals, politicians,
poets, and statesmen who helped shape the nation. The monuments
dedicated to the most famous Americans are west of the Mall on
ground reclaimed from the marshy flats of the Potomac. This is also
the location of Washington's cherry trees, gifts from Japan and focus
of a festival each spring.

On this tour we'll walk clockwise among the monuments and through
the cherry trees. This can be a leisurely, half-day walk, depending on
the speed you travel and the time you spend at each spot. If it's an extremely hot day you may want to hop a Tourmobile bus and travel between the monuments in air-conditioned comfort.

❶ We'll start in front of the tallest of them all, the **Washington Monument** (Metro: Smithsonian). At the western end of the Mall, the Washington Monument punctuates the capital like a huge exclamation
point. Visible from nearly everywhere in the city, it serves as a landmark for visiting tourists and lost motorists alike.

Congress first authorized a monument to General Washington in 1783.
In his 1791 plan for the city, Pierre L'Enfant selected a site (the point
where a line drawn west from the Capitol crossed one drawn south
from the White House), but it wasn't until 1833, after years of quib-
bling in Congress, that a private National Monument Society was
formed to select a designer and to search for funds. Robert Mills's winning design called for a 600-foot-tall decorated obelisk rising from a
circular colonnaded building. The building at the base was to be an
American pantheon, adorned with statues of national heroes and a massive statue of Washington riding in a chariot pulled by snorting horses.

Because of the marshy conditions of L'Enfant's original site, the position of the monument was shifted to firmer ground 100 yards southeast. (If you walk a few steps north of the monument you can see the

stone marker that denotes L'Enfant's original axis.) The cornerstone was laid in 1848 with the same Masonic trowel Washington himself had used to lay the Capitol's cornerstone 55 years earlier. The Monument Society continued to raise funds after construction was begun, soliciting subscriptions of one dollar from citizens across America. It also urged states, organizations, and foreign governments to contribute memorial stones for the construction. Problems arose in 1854, when members of the anti-Papist "Know Nothing" party stole a block donated by Pope Pius IX, smashed it, and dumped its shards into the Potomac. This action, a lack of funds, and the onset of the Civil War kept the monument at a fraction of its final height, open at the top, and vulnerable to the rain. A clearly visible ring about a third of the way up the obelisk testifies to this unfortunate stage of the monument's history: Although all of the marble in the obelisk came from the same Maryland quarry, that used for the second phase of construction came from a different stratum and is of a slightly different shade.

In 1876 Congress finally appropriated $200,000 to finish the monument, and the Army Corps of Engineers took over construction, thankfully simplifying Mills's original design. Work was finally completed in December 1884, when the monument was topped with a 7½-pound piece of aluminum, then one of the most expensive metals in the world. Four years later the monument was opened to visitors, who rode to the top in a steam-operated elevator. (Only men were allowed to take the 20-minute ride; it was thought too dangerous for women, who as a result had to walk up the stairs if they wanted to see the view.)

At 555 feet 5 inches, the Washington Monument is the world's tallest masonry structure. The view from the top takes in most of the District and parts of Maryland and Virginia. Visitors are no longer permitted to climb the 898 steps leading to the top. (Incidents of vandalism and a disturbing number of heart attacks on the steps convinced the Park Service that letting people walk up on their own wasn't such a good idea.) Most weekends at 10 and 2 there are walk-down tours, with a volunteer guide describing the monument's construction and showing the 193 stone and metal plaques that adorn the inside. (The tours are sometimes canceled due to lack of staff. Call the day of your visit to confirm.)

There is usually a wait to take the minute-long elevator ride up the monument's shaft, and the Park Service rangers standing at the head of the line are good at estimating how long. Figure on a wait of approximately 10 to 15 minutes for each side of the monument that is lined with people. If the line goes all the way around the monument, you'll wait anywhere from 40 minutes to an hour. *Constitution Ave. at 15th St. NW,* ☎ *202/426–6840.* ☛ *Free.* ☉ *Apr.–Labor Day, daily 8 AM–midnight; Sept.–Mar., daily 9–5.*

② After your ascent and descent, walk on the path that leads south from the monument. On your right you'll pass the open-air **Sylvan Theater,** scene of a variety of musical performances during the warmer months. Continue south and cross Independence Avenue at 15th Street, passing the redbrick **Auditor's Building,** the **United States Holocaust Memorial Museum,** and the colonnaded **Bureau of Engraving and Printing** (*see* Tour 1, *above*).

③ Carefully cross Maine Avenue at the light and walk down to the **Tidal Basin.** This placid pond was part of the Potomac until 1882, when portions of the river were filled in to improve navigation and create additional parkland, including that upon which the Jefferson Memorial

Tour 2: The Monuments

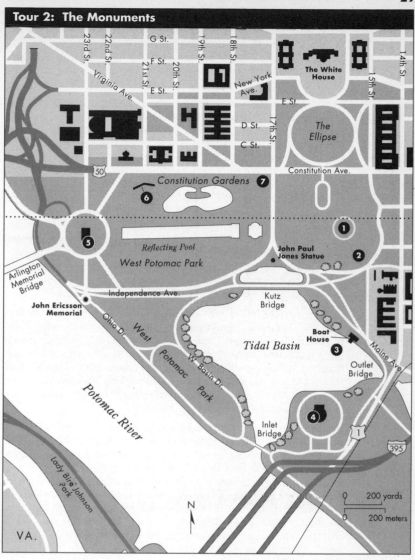

Jefferson Memorial, **4**
Lincoln Memorial, **5**
Lockkeeper's house, **7**
Sylvan Theater, **2**
Tidal Basin, **3**

Vietnam Veterans
Memorial and
Constitution
Gardens, **6**
Washington
Monument, **1**

was later built. Paddleboats have been a fixture on the Tidal Basin for years. You can rent one at the boathouse on the east side of the basin, southwest of the Bureau of Engraving. *Northeast bank of Tidal Basin, ☎ 202/479–2426. Paddleboat rentals: $8 per hr, $1.75 each additional 15 mins. Children under 16 must be accompanied by an adult. ⏲ Daily 10–6, weather permitting.*

Continue down the path that skirts the Tidal Basin and cross the Outlet Bridge to get to the **Jefferson Memorial,** the southernmost of the major monuments in the District. Congress decided that Jefferson deserved a monument positioned as prominently as those in honor of Washington and Lincoln, and this spot directly south of the White House seemed ideal. Jefferson had always admired the Pantheon in Rome—the rotundas he designed for the University of Virginia and his own Monticello were inspired by its dome—so architect John Russell Pope drew from the same source when he designed this memorial to our third president. Dedicated in 1943, it houses a statue of Jefferson. Its walls are lined with inscriptions based on his writings. One of the best views of the White House can be seen from the memorial's top steps, although the view may be obstructed on your visit by the scaffolding that will surround the memorial while it undergoes renovation. *Tidal Basin, south bank, ☎ 202/426–6821. ☛ Free. ⏲ Daily 8 AM–midnight.*

4

After viewing the Jefferson Memorial, continue along the sidewalk that hugs the Tidal Basin. You'll see two grotesque sculpted heads on the sides of the **Inlet Bridge.** The inside walls of the bridge also sport two other interesting sculptures: bronze, human-headed fish that spout water from their mouths. The bridge was refurbished in the 1980s at the same time the chief of the park—a Mr. Jack Fish—was retiring. Sculptor Constantine Sephralis played a little joke: These fish heads are actually Fish's head.

Once you cross the bridge, you have a choice: You can walk to the left, along the Potomac, or continue along the Tidal Basin to the right. The latter route is somewhat more scenic, especially when the cherry trees are in bloom. The first batch of these trees arrived from Japan in 1909. The trees were infected with insects and fungus, however, and the Department of Agriculture ordered them destroyed. A diplomatic crisis was averted when the United States politely asked the Japanese for another batch, and in 1912 Mrs. William Howard Taft planted the first tree. The second was planted by the wife of the Japanese ambassador. About 200 of the original trees still grow near the Tidal Basin. (The Tidal Basin's cherry trees are the single-flowering Akebeno and Yoshino variety. Double-blossom Fugenzo and Kwanzan trees grow in East Potomac Park and flower about two weeks after their more famous cousins.)

The trees are now the centerpiece of Washington's Cherry Blossom Festival, held each spring. The festivities are kicked off by the lighting of a ceremonial Japanese lantern that rests on the north shore of the Tidal Basin, not far from where the first tree was planted. The once-simple celebration has grown over the years to include concerts, fashion shows, and a parade. Park Service experts try their best to predict exactly when the buds will pop. The trees are usually in bloom for about 10–12 days at the beginning of April. When winter refuses to release its grip, the parade and festival are held anyway, without the presence of blossoms, no matter how inclement the weather. And when the weather complies, and the blossoms are at their peak at the time of the festivities, Washington rejoices.

West Potomac Park, the green expanse to the west of the Tidal Basin, is a pleasant place to sit and rest for a while, to watch the paddleboats skim the surface of the Tidal Basin, and to feed the squirrels that usually approach looking for handouts. The character of West Potomac Park will change over the next few years as the $47.2 million Franklin Delano Roosevelt Memorial is constructed. FDR asked for a simple memorial (in fact, one already sits on a wedge of grass in front of the National Archives) but boosters have for years been pushing for something more grandiose. When it's completed in 1996 the memorial will comprise a long sequence of walkways and shaded, exterior "rooms" containing sculptures and inscriptions about the 32nd president. To get to our next stop, the Lincoln Memorial, walk northwest along West Basin Drive, then cut across to Ohio Drive. Cross Independence Avenue at the light; the traffic here can be dangerous.

As you walk north along Ohio Drive you'll pass a series of playing fields. Softball has become as competitive a sport as politics in Washington, and the battle to secure a field here or elsewhere in the city starts long before the season. Farther along Ohio Drive, directly south of the Lincoln Memorial, is a granite sculpture honoring **John Ericsson,** builder of the ironclad *Monitor,* which took on the Confederate *Merrimac* at Hampton Roads off the coast of Virginia during the Civil War.

A memorial to veterans of the Korean War, between Independence Avenue and the Lincoln Memorial, in a grove of trees called Ash Woods, was dedicated on July 27, 1995—the 42nd anniversary of the Korean War armistice. **The Korean War Veterans Memorial** consists of a column of soldiers marching toward an American flag, along with a reflecting pool and a granite wall etched with war scenes.

★ ❺ The **Lincoln Memorial** is considered by many to be the most inspiring monument in the city. It would be hard to imagine Washington without the Lincoln and Jefferson memorials, though they were both criticized when first built. The Jefferson Memorial was dubbed "Jefferson's muffin"; critics lambasted the design as outdated and too similar to that of the Lincoln Memorial. Some also complained that the Jefferson Memorial blocked the view of the Potomac from the White House. Detractors of the Lincoln Memorial thought it inappropriate that the humble Lincoln be honored with what amounts to a modified but nonetheless rather grandiose Greek temple. The white Colorado-marble memorial was designed by Henry Bacon and completed in 1922. The 36 Doric columns represent the 36 states in the Union at the time of Lincoln's death; the names of the states appear on the frieze above the columns. Above the frieze are the names of the 48 states in the Union when the memorial was dedicated. (Alaska and Hawaii are noted by an inscription on the terrace leading up to the memorial.)

Daniel Chester French's somber statue of the seated president, in the center of the memorial, gazes out over the Reflecting Pool. Though the 19-foot-high sculpture looks as if it were cut from one huge block of stone, it actually comprises 28 interlocking pieces of Georgia marble. (The memorial's original design called for a 10-foot-high sculpture, but experiments with models revealed that a statue that size would be lost in the cavernous space.) Inscribed on the south wall is the Gettysburg Address, and on the north wall is Lincoln's second inaugural address. Above each inscription is a mural painted by Jules Guerin: On the south wall is an angel of truth freeing a slave; the unity of North and South are depicted opposite. The memorial served as a fitting backdrop for Martin Luther King's "I have a dream" speech in 1963.

Many visitors look only at the front and inside of the Lincoln Memorial, but there is much more to explore. On the lower level to the left is a display that chronicles the memorial's construction. There is also a set of windows that look onto the huge structure's foundation. Stalactites (hanging from above) and stalagmites (growing from below) have formed underneath the marble tribute to Lincoln. Some parts of the Lincoln Memorial may be off-limits when you visit. Like the Jefferson, the Lincoln is shrouded in scaffolding as it undergoes a three- to five-year program to repair the effects of acid rain, insects, jet fuel, and other destructive elements.

Although visiting the area around the Lincoln Memorial during the day allows you to take in an impressive view of the Mall to the east, the best time to see the memorial itself is at night. Spotlights illuminate the outside while inside, light and shadows play across Lincoln's gentle face. *West end of Mall,* ☎ *202/426–6895.* ☛ *Free.* ☉ *24 hrs; staffed daily 8 AM–midnight.*

❻ Walk down the steps of the Lincoln Memorial and to the left to get to the **Vietnam Veterans Memorial** and **Constitution Gardens.** Constitution Gardens, the area south of Constitution Avenue between 17th and 23rd streets NW, was once home to "temporary" buildings erected by the Navy before World War I and not removed until after World War II. Many ideas were proposed to develop the 50-acre site. President Nixon is said to have favored something resembling Copenhagen's Tivoli Gardens. The final design was a little plainer, with paths winding through groves of trees and, on the lake, a tiny island paying tribute to the signers of the Declaration of Independence, their signatures carved into a low stone wall.

The Vietnam Veterans Memorial is another landmark that encourages introspection. The concept came from Jan Scruggs, a former infantry corporal who had served in Vietnam. The stark design by Maya Ying Lin, a 21-year-old Yale architecture student, was selected in a 1981 competition. Upon its completion in 1982, the memorial was decried by some veterans as a "black gash of shame." With the addition of Frederick Hart's statue of three soldiers and a flagpole just south of the wall, most critics were won over.

The wall is one of the most visited sites in Washington, its black granite panels reflecting the sky, the trees, and the faces of those looking for the names of friends or relatives who died in the war. The names of more than 58,000 Americans are etched on the face of the memorial in the order of their deaths. Directories at the entrance and exit to the wall list the names in alphabetical order. (It was recently discovered that because of a clerical error the names of some two dozen living vets are carved into the stone as well.) For help in finding a specific name, ask a ranger at the blue-and-white hut near the entrance. Thousands of offerings are left at the wall each year: letters, flowers, medals, uniforms, snapshots. The National Park Service collects these and stores them in a warehouse in Lanham, Maryland, where they are fast becoming another memorial. Tents are often set up near the wall by veterans groups; some provide information on soldiers who remain missing in action, and others are on call to help fellow vets deal with the sometimes powerful emotions that overtake them when visiting the wall for the first time. *Constitution Gardens, 23rd St. and Constitution Ave. NW,* ☎ *202/634–1568.* ☛ *Free.* ☉ *24 hrs; staffed 8 AM–midnight.*

After years of debate over its design and necessity, the **Vietnam Women's Memorial**—in honor of the women who served in that conflict—was finally dedicated on Veterans Day 1993. The monument—two uniformed women caring for a wounded male soldier while a third woman kneels nearby—sits in Constitution Gardens, southeast of the Vietnam Veterans Memorial.

The FDR, Korean War, and Vietnam Women's memorials—as well as proposed memorials to military women, black patriots, and George Mason—have troubled some Washingtonians. They feel the city is entering an unnecessary monument-building boom in the 1990s. Each veterans' and special-interest group seems to want its own separate memorial and there's concern that too many grandiose designs (each group, of course, wants its to be the biggest) are clogging Washington's monumental core.

TIME OUT At the circular **snack bar** just west of the Constitution Gardens lake you can get hot dogs, potato chips, candy bars, soft drinks, and beer at prices lower than those charged by most street vendors.

❼ Walk north to Constitution Avenue and head east. The stone **lockkeeper's house** at the corner of Constitution Avenue and 17th Street is the only remaining monument to Washington's unsuccessful experiment with a canal. L'Enfant's design called for a canal to be dug from the Tiber—a branch of the Potomac that extended from where the Lincoln Memorial is now—across the city to the Capitol and then south to the Anacostia River. (L'Enfant even envisioned the president's riding in a ceremonial barge from the White House to the Capitol.) The City Canal became more nuisance than convenience, and by the Civil War it was a foul-smelling cesspool that often overran its banks. The stone building at this corner was the home of the canal's lockkeeper until the 1870s, when the waterway was covered over with B Street, which was renamed Constitution Avenue in 1932.

The nearest Metro station is Federal Triangle, five blocks to the east on 12th Street.

TOUR 3: THE WHITE HOUSE AREA

Numbers in the margin correspond to points of interest on the Tour 3: The White House Area map.

In a city full of immediately recognizable images, perhaps none is more familiar than the White House. This is where the buck stops and where the nation turns in times of crisis. On this tour we'll visit the White House, then strike out into the surrounding streets to explore the president's neighborhood, which includes some of the oldest houses in the city.

To reach the start of our tour, take the Metro to the McPherson Square station. We'll begin our exploration in front of 1600 Pennsylvania Avenue. Pierre L'Enfant called it the President's House; it was known formally as the Executive Mansion; and in 1902 Congress officially

★ **❶** proclaimed it the **White House,** though, contrary to popular belief, it had been given that nickname even before its white sandstone exterior was painted to cover the fire damage it suffered during the War of 1812. Irishman James Hoban's plan, based on the Georgian design of Leinster Hall near Dublin and of other Irish country houses, was selected in a contest, in 1792. The building wasn't ready for its first occupant until 1800, so George Washington never lived here. Completed in 1829, it has undergone many structural changes since then: Thomas Jefferson, who had entered his own design in the contest under an as-

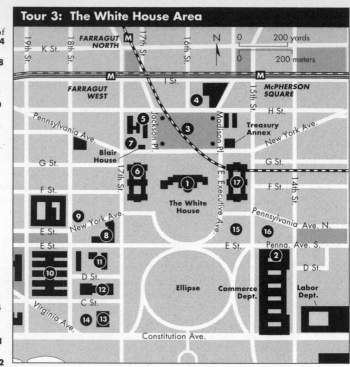

Tour 3: The White House Area

sumed name, added terraces to the east and west wings. Andrew Jackson installed running water. James Garfield put in the first elevator. Between 1948 and 1952, Harry Truman had the entire structure gutted and restored, adding a second-story porch to the south portico. Each family that has called the White House home has left its imprint on the 132-room mansion. George Bush installed a horseshoe pit. Most recently, Bill Clinton had a customized jogging track put in.

② A **White House visitor center** (☎ 202/208–1631) opened in the Commerce Department's Baldrige Hall in March 1995. The official address is 1450 Pennsylvania Avenue NW, but it is physically on E Street between 14th and 15th streets. Run by the Department of Parks, the visitor center's primary function is to disperse tickets to the White House. Tickets are dispensed on a first-come, first-served basis. (They are often gone by 9 AM.) Your ticket will show the approximate time of your tour. The center is open from Memorial Day to Labor Day, Tuesday through Saturday from 7 to 7; the remainder of the year, its hours are 8 to 5. Also at the center are exhibits pertaining to the White House's construction, its decor, and the families who have lived there. Photographs, artifacts, and videos relate the house's history to those who don't have the opportunity to tour the building personally.

Tuesday through Saturday mornings (except holidays), from 10 AM to noon, selected public rooms on the ground floor and first floor of the White House are open to visitors. The center only disperses tickets March through September; in other months, simply join the line that forms along East Executive Avenue, between the White House and the Treasury Building. Expect a long line, but the wait is worthwhile if you're interested in a firsthand look at what is perhaps the most important building in the city. There is seating on the Ellipse for those waiting to see the White House, and volunteer marching bands, drill teams, and other musical groups entertain those who are stuck in line. If you write to your representative or senator's office well in advance of your trip, you can receive special VIP passes for tours between 8 and 10 AM. On selected weekends in April and October, the White House is open for garden tours. In December it's decorated for the holidays.

The **Ellipse** is bounded by Constitution Avenue, E Street, 15th Street, and 17th Street. From this vantage point you can see the Washington Monument and the Jefferson Memorial to the south and the red-tile roof of the Department of Commerce to the east, with the tower of the Old Post Office Building sticking up above it. To the north you have a good view of the back of the White House; the rounded portico and Harry Truman's second-story porch are clearly visible. The south lawn of the White House serves as a heliport for *Marine One,* the president's helicopter. On Easter Monday the south lawn is also the scene of the White House Easter Egg Roll. The **National Christmas Tree** grows on the northern edge of the Ellipse. Each year in mid-December it is lighted by the president during a festive ceremony that marks the beginning of the holiday season.

You'll enter the White House through the East Wing lobby on the ground floor, walking past the Jacqueline Kennedy Rose Garden. Your first stop is the large white-and-gold **East Room,** the site of presidential news conferences. In 1814 Dolley Madison saved the room's full-length portrait of George Washington from torch-carrying British soldiers by cutting it from its frame, rolling it up, and spiriting it out of the White House. (No fool she, Dolley also rescued her own portrait.) A later occupant, Teddy Roosevelt, allowed his children to ride their pet pony in the East Room.

The Federal-style **Green Room,** named for the moss-green watered silk that covers its walls, is used for informal receptions and "photo opportunities" with foreign heads of state. Notable furnishings in this room include a New England sofa that once belonged to Daniel Webster and portraits of Benjamin Franklin, John Quincy Adams, and Abigail Adams. The president and his guests are often shown on TV sitting in front of the Green Room's English Empire mantel, engaging in what are invariably described as "frank and cordial" discussions.

The elliptical **Blue Room,** the most formal space in the White House, is furnished with a gilded Empire-style settee and chairs that were ordered by James Monroe. (Monroe asked for plain wooden chairs, but the furniture manufacturer thought such unadorned furnishings too simple for the White House and took it upon himself to supply chairs more in keeping with their surroundings.) The White House Christmas tree is placed in this room each year. Another well-known elliptical room, the president's **Oval Office,** is in the semidetached West Wing of the White House, along with other executive offices.

The **Red Room** is decorated as an American Empire–style parlor of the early 19th century, with furniture by the New York cabinetmaker Charles-Honoré Lannuier. You'll recognize the marble mantel as the twin of the mantel in the Green Room.

The **State Dining Room,** second in size only to the East Room, can seat 140 guests. The room is dominated by G. P. A. Healy's portrait of Abraham Lincoln, painted after the president's death. The stone mantel is inscribed with a quotation from one of John Adams's letters: "I pray heaven to bestow the best of blessings on this house and all that shall hereafter inhabit it. May none but honest and wise men ever rule

White House Floor Plan: Ground and First Floors

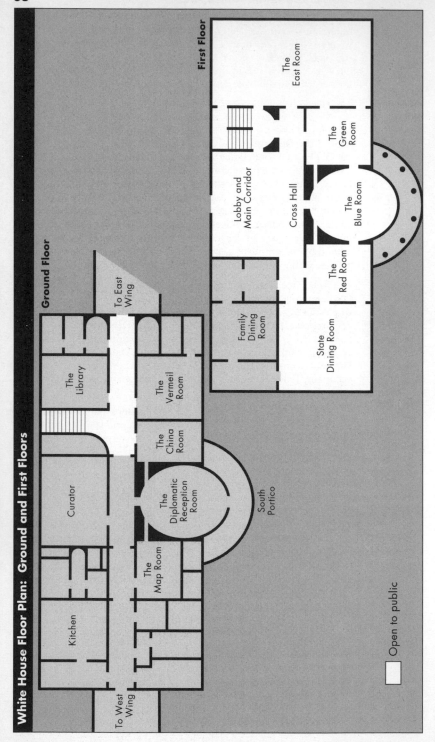

Ground Floor

Kitchen

Curator

The Library

To East Wing

The Map Room

The China Room

The Vermeil Room

The Diplomatic Reception Room

South Portico

To West Wing

First Floor

Lobby and Main Corridor

Cross Hall

The East Room

The Green Room

The Blue Room

The Red Room

Family Dining Room

State Dining Room

Open to public

under this roof." In Teddy Roosevelt's day a stuffed moose head hung over the mantel. *1600 Pennsylvania Ave. NW,* ☎ *202/755–7798, 202/ 456–7041 (recording), or 202/619–7222 (Park Service).* ☛ *Free.* ☉ *Tues.–Sat. 10–noon. White House is occasionally closed without notice for official functions. Baby strollers are not allowed on tour.*

❸ **Lafayette Square,** bordered by Pennsylvania Avenue, Madison Place, H Street, and Jackson Place, is an intimate oasis in the midst of downtown Washington. With such an important resident living across the street, National Capital Park Service gardeners lavish extra attention on the square's trees and flower beds.

When Pierre L'Enfant proposed the location for the Executive Mansion, the only building north of what is today Pennsylvania Avenue was the Pierce family farmhouse, which stood at the northeast corner of the present square. An apple orchard and a family burial ground were the area's two other main features. During the construction of the White House, workers' huts and a brick kiln were set up, and soon private residences began popping up around the square (though sheep would continue to graze on it for years). L'Enfant's original plan for the city designated this area as part of "President's Park"; in essence it was the president's front yard, just as what is now the Ellipse was once the president's backyard. The egalitarian Thomas Jefferson, concerned that large, landscaped White House grounds would give the wrong impression in a democratic country, ordered that the area be turned into a public park. Soldiers camped in the square during the War of 1812 and the Civil War, turning it at both times into a muddy pit. Today, protesters set their placards up in Lafayette Square, jockeying for positions that face the White House. Although the National Park Service can't restrict the protesters' freedom of speech, it does try to restrict the size of their signs.

Standing in the center of the park—and dominating the square—is a large **statue of Andrew Jackson.** Erected in 1853 and cast from bronze cannon that Jackson had captured during the War of 1812, this was the first equestrian statue made in America. (An exact duplicate faces St. Louis Cathedral in New Orleans's Jackson Square.)

Jackson's is the only statue of an American in the park. The other statues are of foreign-born soldiers who helped in America's fight for independence. In the southeast corner is the park's namesake, the **Marquis de Lafayette,** the young French nobleman who came to America to fight in the Revolution. When Lafayette returned to the United States in 1824 he was given a rousing welcome: He was wined and dined in the finest homes and showered with gifts of cash and land.

Head north on **Madison Place.** The colonnaded building across the street at the corner of Pennsylvania Avenue is an annex to the Treasury Department. The modern redbrick building farther on, at 717 Madison Place, houses a variety of judicial offices. Its design—with the squared-off bay windows—is echoed in the taller building that rises behind it and is mirrored in the **New Executive Office Building** on the other side of Lafayette Square. Planners in the '20s recommended that the private houses on Lafayette Square, many built in the Federal period, be torn down and replaced with a collection of uniform neoclassical-style government buildings. A lack of funds providentially kept the neighborhood intact, and in the early '60s John and Jacqueline Kennedy worked to save the historic town houses.

The next house down, yellow with a second-story ironwork balcony, was built in 1828 by Benjamin Ogle Tayloe. During the McKinley administration, Ohio Senator Marcus Hanna lived here, and the president's frequent visits earned it the nickname the "Little White House." Dolley Madison lived in the next-door Cutts-Madison House after her husband died. Both the Tayloe and Madison houses are now part of the Federal Judicial Center.

Continue down Madison Place. The next statue is that of **Thaddeus Kosciuszko,** the Polish general who fought alongside American colonists against the British. If you head east on H Street for half a block, you'll come to the **United States Government Bookstore** (1510 H St. NW, ☎ 202/653–5075), the place to visit if you'd like to buy a few pounds of the millions of tons of paper the government churns out each year. Here is where you'll find a copy of the latest federal budget or *The Surgeon General's Report on Nutrition and Health.*

TIME OUT Presidential adviser Bernard Baruch used to eat his lunch in Lafayette Park, and you can, too. **Loeb's Restaurant** (around the corner at 15th and I streets NW) is a New York–style deli that serves up salads and sandwiches to eat there or to go.

❹ Across from the park, on H Street, is the golden-domed **St. John's Episcopal Church,** the so-called "Church of the Presidents." Every president since Madison has visited the church, and many worshiped here on a regular basis. Built in 1816, the church was the second building on the square. Benjamin Latrobe, who worked on both the Capitol and the White House, designed it in the form of a Greek cross, with a flat dome and a lantern cupola. The church has been altered somewhat since then; later additions include the Doric portico and the cupola tower. You can best sense the intent of Latrobe's design while standing inside under the saucer-shape dome of the original building. Not far from the center of the church is pew 54, where visiting presidents are seated. The kneelers of many of the pews are embroidered with the presidential seal and the names of several chief executives. Brochures are available inside for those who would like to take a self-guided tour. *16th and H Sts. NW,* ☎ *202/347–8766.* ☛ *Free.* ☉ *Mon.–Sat. 8–4. Tours after 11 AM Sun. service and by appointment.*

Just east of the church is the four-story **St. John's Parish House,** built in 1836 by Matthew St. Clair Clark, clerk of the House of Representatives. The house's most famous resident was Lord Alexander Baring Ashburton, the British Minister who lived here in 1842 while negotiating a dispute over the position of the U.S.-Canadian border. The house later served as the British legation.

Across 16th Street stands the **Hay-Adams Hotel,** one of the most opulent hostelries in the city and a favorite with Washington insiders and visiting celebrities. It takes its name from a double house, owned by Lincoln biographer John Hay and historian Henry Adams, that stood on this spot. Next to it is the **Chamber of Commerce of the United States,** its neoclassical facade typical of the type of building that might have surrounded Lafayette Park had JFK not intervened. The statue at the northwest corner of Lafayette Square is of **Baron von Steuben,** the Prussian general who drilled Colonial troops during the Revolution.

❺ The redbrick, Federal-style **Decatur House** on the corner of H Street and Jackson Place was the first private residence on President's Park (the White House doesn't really count as *private*). Designed by Benjamin Latrobe, the house was built for naval hero Stephen Decatur and his wife, Susan, in 1819. Decatur had earned the affection of the nation in battles against the British and the Barbary pirates. Planning to start a political career, he used the prize money Congress awarded him for his exploits to build this home near the White House. Tragically, only 14 months after he moved in, Decatur was killed in a duel with James Barron, a disgruntled former Navy officer who held Decatur responsible for his court-martial. Later occupants of the house included Henry Clay, Martin Van Buren, and the Beales, a prominent family from the West whose modifications of the building include a parquet floor showing the state seal of California. The house is now operated by the National Trust. The first floor is furnished as it was in Decatur's time. The second floor is furnished in the Victorian style favored by the Beale family, who owned it until 1956 (thus making Decatur House both the first and *last* private residence on Lafayette Square). The National Trust store around the corner (entrance on H Street) sells a variety of books, postcards, and gifts. *748 Jackson Pl. NW, ☎ 202/842–0920. ☉ Tues.– Fri. 10–3, weekends noon–4. ☛ $3 adults, $1.50 senior citizens and students, free to children under 6 and National Trust members. Tours on the hr and ½ hr.*

Head south on **Jackson Place.** Many of the row houses on this stretch date from the pre–Civil War or Victorian periods; even the more modern additions, though—such as those at 718 and 726—are designed in a style that blends with their more historic neighbors. **Count Rochambeau,** aide to General Lafayette, is honored with a statue at the park's southwest corner.

❻ Directly across Pennsylvania Avenue, to the west of the White House, is the **Old Executive Office Building,** which has gone from being one of the most detested buildings in the city to one of the most beloved. It was built between 1871 and 1888 and originally housed the War, Navy, and State departments. Its architect, Alfred B. Mullett, patterned it after the Louvre, but detractors quickly criticized the busy French Empire design—with its mansard roof, tall chimneys, and 900 freestanding columns—as an inappropriate counterpoint to the Greek Revival Treasury Building that sits on the other side of the White House. Numerous plans to alter the facade foundered due to lack of money. The granite edifice may look like a wedding cake, but its high ceilings and spacious offices make it popular with occupants, who include members of the executive branch. Dan Quayle had his office in here; Albert Gore, Jr., is a little closer to the action, in the West Wing of the White House, just down the hall from the president. The Old Executive Office Building has played host to numerous historic events. It was here that Secretary of State Cordell Hull met with Japanese diplomats after the bombing of Pearl Harbor, and it was here that Oliver North and Fawn Hall shredded Iran-Contra documents.

The green canopy at 1651 Pennsylvania Avenue marks the entrance to **Blair House,** the residence used by heads of state visiting Washington. Harry S. Truman lived here from 1948 to 1952 while the White House was undergoing its much-needed renovation. A plaque on the fence honors White House policeman Leslie Coffelt, who died in 1950 when Puerto Rican separatists attempted to assassinate President Truman at this site.

❼ Head west on Pennsylvania Avenue. At the end of the block, with the motto "Dedicated to Art" engraved above the entrance, is the **Renwick Gallery.** The French Second Empire–style building was designed by Smithsonian Castle architect James Renwick in 1859 to house the art collection of Washington merchant and banker William Wilson Corcoran. Corcoran was a Southern sympathizer who spent the duration of the Civil War in Europe. While he was away his unfinished building was pressed into service by the government as a quartermaster general's post. In 1874 the Corcoran, as it was then called, opened as the first private art museum in the city. Corcoran's collection quickly outgrew the building and in 1897 it was moved to a new gallery a few blocks south on 17th Street (described below). After a stint as the U.S. Court of Claims, this building was restored, renamed after its architect, and opened in 1972 as the Smithsonian's museum of American decorative arts. Although crafts were once the poor relations of the art world—handwoven rugs and delicately carved tables were considered somehow less "artistic" than, say, oil paintings and sculptures—they have recently come into their own. The Renwick has been at the forefront of the crafts movement, and its collection includes exquisitely designed and made utilitarian items, as well as objects created out of such traditional craft media as fiber and glass. Not everything at the museum is Shaker furniture and enamel jewelry, though. The second-floor Grand Salon is still furnished in the opulent Victorian style Corcoran favored when his collection adorned its walls. Paintings are hung in tiers, one above the other, and in Corcoran's portrait the Renwick itself is visible in the background. *Pennsylvania Ave. and 17th St. NW,* ☎ *202/357–2700, TTY 202/357–1729.* ☛ *Free.* ⊙ *Daily 10–5:30; closed Dec. 25.*

Head south on 17th Street. You'll pass the **Winder Building** (604 17th St.), erected in 1848 as one of the first office blocks in the capital and used during the Civil War as the headquarters of the Union Army. Down another block on the right, at the corner of 17th Street and New York ❽ Avenue, is the **Corcoran Gallery of Art,** one of the few large museums in Washington outside the Smithsonian family. The Beaux Arts–style building, its copper roof green with age, was designed by Ernest Flagg and completed in 1897. The gallery's permanent collection numbers more than 11,000 works, including paintings by the first great American portraitists John Copley, Gilbert Stuart, and Rembrandt Peale. The Hudson River School is represented by such works as *Mount Corcoran* by Albert Bierstadt and Frederic Church's *Niagara.* There are also portraits by John Singer Sargent, Thomas Eakins, and Mary Cassatt. European art is seen in the Walker Collection (late-19th- and early 20th-century paintings, including works by Gustave Courbet, Monet, Pissarro, and Renoir) and the Clark Collection (Dutch, Flemish, and French Romantic paintings, and the restored entire 18th-century Grand Salon of the Hotel d'Orsay in Paris). Be sure to see Samuel Morse's *Old House of Representatives* and Hiram Powers's *Greek Slave,* which scandalized Victorian society. (The latter, a statue of a nude woman with her wrists chained, was considered so shocking by Victorian audiences that separate viewing hours were established for men and women, and children under 16 were not allowed to see it at all.) Photography and works by contemporary American artists are also among the Corcoran's strengths. The adjacent Corcoran School is the only four-year art college in the Washington area. *17th St. and New York Ave. NW,* ☎ *202/638–1439 (recording), 202/638–3211. Suggested donation: $3 adults, $1 students and senior citizens, children under 12 free, $5 for family groups.* ⊙ *Mon., Wed., and Fri.–Sun. 10–5, Thurs. 10–9. Closed Tues., Dec. 25, Jan. 1. Tours of permanent collection are offered daily (except Tues.) at 12:30, Thurs. at 7:30 PM.*

TIME OUT   **The Café at the Corcoran** has a lunch menu that includes a selection of salads, light entrées, desserts, and a refreshing assortment of fruit and vegetable shakes. The café also serves a Continental breakfast, an English tea complete with scones and clotted cream, and dinner on Thursday, when the museum is open late. Sunday brunch features the music of a live jazz band.

❾ A block up New York Avenue, at the corner of 18th Street, is the **Octagon House,** completed in 1801 for John Tayloe III, a wealthy Virginia plantation owner. Designed by William Thornton (the Capitol's architect), the Octagon House actually has only six sides, not eight. Thornton chose the unusual shape to conform to the acute angle formed by L'Enfant's intersection of New York Avenue and 18th Street.

After the White House was burned in 1814 the Tayloes invited James and Dolley Madison to stay in the Octagon House. It was in a second-floor study that the Treaty of Ghent, ending the War of 1812, was signed. By the late 1800s the building was used as a rooming house. In this century the house served as the headquarters of the American Institute of Architects before the construction of AIA's rather unexceptional building behind it.

The Octagon's first restoration, in the 1960s, revealed intricate plaster molding and the original 1799 Coade stone mantels (made using a now-lost method of casting crushed stone). It is currently in the midst of a far more thorough, $4 million restoration that will return it to its 1815 appearance. The exterior work is finished, topped off by a new, and historically accurate, cypress-shingle roof, complete with parapet. Work continues inside, though the second-floor galleries—home to changing exhibits on architecture, city planning, and Washington history—are open to the public. *1799 New York Ave. NW, ☎ 202/638–3105, TTY 202/638–1538. Suggested donation: $2 adults, $1 senior citizens and students, 50¢ children. ☉ Tues.–Fri. 10–4, weekends noon–4; closed Dec. 25 and Jan. 1.*

❿ A block south on 18th Street is the **Department of the Interior** building, designed by Waddy B. Wood. At the time of its construction in 1937 it was the most modern government building in the city and the first with escalators and central air-conditioning. The outside of the building is somewhat plain, but much of the interior is decorated with paintings that reflect the Interior Department's work. Hallways feature heroic oil paintings of dam construction, panning for gold, and cattle drives. You'll pass some of these if you visit the **Department of the Interior Museum** on the first floor. (You can enter the building at its E Street or C Street doors; adults must show photo ID.) Soon after it opened in 1938, the museum became one of the most popular attractions in Washington; evening hours were maintained even during World War II. The small museum tells the story of the Department of the Interior, a huge agency dubbed the "Mother of Departments" because from it grew the Departments of Agriculture, Labor, Education, and Energy. Today Interior oversees most of the country's federally owned land and natural resources, and exhibits in the museum outline the work done by the Bureau of Land Management, the U.S. Geological Survey, the Bureau of Indian Affairs, the National Park Service, and other Interior branches. The museum retains much of its New Deal–era flavor—including meticulously created dioramas depicting various historic events and American locales—and is, depending on your tastes, either quaint or outdated. Still, it's a nice contrast to the high-tech video museums of today. It is in the process of getting a facelift that promises to modernize it. The Indian Craft Shop across the hall from the museum sells Native American pottery, dolls, carvings, jewelry, baskets, and books. It, too, has been part of the Department of the Interior since 1938. *C and E Sts. between 18th and 19th Sts. NW, ☎ 202/208–4743. ☛ Free. ☉ Weekdays 8–5; closed federal holidays. Call at least 2 wks ahead for tour of building's architecture and murals.*

⑪ Walk back east on E Street to 17th Street past the three buildings that house the headquarters of the **American Red Cross.** The main building, a neoclassical structure of blinding white marble built in 1917, commemorates the service and devotion of the women who cared for the wounded on both sides during the Civil War. The building's Georgian-style board of governors hall has three stained-glass windows designed by Louis Tiffany. *430 17th St. NW,* ☎ *202/737–8300.* ☛ *Free.* ☯ *Weekdays 9–4.*

⑫ A block south is **Memorial Continental Hall,** headquarters of the Daughters of the American Revolution. This beaux arts building was the site each year of the DAR's congress until the larger Constitution Hall was built around the corner. An entrance on D Street leads to the **DAR Museum.** Its 50,000-item collection includes fine examples of Colonial and Federal silver, china, porcelain, stoneware, earthenware, and glass. Thirty-three period rooms are decorated in styles representative of various U.S. states, ranging from an 1850 California adobe parlor to a New Hampshire attic filled with toys from the 18th and 19th centuries. *1776 D St. NW,* ☎ *202/879–3240.* ☛ *Free.* ☯ *Weekdays 8:30–4, Sun. 1–5. Docents available for tours weekdays 10:30–2:30.*

⑬ Just across C Street to the south of Continental Hall is the **House of the Americas,** the headquarters of the Organization of American States. The interior of this building features a cool patio adorned with a pre-Columbian–style fountain and lush tropical plants. This tiny rain forest is a good place to rest when Washington's summer heat is at its most oppressive. The upstairs Hall of Flags and Heroes contains, as the name implies, busts of generals and statesmen from the various OAS member countries as well as each country's flag. *17th St. and Constitution Ave. NW,* ☎ *202/458–3000.* ☛ *Free.* ☯ *Weekdays 9–5:30.*

⑭ Behind the House of the Americas is the **Art Museum of the Americas.** The small gallery is in a building that formerly served as the residence for the secretary general of the OAS. It hosts changing exhibits highlighting 20th-century Latin American artists. *201 18th St. NW,* ☎ *202/ 458–6016.* ☛ *Free.* ☯ *Tues.–Sat. 10–5.*

Next, head east on Constitution Avenue and take the first left, following the curving drive that encircles the Ellipse. The rather weather-beaten **gate house** at the corner of Constitution Avenue and 17th Street once stood on Capitol Hill. It was designed in 1828 by Charles Bulfinch, the first native-born American to serve as architect of the Capitol, and was moved here in 1874 after the Capitol grounds were redesigned by Frederick Law Olmsted. A twin of the gate house stands at Constitution Avenue and 15th Street.

⑮ Across E Street to the northeast of the Ellipse, in a small park bounded by E Street, 15th Street, East Executive Avenue, and Alexander Hamilton Place, stands the massive **William Tecumseh Sherman Monument.** Just north of this memorial is the southern facade of the Treasury Building, its entrance guarded by a **statue of Alexander Hamilton,** the department's first secretary.

⑯ Across 15th Street to the east is **Pershing Park,** a quiet, sunken garden that honors General "Blackjack" Pershing, commander of the American expeditionary force in World War I. Engravings on the stone walls recount pivotal campaigns from that war. Ice-skaters glide on the square pool in the winter.

One block to the north is the venerable **Hotel Washington** (*515 15th St.,* ☎ *202/638–5900*). Its lobby is narrow and unassuming, but the view from the rooftop Sky Top Lounge—open May to October—is one of the best in the city.

(17) To your left is the long side of the **Treasury Building,** the largest Greek Revival edifice in Washington. Pierre L'Enfant had intended for Pennsylvania Avenue to stretch in a straight, unbroken line from the White House to the Capitol. This plan was ruined by the construction of the Treasury Building on this site just east of the White House. Robert Mills, the architect responsible for the Washington Monument and the Patent Office (now the National Museum of American Art), designed the grand colonnade that stretches down 15th Street. Construction of the Treasury Building started in 1836 and, after several additions, was finally completed in 1869. Guided 90-minute tours are given every Saturday, except holiday weekends, and take visitors past the Andrew Johnson suite, used by Johnson as the executive office while Mrs. Lincoln moved out of the White House; the two-story marble Cash Room; and a 19th-century burglarproof vault lining that saw duty when the Treasury once stored currency. *15th St. between Pennsylvania and New York Aves. NW,* ☎ *202/622–0896, TTY 202/622–0692.* ☛ *Free. Register at least 1 wk ahead for the tour; visitors must provide name, date of birth, and Social Security number, and show photo ID at start of tour.*

TIME OUT A glittering urban mall, **The Shops** (in the National Press Building, F and G Sts. between 13th and 14th Sts. NW) is home to table-service restaurants such as the **American Café** and the **Boston Seafood Company,** as well as faster and cheaper fare in its top-floor Food Hall.

Continue up 15th Street. The luxurious **Old Ebbitt Grill** (675 15th St. NW, ☎ 202/347–4800) is a popular watering spot for journalists and television news correspondents.

The corner of 15th Street and Pennsylvania Avenue has been dubbed Washington's Wall Street. Adjacent to the imposing Treasury are brokerage firms and buildings belonging to Riggs Bank and Crestar Bank. The location is especially fitting for banks, since this stretch of 15th Street is pictured on the back of every $10 bill. (And if you're wondering what that car is that drives past the Treasury Building on the back of every sawbuck, it's a 1926 Hupmobile.)

The Metro stations nearest to the end of this tour are McPherson Square, at 15th and I streets, and Metro Center, three blocks east on G Street.

TOUR 4: CAPITOL HILL

Numbers in the margin correspond to points of interest on the Tour 4: Capitol Hill map.

The people who live and work on "the Hill" do so in the shadow of the edifice that lends the neighborhood its name: the gleaming white Capitol building. More than just the center of government, however, the Hill also includes charming residential blocks lined with Victorian row houses and a fine assortment of restaurants, bars, and shops. Capitol Hill's boundaries are disputed: It's bordered to the west, north, and south by the Capitol, Union Station, and I Street, respectively. Some argue that Capitol Hill extends east to the Anacostia River, others that it ends at 11th Street near Lincoln Park. The neighborhood does in fact seem to grow as members of Capitol Hill's active historic-preservation movement restore more and more 19th-century houses.

① Start your exploration of the Hill inside the cavernous main hall of **Union Station,** which sits on Massachusetts Avenue north of the Capitol. In 1902 the McMillan Commission—charged with suggesting ways to improve the appearance of the city—recommended that the many train lines that sliced through the capital share one main depot. Union Station was opened in 1908 and was the first building completed under the commission's plan. Chicago architect and commission member Daniel H. Burnham patterned the station after the Roman Baths of Diocletian.

For many visitors to Washington, the capital city is first seen framed through the grand station's arched doorways. In its heyday, during World War II, more than 200,000 people swarmed through the station daily. By the '60s, however, the decline in train travel had turned the station into an expensive white-marble elephant. It was briefly, and unsuccessfully, transformed into a visitor center for the Bicentennial; but by 1981 rain was pouring in through the neglected station's roof, and passengers boarded trains at a ramshackle depot behind the station.

The Union Station you see today is the result of a restoration completed in 1988, an effort intended to be the beginning of a revival of Washington's east end. It's hoped that the shops, restaurants, and nine-screen movie theater in Union Station will draw more than just train travelers to the beaux arts building. The jewel of the structure remains its meticulously restored main waiting room. With its 96-foot-high coffered ceiling gilded with eight pounds of gold leaf, it is one of the city's great spaces and is used for inaugural balls and other festive events. Forty-six statues of Roman legionnaires, one for each state in the Union when the station was completed, ring the grand room. The statues were the subject of controversy when the building was first opened. Pennsylvania Railroad president Alexander Cassatt (brother of artist Mary) ordered sculptor Louis Saint-Gaudens to alter the statues, convinced that the legionnaires' skimpy outfits would scandalize female passengers. The sculptor obligingly added a shield to each figure, obscuring any offending body parts.

The east hall, now filled with vendors, was once an expensive restaurant. It is decorated with Pompeiian tracery and plaster walls and columns painted to look like marble. At one time the station also featured a secure presidential waiting room, now restored. The private waiting room was by no means a frivolous addition: Twenty years before Union Station was built, President Garfield was assassinated in the public waiting room of the old Baltimore and Potomac terminal on 6th Street. Group tours of Union Station are available by appointment (☎ 202/289–1908).

TIME OUT   On Union Station's lower level you'll find more than 20 food stalls, offering everything from pizza to sushi. On the main level are Capitol Hill favorite the **American Cafe,** the trendy Italian restaurant **Sfuzzi,** and **America,** which has a menu as expansive as its name: everything from Albuquerque blue corn enchiladas to New York Reuben sandwiches.

As you walk out Union Station's front doors, glance to the right. At the end of a long succession of archways is the Washington **City Post Office,** also designed by Daniel Burnham and completed in 1914. Nostalgic odes to the noble mail carrier are inscribed on the exterior of the marble building; one of them eulogizes the "Messenger of sympathy and love, servant of parted friends, consoler of the lonely, bond of the scattered family, enlarger of the common life." After extensive **②** renovation, the building reopened in 1993 as the **National Postal Museum,** the newest member of the Smithsonian family. Exhibits under-

Tour 4: Capitol Hill

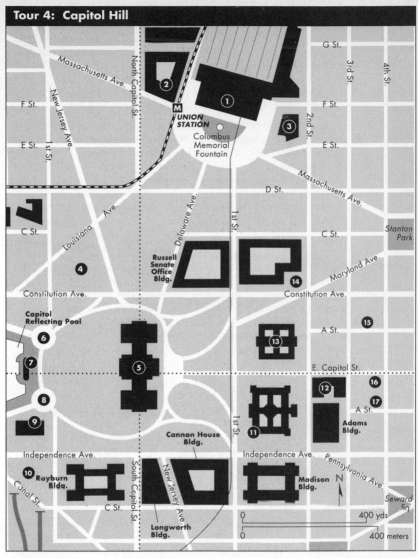

Bartholdi Fountain, **10**
Capitol, **5**
Folger Shakespeare Library, **12**
Frederick Douglass Townhouse, **15**
Grant Memorial, **7**

James Garfield Memorial, **8**
Library of Congress/Jefferson Building, **11**
National Postal Museum, **2**
Peace Monument, **6**

Robert A. Taft Memorial, **4**
Sewall-Belmont House, **14**
South side of East Capitol Street, **16**
Supreme Court Building, **13**

326 A Street, **17**
Thurgood Marshall Federal Judiciary Building, **3**
Union Station, **1**
United States Botanic Gardens, **9**

score the important part the mail played in the development of America and include horse-drawn mail coaches, railway mail cars, actual airmail planes, every U.S. stamp issued, many foreign stamps, and a collection of philatelic rarities. The National Museum of Natural History may have the Hope Diamond, but the National Postal Museum has in its collection the container used to mail the priceless gem to the Smithsonian. *2 Massachusetts Ave. NE,* ☎ *202/357–2700.* ☛ *Free.* ☉ *Daily 10–5:30; closed Dec. 25.*

❸ Return to Union Station and walk the length of the arcade, at the end of which is the **Thurgood Marshall Federal Judiciary Building.** The spectacular atrium, a signature work for architect Edward Larabee Barnes, has a bamboo garden. Turn back toward the center of Union Station's plaza and the **Columbus Memorial Fountain,** designed by Lorado Taft. A caped, steely-eyed Christopher Columbus stares into the distance, flanked by a hoary, bearded figure (the Old World) and an Indian brave (the New).

Head south from the fountain, away from Union Station, cross Massachusetts Avenue, and walk down Delaware Avenue. On the left you'll pass the **Russell Senate Office Building.** Note the delicate treatment below the second-story windows that resembles twisted lengths of fringed cloth. Completed in 1909, this was the first of the Senate office buildings. Beyond it are the Dirksen and Hart office buildings.
❹ To the right, sticking up above the trees, is a monolithic carillon, a **memorial to Robert A. Taft,** son of the 27th president and longtime Republican senator.

★ **❺** Cross Constitution Avenue and enter the **Capitol** grounds, landscaped in the late-19th century by Frederick Law Olmsted, Sr., who, along with Calvert Vaux, created New York City's Central Park. On these 68 acres you will find both the tamest squirrels in the city and the highest concentration of television news correspondents, jockeying for a good position in front of the Capitol for their "stand-ups." A few hundred feet northeast of the Capitol are two cast-iron car shelters, left over from the days when horse-drawn trolleys served the Hill. Olmsted's six pinkish, bronze-topped lamps directly east from the Capitol are a treat, too.

When planning the city, Pierre L'Enfant described the gentle rise on which the Capitol sits, known then as Jenkins Hill, as "a pedestal waiting for a monument." The design of this monument was the result of a competition held in 1792; the winner was William Thornton, a physician and amateur architect from the West Indies. With its central rotunda and dome, Thornton's Capitol is reminiscent of Rome's Pantheon, a similarity that must have delighted the nation's founders, who felt the American government was based on the principles of the Republic of Rome.

The cornerstone was laid by George Washington in a Masonic ceremony on September 18, 1793, and in November 1800, both the Senate and the House of Representatives moved down from Philadelphia to occupy the first completed section of the Capitol: the boxlike portion between the central rotunda and today's north wing. (Subsequent efforts to find the cornerstone Washington laid have been unsuccessful, though when the east front was extended in the 1950s, workmen found a knee joint thought to be from a 500-pound ox that was roasted at the 1793 celebration.) By 1806 the House wing had been completed, just to the south of what is now the domed center, and a covered wooden walkway joined the two wings.

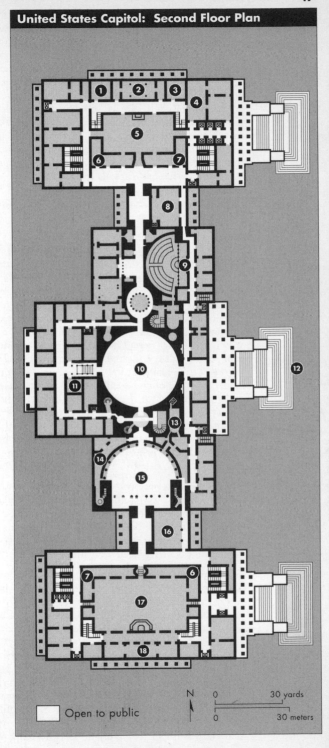

United States Capitol: Second Floor Plan

N

0   30 yards

0   30 meters

Open to public

The Congress House grew slowly and suffered a grave setback on August 24, 1814, when British troops led by Sir George Cockburn marched on Washington and set fire to the Capitol, the White House, and numerous other government buildings. (Cockburn reportedly stood on the House Speaker's chair and asked his men, "Shall this harbor of Yankee democracy be burned?" The question was rhetorical; the building was torched.) The wooden walkway was destroyed and the two wings gutted, but the walls were left standing after a violent rainstorm doused the flames. Fearful that Congress might leave Washington, residents raised money for a hastily built "Brick Capitol" that stood where the Supreme Court is today. Architect Benjamin Henry Latrobe supervised the rebuilding of the Capitol, adding such American touches as the corncob-and-tobacco-leaf capitals to columns in the east entrance to the Senate wing. He was followed by Boston-born Charles Bulfinch, and in 1826 the Capitol, its low wooden dome sheathed in copper, was finally finished.

North and south wings were added in the 1850s and '60s to accommodate a growing government trying to keep pace with a growing country. The elongated edifice extended farther north and south than Thornton had planned, and in 1855, to keep the scale correct, work began on a tall cast-iron dome. President Lincoln was criticized for continuing this expensive project while the country was in the throes of the bloody Civil War, but he called the construction "a sign we intend the Union shall go on." This twin-shelled dome, a marvel of 19th-century engineering, rises 285 feet above the ground and weighs 9 million pounds. It expands and contracts up to 4 inches a day, depending on the outside temperature. The figure on top of the dome, often mistaken for Pocahontas, is called *Freedom.* Sculptor Thomas Crawford had first planned for the 19-foot-tall bronze statue to wear the cloth liberty cap of a freed Roman slave, but southern lawmakers, led by Jefferson Davis, objected. An "American" headdress composed of a star-encircled helmet surmounted with an eagle's head and feathers was substituted. After being plucked from the dome by helicopter, *Freedom* received a much needed sprucing up in 1993.

The Capitol has continued to grow. In 1962 the east front was extended 34 feet, creating 100 additional offices. Preservationists have fought to keep the west front from being extended, since it is the last remaining section of the Capitol's original facade. A compromise was reached in 1983, when it was agreed that the facade's crumbling sandstone blocks would simply be replaced with stronger limestone.

Guided tours of the Capitol usually start beneath the dome in the Rotunda, but if there's a crowd you may have to wait in a line that forms at the top of the center steps on the east side. If you want to forgo the tour, which is brief but informative, you may look around on your own. Enter through one of the lower doors to the right or left of the main steps. Start your exploration under Constantino Brumidi's *Apotheosis of Washington,* the fresco in the center of the dome. Working as Michelangelo did in the Sistine Chapel, applying paint to wet plaster, Brumidi completed this fresco in 1865. The figures in the inner circle represent the 13 original states of the Union; those in the outer ring symbolize arts, sciences, and industry. The flat, sculpture-style frieze around the rim of the Rotunda depicting 400 years of American history was started by Brumidi. While painting Penn's treaty with the Indians, the 74-year-old artist slipped on the 58-foot-high scaffold and almost fell off. Brumidi managed to hang on until help arrived, but he died a few months later from shock brought on by the incident. The work was continued by another Italian, Filippo Costaggini, but the frieze wasn't finished until American Allyn Cox added the final touches in 1953.

Notice the Rotunda's eight immense oil paintings of scenes from American history. The four scenes from the Revolutionary War are by John Trumbull, who served alongside George Washington and painted the first president from life. Twenty-six people have lain in state in the Rotunda, including nine presidents, from Abraham Lincoln to Lyndon Baines Johnson. Underneath the Rotunda, above an empty crypt that was designed to hold the remains of George and Martha Washington, is an exhibit chronicling the construction of the Capitol.

South of the Rotunda is Statuary Hall, once the legislative chamber of the House of Representatives. The room has an interesting architectural feature that maddened early legislators: A slight whisper uttered on one side of the hall can be heard on the other. (Don't be disappointed if this parlor trick doesn't work when you're visiting the Capitol; sometimes the hall is just too noisy.) When the House moved out, Congress invited each state to send statues of two great deceased citizens for placement in the former chamber. Because the weight of the accumulated statues threatened to cave the floor in, some of the sculptures were dispersed to various other spots throughout the Capitol.

To the north, on the Senate side, you can look into the chamber once used by the Supreme Court and into the splendid Old Senate Chamber above it, both of which have been restored. Also be sure to see the Brumidi Corridor on the ground floor of the Senate wing. Frescoes and oil paintings of birds, plants, and American inventions adorn the walls and ceilings, and an intricate, Brumidi-designed bronze stairway leads to the second floor. The Italian artist also memorialized several American heroes, painting them inside trompe l'oeil frames. Trusting that America would continue to produce heroes long after he was gone, Brumidi left some frames empty. The most recent one to be filled, in 1987, honors the crew of the space shuttle *Challenger*.

If you want to watch some of the legislative action in the **House** or **Senate chambers** while you're on the Hill you'll have to get a gallery pass from the office of your representative or senator. (To find out where those offices are, ask any Capitol police officer, or dial 202/224–3121.) In the chambers you'll notice that Democrats sit to the right of the presiding officer, Republicans to the left—the opposite, it's often noted, of their political leanings. You may be disappointed by watching from the gallery. Most of the day-to-day business is conducted in the various legislative committees, many of which meet in the congressional office buildings. The *Washington Post's* daily "Today in Congress" lists when and where the committees are meeting. To get to a house or Senate office building, go to the Capitol's basement and ride the miniature subway used by legislators. *East end of Mall,* ☎ *202/224–3121. For guide service,* ☎ *202/225–6827.* ☛ *Free.* ☼ *Daily 9–4:30; summer hrs determined annually, but Rotunda and Statuary Hall usually open daily 9–8.*

TIME OUT   A meal at a **Capitol cafeteria** may give you a glimpse of a well-known politician or two. A public dining room on the first floor, Senate-side, is open 7:30 AM–3:30 PM. A favorite with legislators is the Senate bean soup, made and served every day since 1901 (no one is sure exactly why, though the menu, which you can take with you, outlines a few popular theories).

When you're finished exploring the inside of the Capitol, make your way to the **west side.** In 1981, Ronald Reagan broke with tradition and moved the presidential swearing-in ceremony to this side of the Capitol, which offers a dramatic view of the Mall and monuments below and can accommodate more guests than the east side, where all previous presidents took the oath of office. Walk down the northernmost flight of steps and follow the red-and-black path that leads to Pennsylvania Avenue. The white-marble memorial in the center of the traf-
❻ fic circle in front of you is the **Peace Monument,** which depicts America, grief-stricken over sailors lost at sea, weeping on the shoulder of History. Cross First Street carefully and walk to the left along the **Capitol**
❼ **Reflecting Pool.** As you continue south you'll pass the **Grant Memorial.** At a length of 252 feet, it's the largest sculpture group in the city. The statue of Ulysses S. Grant on horseback is flanked by Union artillery and cavalry. Further south, in the intersection of First Street and
❽ Maryland Avenue SW, is the **James Garfield Memorial.** The 20th president of the United States, Garfield was assassinated in 1881 after only a few months in office.

❾ Across Maryland Avenue is the **United States Botanic Gardens,** a peaceful, plant-filled oasis between Capitol Hill and the Mall. The conservatory includes a cactus house, a fern house, and a subtropical house filled with orchids. Seasonal displays include blooming plants at Easter, chrysanthemums in the fall, and Christmas greens and poinsettias in December and January. Brochures just inside the doorway offer helpful gardening tips. *1st St. and Maryland Ave. SW, ☎ 202/225–8333.*
☛ *Free.* ☺ *May–July, daily 9–8; Aug.–Apr., daily 9–5.*

When you exit the Botanic Gardens, walk away from the Capitol, take the first left along the pebbled sidewalk, and cross Independence Avenue. To the right is the **Hubert H. Humphrey Building,** home of the Department of Health and Human Services. The beige building gets a much-needed splash of color from *Shorepoints I,* the red abstract sculpture by James Rosati that sits in front of it.

Walk east on Independence Avenue. On the right, in a park that is part
❿ of the Botanic Garden, you'll pass the **Bartholdi Fountain.** Frédéric-Auguste Bartholdi, sculptor of the more famous—and much larger— Statue of Liberty, created this delightful fountain for the Philadelphia Centennial Exhibition of 1876. With its aquatic monsters, sea nymphs, tritons, and lighted globes (once gas, now electric), the fountain represents the elements of water and light. The U.S. government purchased the fountain after the exhibition and placed it on the grounds of the old Botanic Garden on the Mall. It was moved to its present location in 1932.

Cross 1st Street SW and continue east on Independence Avenue past the **Rayburn, Longworth,** and **Cannon House office buildings.** At In-
⓫ dependence Avenue and 1st Street SE is the green-domed **Jefferson Building** of the **Library of Congress.** Like many buildings in Washington that seem a bit overwrought (the Old Executive Office Building is another example), the library was criticized when it was completed, in 1897. Some detractors felt its Italian Renaissance design was a bit too florid. Congressmen were even heard to grumble that its dome—topped with the gilt "Flame of Knowledge"—competed with that of their Capitol. It is certainly decorative, with busts of Dante, Goethe, Hawthorne, and other great writers perched above its entryway. *The Court of Neptune,* Roland Hinton Perry's fountain at the base of the front steps, rivals some of Rome's best fountains.

Provisions for a library to serve members of Congress were originally made in 1800, when the government set aside $5,000 to purchase and house books that legislators might need to consult. This small collection was housed in the Capitol but was destroyed in 1814, when the British burned the city. Thomas Jefferson, then in retirement at Monticello, offered his personal library as a replacement, noting that "there is, in fact, no subject to which a Member of Congress may not have occasion to refer." Jefferson's collection of 6,487 books, for which Congress eventually paid him $23,950, laid the foundation for the great national library. (Sadly, another fire in 1851 wiped out two-thirds of Jefferson's books.) By the late 1800s it was clear the Capitol building could no longer contain the growing library, and the Jefferson Building was constructed. The **Adams Building,** on 2nd Street behind the Jefferson, was added in 1939. A third structure, the **James Madison Building,** opened in 1980; it is just south of the Jefferson Building, between Independence Avenue and C Street.

The **Library of Congress** today holds some 103 million items, of which only a quarter are books. The remainder includes manuscripts, prints, films, photographs, sheet music, and the largest collection of maps in the world. Also part of the library is the Congressional Research Service, which, as the name implies, works on special projects for senators and representatives.

The Jefferson and Adams buildings are nearing the end of an extensive renovation and some parts may be closed on your visit. The gem of the Jefferson Building is the richly decorated Great Hall, adorned with mosaics, paintings, and curving marble stairways. The grand, octagonal Main Reading Room, its central desk surrounded by mahogany readers' tables, is either inspiring or overwhelming to researchers. Computer terminals have replaced the wooden card catalogues, but books are still retrieved and dispersed the same way: Readers (18 years or older) hand request slips to librarians and wait patiently for their materials to be delivered. Researchers aren't allowed in the stacks and only members of Congress can check books out.

But books are only part of the story. Family trees are explored in the Local History and Genealogy Reading Room. In the Folklife Reading Room, patrons can listen to LP recordings of American Indian music or hear the story of B'rer Rabbit read in the Gullah dialect of Georgia and South Carolina. Items from the library's collection—which includes a Gutenberg Bible—are often on display in the Jefferson and Madison buildings. Classic films are shown for free in the 64-seat Mary Pickford Theater (☎ 202/707–5677 for information). *Jefferson Bldg., 1st St. and Independence Ave. SE,* ☎ *202/707–8000.* ☛ *Free. Most reading rooms open Mon., Wed., and Thurs. 8:30–9:30, Tues., Fri., and Sat. 8:30–5, Sun. 1–5.* ☎ *202/707–6400 for special hrs. Tours leave weekdays at 10, 1, and 3 from Madison Building, Independence Ave. between 1st and 2nd Sts. SE; groups of 10 or more should call ahead for reservations.*

⓬ Behind the Jefferson Building stands the **Folger Shakespeare Library.** The Folger Library's collection of works by and about Shakespeare and his times is second to none. The white-marble Art Deco building, designed by architect Paul Philippe Cret, is decorated with scenes from the Bard's plays. Inside is a reproduction of an inn-yard theater, which is the setting for performances of chamber music, baroque opera, and other events appropriate to the surroundings, and a gallery, designed in the manner of an Elizabethan Great Hall, which hosts rotating exhibits from the library's collection. *201 E. Capitol St. SE,* ☎ *202/544–4600.* ☛ *Free.* ☉ *Mon.–Sat. 10–4.*

⓭ Walk back down East Capitol Street and turn right onto 1st Street. The stolid **Supreme Court Building** faces 1st Street here. The justices arrived in Washington in 1800 along with the rest of the government but were for years shunted around various rooms in the Capitol; for a while they even met in a tavern. It wasn't until 1935 that the court got its own building, this white-marble temple with twin rows of Corinthian columns, designed by Cass Gilbert. William Howard Taft, the only man to serve as both president and chief justice, was instrumental in getting the court a home of its own, though he died before it was completed.

The Supreme Court convenes on the first Monday in October and remains in session until it has heard all of its cases and handed down all its decisions (usually the end of June). On Monday through Wednesday of two weeks in each month, the justices hear oral arguments in the velvet-swathed court chamber. Visitors who want to listen can choose to wait in either of two lines. One, the "three-to-five-minute" line, shuttles visitors through, giving them a quick impression of the court at work. If you choose the other, for those who'd like to stay for the whole show, it's best to be in line by 8:30 AM. The main hall of the Supreme Court is lined with busts of former chief justices; the courtroom itself is decorated with allegorical friezes. Perhaps the most interesting appurtenance in the imposing building, however, is a basketball court on one of the upper floors (it's been called the highest court in the land). *1st and E. Capitol Sts. NE,* ☎ *202/479–3000.* ☛ *Free.* ☉ *Weekdays 9–4:30.*

⓮ One block north of the Supreme Court, at the corner of Constitution Avenue and 2nd Street, is the redbrick **Sewall-Belmont House,** built in 1800 by Robert Sewall. Part of the house dates from the early 1700s, which makes it the oldest home on Capitol Hill. From 1801 to 1813 Secretary of the Treasury Albert Gallatin lived here. He finalized the details of the Louisiana Purchase in his front-parlor office. The house became the only private residence burned in Washington during the British invasion of 1814, after a resident fired on advancing British troops from an upper-story window. (It was, in fact, the only resistance the British met. The rest of the country was disgusted at Washington's inability to defend itself.) The house, now the headquarters of the National Woman's Party, has a museum that chronicles the early days of the women's movement and is filled with period furniture and portraits and busts of such suffrage-movement leaders as Lucretia Mott, Elizabeth Cady Stanton, and Alice Paul. *144 Constitution Ave. NE,* ☎ *202/ 546–3989.* ☛ *Free.* ☉ *Nov.–Feb., Tues.–Fri. 10–3, Sat. 12–4; Mar.–Oct., Tues.–Fri. 10–3, Sat. 10–4, Sun. noon–4.*

After seeing the Sewall-Belmont House, continue east on Maryland Avenue, past the headquarters of the **Veterans of Foreign Wars.** Only three blocks from the Capitol, the Hill's residential character asserts itself. At Stanton Square turn right onto 4th Street NE, walk south two blocks, and then turn right onto A Street. The gray house with the ⓯ mansard roof at 316 A Street is the **Frederick Douglass Townhouse** (not open to the public). The first Washington home of the famous abolitionist and writer, this structure housed the National Museum of African Art until 1987, when the museum was moved to a new building on the Mall (*see* Tour 1, *above*).

Walk back to 4th Street and down another block to East Capitol Street, the border between the northeast and southeast quadrants of the city. The orange and yellow trash cans, emblazoned with the silhouette of an Indian, are reminders that East Capitol street is a main thoroughfare to RFK Stadium, home turf of the Washington Redskins. In the '50s there was a plan to construct government office buildings on both sides of East Capitol Street as far as Lincoln Park, seven blocks to the east. The neighborhood's active historic-preservation supporters successfully fought the proposal. The houses on the-

16 **south side of East Capitol Street** are a representative sampling of homes on the Hill. The corner house, No. 329, has a striking tower with a bay window and stained glass. Next door are two Victorian houses with iron trim below the second floor. A pre–Civil War Greek-Revival

17 frame house sits behind a trim garden at No. 317. At **326 A Street,** in a quiet neighborhood behind the Library of Congress's Adams Building, is the stucco house that artist Constantino Brumidi lived in while he was working on the Capitol.

TIME OUT   **Le Bon Cafe** (210 2nd St. SE) is a cozy French bistro serving excellent coffees, pastries, and light lunches. The sixth floor dining halls of the **Library of Congress, Madison Building** (see above) offer great views and inexpensive fare.

Turn right on Pennsylvania Avenue and head back toward the Capitol's familiar white dome. The south side of the street is lined with restaurants and bars frequented by those who live and work on the Hill.

You'll find the nearest Metro stop, Capitol South, on the corner of 1st and D streets SE.

TOUR 5: OLD DOWNTOWN AND FEDERAL TRIANGLE

Numbers in the margin correspond to points of interest on the Tour 5: Old Downtown and Federal Triangle map.

Just because Washington is a planned city doesn't mean the plan was executed flawlessly. Pierre L'Enfant's design has been alternately shelved and rediscovered several times in the last 200 years. Nowhere have the city's imperfections been more visible than on L'Enfant's grand thoroughfare, Pennsylvania Avenue. By the early '60s it had become a national disgrace, the dilapidated buildings that lined it home to pawn shops and cheap souvenir stores. While riding up Pennsylvania Avenue in his inaugural parade, a disgusted John F. Kennedy is said to have turned to an aide and said, "Fix it!" Washington's downtown—once within the diamond formed by Massachusetts, Louisiana, Pennsylvania, and New York avenues—had its problems, too, many as a result of the riots that rocked the capital in 1968 after the assassination of Martin Luther King, Jr. In their wake, many downtown businesses left the area and moved north of the White House.

In recent years developers have rediscovered "old downtown," and buildings are now being torn down or remodeled at an amazing pace. After several false starts Pennsylvania Avenue is shining once again. This tour explores the old downtown section of the city, then swings around to check the progress on the monumental street that links the Congress House—the Capitol—with the President's House.

1 Start your exploration in front of the **Pension Building,** on F Street between 4th and 5th streets (Metro: Judiciary Square). The massive redbrick edifice was built between 1882 and 1887 to house workers who processed the pension claims of veterans and their survivors, an activity that intensified after the Civil War. The architect was U.S. Army Corps of Engineers General Montgomery C. Meigs, who took as his inspiration the Italian Renaissance–style Palazzo Farnese in Rome.

Before entering the building, walk down its F Street side. The terracotta frieze by Caspar Buberl between the first and second floors depicts soldiers marching and sailing in an endless procession around the building. Architect Meigs lost his oldest son in the Civil War, and, though the frieze depicts Union troops, he intended it as a memorial to all who were killed in the bloody war. Meigs designed the Pension Building with workers' comfort in mind, long before anyone knew that cramped, stuffy offices could cause "sick building syndrome." Note the three "missing" bricks under each window that helped keep the building cool by allowing air to circulate.

The open interior of the building is one of the city's great spaces and has been the site of inaugural balls for more than 100 years. (The first ball was for Grover Cleveland in 1885; because the building wasn't finished at the time, a temporary wooden roof and floor were erected.) The eight central Corinthian columns are the largest in the world, rising to a height of 75 feet. Though they look like marble, each is made of 75,000 bricks, covered with plaster and painted to resemble Siena marble. Each year NBC tapes its "Christmas in Washington" TV special in the breathtaking hall.

The Pension Building now houses the **National Building Museum,** devoted to architecture and the building arts. "Washington: Symbol and City" is a permanent exhibit that outlines the capital's architectural history, from monumental core to residential neighborhoods. Recent temporary exhibits have explored the construction of the Statue of Liberty, the history of Washington's apartment buildings, and the national effects of wartime construction. *F St. between 4th and 5th Sts. NW,* ☎ *202/272–2448.* ☛ *Free.* ☉ *Mon.–Sat. 10–4, Sun. noon–4; closed Thanksgiving, Dec. 25, Jan. 1. Tours weekdays at 12:30, weekends at 12:30 and 1:30.*

Two blocks east and a block north is another redbrick building, though one on a smaller scale. The Federal Revival–style **Old Adas Israel Synagogue** is the oldest synagogue in Washington. Built in 1876 at 6th and G streets NW, it was moved to its present location in 1969 to make way for an office building. Exhibits in the Lillian and Albert Small Jewish Museum inside explore Jewish life in Washington. *3rd and G Sts. NW,* ☎ *202/789–0900. Suggested donation: $2 adults, $1 children.* ☉ *Sun.–Thurs. 10–4, Fri. by appointment.*

2 Back across F Street from the Pension Building is **Judiciary Square.** As the name implies, this is the District's judicial core, with both city and federal courthouses arranged around it. The **National Law Enforcement Officers Memorial** was dedicated here in October 1991. A 3-foot-high wall bears the names of more than 15,000 American police officers killed in the line of duty since 1794. On the third line of panel 13W are the names of six officers killed by William Bonney, better known as Billy the Kid. J. D. Tippit, the Dallas policeman killed by Lee Harvey Oswald, is honored on the ninth line of panel 63E. Given the dangerous nature of police work, it will be one of the few memorials to which names will continue to be added. Two blocks away is a visitor center with exhibits on the history of the memorial and computers that allow you to look up officers by name, date of death, state, and department. A small shop sells souvenirs. *Visitor center, 605 E St. NW,* ☎ *202/737–*

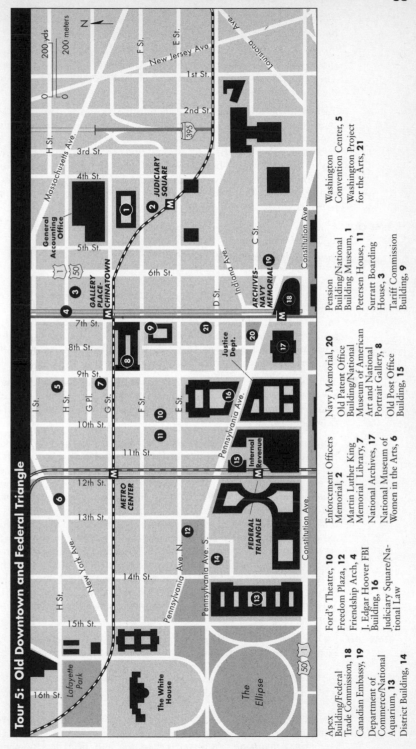

Tour 5: Old Downtown and Federal Triangle

N

200 yds
200 meters

New Jersey Ave
Louisiana Ave.
E St.
F St.
1st St.
2nd St.
3rd St.
H St.
Massachusetts Ave.
Massachusetts Ave.
395
4th St.
JUDICIARY SQUARE
M
General Accounting Office
1
2
5th St.
C St.
6th St.
Constitution Ave.
D St.
Indiana Ave.
ARCHIVES-NAVY MEMORIAL 19
18
M
1
50
GALLERY PLACE-CHINATOWN
3
4
M
7th St.
9
21
Justice Dept.
20
17
8th St.
Pennsylvania Ave.
8
9th St.
5
H St.
G Pl.
G St.
7
16
10
F St.
E St.
I St.
10th St.
Internal Revenue
11
M
15
11th St.
12th St.
M
METRO CENTER
6
13th St.
FEDERAL TRIANGLE
12
Constitution Ave.
New York Ave.
H St.
14
Pennsylvania Ave. N.
Pennsylvania Ave. S.
14th St.
13
15th St.
The White House
Lafayette Park
16th St.
50
1
The Ellipse

Apex Building/Federal Trade Commission, **18**
Canadian Embassy, **19**
Department of Commerce/National Aquarium, **13**
District Building, **14**

Ford's Theatre, **10**
Freedom Plaza, **12**
Friendship Arch, **4**
J. Edgar Hoover FBI Building, **16**
Judiciary Square/National Law

Enforcement Officers Memorial, **2**
Martin Luther King Memorial Library, **7**
National Archives, **17**
National Museum of Women in the Arts, **6**

Navy Memorial, **20**
Old Patent Office Building/National Museum of American Art and National Portrait Gallery, **8**
Old Post Office Building, **15**

Pension Building/National Building Museum, **1**
Petersen House, **11**
Surratt Boarding House, **3**
Tariff Commission Building, **9**

Washington Convention Center, **5**
Washington Project for the Arts, **21**

3400. ☛ Free. ⊙ Weekdays 9–5, Sat. 10–5, Sun. noon–5. Call to arrange free tour.

Head west on F Street. After you cross 5th Street, look back at the Pension Building. It's easier to see the interesting roof from this distance. The prison block–like structure north of the Pension Building houses the General Accounting Office.

Turn right on 6th Street and walk two blocks north. The Chinese characters on the street signs signal that you're entering Washington's compact **Chinatown,** bordered by G, E, 5th, and 8th streets. The area is somewhat down-at-the-heels—you'll find boarded-up buildings and graffiti-covered walls—but this is the place to go for Chinese food in the District. Nearly every restaurant has a roast duck hanging in the window, and the shops here sell a wide variety of Chinese goods, from paperback books to traditional medicines.

TIME OUT If the smells of Chinese cooking have activated your taste buds, try the highly rated **Mr. Yung's** (740 6th St. NW). It specializes in Cantonese cuisine, and if you're lucky enough to be in the neighborhood between 11 and 3, be sure to sample the dim sum.

❸ Turn left off 6th Street onto H Street. The **Surratt Boarding House,** where John Wilkes Booth and his co-conspirators plotted the assassination of Abraham Lincoln, is at 604 H Street NW. (It's now a Chinese restaurant called Go-Lo's.) The colorful and ornate 75-foot-wide
❹ **Friendship Arch** that spans H Street at 7th Street is a reminder of Washington's sister-city relationship with Beijing.

❺ To the west, at 9th and H streets, is the **Washington Convention Center.** Opened in 1983, the center pumped much-needed life into this part of downtown and spurred the development of nearby hotels and office buildings.

Continue west on H Street and turn right on 13th Street. At 13th and
❻ New York Avenue NW is the **National Museum of Women in the Arts,** a showcase of works by prominent female artists from the Renaissance to the present. The beautifully restored 1907 Renaissance Revival building was designed by Waddy Wood and, ironically, was once a men-only Masonic temple. When the museum opened in 1987 some questioned the wisdom of segregating artists by sex. Since then its acclaimed exhibitions have won over most naysayers. In addition to displaying traveling shows, the museum houses a permanent collection that includes paintings, drawings, sculpture, prints, and photographs by such artists as Georgia O'Keeffe, Mary Cassatt, Élisabeth Vigée-Lebrun, Frida Kahlo, and Judy Chicago. *1250 New York Ave. NW, ☎ 202/783–5000. Suggested donation: $3 adults; $2 students, senior citizens, and children. ⊙ Mon.–Sat. 10–5, Sun. noon–5.*

TIME OUT For a casual lunch in an elegant setting try the cafe in the **National Museum of Women in the Arts** (see above). Another interesting lunch spot nearby is the **Sphinx Club** (1315 K St. NW), with its preserved 1914 Turkish-style tile front and cathedral-like interior. The kitchen produces salads and sandwiches and a daily grilled meal that's always worth trying.

Across the street, at 1300 New York Avenue NW, is the **InterAmerican Development Bank Cultural Center.** Founded in 1959, the IADB is an international bank that finances economic and social development in Latin America and the Caribbean. Its small cultural center hosts changing exhibits of paintings, sculptures, and artifacts from member countries. *1300 New York Ave. NW,* ☎ *202/623–3287.* ☛ *Free.* ۞ *Weekdays 11–6.*

Head south on 12th Street. Two of the Washington area's largest department stores are nearby—Woodward & Lothrop, at 11th and F, and Hecht's, at 12th and G. Turn left on G Street.

❼ The squat black building at 9th and G streets is the **Martin Luther King Memorial Library,** designed by Mies van der Rohe, the largest public library in the city. A mural on the first floor depicts events in the life of the Nobel Prize–winning civil rights activist. Used books are almost always on sale at bargain prices in the library's gift shop. *901 G St. NW,* ☎ *202/727–1111.* ۞ *Mon.–Thurs. 9–9, Fri.–Sat. 9–5:30, Sun. 1–5.*

Across 9th Street, on the block bounded by F, G, 7th, and 9th streets,
❽ stands the **Old Patent Office Building,** which now houses two Smithsonian museums: the **National Portrait Gallery** on the south and the **National Museum of American Art** on the north. Construction on the south wing, which was designed by Washington Monument architect Robert Mills, started in 1836. When the huge Greek-Revival quadrangle was completed in 1867 it was the largest building in the country. Many of its rooms housed glass display cabinets filled with the models that inventors were required to submit with their patent applications.

During the Civil War, the Patent Office, like many other buildings in the city, was turned into a hospital. Among those caring for the wounded here were Clara Barton and Walt Whitman. In the 1950s the building was threatened with demolition to make way for a parking lot, but the efforts of preservationists saved it. The Smithsonian opened it to the public in 1968.

The first floor of the National Museum of American Art holds displays of early American art and art of the West, as well as a gallery of painted miniatures. Be sure to see *The Throne of the Third Heaven of the Nations' Millennium General Assembly,* by James Hampton. Discarded materials, such as chairs, bottles, and light bulbs, are sheathed in aluminum and gold foil in this strange and moving work of religious art. On the second floor are works by the American Impressionists, including John Henry Twachtman and Childe Hassam. There are also plaster models and marble sculptures by Hiram Powers, including the plaster cast of his famous work *The Greek Slave,* the original of which is housed in the Corcoran Gallery (*see* Tour 3, *above*). Just outside the room containing Powers's work is a copy of a sculpture Augustus Saint-Gaudens created for Henry Adams. Adams's wife had committed suicide and the original of this moving, shroud-draped figure sits above her grave in Rock Creek Cemetery. Also on this floor are massive landscapes by Albert Bierstadt and Thomas Moran. The third floor is filled with modern art, including works by Leon Kroll and Edward Hopper that were commissioned during the '30s by the federal government. The Lincoln Gallery—site of the receiving line at Abraham Lincoln's 1865 inaugural ball—has been restored to its original appearance and contains modern art by Jasper Johns, Robert Rauschenberg, Milton Avery, Kenneth Noland, and others. *8th and G Sts. NW,* ☎ *202/357–2700, TTY 202/357–1729.* ☛ *Free.* ۞ *Daily 10–5:30; closed Dec. 25.*

You can enter the National Portrait Gallery from any floor of the National Museum of American Art or walk through the courtyard between the two wings. The best place to start a circuit of the Portrait Gallery is on the restored third floor. The mezzanine level of the wonderfully busy room features a **Civil War exhibition,** with portraits, photographs, and lithographs of such wartime personalities as Julia Ward Howe, Frederick Douglass, Ulysses S. Grant, and Robert E. Lee. There are also life casts of Abraham Lincoln's hands and face. The Renaissance-style gallery has been restored to its original splendor, complete with colorful tile flooring and a stained-glass skylight. Highlights of the Portrait Gallery's second floor include the **Hall of Presidents** (featuring a portrait or sculpture of each chief executive) and the George Washington "Lansdowne" portrait. The first floor features portraits of well-known American athletes and performers. *Time* magazine gave the museum its collection of Person of the Year covers and many other photos and paintings that the magazine has commissioned over the years. Parts of this collection are periodically on display. *8th and F Sts. NW,* ☎ *202/357–2700, TTY 202/357–1729.* ☛ *Free.* ☉ *Daily 10–5:30; closed Dec. 25.*

TIME OUT   The **Patent Pending** restaurant, between the two museums, serves an ample selection of salads, sandwiches, hot entrées, and other treats. Tables and chairs in the large museum courtyard make sitting outside the thing to do when the weather is pleasant.

If you leave the pair of museums in the Patent Office Building by way of the National Portrait Gallery's F Street doors, you'll come upon another of Washington's beautiful views. Directly ahead, four blocks away in the Federal Triangle, is the **National Archives** building. To the east is the green barrel-roof of **Union Station,** and to the west you can see the **Treasury Department Building.** Just across the F Street pedestrian

9 mall and to the left is the **Tariff Commission Building,** designed by Robert Mills and finished in 1866. When the Capitol was burned by the British in 1814, Congress met temporarily in a hotel that stood on this site. Another earlier building on the site housed the nation's first public telegraph office, operated by Samuel F. B. Morse.

The block of F Street between 9th and 10th streets has long been a center of shopping in the District. It's dotted with cut-rate electronics stores, pawn shops, and lingerie stores, and the sidewalks are usually crowded with shoppers looking over the wares of street vendors, who hawk everything from sweatshirts and sunglasses to perfumes and panty hose. Many residents fear that developers' new-found interest in old downtown may threaten this lively part of the city.

Turn left off F Street onto 10th Street. Halfway down the block on the

10 left is **Ford's Theatre.** In 1861, Baltimore theater impresario John T. Ford leased the First Baptist Church building that stood on this site and turned it into a successful music hall. The building burned down late in 1862, and Ford rebuilt it. The events of April 14, 1865, would shock the nation and close the theater. On that night, during a production of *Our American Cousin,* John Wilkes Booth entered the presidential box and assassinated Abraham Lincoln. The stricken president was carried across the street to the house of tailor William Petersen. Charles Augustus Leale, a 23-year-old doctor, attended to the president, whose injuries would have left him blind had he ever regained consciousness. To let Lincoln know that someone was nearby, Leale

11 held his hand throughout the night. Lincoln died in the **Petersen House** (516 10th St. NW, ☎ 202/426–6830; open daily 9–5) the next morning. Visitors can see the restored front and back parlors of the house, as well as the bedroom where the president died. Most of the furnishings are not original, but the pillow and bloodstained pillowcases are those used on that fateful night.

The federal government bought Ford's Theatre in 1866 for $100,000 and converted it into office space. It was remodeled as a Lincoln museum in 1932 and was restored to its 1865 appearance in 1968. The basement museum—with artifacts such as Booth's pistol and the clothes Lincoln was wearing when he was shot—reopened in 1990 after a complete renovation. The theater itself continues to present a complete schedule of plays. *A Christmas Carol* is an annual holiday favorite. *511 10th St. NW,* ☎ *202/426–6924.* ☛ *Free.* ☉ *Daily 9–5. Theater closed when rehearsals or matinees are in progress (generally Thurs. and weekends); Lincoln Museum in basement remains open at these times. Closed Dec. 25.*

Continue south on 10th Street and turn right on E Street. Most people would consider this E Street, but you'll notice that some of the buildings on this stretch—including both the Warner Theatre and the National Theatre—boast "Pennsylvania Avenue" on their entrances. There's a certain cachet to sharing a street address with the president.

TIME OUT   The **Hard Rock Cafe** (999 E St. NW, ☎ 202/737-7625) opened its Washington branch in 1989, bringing hearty American food, a modest selection of beers, and lots of those famous T-shirts (the Hard Rock's gift shop opened a full year before the restaurant did). This is a popular spot for tourists, so if you're not up to waiting in line, try to arrive early for lunch or dinner.

⑫ **Freedom Plaza** (the former Western Plaza) is bounded by 13th, 14th, and E streets and Pennsylvania Avenue. Its east end is dominated by a **statue of General Casimir Pulaski,** the Polish nobleman who led an American cavalry corps during the Revolutionary War and was mortally wounded in 1779 at the Siege of Savannah. He gazes over a plaza that is inlaid in bronze with a detail from L'Enfant's original 1791 plan for the Federal City. Bronze outlines the President's Palace and the Congress House; the Mall is represented by a green lawn. Cut into the edges are quotations about the capital city, not all of them complimentary. To compare L'Enfant's vision with today's reality, stand in the middle of the map's Pennsylvania Avenue and look west. L'Enfant had planned an unbroken vista from the Capitol to the White House, but the Treasury Building, begun in 1836, ruined the view. Turning to the east you'll see the U.S. Capitol sitting on Jenkins Hill like an American Taj Mahal.

There's a lot to see and explore in the blocks near Freedom Plaza. The beaux arts **Willard Hotel** is on the corner of 14th Street and Pennsylvania Avenue. There was a Willard Hotel on this spot long before this ornate structure was built in 1901. The original Willard was the place to stay in Washington if you were rich or influential (or wanted to give that impression). Abraham Lincoln stayed there while waiting to move into the nearby White House. Julia Ward Howe stayed there during the Civil War and wrote "The Battle Hymn of the Republic" after gazing down from her window to see Union troops drilling on Pennsylvania Avenue. It's said the term "lobbyist" was coined to describe the favor seekers who would buttonhole President Ulysses S. Grant in the hotel's public rooms. The second Willard, with its mansard roof dotted with circular windows, was designed by Henry Hardenbergh, architect of New York's Plaza Hotel. Although it was just as opulent as the hotel it replaced, it fell on hard times after World War II. In 1968 it closed, standing empty until 1986, when it reopened, amid much fanfare, after an ambitious restoration. The Willard's rebirth is one of the most visible successes of the Pennsylvania Avenue Development Corporation, the organization charged with reversing the decay of America's Main Street.

Just north of Freedom Plaza, on F Street between 13th and 14th streets, are **The Shops,** a collection of stores in the National Press Building, itself home to dozens of domestic and foreign media organizations. The Shops has sit-down restaurants and fast food in its upstairs Food Hall. Washington's oldest stage, the **National Theatre,** also overlooks the plaza. This National has been here since 1922, though there has been a theater on this spot since 1835. After seeing her first play here at the age of six, Helen Hayes vowed to become an actress. If you plan ahead you can take a free tour of the historic theater that takes in the house, stage, backstage, wardrobe room, dressing rooms, the area under the stage, the Helen Hayes Lounge, and the memorabilia-filled archives. *1321 Pennsylvania Ave. NW,* ☎ *202/783–3370.* ☛ *Free. Minimum of 10 people on tour; make reservations at least 1 wk ahead.*

To the south of Freedom Plaza is **Federal Triangle,** the mass of government buildings constructed from 1929 to 1938 between 15th Street, Pennsylvania Avenue, and Constitution Avenue. Before Federal Triangle was developed, government workers were scattered throughout the city, largely in rented offices. Looking for a place to consolidate this work force, city planners hit on the area south of Pennsylvania Avenue known, at the time, as "Murder Bay," a notorious collection of rooming houses, taverns, tattoo parlors, and brothels. A uniform classical architectural style, with Italianate red-tile roofs and interior plazas reminiscent of the Louvre, was chosen for the building project.

The western base of the triangle, and the first part completed, is the
⑬ **Department of Commerce** building, between 14th and 15th streets. When it opened in 1932 it was the world's largest government office building. It also houses the **National Aquarium,** established in 1873, the oldest public aquarium in the United States. Its tanks display tropical and freshwater fish, moray eels, frogs, turtles, piranhas, even sharks, and a "touch tank" lets visitors handle sea creatures such as crabs and oysters. *14th St. and Pennsylvania Ave. NW,* ☎ *202/482–2825.* ☛ *$2 adults, 75¢ children 4–10 and senior citizens.* ⊙ *Daily 9–5; closed Dec. 25. Sharks are fed Mon., Wed., Sat. at 2; piranhas Tues., Thurs., Sun. at 2.*

Federal Triangle's planners envisioned interior courts filled with plazas and parks, but the needs of the motor car foiled any such grand plans. A park was planned for the spot of land between 13th and 14th streets across from the Commerce Building, but for many years it was an immense parking lot; now a federal office building containing an international cultural and trade center is being built there. The beaux arts
⑭ **District Building,** at the corner of 14th Street and Pennsylvania Avenue South, is home to the city council. It was erected in 1908, and, though it didn't fit in with the original 1929 Federal Triangle plans, it survived. (The building is in poor shape, however, and in 1992, Mayor Sharon Pratt Kelly moved several city agencies to tony digs near Judiciary Square. The inclusion in her own office of such amenities as a gas fireplace and granite countertops did not endear her to taxpayers.)

This tour continues east on Pennsylvania Avenue, against the direction taken by newly inaugurated presidents on their way to the White House. Thomas Jefferson started the parade tradition in 1805 after taking the oath of office for his second term. He was accompanied by a few friends and a handful of congressmen. Four years later James Madison made things official by instituting a proper inaugural celebration. The flag holders on the lamp posts are clues that Pennsylvania Avenue remains the city's most important parade route. With the Capitol at one end and the White House at the other, the avenue symbolizes both the distance and the connection between these two branches of government.

Such symbolism may have been lost on early inhabitants of Washington. When Pennsylvania Avenue first opened in 1796, it was an ugly and dangerous bog. Attempts by Jefferson to beautify the road by planting poplar trees were only partially successful: Many were chopped down for firewood. In the mid-19th century, crossing the rutted thoroughfare was a dangerous proposition, and rainstorms often turned the street into a river. The avenue was finally paved with wooden blocks in 1871.

TIME OUT   The Hard Rock Cafe is not the only memorabilia- and souvenir-filled eatery downtown. At **Planet Hollywood** (1101 Pennsylvania Ave. NW, ☎ 202/783-7827) you can eat and drink surrounded by such Hollywood set pieces and costumes as Darth Vader's shiny black mask, and a Klingon battle cruiser from the *Star Trek* movies. Meanwhile, film clips run on drop-down movie screens. (The works of chain co-owners Bruce Willis and Arnold Schwarzenegger are curiously well represented.)

Farther down Pennsylvania Avenue, across 12th Street, is the Romanesque **Old Post Office Building.** When it was completed, in 1899, it was the largest government building in the District, the first with a clock tower, and the first with an electric power plant. Despite these innovations, it earned the sobriquet "old" after only 18 years, when a new District post office was constructed near Union Station. When urban planners in the '20s decided to impose a uniform design on Federal Triangle, the Old Post Office was slated for demolition (some critics said it stood out like an "old tooth"). First a lack of money during the Depression, then the intercession of preservationists, headed by Nancy Hanks of the National Endowment for the Arts, saved the fanciful granite building. Major renovation was begun in 1978, and in 1984 the public areas in the Old Post Office Pavilion—an assortment of shops and restaurants inside the airy central courtyard—were opened. Other shops and restaurants were added to the pavilion's three-story, glass-enclosed East Atrium in 1992, along with City Golf, an indoor miniature golf course and bar.

Park Service rangers who work at the Old Post Office consider a trip to the observation deck in the **clock tower** to be one of Washington's best-kept secrets. Although not as tall as the Washington Monument, it offers nearly as impressive a view. Even better, it's usually not as crowded, the windows are bigger, and—unlike the monument's windows—they're open, allowing cool breezes to waft through. (The tour is about 15 minutes long.) On the way down be sure to look at the Congress Bells, cast at the same British foundry that made the bells in London's Westminster Abbey. The bells are rung to honor the opening and closing of Congress and on other important occasions, such as when the Redskins win the Super Bowl. *Pennsylvania Ave. and 12th St. NW, tower* ☎ *202/606-8691, pavilion* ☎ *202/289-4224.* ☛ *Free. Tower open Easter–Labor Day, daily 8 AM–11 PM (last tour 10:45); Sept.–Mar., daily 10–6 (last tour 5:45).*

TIME OUT   The waffle-cone ice-cream confections available at **Scoops Homemade Cones,** on the lower level of the Post Office Pavilion, are especially refreshing on a hot, humid day.

As you cross 10th Street look to your left at the delightful trompe l'oeil mural on the side of the **Lincoln Building,** two blocks up. It looks as if there's a hole in the building. There's also a portrait of the building's namesake. Closer to Pennsylvania Avenue on 10th Street is an example of one of Washington's strangest and most popular architectural conceits: a "façademy." The multi-arched, redbrick facade of a 1909 building has been retained—like a bug stuck in amber—on the front of a massive shop-and-office block.

Continuing down Pennsylvania Avenue, the next big building on the right is the **Department of Justice.** Like the rest of Federal Triangle, it boasts some Art Deco features, including the cylindrical aluminum torches outside the doorways, adorned with bas-relief figures of bison, dolphins, and birds.

🔟 Across from the Justice building is the **J. Edgar Hoover Federal Bureau of Investigation Building.** A hulking presence on the avenue, it was decried from birth as hideous. Even Hoover himself is said to have called it the "ugliest building I've ever seen." Opened in 1974, it hangs over 9th Street like a poured-concrete Big Brother. One thing is certain, it is secure. The one-hour tour of the building remains one of the most popular tourist activities in the city. A brief film outlines the Bureau's work, while exhibits describe famous past cases and illustrate the FBI's fight against organized crime, terrorism, bank robbery, espionage, extortion, and other criminal activities. There's everything from gangster John Dillinger's death mask to a poster display of the 10 Most Wanted criminals. (Look carefully: Two bad guys were apprehended as a result of tips from tour takers!) You'll also see the laboratories where the FBI painstakingly studies evidence. The high point of the tour comes right at the end: A special agent gives a live-ammo firearms demonstration in the building's indoor shooting range. *10th St. and Pennsylvania Ave. NW (tour entrance on E St. NW),* ☎ *202/324–3447.* ☛ *Free. Tours weekdays 8:45–4:15. Closed federal holidays. At peak times, there may be an hr wait for tour.*

🔢 The classical **National Archives** building fills the area between 7th and 9th streets and Pennsylvania and Constitution avenues. Beside it is a small park with a modest **memorial to Franklin Roosevelt.** The desk-size piece of marble on the sliver of grass is exactly what the president asked for (though this hasn't stopped fans of the 32nd president in their successful efforts to secure a grander memorial to FDR in West Potomac Park, due to be completed in 1996). Designed by John Russell Pope, the Archives building was erected in 1935 on the site of the old Center Market. This large block had been a center of commerce since the early 1800s, when barges plying the City Canal (which flowed where Constitution Avenue is now) were loaded and unloaded here. A vestige of this mercantile past lives on in the name given to the two semicircular developments across Pennsylvania Avenue from the Archives—**Market Square.** City planners hope that the residential development will enliven this stretch of Pennsylvania Avenue.

Turn right onto 9th Street and head to the Constitution Avenue side of the Archives. All the sculpture that adorns the building was carved on the site, including the two statues that flank the flight of steps facing the Mall, *Heritage* and *Guardianship,* by James Earle Fraser. Fraser also carved the scene on the pediment, which represents the transfer of historic documents to the recorder of the Archives. (Like nearly all pediment decorations in Washington, the scene is bristling with electric wires designed to thwart the advances of destructive pigeons.)

The Declaration of Independence, the Constitution, and the Bill of Rights are on display in the Rotunda of the Archives building, in a case made of bulletproof glass, illuminated with green light, and filled with helium gas (to protect the irreplaceable documents). At night and on Christmas—the only day the Archives are closed—they are lowered into a vault. If the Smithsonian Institution is the nation's attic, the Archives is the nation's basement, and it bears responsibility for the cataloguing and safekeeping of important government documents and other items. Objects in its vast collection include bureaucratic correspondence, veterans and immigration records, treaties, even Richard Nixon's resignation letter and the rifle Lee Harvey Oswald used to assassinate John F. Kennedy. *Constitution Ave. between 7th and 9th Sts. NW,* ☎ *202/501–5000.* ☛ *Free.* ☼ *Apr.–Labor Day, daily 10–9:30; Sept.–Mar., daily 10–5:30. Behind-the-scenes tours by reservation weekdays at 10:15 and 1:15,* ☎ *202/501–5205 well in advance.*

⑱ Continuing down Constitution Avenue you'll come to the tip of Federal Triangle. The **Apex Building,** completed in 1938, is the home of the **Federal Trade Commission.** The carving that adorns this triangular building depicts various aspects of trade. Note the relief decorations representing *Agriculture* (the harvesting of grain, by Concetta Scaravaglione) and *Trade* (two men bartering over an ivory tusk, by Carl Schmitz) over the doorways on the Constitution Avenue side. Two heroic statues by Michael Lantz on either side of the rounded eastern portico, each depicting a muscular, shirtless workman wrestling with a wild horse, represent *Man Controlling Trade.* Just across 6th Street is a three-tier fountain decorated with the signs of the zodiac; it is a memorial to Andrew Mellon, who as secretary of the treasury oversaw construction of the $125 million Federal Triangle (and who, as a deep-pocketed philanthropist, was the driving force behind the National Gallery of Art, just across Constitution Avenue). The impressive whitestone-and-glass building across Pennsylvania Avenue from Mellon's foun-

⑲ tain is the **Canadian Embassy,** designed by Arthur Erickson and completed in 1988. Inside, a gallery periodically displays exhibits on Canadian culture and history. *501 Pennsylvania Ave. NW,* ☎ *202/682–1740.* ☛ *Free.* ☼ *Weekdays 10–5 when an exhibition is mounted; otherwise closed.*

Backtrack a bit by circling the rounded end of the Federal Trade Commission Building, crossing Pennsylvania Avenue, and heading west. Pioneering photographer Mathew Brady had his studio in the twin-tower building at **625 Pennsylvania Avenue.** He's thought to have snapped some of his pictures of the city from the building's upper windows. For years after that it was better known as the home of Apex Liquors. Sears, Roebuck and Co. now owns the building, which serves as the huge retailer's Washington lobbying office and is sometimes called Sears House.

There is a multitude of statues and monuments at this confluence of 7th Street and Pennsylvania and Indiana avenues. The **Grand Army of the Republic** memorial pays tribute to the men who won the Civil War. Less conventional is the nearby stork-surmounted **Temperance Fountain.** It was erected in the 19th century by a teetotaling physician named Cogswell who hoped the fountain, which once dispensed icecold water, would lure people from the evils of drink.

⑳ Across 7th Street, close by a memorial to **General Winfield Scott,** is the **Navy Memorial,** a massive granite map of the world with a statue of a lone sailor. In the summer, the memorial's concert stage is the site of military band performances. To the northeast, in the Market Square Development, is the memorial's visitor center, complete with gift shop and "Navy Memorial Log Room," where visitors can use computers to look up the service records of sailors entered into the log. There's also the 250-seat, wide-screen Arleigh & Roberta Burke Theater, home of continuous screenings of the 30-minute, 70-millimeter film *At Sea*. Produced by the same company that made the IMAX hit *To Fly*, *At Sea* is a visually stunning look at life aboard a modern aircraft carrier. *701 Pennsylvania Ave. NW*, ☎ *202/737–2300. Visitor center open Mar.–Oct., Mon.–Sat. 10–6, Sun. noon–5; Nov.–Feb., Mon.–Sat. 10–5, Sun. noon–5.* ☛ *To At Sea: $3.50 adults, $2.50 senior citizens, students 18 and under, and military personnel; advance tickets available from TicketMaster,* ☎ *202/432–7328; group tickets, tel 202/628–3557 or 800/723–3557.*

The redevelopment that has rejuvenated Pennsylvania Avenue hasn't been confined solely to that famous street. **Pennsylvania Quarter** is the name given to the mix of condominiums, apartments, retail spaces, and restaurants in the blocks bounded by Pennsylvania Avenue and 6th, 9th, and G streets. The area includes the Lansburgh complex, at the corner of 8th and E streets. Built around three existing buildings (including the defunct Lansburgh department store), the complex includes the Shakespeare Theatre, which in 1992 moved from its former home in the Folger Library to this state-of-the-art, 447-seat space.

㉑ The **Washington Project for the Arts** shows the challenging work of contemporary artists, many of them from the Washington area. The two floors of gallery space usually include displays of avant-garde media (photography and video) as well as visual art (paintings and sculpture). WPA's **Bookworks** sells an exhaustive selection of art books—both books about art and limited edition books created by artists that are works of art themselves. *400 7th St. NW (entrance on D St.),* ☎ *202/ 347–4813, Bookworks* ☎ *202/347–4590.* ☛ *Free.* ☉ *Tues.–Sat. 11–6, Sun. 12–5.*

The nearest Metro stations are Gallery Place, on G Street, and National Archives on 7th.

TOUR 6: GEORGETOWN

Numbers in the margin correspond to points of interest on the Tour 6: Georgetown map.

Long before the District of Columbia was formed, Georgetown, Washington's oldest neighborhood, was a separate city that boasted a harbor full of ships and warehouses filled with tobacco. Washington has filled in around Georgetown over the years, but the former tobacco port retains an air of aloofness. Its narrow streets, which refuse to conform to Pierre L'Enfant's plan for the Federal City, make up the capital's wealthiest neighborhood and are the nucleus of its nightlife.

The area that would come to be known as George (after George II), then George Towne and, finally, Georgetown, was part of Maryland when it was settled in the early 1700s by Scottish immigrants, many of whom were attracted to the region's tolerant religious climate. Georgetown's position at the farthest point up the Potomac one could reach by boat made it an ideal transit-and-inspection point for farmers who grew tobacco in Maryland's interior. In 1789 the state granted the town a charter, but two years later Georgetown—along with Alexandria, its counterpart in Virginia—was included by George Washington in the Territory of Columbia, site of the new capital.

While Washington struggled, Georgetown thrived. Wealthy traders built their mansions on the hills overlooking the river; merchants and the working class lived in more modest homes closer to the water's edge. In 1810 a third of Georgetown's population was black—both free people and slaves. The **Mt. Zion United Methodist Church** on 29th Street is the oldest black church in the city and was a stop on the Underground Railroad. Georgetown's rich history and success instilled in citizens of both colors feelings of superiority that many feel linger today. (When Georgetowners thought the dismal capital was dragging them down, they asked to be given back to Maryland, the way Alexandria was given back to Virginia in 1845). Tobacco eventually became a less important commodity, and Georgetown became a milling center, using water power from the Potomac. When the Chesapeake & Ohio (C&O) Canal was completed in 1850, the city intensified its milling operations and became the eastern end of a waterway that stretched 184 miles to the west. The canal took up some of the slack when Georgetown's harbor began to fill with silt and the port lost business to Alexandria and Baltimore, but the canal never became the success it was meant to be.

In the years that followed, Georgetown was a far cry from the fashionable spot it is today. Clustered near the water were a foundry, a fish market, paper and cotton mills, and a power station for the city's streetcar system, all of which made Georgetown a smelly industrial district. It still had its Georgian, Federal, and Victorian homes, though, and when the New Deal and World War II brought a flood of newcomers to Washington, Georgetown's tree-shaded streets and handsome brick houses were rediscovered. Pushed out in the process were Georgetown's blacks, most of whom rented the houses they lived in.

Today some of Washington's most famous citizens call Georgetown home, including *Washington Post* matriarch Katherine Graham, former *Post* editor Ben Bradlee, celebrity biographer Kitty Kelley, and political insider Pamela Churchill Harriman. Georgetown's historic preservationists are among the most vocal in the city. Part of what the activists want protection from is the crush of people who descend on their community every night. This is Washington's center for restaurants, bars, nightclubs, and trendy boutiques. On M Street and Wisconsin Avenue, visitors can indulge just about any taste and take home almost any upmarket souvenir. Harder to find is a parking place. The lack of a Metro station in Georgetown means you'll have to take a bus or walk to this part of Washington. It's about a 15-minute walk from the Dupont Circle or Foggy Bottom Metro station. (If you'd rather take a bus, the G2 Georgetown University bus goes from Dupont Circle west along P Street. The 34 and 36 Friendship Heights buses leave from 22nd and Pennsylvania and deposit you at 31st and M.)

Georgetown owes some of its charm and separate growth to geography. This town-unto-itself is separated from Washington to the east by Rock Creek. On the south it's bordered by the Potomac, on the west by Georgetown University. How far north does Georgetown reach? Probably not much farther than the large estates and parks above R Street, though developers and real estate agents would be happy to take Georgetown right up to the Canadian border if it increased the value of property along the way.

❶ Start your exploration of Georgetown in front of the **Old Stone House** (M Street between 30th and 31st streets), thought to be Washington's only surviving pre-Revolutionary building. Begun in 1764 by a cabinetmaker named Christopher Layman, this fieldstone house was used as both a residence and a place of business by a succession of occupants. Five of the house's rooms are furnished with the sort of sturdy beds, spinning wheels, and simple tables associated with middle-class Colonial America. The National Park Service maintains the house and its lovely gardens in the rear, which are planted with fruit trees and perennials. Costumed guides answer questions about the house and its history. *3051 M St. NW,* ☎ *202/426–6851.* ☛ *Free.* ☉ *Wed.–Sun. 8– 4:30; closed major holidays.*

2 Around the corner, at 1221 31st Street, is the old Renaissance Revival–style **Customs House.** Built in 1858 to serve the port of Georgetown, it's been transformed into the Georgetown branch of the U.S. Postal Service, and there's really no reason to go inside unless you want to buy stamps or mail postcards.

Go back to M Street and cross over to Thomas Jefferson Street (between 30th and 31st streets). For most of its history, Georgetown was a working city, and the original names of its streets—Water Street, The Keys, Fishing Lane—bear witness to the importance of the harbor. The area south of M Street (originally called Bridge Street because of the bridge that spanned Rock Creek to the east) was inhabited by tradesmen, laborers, and merchants. Their homes were modest and close to Georgetown's industrial heart. The two-story brick building at **1083 Thomas Jefferson Street** was built around 1865 as a stable for the horses and hearses of a nearby undertaker and cabinetmaker. The wide doors on the right let the horses in; the hoist beam above the right-most window was used to lift hay and wood to the second floor. Three fine brick Federal houses stand south of the Georgetown Dutch Inn, at 1069, 1067, and 1063 Thomas Jefferson Street. The last has attractive flat lintels with keystones and a rounded keystone arch above the doorway. Across the street, at No. 1058, is a two-story brick structure built around **3** 1810 as a **Masonic lodge.** Its interesting details include a pointed facade and recessed central arch, proof of the Masons' traditional attachment to the building arts.

As you walk south on Thomas Jefferson Street, you'll pass over the **4** **C&O Canal,** the waterway that kept Georgetown open to shipping after its harbor had filled with silt. George Washington was one of the first to advance the idea of a canal linking the Potomac with the Ohio River across the Appalachians. Work started on the C&O Canal in 1828, and when it opened in 1850, its 74 locks linked Georgetown with Cumberland, Maryland, 184 miles to the northwest (still short of its intended destination). Lumber, coal, iron, wheat, and flour moved up and down the canal, but it was never as successful as its planners had hoped it would be. Many of the bridges spanning the canal in Georgetown were too low to allow anything other than fully loaded barges to pass underneath, and competition from the Baltimore & Ohio Railroad eventually spelled an end to profitability. Today the canal is a part of the National Park system, and walkers follow the towpath once used by mules while canoeists paddle the canal's calm waters. Between April and October you can go on a leisurely, mule-drawn trip aboard the *Georgetown* canal barge. Tickets are available across the canal, in the **5** **Foundry Mall.** The mall gets its name from an old foundry that overlooked the canal at 30th Street. Around the turn of the century it was turned into a veterinary hospital that cared for mules working on the canal. Today it's a restaurant. *1057 Thomas Jefferson St. NW,* ☎ *202/ 653–5190, 301/299–2026 (recorded information), or 301/299–3613 for group reservations and rates.* ☛ *$5 adults, $3.50 senior citizens and children under 13. 90-min barge trips mid-Apr.–early Nov., Wed.–Fri. and Sun. 10:30, 1, and 3; Sat. 10:30, 1, 3, and 5.*

Tour 6: Georgetown

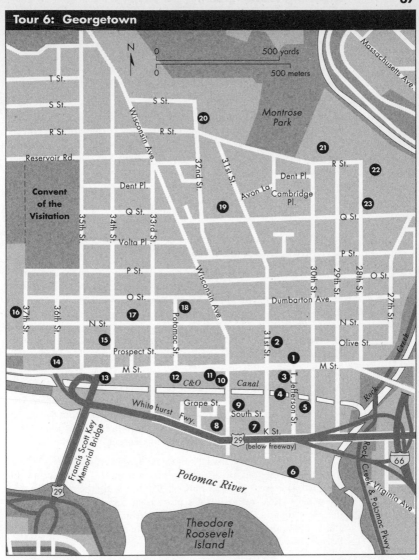

N

0   500 yards
0   500 meters

6 Continue south, across K Street, and into **Washington Harbour,** a glittering, postmodern riverfront development designed by Arthur Cotton Moore that includes restaurants, offices, apartments, and upscale shops. The plazas around its large central fountain and gardens are dotted with the eerily realistic sculptures of J. Seward Johnson, Jr. From the edge of Washington Harbour you can see the Watergate complex and Kennedy Center to the east.

Georgetown's **K Street** is lined with the offices of architects, ad agencies, and public relations companies. In many of these offices you can hear the rumble of cars on the Whitehurst Freeway, the elevated road above K Street that leads to the Francis Scott Key Memorial Bridge. Though you'll probably have to peer through a vine-covered fence to see it, at the corner of 31st and K streets is a **plaque** commemorating **7** **Suter's Tavern.** In March 1791, in the one-story hostelry that stood on this spot, George Washington met with the men who owned the tobacco farms and swampy marshes to the east of Georgetown and persuaded them to sell their land to the government so construction of the District of Columbia could begin.

At the foot of Wisconsin Avenue is another legacy from the area's mercantile past. The last three buildings on the west side were built around 1830 by trader and merchant **Francis Dodge.** Note the heavy stone foun- **8** dation of the southernmost **warehouse,** its star-end braces and the broken hoist in the gable end. According to an 1838 newspaper ad, Georgetown shoppers could visit Dodge's grocery to buy such items as "Porto Rico Sugar, Marseilles soft-shelled Almonds and Havanna Segars."

A short way up Wisconsin Avenue, on the other side of the street, stands **9** the Gothic Revival **Grace Episcopal Church.** In the mid- to late-19th century this church served the boatmen and workers from the nearby C&O Canal. At the time this was one of the poorest sections of Georgetown. (There are no "poor" sections in Georgetown anymore.)

Walking farther up Wisconsin Avenue you'll again cross the C&O Canal, this time via the only bridge that remains from the 19th century. On the north side is a simple granite obelisk honoring the men who built the waterway. A memorial of a more poignant sort can be found at **10** the 1840 **Vigilant Firehouse,** north of the canal at 1066 Wisconsin Avenue. A plaque set in the wall reads: "Bush, the Old Fire Dog, died of Poison, July 5th, 1869, R.I.P."

The intersection of Wisconsin Avenue and M Street is the heart of boisterous Georgetown. This spot—under the gleaming, golden dome of Riggs Bank on the northeast corner—is mobbed every weekend.

11 Turning left on M Street you'll come to the entrance to **Georgetown Park** (3222 M St. NW), a multilevel shopping extravaganza that answers the question "If the Victorians had invented shopping malls, what would they look like?" Such high-ticket stores as F.A.O. Schwarz, Williams-Sonoma, Polo/Ralph Lauren, and Godiva Chocolates can be found within this artful, skylit mass of polished brass, tile flooring, and potted plants. If you've always looked down your nose at mall architecture, Georgetown Park might win you over.

TIME OUT Pizzeria Uno (3211 M St. NW) has brought Chicago-style pizza to the heart of Georgetown. The deep-dish pies take a while to cook, but the wait is worth it. Those in a hurry may want to order the "personal-size" pizza: It's ready in five minutes and costs less than $6.

A stroll up either M Street or Wisconsin Avenue will take you past a dizzying array of merchandise, from expensive bicycling accessories to ropes of gold, from antique jewelry and furniture to the latest fashions in clothes and records. Walking west on M Street to Potomac Street **(12)** you'll come to the **Markethouse,** an 1865 brick building that once housed a market filled with victual stalls. There has been some sort of market on this spot since 1795, and in 1993 Dean & Deluca, the trendy Manhattan specialty grocer, moved in. In addition to expensive meats and cheeses, espressos, lattes, and cappuccinos are available, along with sandwiches and pastries.

M Street west leads to the **Key Bridge** into Rosslyn, Virginia. A house owned by Francis Scott Key, author of the national anthem, was demolished in 1947 to make way for the bridge that would bear his name.

(13) The **Francis Scott Key Memorial Park** (on M Street between 34th Street and Key Bridge) honors the Washington attorney who "by dawn's early light" penned the national anthem, upon seeing that the flag had survived the night's British bombardment of Ft. McHenry in Baltimore harbor during the War of 1812. A replica of the 15-star, 15-stripe flag that inspired Key flies over the park 24 hours a day. It's a noisy spot for a park, hard by busy Key Bridge, washed in the sounds of jets thundering into National Airport. Here Georgetown's quaint demeanor contrasts with the silvery skyscrapers of Rosslyn, Virginia, across the Potomac.

The heights of Georgetown to the north above N Street contrast with the busy jumble of the old waterfront. To reach the higher ground you can walk up M Street past the old brick streetcar barn at No. 3600 **(14)** (now a block of offices), turn right, and climb the 75 **steps** that figured prominently in the eerie climax of the movie **The Exorcist.** If you prefer a less demanding climb, walk up 34th Street instead.

(15) **Halcyon House,** at the corner of 34th and Prospect streets, was built in 1783 by Benjamin Stoddert, first secretary of the Navy. The object of many subsequent additions and renovations, the house is now a concatenation of architectural styles. Prospect Street gets its name from the fine views it affords of the waterfront and the river below.

The sounds of traffic diminish the farther north one walks from the **(16)** bustle of M Street. To the west is **Georgetown University,** the oldest Jesuit school in the country. It was founded in 1789 by John Carroll, first American bishop and first archbishop of Baltimore. About 12,000 students attend Georgetown, known now as much for its perennially successful basketball team as for its fine programs in law, medicine, and the liberal arts. When seen from the Potomac or from Washington's high ground, the Gothic spires of Georgetown's older buildings give the university an almost medieval look.

Architecture buffs, especially those interested in Federal and Victorian houses, enjoy wandering along the redbrick sidewalks of upper Georgetown. The average house here has two signs on it: a brass plaque notifying passersby of the building's historic interest and a window decal that warns burglars of its state-of-the-art alarm system. To get a representative taste of the houses in the area, continue north for a block on 34th Street and turn right onto N Street. The group of five Federal **(17)** houses between 3339 and 3327 N Street are known collectively as **Cox's Row,** after John Cox, a former mayor of Georgetown, who built them in 1817.

The flat-front, redbrick Federal house at **3307 N Street** was the home of then-Senator John F. Kennedy and his family before the White House beckoned. Turn left onto Potomac Street and walk a block up to O Street. O Street still has two leftovers from an earlier age: cobblestones and streetcar tracks. Residents are proud of the cobblestones, and you'll notice that even some of the concrete patches have been scored to resemble the paving stones. **St. John's Church** (3240 O St. NW, ☎ 202/338–1796) was built in 1809 and is attributed to Dr. William Thornton, architect of the Capitol. Later alterations have left it looking more Victorian than Federal. At the corner of the churchyard is a memorial to Colonel Ninian Beall, the Scotsman who received the original patent for the land that would become Georgetown.

Georgetown's largest estates sit farther north, commanding fine views of Rock Creek to the east and of the old tobacco town spread out near the river below. Depending on your mood, you can walk north either on Wisconsin Avenue (the bustling commercial route) or a block east, on 31st Street (a quieter residential street). Strolling 31st Street will give you a chance to admire more of the city's finest houses.

Whichever way you go, stop at Q Street between 31st and 32nd streets. Through the trees to the north, at the top of a sloping lawn, you'll see the neoclassical **Tudor Place,** designed by Capitol architect William Thornton and completed in 1816. The house was built for Thomas Peter, son of Georgetown's first mayor, and his wife, Martha Custis, Martha Washington's granddaughter. It was because of this connection to the president's family that Tudor Place came to house many items from Mount Vernon. The yellow stucco house is interesting for its architecture—especially the dramatic, two-story domed portico on the south side—but its familial heritage is even more remarkable: Tudor Place stayed in the same family for 178 years, until 1983, when Armistead Peter III died. Before his death, Peter established a foundation to restore the house and open it to the public. On a house tour you'll see chairs that belonged to George Washington, Francis Scott Key's desk, and spurs of members of the Peter family who were killed in the Civil War (although the house was in Washington, the family was true to its Virginia roots and fought for Dixie). The grounds contain many specimens planted in the early 19th century. *1644 31st St. NW, ☎ 202/965–0400. Suggested donation: $5. Tours Tues.–Fri. 10, 11:30, 1, and 2:30; Sat. hourly 10–4 (last tour at 3). Reservations advised.*

Dumbarton Oaks—not to be confused with the nearby Dumbarton House—is on 32nd Street, north of R Street. Career diplomat Robert Woods Bliss and his wife, Mildred, bought the property in 1920 and set about taming the sprawling grounds and removing 19th-century additions that had marred the Federal lines of the 1801 mansion. In 1940 the Blisses conveyed the estate to Harvard University, which maintains world-renowned collections of Byzantine and pre-Columbian art there. Both are small but choice, reflecting the enormous skill and creativity going on at roughly the same time on two sides of the Atlantic. The Byzantine collection includes beautiful examples of both religious and secular items executed in mosaic, metal, enamel, and ivory. Pre-Columbian works—artifacts and textiles from Mexico and Central and South America by such peoples as the Aztec, Maya, and Olmec—are arranged in an enclosed glass pavilion designed by Philip Johnson. Also on view to the public are the lavishly decorated music room and selections from Mrs. Bliss's collection of rare, illustrated garden books. Events at Dumbarton Oaks have not been confined to the study of the past. In 1944 representatives of the United States, Great

Britain, China, and the Soviet Union met in the music room here to lay the groundwork for the United Nations.

Anyone with even a mild interest in flowers, shrubs, trees—anything that grows out of the ground—will enjoy a visit to Dumbarton Oaks's 10 acres of formal gardens, one of the loveliest spots in all of Washington (enter via R Street). Designed by noted landscape architect Beatrix Farrand, the gardens incorporate elements of traditional English, Italian, and French styles. A full-time crew of a dozen gardeners toils to maintain the stunning collection of terraces, geometric gardens, tree-shaded brick walks, fountains, arbors, and pools. Plenty of well-positioned benches make this a good place for resting weary feet, too. *Art collections: 1703 32nd St. NW,* ☎ *202/338–8278 (recorded information) or 202/342–3200. Suggested donation: $1.* ⊘ *Tues.–Sun. 2–5. Gardens: 31st and R Sts. NW.* ☛ *Apr.–Oct., $3 adults, $2 senior citizens and children under 12, senior citizens free on Wed.; Nov.–Mar., free.* ⊘ *Apr.–Oct., daily 2–6; Nov.–Mar., daily 2–5. Gardens and collections closed on national holidays and Dec. 24.*

Three other sylvan retreats lie north of R Street in upper Georgetown. Originally part of the Bliss estate, **Dumbarton Oaks Park** sprawls to the north and west. **Montrose Park** lies to the east of the estate. Further east is **Oak Hill Cemetery,** its funerary obelisks, crosses, and gravestones spread out like an amphitheater of the dead on a hill overlooking Rock Creek. Near the entrance is an 1850 Gothic-style chapel designed by Smithsonian Castle architect James Renwick. Across from the chapel is the resting place of actor, playwright, and diplomat John H. Payne, who is remembered today primarily for his song "Home Sweet Home." A few hundred feet to the north is the circular tomb of William Corcoran, founder of the Corcoran Gallery of Art. *30th and R Sts. NW,* ☎ *202/337–2835.* ☛ *Free.* ⊘ *Weekdays 10–4; closed major holidays.*

Walking south on 28th Street you'll pass **Evermay** (1623 28th St. NW). The Georgian manor house, built around 1800 by real estate speculator Samuel Davidson, is almost hidden by its black-and-gold gates and high brick wall. Davidson wanted it that way. He sometimes took out advertisements in newspapers warning sightseers to avoid his estate "as they would a den of devils or rattlesnakes." The mansion is in private hands, but its grounds are often opened for garden tours.

A few steps east of 28th Street on Q Street is **Dumbarton House,** the headquarters of the National Society of the Colonial Dames of America. Its symmetry and the two curved wings on the north side make Dumbarton, built around 1800, a distinctive example of Georgian architecture. The man who built the house, Joseph Nourse, was registrar of the U.S. Treasury. Other well-known Americans have spent time at the house, including Dolley Madison, who is said to have stopped here when fleeing Washington in 1814. One hundred years later, the house was moved 50 feet up the hill, when Q Street was cut through to the Dumbarton Bridge.

Eight rooms inside Dumbarton House have been restored to their Colonial splendor and are decorated with period furnishings, such as mahogany American Chippendale chairs, hallmark silver, Persian rugs, and a breakfront cabinet filled with rare books. Notable items include a 1789 Charles Willson Peale portrait of Benjamin Stoddert's children (with an early view of Georgetown harbor in the background), Martha Washington's traveling cloak, and a British redcoat's red coat. *2715 Q St. NW,* ☎ *202/337–2288. Suggested donation: $3.* ⊘ *Tues.–Sat. 10–1. Group tours by appointment.*

TOUR 7: DUPONT CIRCLE

Numbers in the margin correspond to points of interest on the Tour 7: Dupont Circle map.

Three of Washington's main thoroughfares intersect at Dupont Circle: Connecticut, New Hampshire, and Massachusetts avenues. With a handsome small park and a splashing fountain in the center, Dupont Circle is more than a deserted island around which traffic flows, making it an exception among Washington circles. The activity on the circle spills over into the surrounding streets, one of the liveliest, most vibrant neighborhoods in Washington.

Development near Dupont Circle started during the post–Civil War boom of the 1870s. As the city increased in stature, the nation's wealthy and influential citizens began building their mansions near the circle. The area underwent a different kind of transformation in the middle of this century, when the middle and upper classes deserted Washington for the suburbs, and in the '60s the circle became the starting point for marches sponsored by various counterculture groups. Today the neighborhood is once again fashionable, and its many restaurants, offbeat shops, and specialty bookstores lend it a distinctive, cosmopolitan air.

❶ Start your exploration in **Dupont Circle** itself (Metro: Dupont Circle). Originally known as Pacific Circle, this hub was the westernmost circle in Pierre L'Enfant's original design for the Federal City. The name was changed in 1884, when Congress authorized construction of a bronze statue honoring Civil War hero Admiral Samuel F. Dupont. The statue fell into disrepair, and Dupont's family—who had never liked it anyway—replaced it in 1921 with the fountain you see today. The marble fountain, with its allegorical figures Sea, Stars, and Wind, was created by Daniel Chester French, the sculptor of Lincoln's statue in the Lincoln Memorial.

As you look around the circumference of the circle, you'll be able to see the special constraints within which architects in Washington must work. Since a half-dozen streets converge on Dupont Circle, the buildings around it are, for the most part, wedge shaped and set on oddly shaped plots of land like massive slices of pie.

Only two of the great houses that stood on the circle in the early 20th century remain today. The Renaissance-style house at **15 Dupont Circle,** next to P Street, was built in 1903 for Robert W. Patterson, publisher of the *Washington Times-Herald*. Patterson's daughter, Cissy, who succeeded him as publisher of the paper, was known for hosting parties that attracted such notables as William Randolph Hearst, Douglas MacArthur, and J. Edgar Hoover. In 1927, while Cissy was living in New York City and the White House was being refurbished, Calvin Coolidge and his family stayed in this Dupont Circle home. The Coolidges received American flier Charles Lindbergh here; some of the most famous photographs of Lindy were taken as he stood on the house's balcony and smiled down at the crowds below. After Patterson's death the house was bought by the Washington Club. The **Sulgrave Club,** at the corner of Massachusetts Avenue, was also once a private home and is now likewise a club. Neither is open to the public.

❷ Cross the traffic circle carefully and head south on New Hampshire Avenue. A block down on the left is the impressive **Heurich Mansion,** home to the **Historical Society of Washington, D.C.** This severe Romanesque Revival mansion was the home of Christian Heurich, a German orphan who made his fortune in this country in the beer business.

Heurich's brewery was in Foggy Bottom, where the Kennedy Center stands today. Brewing was a dangerous business in the 19th century, and fires had more than once reduced Heurich's beer factory to ashes. Perhaps because of this he insisted that his home, completed in 1894, be fireproof. Although 17 fireplaces were installed—some with onyx facings, one with the bronze image of a lion staring out from the back—not a single one ever held a fire.

After Heurich's widow died, in 1955, the house was turned over to the Historical Society and today is its headquarters and houses its voluminous archives. All the furnishings in the house were owned and used by the Heurichs. The interior of the house is an eclectic Victorian treasure trove of plaster detailing, carved wooden doors, and painted ceilings. The downstairs breakfast room, where Heurich, his wife, and their three children ate most of their meals, is decorated like a rathskeller and is adorned with such German sayings as "A good drink makes old people young."

Heurich must have taken the German proverbs seriously. He drank his beer every day, had three wives (not all at once), and lived to be 102. (In 1986 Heurich's grandson Gary started brewing the family beer again. Though it's made in Utica, New York, he vows to someday build another Heurich brewery near Washington.) Docents who give tours of the house are adept at answering questions about other Washington landmarks, too. *1307 New Hampshire Ave. NW, ☎ 202/785–2068. Exhibits free. ⊙ Tues.–Sat. 10–4. 45-min house tours: $3 adults, $1.50 senior citizens, Wed.–Sat. at noon, 1, 2, and 3.*

Cross New Hampshire Avenue and turn left on O Street. The row houses on this block are a little less impressive than Heurich's castle, but they are examples of what makes Dupont Circle so attractive to Washington's young professionals: spacious brick Victorian town houses close to nightlife, offices, and public transportation.

Turn north on 21st Street and cross P Street. This area has a high concentration of restaurants and bars and is crowded and boisterous at night. It also serves as an informal crossroads for Washington's gay community. (There are several gay night spots farther up P Street.)

TIME OUT This Dupont Circle branch of **Pan Asian Noodles & Grill** (2020 P St. NW, ☎ 202/872–8889) is one of three locations in Washington. All offer reasonably priced noodle dishes from the Orient.

At the corner of Massachusetts Avenue and 21st Street is the opulent
❸ Walsh-McLean House. Tom McLean was an Irishman who made a fortune with a Colorado gold mine and came to Washington to show his wealth. Washington was the perfect place to establish a presence for America's late-19th-century nouveau riche. It was easier to enter "society" in the nation's planned capital than in New York or Philadelphia, and wealthy industrialists and lucky entrepreneurs flocked to the city on the Potomac. Walsh announced his arrival with this 60-room mansion. His daughter, Evalyn Walsh-McLean, the last private owner of the Hope Diamond (now in the Smithsonian's Museum of Natural History), was one of the city's leading hostesses. Today the house is used as an embassy by the Indonesian government. The **Jockey Club** restaurant in the redbrick Ritz-Carlton Hotel across the street is a favorite lunching spot of Washington power brokers.

Head west on Massachusetts Avenue. The palatial home at No. 2118 is a mystery even to many longtime Washingtonians, who assume it's
❹ just another embassy. **Anderson House** is not an embassy, though it does have a link to the diplomatic world. Larz Anderson was a diplomat

whose career included postings to Japan and Belgium. Anderson and his heiress wife, Isabel, toured the world, picking up objects that struck their fancy. They filled their residence, which was constructed in 1905, with the booty of their travels, including choir stalls from an Italian Renaissance church, Flemish tapestries, and a large—if spotty—collection of Asian art. All this remains in the house, for visitors to see.

In accordance with Anderson's wishes, the building also serves as the headquarters of a group he belonged to: the **Society of the Cincinnati.** The oldest patriotic organization in the country, the society was formed in 1783 by a group of officers who had served with George Washington during the Revolutionary War. The group took the name Cincinnati from Cincinnatus, a distinguished Roman who, circa 500 BC, led an army against Rome's enemies and later quelled civil disturbances in the city. After each instance he returned to the simple life on his farm. The story impressed the American officers, who saw in it a mirror of their own situation: They too would leave the battlefields behind to get on with the business of forging a new nation. (One such member went on to name the city in Ohio.) Today's members are direct descendants of those American revolutionaries.

Many of the displays in the society's museum focus on the Colonial period and the Revolutionary War. One room—painted in a marvelous trompe l'oeil style that deceives visitors into thinking the walls are covered with sculpture—is filled with military miniatures from the United States and France. (Because of the important role France played in defeating the British, French officers were invited to join the society. Pierre L'Enfant, "Artist of the Revolution" and planner of Washington, designed the society's eagle medallion.)

The house is often used by the federal government to entertain visiting dignitaries. Amid the glitz, glamour, beauty, and patriotic spectacle of the mansion are two delightful painted panels in the solarium that depict the Andersons' favorite motor-car sightseeing routes around Washington. *2118 Massachusetts Ave. NW,* ☎ *202/785–2040.* ☛ *Free.* ☉ *Tues.–Sat. 1–4.*

Across the street at 2121 Massachusetts Avenue is the **Cosmos Club,** founded in 1878 and perhaps the most exclusive private club in the city. Neither money nor influence will get you on the membership rolls. It takes brains. Different rooms in the club celebrate members who have won Nobel Prizes or appeared on postage stamps. The formerly men-only club started accepting women in 1988. Judith Martin (a.k.a. Miss Manners) was one of the first admitted.

Head west on Q Street, past a row of expensive town houses, to the ❺ **Bison Bridge.** Tour guides at the Smithsonian's Museum of Natural History are quick to remind visitors that America never had buffalo; the big animals that roamed the plains were bison. Though many maps and guidebooks call this the Buffalo Bridge, the four bronze statues by A. Phimister Proctor are of bison. Officially called the **Dumbarton Bridge,** the structure stretches across Rock Creek Park into Georgetown. Its sides are decorated with busts of Native Americans, the work of architect Glenn Brown, who, along with his son Bedford, designed the bridge in 1914. The best way to see the busts is to walk the footpath along Rock Creek or to lean over the green railings beside the bison and peer through the trees.

Walking north on 23rd Street you'll pass between two more embassies, those of Turkey and Romania, both of which sit on **Sheridan Circle** and

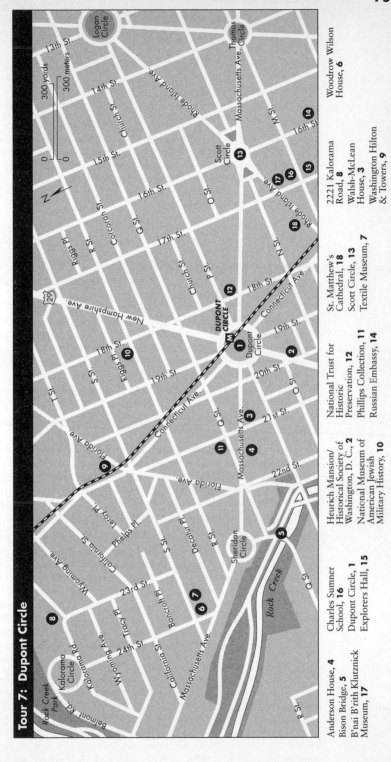

Tour 7: Dupont Circle

Anderson House, **4**
Bison Bridge, **5**
B'nai B'rith Klutznick
Museum, **17**

Charles Sumner
School, **16**
Dupont Circle, **1**
Explorers Hall, **15**

Heurich Mansion/
Historical Society of
Washington, D. C., **2**
National Museum of
American Jewish
Military History, **10**

National Trust for
Historic
Preservation, **12**
Phillips Collection, **11**
Russian Embassy, **14**

St. Matthew's
Cathedral, **18**
Scott Circle, **13**
Textile Museum, **7**

2221 Kalorama
Road, **8**
Walsh-McLean
House, **3**
Washington Hilton
& Towers, **9**

Woodrow Wilson
House, **6**

are topped with antennae as big as trampolines used to send messages back to the homeland.

Turn left on Massachusetts Avenue. Although the entire Dupont Circle area is dotted with embassies, the stretch of Massachusetts Avenue on either side of Sheridan Circle is known as Embassy Row proper. The area is rife with delegations from foreign countries, and a stroll down the street will provide you with an opportunity to test your knowledge of the world's flags.

Continue west on Massachusetts Avenue. The **Cameroon Embassy** is housed in the mansion at 2349 Massachusetts Avenue. This fanciful castle, with its conical tower, bronze weather vane, and intricate detailing around the windows and balconies, is the westernmost of the beaux arts–style mansions built along Massachusetts Avenue in the late-19th and early 20th centuries.

Turn right on S Street. The statue on the left commemorates Irish patriot **Robert Emmet;** it was dedicated in 1966 to mark the 50th anniversary of Irish independence. A small reproduction can be found in
❻ the **Woodrow Wilson House,** a few hundred feet down S Street. Wilson is the only president who stayed in Washington after leaving the White House. (He's also the only president buried in the city, inside the Washington Cathedral.) He and his second wife, Edith Bolling Wilson, retired in 1920 to this Georgian Revival house designed by Washington architect Waddy B. Wood. (Wood also designed the Department of the Interior Building on C Street and the National Museum of Women in the Arts building) The house had been built in 1915 for a carpet magnate, and on the first and third floors you can still see the half-snaps that run along the edges of the floors to hold down the long-gone wall-to-wall carpeting.

President Wilson suffered a stroke toward the end of his second term, in 1919, and he lived out the last few years of his life on this quiet street. Edith made sure he was comfortable; she had a bed constructed that was the same dimensions as the large Lincoln bed Wilson had slept in while in the White House. She also had the house's trunk lift electrified so the partially paralyzed president could move from floor to floor. When the streetcars stopped running in 1962 the elevator stopped working. It had received its electricity directly from the streetcar line.

After Edith died, in 1961, the house and its contents were bequeathed to the National Trust for Historic Preservation. On view inside are such items as a Gobelins tapestry, a baseball signed by King George V, and the shell casing from the first shot fired by U.S. forces in World War I. The house also contains memorabilia related to the history of the short-lived League of Nations, including the colorful flag Wilson hoped would be adopted by that organization. *2340 S St. NW,* ☎ *202/387–4062.* ☛ *$4 adults, $2.50 senior citizens and students, children under 7 free.* ☉ *Tues.–Sun. 10–4; closed major holidays.*

Just next door, in a house that was also designed by Waddy Wood, is
❼ the **Textile Museum.** In the 1890s, founder George Hewitt Myers purchased his first Oriental rug for his dorm room at Yale and subsequently collected more than 12,000 textiles and 1,500 carpets. An heir to the Bristol-Myers fortune, Myers and his wife lived two houses down from Wilson, at 2310 S Street, in a home designed by John Russell Pope, architect of the National Archives and Jefferson Memorial. Myers bought the house next door, at No. 2320, and opened his museum to the public in 1925. Rotating exhibits are taken from a permanent collection of historic and ethnographic items that include Coptic and

pre-Columbian textiles, Kashmir embroidery, and Turkman tribal rugs. At least one show of modern textiles—such as quilts or fiber art—is mounted each year. *2320 S St. NW, ☎ 202/667–0441. Suggested donation: $5. ☾ Mon.–Sat. 10–5, Sun. 1–5; closed major holidays. Highlight tours: Sept.–May; Wed., Sat., and Sun. at 2.*

S Street is an informal dividing line between the Dupont Circle area to the south and the exclusive **Kalorama** neighborhood to the north. The name for this peaceful, tree-filled enclave—Greek for "beautiful view"—was contributed by politician and writer Joel Barlow, who bought the large tract in 1807. Kalorama is filled with embassies and luxurious homes. Walk north on 23rd Street until it dead-ends at the (8) Tudor mansion at **2221 Kalorama Road.** This imposing house was built in 1911 for mining millionaire W. W. Lawrence, but since 1936 it has been the residence of the French ambassador. For a taste of the beautiful view that so captivated Barlow, walk west on Kalorama Road, then turn right on Kalorama Circle. At the bottom of the circle you can look down over Rock Creek Park, the finger of green that pokes into northwest Washington.

Walk back down Kalorama, and continue on to Connecticut. The large, beige institutional building on the left near Connecticut Avenue is the Chinese Embassy. Turn right and walk south down Connecticut (9) Avenue. On the left at 1919 Connecticut is the **Washington Hilton & Towers,** home of the largest ballroom on the East Coast and site of John Hinckley's 1981 assassination attempt on Ronald Reagan.

(10) Two blocks off Connecticut to the left is the **National Museum of American Jewish Military History.** The message here is that Jews in this country are first and foremost American citizens and have served in every war the nation has fought. It is primarily a military museum, with displays of weapons, uniforms, medals, recruitment posters, and other memorabilia. The few specifically religious items—a camouflage yarmulke, rabbinical supplies fashioned from shell casings and parachute silk—underscore the strange demands placed on religion during war. *1811 R St. NW, ☎ 202/265–6280. ☛ Free. ☾ Weekdays 9–5, Sun. 1–5; closed Sat. and federal and Jewish holidays.*

On R street on the other side of Connecticut is the **Fondo Del Sol Visual Art and Media Center,** a nonprofit center devoted to the cultural heritage of the Americas. Changing exhibitions cover contemporary, pre-Columbian, and folk art. The center also offers a program of lectures, concerts, poetry readings, exhibit tours, and an annual summer festival featuring salsa and reggae music. *2112 R St. NW, ☎ 202/483–2777. ☛ $2–$3 adults (depending on exhibit), children under 16 free. ☾ Wed.–Sat. 12:30–5.*

Walk south on 21st Street. Many private art galleries—selling the work of local, national, and international artists—have sprung up around here, perhaps to bask in the glow of our next stop.

Washington has many museums that are the legacy of one great patron, but the **Phillips Collection,** at 21st and Q streets, is among the most (11) beloved. In 1918 Duncan Phillips, grandson of a founder of the Jones and Laughlin Steel Company, started to collect art for a museum that would stand as a memorial to his father and brother, who had died within 13 months of each other. Three years later what was first called the Phillips Memorial Gallery opened in two rooms of this Georgian-Revival home near Dupont Circle. It was the first permanent museum of modern art in the country.

Not interested in a painting's market value or its faddishness, Phillips searched for works that impressed him as outstanding products of a particular artist's unique vision. Holdings include works by Georges Braque, Paul Cézanne, Paul Klee, Henri Matisse, John Henry Twachtman, and the largest museum collection in the country of the work of Pierre Bonnard. The exhibits change regularly. The collection's best-known paintings include Renoir's *Luncheon of the Boating Party, Repentant Peter* by both Goya and El Greco, *A Bowl of Plums* by 18th-century artist Jean-Baptiste Siméon Chardin, Degas's *Dancers at the Bar,* Van Gogh's *Entrance to the Public Garden at Arles,* and Cézanne's self-portrait, the painting Phillips said he would save first if his gallery caught fire. During the '20s, Phillips and his wife, Marjorie, started to support American Modernists such as John Marin, Georgia O'Keeffe, and Arthur Dove.

The Phillips is a comfortable museum. Works of a favorite artist are often grouped together in "exhibition units," and, unlike most other galleries (where uniformed guards appear uninterested in the masterpieces around them), the Phillips employs students of art, many of whom are artists themselves, to sit by the paintings and answer questions.

The Phillips family moved out of the house in 1930. An addition was built in 1960 and renovated and renamed the Goh Annex in 1989. It gave the Phillips 50% more exhibit space and is host to traveling exhibits and rotating selections from the museum's permanent collection. On Thursdays, the museum stays open late, enticing people with chamber music or jazz, and a café that serves light dinners. *1600–1612 21st St. NW,* ☎ *202/387–2151.* 🞀 *$6.50 adults, $3.25 students and senior citizens, under 18 free; Thurs. eve, $5.* ☉ *Tues.–Wed. and Fri.–Sat. 10–5, Thursday, 10–8:30, Sun. noon–7. Tours Wed. and Sat. at 2. Gallery talks 1st and 3rd Thurs. at 12:30.*

After visiting the Phillips, walk east on Q Street and turn south on Connecticut Avenue.

TIME OUT   Connecticut Avenue near Dupont Circle is chockablock with restaurants. The **Chesapeake Bagel Bakery** (1636 Connecticut Ave. NW) is a low-key lunchroom that serves a wide variety of bagel sandwiches. **Ferrara** (above the Q St. entrance to the Metro) and **Starbucks** (at Connecticut Ave. NW above Dupont Circle) are part of the invasion of specialty coffee shops that also serve sweets. At **Kramerbooks** (1517 Connecticut Ave. NW, open 24 hours on weekends) relax over dinner or a drink after browsing the stocked shelves. One of the best Chinese restaurants in the city is **City Lights of China** (1731 Connecticut Ave. NW).

⑫ Skirt the circle and walk east on Massachusetts Avenue. The **National Trust for Historic Preservation** sits at the corner of 18th Street and Massachusetts Avenue in, naturally, a building that has been historically preserved. The building once housed some of the most luxurious apartments in the city. The beaux arts–style McCormick Apartments, designed by Jules H. de Sibour, were built in 1917 and contained only six apartments, one on each floor, each with 11,000 square feet of space. Some of Washington's most prominent citizens lived here, including hostess Perle Mesta and Andrew Mellon, secretary of the treasury under three presidents, whose top-floor flat contained many of the paintings that would later go to the National Gallery of Art. During World War II the building was converted to office space, and in 1977 it was bought by the National Trust. The building is closed to the public, but a quick peek at the circular lobby will give you an idea of the lavish world its one-time residents inhabited.

Continue down Massachusetts Avenue. On the left is the **Brookings Institution,** one of dozens of think tanks in Washington that offer their partisan and nonpartisan advice to whomever is in power or whomever would like to be. Farther east on the left you'll spot the **Australian Embassy,** containing a gallery that periodically shows works of art of an antipodean nature. *1601 Massachusetts Ave. NW,* ☎ *202/797–3000.* ☛ *Free.* ⊙ *Weekdays 8:30–4:30.*

⑬ **Scott Circle** is at the center of the intersections of Massachusetts and Rhode Island avenues and 16th Street. The equestrian statue of **General Winfield Scott** was cast from cannon captured in the Mexican War. On the west side of Scott Circle there is a statue of fiery orator **Daniel Webster.** If you walk to the south side of the circle and look down 16th Street you'll get a familiar view of the columns of the White House, six blocks away. Across the circle is an interesting memorial to **S. C. F. Hahnemann,** his statue sitting in a recessed wall, his head surrounded by a mosaic of colorful tiles. (Who, you ask, was S. C. F. Hahnemann? He was the founder of the homeopathic school of medicine.)

One block south on 16th Street stands the **Jefferson Hotel.** Designed by Jules H. de Sibour, the man responsible for the McCormick Apartments, it too started out as apartments but was converted to a hotel in the '50s. It has a reputation for luxury and discretion and is a favorite temporary home for White House cabinet members awaiting confirmation. Farther down 16th Street, the red, white, and blue flag of
⑭ Russia flies before the **Russian Embassy** (1125 16th St. NW), housed in an ornate mansion that was built for the widow of George Pullman of railroad-car fame. It first did diplomatic duty as the Imperial Russian Embassy, then became the Soviet Embassy, and now it's Russian once again. The rest of the ex-Soviet republics were left scrambling for their own embassies after the breakup of the USSR in 1991.

Turn right onto M Street. On the southwest corner of 16th and M streets sits the headquarters of the **National Geographic Society.** Founded in 1888, the society is best known for its yellow-border magazine, found in family rooms and attics across the country. The society has sponsored numerous expeditions throughout its 100-year history, including those of Admirals Peary and Byrd and underwater explorer Jacques
⑮ Cousteau. **Explorers Hall,** entered from 17th Street, is the magazine come to life. Recently renovated, Explorers Hall invites visitors to learn about the world in a decidedly interactive way. You can experience everything from a minitornado to video "touch-screens" that explain various geographic concepts and then quiz you on what you've learned. The most dramatic events take place in Earth Station One, a 72-seat amphitheater that sends the audience on a journey around the world. The centerpiece is a hand-painted globe, 11 feet in diameter, that floats and spins on a cushion of air, showing off different features of the planet. *17th and M Sts.,* ☎ *202/857–7588 (recorded information), 202/857–7689 (group tour information).* ☛ *Free.* ⊙ *Mon.–Sat. and holidays 9–5, Sun. 10–5.*

⑯ Across M Street is the **Charles Sumner School,** built in 1872 for the education of black children in the city. It takes its name from the Massachusetts senator who delivered a blistering attack against slavery in 1856 and was savagely caned as a result by a congressman from South Carolina. The building was designed by Adolph Cluss, who created the Arts and Industries Building on the Mall. It is typical of the District's Victorian-era public schools. Beautifully restored in 1986, the school serves mainly as a conference center, though it hosts changing art exhibits and houses a permanent collection of memorabilia relating to the city's public school system. *1201 17th St. NW, ☎ 202/727–3419.* ☛ *Free.* ☉ *Weekdays 10–5. Often closed for conferences; call ahead to arrange tours.*

Farther up 17th Street, at the corner of Rhode Island Avenue, is the
⑰ B'nai B'rith Klutznick Museum, devoted to the history of the Jewish people. The museum's permanent exhibits span 20 centuries and highlight Jewish festivals and the rituals employed to mark the various stages of life. A wide variety of Jewish decorative art, adorning such items as spice boxes and Torah wrappers, is on display. Changing exhibits highlight the work of contemporary Jewish artists. *1640 Rhode Island Ave. NW, ☎ 202/857–6583. Suggested donation: $2.* ☉ *Sun.–Fri. 10–5; closed Sat. and federal and Jewish holidays.*

Half a block west on Rhode Island Avenue, across from a memorial
⑱ to nuns who served as nurses during the Civil War, is **St. Matthew's Cathedral,** the seat of Washington's Catholic archbishop. John F. Kennedy frequently worshiped in this Renaissance-style church, and in 1963 his funeral mass was held within its richly decorated walls. Set in the floor, directly in front of the main altar, is a memorial to the slain president: "Here rested the remains of President Kennedy at the requiem mass November 25, 1963, before their removal to Arlington where they lie in expectation of a heavenly resurrection." *1725 Rhode Island Ave. NW, ☎ 202/347–3215.* ☛ *Free.* ☉ *Weekdays and Sun. 6:30–6:30, Sat. 7:30–6:30. Tours Sun. 2:30–4:30.*

You are now between two Metro stations. Dupont Circle is two blocks north on Connecticut Avenue, and Farragut North is one block south.

TOUR 8: FOGGY BOTTOM

Numbers in the margin correspond to points of interest on the Tour 8: Foggy Bottom map.

The Foggy Bottom area of Washington—bordered roughly by the Potomac and Rock Creek to the west, 20th Street to the east, Pennsylvania Avenue to the north, and Constitution Avenue to the south—has three main claims to fame: the State Department, the Kennedy Center, and George Washington University. In 1763 a German immigrant named Jacob Funk purchased this land, and a community called Funkstown sprang up on the Potomac. This nickname is only slightly less amusing than the present one, an appellation that is derived from the wharves, breweries, lime kilns, and glassworks that were near the water. Smoke from these factories combined with the swampy air of the low-lying ground to produce a permanent fog along the waterfront.

The smoke-belching factories ensured work for the hundreds of German and Irish immigrants who settled in Foggy Bottom in the 19th century. By the 1930s, however, industry was on the way out, and Foggy Bottom had become a poor, predominantly black part of Washington. The opening of the State Department headquarters in 1947 reawakened middle-class interest in the neighborhood's modest row houses. Many of them are now gone, and Foggy Bottom today suffers from a split personality, and tiny, one-room-wide row houses sit next to large, mixed-use developments.

Start your exploration near the Foggy Bottom Metro station on 23rd
❶ Street near I Street. The campus of **George Washington University** covers much of Foggy Bottom south of Pennsylvania Avenue between 19th and 24th streets. George Washington had always hoped the cap-

ital would be home to a world-class university. He even left 50 shares of stock in the Patowmack Canal Co. to endow it. Congress never acted upon his wishes, however, and it wasn't until 1822 that the university that would eventually be named after the first president began to take shape. The private Columbian College in the District of Columbia opened that year with the aim of training students for the Baptist ministry. In 1904 the university shed its Baptist connections and changed its name to George Washington University. In 1912 it moved to its present location and since that time has become the second largest landholder in the District (after the federal government). Students have ranged from J. Edgar Hoover to Jacqueline Kennedy Onassis. In addition to modern university buildings GWU occupies many 19th-century houses.

Walk west from the Metro station on the I Street pedestrian mall, then ❷ turn left on New Hampshire Avenue. Across Virginia Avenue is the **Watergate,** possibly the world's most notorious apartment-office complex, famous for the events that took place here on June 17, 1972. As Nixon aides E. Howard Hunt, Jr., and G. Gordon Liddy sat in the Howard Johnson Motor Lodge across the street, five men were caught trying to bug the headquarters of the Democratic National Committee on the sixth floor of 2600 Virginia Avenue. (There's a marketing company in that space today.)

Even before the break-in, the Watergate—which first opened in 1965—was well known in the capital. Within its distinctive curving lines and behind its "toothpick" balusters have lived some of Washington's famous, including John Mitchell and Rose Mary Woods of Nixon White House fame, and such politicians as Jacob Javits, Alan Cranston, and Robert and Elizabeth Dole. The embassies of Qatar, the United Arab Emirates, Sweden, and Yemen are also in the Watergate. The suffix "-gate" is attached to any political scandal nowadays, but the Watergate itself was named after a monumental flight of steps that lead down to the Potomac behind the Lincoln Memorial. The original Watergate was the site of band concerts until airplane noise from nearby National Airport made the locale impractical.

Walk south on New Hampshire Avenue, past the Saudi Arabian Em- ❸ bassy, to the **John F. Kennedy Center for the Performing Arts.** Its opening in 1971 established Washington as a cultural city to be reckoned with. Concerts, ballets, opera, musicals, and drama are presented in the center's five theaters, and movies are screened almost every night in the theater of the American Film Institute.

The idea for a national cultural center had been proposed by President Eisenhower in 1958. John F. Kennedy had also strongly supported the idea, and after his assassination it was decided to dedicate the center to him as a living memorial. Some critics have called the center's square design unimaginative—it's been dubbed the cake box that the more decorative Watergate came in—but no one has denied that the building is immense. The Grand Foyer, lighted by 18 1-ton Orrefors crystal chandeliers, is 630 feet long. (Even at this size it is mobbed at intermission.) Many of the center's furnishings were donated by foreign countries: The chandeliers came from Sweden, the Matisse tapestries outside the Opera House came from France, and the 3,700 tons of white Carrara marble for the interior and exterior of the building were a gift from Italy. Flags fly in the Hall of Nations and the Hall of States, and in the center of the foyer is a 7-foot-high bronze **bust of Kennedy** by sculptor Robert Berks.

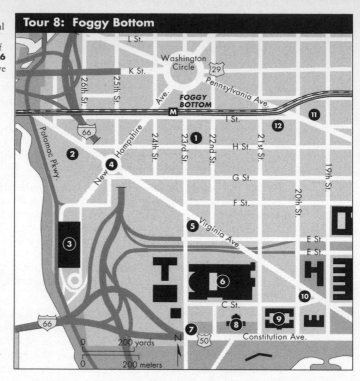

Tour 8: Foggy Bottom

The Library of Congress maintains a **Performing Arts Library** on the roof terrace level, mounting periodic theatrical and musical exhibits (original Mozart manuscripts were a recent offering). If you can tolerate the sound of jets screaming up the Potomac to National Airport, you can get one of the city's better views from the rooftop terrace: To the north are Georgetown and the National Cathedral; to the west Theodore Roosevelt Island and Rosslyn, Virginia; and to the south the Lincoln and Jefferson memorials. *New Hampshire Ave. and Rock Creek Pkwy. NW,* ☎ *202/467–4600.* ☛ *Free.* ☉ *Daily 10–9 (or until last show lets out). Box office open Mon.–Sat. 10–9, Sun. and holidays noon–9. Free tours daily 10–1;* ☎ *202/416–8341 for tour information. Performing Arts Library,* ☎ *202/707–8780.* ☉ *Tues.–Sat. noon–8.*

TIME OUT   There are two restaurants on the top floor of the Kennedy Center. The **Roof Terrace Restaurant** is the more expensive, with a lunch menu that offers open-face sandwiches and salads. The **Encore Café** has soups, chili, salads, and hot entrées starting at under $5.

④ Walk back up New Hampshire Avenue; then turn right on G Street, right on Virginia Avenue (follow the outstretched arm of the **statue of Benito Juárez**, the 19th-century Mexican statesman) and right on 23rd
⑤ Street. The **Pan American Health Organization,** American headquarters of the World Health Organization, is at 23rd Street and Virginia Avenue, in the building that looks like a huge car air filter.

⑥ Two blocks down 23rd Street is the massive **Department of State building.** On the top floor are the opulent **Diplomatic Reception Rooms,** decorated in the manner of great halls of Europe and the rooms of Colonial American plantations. The museum-quality furnishings include a Philadelphia highboy, a Paul Revere bowl, and the desk on which the

Treaty of Paris was signed. The largest room boasts a specially loomed carpet so heavy and large it had to be airlifted in by helicopter. The rooms are used 15–20 times a week to entertain foreign diplomats and heads of state; you can see them, too, but you need to register for a tour well in advance of your visit. *23rd and C Sts. NW,* ☎ *202/647– 3241, TTY 202/736–4474.* ☛ *Free. Tours weekdays at 9:30, 10:30, and 2:45 (not recommended for children under 12). Summer tours must be booked up to 3 months in advance.*

On a hill across C Street is the **U.S. Naval Medical Command.** In an early sketch of Washington, Thomas Jefferson placed the Capitol here. One of the federal government's earliest scientific installations was a naval observatory built here in 1844. By the 1880s, however, Foggy Bottom's smoke and haze forced officials to move the observatory to higher ground, in northwest Washington.

Continue down 23rd Street and turn left onto Constitution Avenue. On the south side of Constitution are the Lincoln and Vietnam Veterans memorials (*see* Tour 2, *above*). The **American Pharmaceutical Association** building is on the corner of Constitution Avenue and 23rd Street. This white-marble building was designed by John Russell Pope and completed in 1934. The APA is one of more than 3,000 trade and professional associations (as obscure as the Cast Iron Soil Pipe Institute and as well-known as the National Association of Broadcasters) that have chosen Washington for their headquarters, eager to represent their members' interests before the government.

❽ One block east is the **National Academy of Sciences.** Inscribed in Greek under the cornice is a quotation from Aristotle on the value of science. Inside, there are often free art exhibits—not all of them relating to science. In front of the academy is Robert Berks's **sculpture of Albert Einstein,** done in the same lumpy, mashed-potato style as the artist's bust of JFK in the Kennedy Center. *2101 Constitution Ave. NW,* ☎ *202/334– 2000.* ☛ *Free.* ⊘ *Weekdays 8:30–5.*

❾ The **Federal Reserve Building** (designed by Folger Library architect Paul Cret) is on Constitution Avenue between 21st and 20th streets. The imposing marble edifice, its bronze entryway topped by a massive eagle, seems to say, "Your money's safe with us." Even so, there isn't any money here. Ft. Knox and New York's Federal Reserve Bank hold most of the Federal Reserve System's gold. The stolid building is a bit more human inside, with a varied collection of art and four special art exhibitions every year. A 45-minute tour includes a film that attempts to explain exactly what it is that "the Fed" does. *Enter on C St., between 20th and 21st Sts.,* ☎ *202/452–3686.* ☛ *Free.* ⊘ *Weekdays 11:30–2. Tours Thurs. at 2:30 (not recommended for children under high school age),* ☎ *202/452–2526.*

❿ Turn left on 20th Street. The fountain one block up in **Robert Owen Park** is perfect for cooling hot and tired feet. Crossing Virginia Avenue and continuing north on 20th Street will take you back onto the campus of George Washington University. Foggy Bottom's immigrant past is apparent in the **United Church** at 20th and G streets. Built in 1891 for blue-collar Germans in the neighborhood, the church still conducts services in German the first and third Sunday of every month.

Walk north to Pennsylvania Avenue. To the right—near No. 1901— are the only two survivors of a string of 18th-century row houses
⓫ known as the **Seven Buildings.** One of the five that have been demolished had served as President Madison's executive mansion after the

British burned the White House in 1814. The two survivors are now dwarfed by the taller office block behind them.

A similar fate befell a row of residences farther west on Pennsylvania Avenue between 20th and 21st streets. These Victorian houses have been hollowed out and refurbished and serve as the entryway for a modern glass office building at **2000 Pennsylvania Avenue.** The backs of the buildings are under the sloping roof of the new development, preserved as if in an urban terrarium.

To get to the Foggy Bottom Metro station, walk three blocks west on I Street.

TOUR 9: CLEVELAND PARK AND THE NATIONAL ZOO

Numbers in the margin correspond to points of interest on the Tour 9: Cleveland Park and the National Zoo map.

Cleveland Park, a tree-shaded neighborhood in northwest Washington, owes its name to onetime summer resident Grover Cleveland and its development to the streetcar line that was laid along Connecticut Avenue in the 1890s. President Cleveland and his wife, Frances Folson, escaped the heat of downtown Washington in 1886 by establishing a summer White House on Newark Street between 35th and 36th streets. Many prominent Washingtonians followed suit. When the streetcar came through in 1892, construction in the area snowballed. Developer John Sherman hired local architects to design houses and provided amenities such as a fire station and a streetcar-waiting lodge to entice home buyers out of the city and into "rural" Cleveland Park. Today the neighborhood's attractive houses and suburban character are popular with Washington professionals.

Start your exploration at the Cleveland Park Metro station at Connecticut Avenue and Ordway Street NW. The colonial-style **Park and Shop** on the east side of Connecticut Avenue has the distinction of being the first shopping center with off-street parking in the city. Built in 1930, it was at the time one of only a handful of shopping centers on the East Coast to offer this convenience. Off-street parking was then a rather revolutionary notion, and business and architectural publications of the day followed the center's progress with interest. A 1930 industry magazine explained, "Customers can leave their cars here without fear of violating traffic regulations," and the *Washington Post* gushed that the development was "modern to the nth degree." The Park and Shop sat empty for several years in the 1980s as the very active Cleveland Park Historical Society—fearful that the building might be torn down and replaced with a high-rise—lobbied to preserve it in some way. They were successful, and in 1991 the restored Park and Shop, with new green awnings and a tasteful addition, reopened with such modern-day draws as a bagel bakery and a video store.

Half a block south is the **Cineplex Odeon Uptown** (3426 Connecticut Ave. NW, ☎ 202/966–5400), a marvelous vintage-1936 Art Deco movie house. Although many other big-screen theaters in the city have been chopped up and transformed into multiplexes, the Uptown still has a single huge screen and an inviting balcony.

Continue south on Connecticut Avenue. You'll cross over a finger of Rock Creek Park via a span decorated with eight Art Deco bridge lights. Beyond the bridge on the left is the city's finest Art Deco apartment

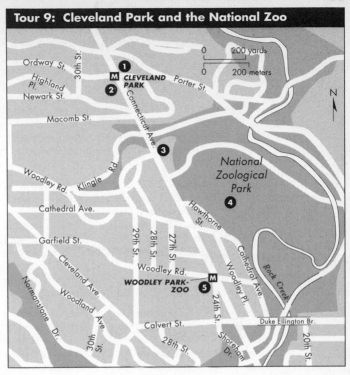

Tour 9: Cleveland Park and the National Zoo

3 house, the **Kennedy-Warren** (3133 Connecticut Ave. NW). Opened in 1931, it features such period detailing as decorative aluminum panels and a streamlined entryway, stone griffins under the pyramidal copper roof, and stylized carved eagles flanking the driveways. Perhaps in keeping with its elegant architecture, the Kennedy-Warren is one of the last apartment buildings in town to still have a doorman.

4 On the same side of Connecticut Avenue is the **National Zoological Park,** part of the Smithsonian Institution and one of the foremost zoos in the world. Created by an Act of Congress in 1889, the 160-acre zoo was designed by landscape architect Frederick Law Olmsted, the man who designed the U.S. Capitol grounds. (Before the zoo opened in 1890, live animals used as taxidermists' models had been kept on the Mall.) For years the zoo's most famous residents were giant pandas Hsing-Hsing and Ling-Ling, gifts from China in 1972. But female Ling-Ling died of heart failure in 1993 at age 23. Sympathy cards poured in from all over the country, the zoo tried in vain to fertilize some of Ling-Ling's extracted eggs, and her body was donated to the Smithsonian's Museum of Natural History. Hsing-Hsing is now the only giant panda in the United States. The zoo has had breeding success with numerous other species, however, including red pandas, Pere David's deer, golden lion tamarins, and pygmy hippopotamuses. The only Komodo dragons in the country are at the National Zoo. Innovative compounds show many animals in naturalistic settings, including the Great Flight Cage—a walk-in aviary in which birds fly unrestricted. Giant crabs, octopuses, cuttlefish, and worms are displayed in an invertebrate exhibit. Zoolab, the Reptile Discovery Center, and the Bird Resource Center all offer activities that teach young visitors about biology. The most ambitious addition to the zoo is Amazonia, a reproduction of a South American rain forest ecosystem. Such fish as twig cats and arowanas swim behind glass walls, while overhead, monkeys and birds flit from tree to tree. The temperature is a constant 85 degrees, with 85% humidity. Also new to the zoo is the Cheetah Conservation Area, a grassy compound that's home to a family of the world's fastest cats. Amazonia and the Cheetah Conservation Area are the most visible attempts by the zoo to show animals in more naturalistic settings and heighten visitors' appreciation of those environments. *3001 Connecticut Ave. NW, ☎ 202/673–4800 or 202/673–4717. ☛ Free. ☉ Apr. 15–Oct. 15, daily: grounds 8–8, animal buildings 9–6, Amazonia 10–4; Oct. 16–Apr. 14, daily: grounds 8–6, animal buildings 9–4:30, Amazonia 10–4. Closed Dec. 25.*

The stretch of Connecticut Avenue south of the zoo is bordered by more venerable apartment buildings. Passing Cathedral Avenue (the first cross-street south of the zoo) you enter a part of town known as **Woodley Park.** Like Cleveland Park to the north, Woodley Park grew as the street-car advanced into this part of Washington. In 1800 Philip Barton Key, uncle of Francis Scott Key, built Woodley, a Georgian mansion on Cathedral Avenue between 29th and 31st streets. The white stucco mansion was the summer home of four presidents: Van Buren, Tyler, Buchanan, and Cleveland. It is now owned by the private Maret School.

At the corner of Connecticut Avenue and Woodley Road is the cross-shape **Wardman Tower.** The Georgian-style tower was built by developer Harry Wardman in 1928 as a luxury apartment building to accompany a now-demolished luxury hotel he had built nearby 10 years earlier. Washingtonians called the project "Wardman's Folly," convinced no one would want to stay in a hotel so far from the city. The Wardman Tower was famous for its well-known residents, who included Dwight D. Eisenhower, Herbert Hoover, Clare Booth Luce, Dean Rusk, Earl Warren, and Caspar Weinberger. It is now part of the Sheraton Washington Hotel (*see* Northwest/Upper Connecticut Avenue *in* Chapter 7, Lodging).

Wardman's success spurred the development of the neighborhood's other large hotel, the **Omni Shoreham** (*see* Northwest/Upper Connecticut Avenue *in* Chapter 7, Lodging) on Calvert Street west of Connecticut Avenue. The Shoreham was known for the entertainers who appeared here, including Rudy Vallee, who performed at its grand opening in 1930. The Shoreham and the nearby Sheraton Washington are two of the city's main convention hotels; you'll notice that many of the people on the streets around you have a plastic name badge pinned to their lapel.

The nearest Metro station is Woodley Park/Zoo, at Connecticut Avenue and Woodley Road.

TOUR 10: ADAMS-MORGAN

To the young, the hip, the cool, and the postmodern, Washington has the reputation of being a rather staid town, more interested in bureaucracy than boogie, with all the vitality of a seersucker suit. It may have the Hope Diamond, these detractors say, but that's about the only thing that really sparkles. What they mean, of course, is that Washington isn't New York City. And thank goodness, say Washingtonians, who wouldn't want to give up their clean subway, comfortable standard of living, or place in the political spotlight, even if it did mean being able to get a decent corned beef sandwich or a double espresso at three in the morning. Besides, Washington does have **Adams-Mor-**

gan. It may not be Greenwich Village, but it's close enough in spirit to satisfy all but the most hardened black-clad, shade-sporting cynics.

Adams-Morgan (roughly, the blocks north of Florida Avenue, between Connecticut Avenue and 16th Street NW) is Washington's most ethnically diverse neighborhood. And as is so often the case, that means it's one of Washington's most interesting areas, home to a veritable United Nations of cuisines, offbeat shops, and funky bars and clubs. The name itself, fashioned in the 1950s by neighborhood civic groups, serves as a symbol of the area's melting pot character: It's a conjunction of the names of two local schools, the predominantly white Adams School and the largely black Morgan School. Today Adams-Morgan is home to every shade in between, too, with large Latino and West African populations.

The neighborhood's grand 19th-century apartment buildings and row houses and its bohemian atmosphere have attracted young urban professionals, the businesses that cater to them, the attendant parking and crowd problems, and the inevitable climb in real estate values. It's all caused some longtime Adams-Morganites to wonder if their neighborhood is in danger of mutating into another Georgetown.

Adams-Morgan already has one thing in common with Georgetown: There's no Metro stop. It's a 15-minute walk from the Woodley Park/Zoo Metro station: Walk south on Connecticut, then turn left on Calvert Street, and cross over Rock Creek Park on the Duke Ellington Bridge. The heart of Adams-Morgan is at the crossroads of Adams Mill Road, Columbia Road, and 18th Street.

What follows is more of a leisurely ramble than a tour. Visitors may want to deviate from the path described here and make their own discoveries, in a spirit in keeping with the serendipity of this fascinating area.

Turn left on **Columbia Road.** At tables stretched along the street, vendors hawk watches, leather goods, knockoff perfumes, cassette tapes (blank and prerecorded), sneakers, clothes, and handmade jewelry. The store signs—Casa Lebrato, Urgente Express (the latter the name of a business that specializes in shipping to and from Central America)—are a testament to the area's Latin flavor; on these blocks you'll hear as much Spanish as English.

Cross Columbia at Ontario Road and backtrack. If you'd rather see the neighborhood on two wheels than two feet, turn left onto Champlain Street and rent a bicycle at **City Bikes** (2501 Champlain St. NW, ☎ 202/265–1564; call ahead to reserve a bike on weekends).

Continue west on Columbia Road to its intersection with 18th Street. On Saturday mornings a **market** springs up on the plaza in front of the Crestar bank, at the southwest corner of 18th and Columbia, with vendors selling fruits, vegetables, flowers, and breads.

If Columbia Road east of 18th is Adams-Morgan's Latin Quarter, 18th Street south of Columbia is its restaurant corridor. In the next few blocks you'll pass—besides McDonald's—restaurants serving the cuisines of China, Mexico, India, El Salvador, Ethiopia, France, the Caribbean, Thailand, Argentina, Italy, Vietnam, and, believe it or not, America. If you can't make up your mind, there's even a palm reader who can help decide what your future has in store.

You can also feed your hunger for the outré or offbeat with the funky shops on 18th Street. Here you'll find the mission-style furniture, Russell Wright crockery and Fiestaware, aerodynamic art deco armchairs,

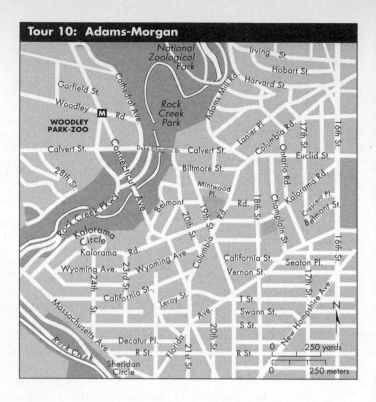

Tour 10: Adams-Morgan

Bakelite telephones, massive chromium toasters, kidney-shape Formica-top coffee tables, skinny neckties, and tacky salt-and-pepper shakers that, through time and television reruns, have been transformed from kitsch into collectible. Among stores carrying these are **Homeworks** (2405 18th St. NW, ☎ 202/483–5857) and **Retrospective** (2324 18th St. NW, ☎ 202/483–8112).

Once you've had your fill of Jetsons lunchboxes and gloopy lava lamps, proceed to the souklike **Bazaar Atlas** (2405 18th St. NW, ☎ 202/332-4911), above Homeworks. It specializes in ethnic goods such as geometric-pattern sweaters from Ecuador and Bolivia, and leather, carved wood, rugs, and hammered metal from Morocco. Nearby is **Kobos** (2444 18th St. NW, ☎ 202/332–9580), owned by a Ghanaian immigrant who sells African jewelry, and clothes fashioned from colorful *kente* cloth.

The spirit of the neighborhood is alive in **1800 Belmont Arts** (1800 Belmont Rd., ☎ 202/265–9341 or 202/319–1940), home to nearly a dozen Afrocentric artists and vendors. Inside are clothing stores, galleries, and a goldsmith.

Down the block and across the street, **Idle Time Books** (2410 18th St. NW, ☎ 202/232–4774) stocks used and out-of-print titles.

The west side of 18th Street is home to a gamut of antiques shops, including **Chenonceau Antiques** (2314 18th St. NW, ☎ 202/667–1651) and its classic 19th- and 20th-century American pieces. Antiques shoppers should also keep an eye out for secondhand shops set up in alleys or warehouses here.

Nearby is the **District of Columbia Arts Center** (DCAC), a combination art gallery-performance space. DCAC exhibits the cutting-edge work of local artists and is the home of offbeat plays, including that uncategorizable category known as performance art. *2438 18th St. NW,* ☎ *202/462–7833.* ☛ *Free to gallery, performance costs vary.* ☉ *Tues.–Fri. 2–6 and during performances (generally Thurs.–Sun. 7 PM–midnight).*

Of course, the measure of any neighborhood is the tone it takes when the sun goes down. In the spring and summer, restaurants open their windows or set out tables on the sidewalks. Those lucky enough to have rooftop seating find diners lining up to eat under the stars. (Washington can be notoriously hot in the summer, but one of Adams-Morgan's charms has always been that its slight elevation wraps it in cooling breezes.)

Although the neighborhood's bar and club scene isn't as varied as its restaurant scene, there are some standouts. Tap dancers use the bar as a stage Friday and Saturday evenings at the decidedly Gallic jazz club **Café Lautrec** (2431 18th St. NW, ☎ 202/265–6436). **Chief Ike's Mambo Room** (1725 Columbia Rd. NW, ☎ 202/332–2211) is as eclectic as its name, with DJs playing everything from R&B to disco and a mural of its namesake, Dwight Eisenhower, in a Native American headdress. Locals cue them up at **Bedrock Billiards** (1841 Columbia Rd. NW, ☎ 202/667–7665), a pool hall with eight tables and a '50s fashion sense. **Club Heaven** is upstairs from a bar named **Hell** (2327 18th St. NW, ☎ 202/667–4355) and has dancing to live and recorded synth-pop music. More in keeping with Adams-Morgan's international flavor is **Bukom Cafe** (2442 18th St. NW, ☎ 202/265–4600), home on weekends to West African music.

Remember that the last trains leave the Woodley Park Metro station at around midnight, so if you can't tear yourself away, be prepared to take a cab.

TOUR 11: ARLINGTON

Numbers in the margin correspond to points of interest on the Tour 11: Arlington map.

The Virginia suburb of Arlington County was once part of the District of Columbia. Carved out of the Old Dominion when Washington was created, it was returned to Virginia along with the rest of the land west of the Potomac in 1845. Washington hasn't held a grudge, though, and there are three attractions in Arlington—each linked to the military— that should be a part of any complete visit to the nation's capital: Arlington National Cemetery, the U.S. Marine Corps War Memorial, and the Pentagon. All are accessible by Metro, and a trip across the Potomac makes an enjoyable half day of sightseeing.

Begin your exploration in **Arlington National Cemetery.** To get there, you can take the Metro to the Arlington Cemetery station, travel on a Tourmobile bus (*see* Sightseeing *in* Important Contacts A to Z), or walk across Memorial Bridge from the District (southwest of the Lincoln Memorial). If you're driving, there's a large paid parking lot at the skylit **visitor center** on Memorial Drive. Stop at the center for a free brochure with a detailed map of the cemetery's 612 acres. (If you're looking for a specific grave, the staff will consult microfilm records and give you directions on how to find it. You should know the deceased's full name and, if possible, his or her branch of service and year of death.) ☎ *703/692–0931.* ☛ *Free.* ☉ *Apr.–Sept., daily 8–7; Oct.–*

*Mar., daily 8–5. Parking lot open Apr.–Sept., daily 8–8; Oct.–Mar.,
daily 8–6. Parking $1.25/hr for 1st 3 hrs, $2/hr thereafter.*

Tourmobile tour buses leave from just outside the visitor center mid-
June–early September, daily 8:30–6:30; early September–mid-June,
daily 8:30–4:30. You can buy tickets here (adults $2.75, children
$1.25) for the 40-minute tour of the cemetery, which includes stops at
the Kennedy grave sites, the Tomb of the Unknowns, and Arlington
House. Touring the cemetery on foot means a fair bit of hiking, but it
will give you a closer look at some of the 200,000 graves spread over
these rolling Virginia hills. If you decide to walk, head west from the
visitor center on Roosevelt Drive and then turn right on Weeks Drive.

While you are at Arlington you will probably hear the clear, doleful
sound of a trumpet playing taps or the sharp reports of a gun salute.
Approximately 15 funerals are held here daily. It is projected the cemetery will be filled in 2020. Although not the largest cemetery in the country, Arlington is certainly the best known, a place where visitors can
trace America's history through the aftermath of its battles.

2 The **Kennedy graves** are just west of the visitor center. John F. Kennedy
is buried under an eternal flame near two of his children who died in
infancy, and his wife Jacqueline Bouvier Kennedy Onassis. Across
from the graves is a low wall engraved with quotations from Kennedy's
inaugural address. JFK's grave was opened to the public in 1967 and
since that time has become the most-visited grave site in the country.
Nearby, marked by a simple white cross, is the grave of his brother,
Robert Kennedy.

This somber plot of land hasn't always been a cemetery. It was in Arlington that the two most famous names in Virginia history—Wash-
ington and Lee—became intertwined. George Washington Parke
Custis—raised by Martha and George Washington, his grandmother
3 and step-grandfather—built **Arlington House** (also known as the Custis-
Lee Mansion) between 1802 and 1817 on his 1,100-acre estate over-
looking the Potomac. After his death, the property went to his daughter,
Mary Anna Randolph Custis. In 1831, Mary Custis married Robert
E. Lee, a recent graduate of West Point. For the next 30 years the Custis-
Lee family lived at Arlington House.

In 1861, Lee was offered command of the Union forces. He declined,
insisting that he could never take up arms against his native Virginia.
The Lees left Arlington House that spring, never to return. Union
troops soon occupied the estate, making it the headquarters of the officers who were charged with defending Washington. When Mrs. Lee
was unable to appear in person to pay a $92.07 property tax the gov-
ernment had assessed, the land was confiscated and a portion set aside
as a military cemetery.

Its heavy Doric columns and severe pediment make Arlington House
one of the area's best examples of Greek Revival architecture. The plantation home was designed by George Hadfield, a young English architect
who for a while supervised construction of the Capitol. The view of
Washington from the front of the house is superb. In 1955 Arlington
House was designated a memorial to Robert E. Lee. It looks much as
it did in the 19th century, and a quick tour will take you past objects
once owned by the Custises and the Lees. *Between Lee and Sherman
Drs.,* ☎ *703/557–0613.* ☛ *Free.* ☉ *Apr.–Sept., daily 9:30–6; Oct.–Mar.,
daily 9:30–4:30; closed Dec. 25 and Jan. 1.*

Tour 11: Arlington

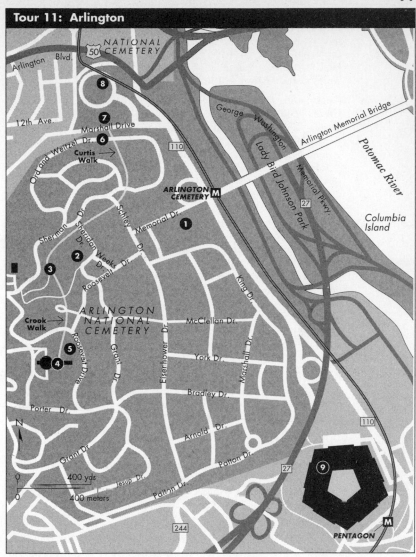

Arlington House, **3**

Kennedy graves, **2**

Netherlands
Carillon, **7**

Pentagon, **9**

Section 7A, **5**

Section 27, **6**

Tomb of the
Unknowns, **4**

United States Marine
Corps War
Memorial, **8**

Visitor Center, **1**

In front of the house, next to a flag that flies at half staff whenever there is a funeral in the cemetery, is the flat-top grave of Pierre L'Enfant, designer of the Federal City. L'Enfant died in 1825, a penniless, bitter man who felt he hadn't been recognized for his planning genius. He was originally buried in Maryland, but his body was moved here with much ceremony in 1909.

After visiting Arlington House and the Kennedy graves, walk south on Crook Walk past the seemingly endless rows of simple white headstones—arranged like soldiers on parade—and follow the signs to the

④ **Tomb of the Unknowns.** The first burial at the Tomb of the Unknowns was on November 11, 1921, when the Unknown Soldier from World War I was interred under the large white-marble sarcophagus. Unknown servicemen killed in World War II and Korea were buried in 1958. The unknown serviceman killed in Vietnam was laid to rest on the plaza on Memorial Day 1984. Soldiers from the Army's U.S. 3rd Infantry ("The Old Guard," portrayed in the movie *Gardens of Stone*) keep watch over the tomb 24 hours a day, regardless of weather conditions. Each sentinel marches exactly 21 steps, then faces the tomb for 21 seconds, symbolizing the 21-gun salute, America's highest military honor. The guard is changed with a precise ceremony during the day—every half-hour from April 1 to September 30 and every hour the rest of the year. At night the guard is changed every two hours. The **Memorial Amphitheater** west of the tomb is the scene of special ceremonies on Veterans Day, Memorial Day, and Easter. Decorations awarded to the unknowns by foreign governments and U.S. and foreign organizations are displayed in an indoor trophy room.

Across from the amphitheater are memorials to the astronauts killed in the *Challenger* shuttle explosion and to the servicemen killed in 1980 while trying to rescue American hostages in Iran. Rising beyond that is the mast from the USS *Maine,* the American ship that was sunk in Havana Harbor in 1898, killing 299 men and sparking the Spanish-American War.

⑤ Below the Tomb of the Unknowns is **section 7A,** where you can find the graves of many distinguished veterans, including boxing champ Joe Louis, ABC newsman Frank Reynolds, actor Lee Marvin, and World War II fighter pilot Col. "Pappy" Boyington.

To reach the sites at the northern end of the cemetery and to make your way into the city of Arlington, first walk north along Roosevelt Drive to Schley Drive (you'll pass the Memorial Gate), then turn right on Custis
⑥ Walk to the Ord & Weitzel Gate. On your way you'll pass **section 27,** where 3,800 former slaves are buried. They lived at Freedman's Village, established at Arlington in 1863 to provide housing, education, and employment training for ex-slaves who had traveled to the capital. The headstones are marked with their names and the word "Civilian" or "Citizen." Buried at grave 19 in the first row of section 27 is William Christman, a Union private who died of peritonitis in Washington on May 13, 1864. He was the first soldier interred at Arlington National Cemetery during the Civil War. *West end of Memorial Bridge, Arlington, VA,* ☎ *703/692–0931.* ☛ *Free.* ☉ *Apr.–early Sept., daily 8–7; mid-Sept.–Mar., daily 8–5.*

Leaving the cemetery through the Ord & Weitzel Gate, cross Marshall
⑦ Drive carefully, and walk to the **Netherlands Carillon.** The 49-bell carillon was presented to the United States by the Dutch people in 1960 as thanks for aid received during World War II. A performance season featuring guest carillonneurs begins Easter Sunday and runs through

August. For one of the most inclusive views of Washington, look to the east across the Potomac. From this vantage point, the Lincoln Memorial, the Washington Monument, and the Capitol are bunched together in a side-by-side formation. *For carillon performance information, call 703/285–2030.*

8 To the north is the **United States Marine Corps War Memorial,** honoring marines who have given their lives since the corps was formed in 1775. The memorial statue, sculpted by Felix W. de Weldon, is based on Joe Rosenthal's Pulitzer Prize–winning photograph of five marines and a Navy corpsman raising a flag atop Mount Suribachi on Iwo Jima on February 19, 1945. By executive order, a real flag flies 24 hours a day from the 78-foot-high memorial. On Tuesday evenings at 7 from late May to late August there is a Marine Corps sunset parade on the grounds of the memorial. On parade nights a free shuttle bus runs from the Arlington Cemetery visitor parking lot (for information, call 202/433–6060). A few words of caution: It is dangerous to visit the memorial after dark.

The Arlington neighborhood of Rosslyn is north of the memorial. Like parts of downtown Washington and Crystal City farther to the south, Rosslyn is almost empty at night once the thousands of people who work there have gone home. Its tall buildings do provide the preternaturally horizontal Washington with a bit of a skyline, but this has come about not without some controversy: Some say the silvery, wing-shape Gannett Buildings are too close to the flight path followed by jets landing at National Airport.

9 To get to the **Pentagon,** take the Metro to the Pentagon station; its escalator surfaces right into the humongous office building. The headquarters of the Department of Defense, the Pentagon was completed in 1943 after just two years of construction. The five-sided building is an exercise in immensity: 23,000 military and civilian employees work here; it is as wide as three Washington Monuments laid end to end; inside are 17½ miles of corridors, 7,754 windows, and 691 drinking fountains. The 75-minute tour of the Pentagon takes you past only those areas that are meant to be seen by outside visitors. In other words, you won't see situation rooms, communications centers, or gigantic maps outlining U.S. and foreign troop strengths. A uniformed serviceman or -woman (who conducts the entire tour walking backward, lest anyone slip away down a corridor) will take you past hallways lined with the portraits of past and present military leaders, scale models of Air Force planes and Navy ships, and the Hall of Heroes, where the names of all the Congressional Medal of Honor winners are inscribed. Occasionally you will catch a glimpse through an interior window of the Pentagon's 5-acre interior courtyard. In the center—at ground zero—is a hot dog stand. *Pentagon, off I–395, Arlington, VA,* ☎ *703/695–1776.* ☛ *Free. Tours: spring and summer, weekdays every ½ hr 9:30–3:30; fall and winter, weekdays every hr 9–3. Photo ID required. Closed federal holidays.*

TOUR 12: ALEXANDRIA

Numbers in the margin correspond to points of interest on the Tour 12: Old Town Alexandria map.

Just a short Metro ride (or bike ride) away from Washington, Old Town Alexandria today attracts visitors seeking a break from the monuments and hustle-and-bustle of the District and interested in an encounter with America's Colonial heritage. Founded in 1749 by Scottish merchants eager to capitalize on the booming tobacco trade, Alexandria emerged as one of the most important ports in Colonial America. The city's history is linked to the most significant events and personages of the Colonial and Revolutionary periods. This colorful past is still alive in restored 18th- and 19th-century homes, churches, and taverns; on the cobbled streets; and on the revitalized waterfront, where clipper ships dock and artisans display their wares.

The quickest way to get to Old Town is to take the Metro to the King Street stop (about 25 minutes from Metro Center). If you're driving you can take either the George Washington Memorial Parkway or Jefferson Davis Highway (Route 1) south from Arlington.

❶ The best place to start a tour of Old Town is at the **Alexandria Convention & Visitors Bureau,** which is in **Ramsay House,** the home of the town's first postmaster and lord mayor, William Ramsay. The structure is believed to be the oldest house in Alexandria. Ramsay was a Scotsman, as a swatch of his tartan on the door proclaims. Travel counselors here provide information, brochures, and self-guided walking tours of the town. *221 King St., 22314, ☎ 703/838–4200, TTY 703/ 838–6494. ☉ Daily 9–5; closed Thanksgiving, Dec. 25, and Jan. 1. Visitors are given a 24-hr permit that allows them to park free at any 2-hr metered spot.*

❷ Across the street, at the corner of Fairfax and King streets, is the **Stabler-Leadbeater Apothecary,** the second-oldest apothecary in the country. It was patronized by George Washington and the Lee family, and it was here, on October 17, 1859, that Lt. Col. Robert E. Lee received orders to move to Harper's Ferry to suppress John Brown's insurrection. The shop now houses a small museum of 18th-century apothecary memorabilia, including one of the finest collections of apothecary bottles in the country (some 800 bottles in all). *105–107 S. Fairfax St., ☎ 703/836–3713. ☛ $1. ☉ Mon.–Sat. 10–4, Sun. 1–5; closed Thanksgiving, Dec. 25, Jan. 1.*

❸ Two blocks south on Fairfax Street, just beyond Duke Street, stands the **Old Presbyterian Meetinghouse.** Built in 1774, this was an important meeting place for Scottish patriots during the Revolution. Eulogies for George Washington were delivered here on December 29, 1799. In a corner of the churchyard you'll find the **Tomb of the Unknown Soldier of the American Revolution.** *321 S. Fairfax St., ☎ 703/549–6670. ☛ Free. Sanctuary open weekdays 10–3 (if locked, obtain key from church office at 316 S. Royal St.); graveyard always open.*

❹ Next walk back up Fairfax Street one block and turn right on Prince
❺ Street. The block between Fairfax and Lee streets is known as **Gentry Row.** One of the most noteworthy structures in the city is the **Athenaeum,** at the corner of Prince and Lee streets. The striking, reddish-brown Greek Revival edifice was built as a bank in the 1850s.

❻ The next block east on Prince Street between Lee and Union, known as **Captain's Row,** was where many of the city's sea captains built their homes. The cobblestones in the street were allegedly laid by Hessian mercenaries who had fought for the British during the Revolution and were held in Alexandria as prisoners of war.

❼ Continuing east on Prince Street you'll come to Alexandria's lively waterfront. One block to the north up Union Street (at the foot of King Street) is one of the most popular destinations in the city, the **Torpedo Factory Arts Center.** This former munitions plant (yes, naval torpedoes were actually manufactured here during World War I and World War

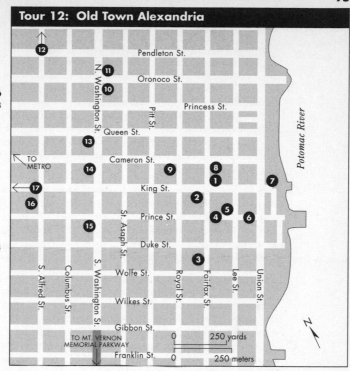

Tour 12: Old Town Alexandria

II) has now been converted into studios and galleries for some 175 professional artists and artisans. Almost every imaginable medium is represented, from printmaking and sculpture to jewelry making, pottery, and stained glass. Visitors can view the workshops, and most of the art and crafts are for sale at reasonable prices. *105 N. Union St., ☎ 703/838–4565. ☛ Free. ⊙ Daily 10–5.*

The Torpedo Factory complex also houses the **Alexandria Archaeology Program,** a city-operated research facility devoted to urban archaeology and conservation. Artifacts from excavations dug in Alexandria are on display. *105 N. Union St., ☎ 703/838–4399. ☛ Free. ⊙ Tues.–Fri. 10–3, Sat. 10–5, Sun. 1–5.*

⑧ Walk back into the town, two blocks up Cameron Street, to reach **Carlyle House,** at the corner of North Fairfax Street, the grandest of Alexandria's older houses. Patterned after a Scottish country manor house, the structure was completed in 1753 by Scottish merchant John Carlyle. This was General Braddock's headquarters and the place where he met with five royal governors in 1755 to plan the strategy and funding of the early campaigns of the French and Indian War. *121 N. Fairfax St., ☎ 703/549–2997. ☛ $3 adults, $1 students 11–17. ⊙ Tues.–Sat. 10–5, Sun. noon–5. Tours every ½ hr.*

⑨ One block west, on Royal Street, is **Gadsby's Tavern Museum,** housed in the old City Tavern and Hotel, which was a center of political and social life in the late 18th century. George Washington attended birthday celebrations in the ballroom here. A tour of the facilities takes you through the taproom, game room, assembly room, ballroom, and communal bedrooms. *134 N. Royal St., ☎ 703/838–4242. ☛ $3 adults, $1 students 11–17. ⊙ Oct.–Mar., Tues.–Sat. 11–4, Sun. 1–4;*

Apr.–Sept., Tues.–Sat. 10–5, Sun. 1–5. Tours 15 mins before and 15 mins after the hr.

Continue west on Cameron Street for three blocks and turn right on Washington Street. The corner of Washington and Oronoco streets (three blocks north) is known as **Lee Corner** because at one time a Lee-owned house stood on each of the four corners. Two survive. One is the **Lee-Fendall House,** the home of several illustrious members of the Lee family, including Richard Henry Lee, signer of the Declaration of Independence, and cavalry commander Henry "Light Horse Harry" Lee. *614 Oronoco St., ☎ 703/548–1789. ☛ $3 adults, $1 students 11–17. ☉ Tues.–Sat. 10–4, Sun. noon–4. Occasionally closed weekends for private events.*

Directly across the street is the **boyhood home of Robert E. Lee,** a fine example of a 19th-century town house. It features Federal architecture and antique furnishings and paintings. *607 Oronoco St., ☎ 703/ 548–8454. ☛ $3 adults, $1 students 11–17. ☉ Mon.–Sat. 10–4, Sun. 1–4; closed Dec. 15–Feb. 1 except on Sun. closest to Jan. 19 for Lee's birthday celebration. Occasionally closed weekends for private events.*

Alexandria's history isn't all Washingtons and Lees, however. The federal census of 1790 recorded 52 free blacks living in the city, and the port town was one of the largest slave exportation points in the South, with at least two bustling slave markets. The history of African Americans in Alexandria and Virginia from 1749 to the present is recounted at the **Alexandria Black History Resource Center,** two blocks north and two blocks west of Lee's boyhood home. *638 North Alfred St., ☎ 703/ 838–4356. ☛ Free. ☉ Tues.–Sat. 10–4.*

Head back to Washington Street and go south now to the corner of Queen Street. Here you'll find the **Lloyd House,** a fine example of Georgian architecture. Built in 1797, it is now operated as part of the Alexandria Library and houses a collection of rare books and documents relating to city and state history. *220 N. Washington St., ☎ 703/ 838–4577. ☛ Free. ☉ Weekdays 9–6, Sat. 9–5.*

At the corner of Cameron and Washington streets, one block south, stands **Christ Church,** where both Washington and Lee were pewholders (Washington paid 36 pounds and 10 shillings—a lot of money in those days—for Pew 60). Built in 1773, it is a fine example of an English Georgian country-style church. It has a fine Palladian window, an interior balcony, and a wrought-brass-and-crystal chandelier brought from England at Washington's expense. *118 N. Washington St., ☎ 703/ 549–1450. ☛ Free. ☉ Weekdays 9–4, Sat. 9–noon, Sun. 2–4:30. Occasionally closed weekends for private events.*

From Christ Church, walk two blocks south to the **Lyceum** at the corner of South Washington and Prince streets. Built in 1839, the structure served alternately as the Alexandria Library, a Civil War hospital, a residence, and an office building. It was restored in the 1970s and now houses two art galleries, a gift shop, and a museum devoted to the area's history. A limited amount of travel information for the entire state is also available here. *201 S. Washington St., ☎ 703/838– 4994. ☛ Free. ☉ Mon.–Sat. 10–5, Sun. 12–5; closed Thanksgiving, Dec. 25, and Jan. 1.*

In 1861, when the city was occupied by Union forces, the 800 soldiers of Alexandria's garrison marched out of town to join the Confederate Army. In the middle of Washington and Prince streets stands the **Confederate Statue,** marking the point at which they assembled. In 1885,

Confederate veterans proposed a memorial to honor their fallen comrades. This statue, based on John A. Elder's painting *Appomattox,* is of a lone soldier glumly surveying the battlefields after General Robert E. Lee's surrender. The names of 100 Alexandria Confederate dead are carved on the base.

⑯ Two blocks to the west on South Alfred Street is the **Friendship Fire Company.** The building was recently renovated and is now outfitted like a typical 19th-century firehouse. *107 S. Alfred St.,* ☎ *703/838–3891. Suggested donation: $1.* ☉ *Thurs.–Sat. 10–4, Sun. 1–4.*

⑰ A little far to walk but well worth visiting is the **George Washington Masonic National Memorial** on Callahan Drive at King Street, a mile west of the center of the city. (You can take Bus 2 or 5 west on King Street; from here, you are only two blocks from the King Street Metro.) The memorial's spire dominates the surroundings, and from the 9th floor observation deck visitors get a spectacular view of Alexandria and Washington in the distance. Among other things, the building contains furnishings from the first Masonic lodge in Alexandria, in which George Washington was Worshipful Master at the same time he served as president. *101 Callahan Dr.,* ☎ *703/683–2007.* ☛ *Free.* ☉ *Daily 9:30–4:50; closed Thanksgiving, Dec. 25, and Jan. 1. Free 50-min guided tours of building and observation deck daily at 9:30, 10:30, 11:30, 1, 2, 3, and 4.*

OFF THE BEATEN TRACK

Anacostia Museum. African-American culture is explored at this Smithsonian museum in a historic Southeast Washington neighborhood. Past exhibits have covered black inventors and aviators, the influential role of black churches, the history of the civil rights movement, African-American life in the antebellum South, and the richness of African-American quilts. *1901 Fort Pl. SE,* ☎ *202/287–3369.* ☛ *Free.* ☉ *Daily 10–5. Closed Dec. 25.*

The **Ansel Adams Collection,** a permanent exhibit of the famous photographer's most important landscapes, is on display at the Wilderness Society's headquarters. *900 17th St. NW,* ☎ *202/833–2300.* ☉ *Weekdays 10–5; closed major holidays and day after Thanksgiving. Large groups should call ahead. Metro: Farragut North and Farragut West.*

Bethune Museum and Archives. Mary McLeod Bethune founded Florida's Bethune-Cookman College, established the National Council of Negro Women, and served as an adviser to President Franklin D. Roosevelt. Exhibits in the museum focus on the achievements of black women. The museum also hosts free weekly concerts as part of its "Black Women in Jazz" series, March through June and September through December. *1318 Vermont Ave. NW,* ☎ *202/332–1233.* ☛ *Free.* ☉ *Weekdays 10–4. Metro: McPherson Square.*

College Park Airport Museum. Opened in 1909, College Park is the world's oldest operating airport and was the site of numerous aviation firsts. Orville and Wilbur Wright tested military planes here and their presence is evident in the museum's early aviation memorabilia. The airport's Air Fair every September features antique airplanes, hot-air balloons, and a Wright Brothers look-alike contest. *1909 Cpl. Frank Scott Dr., College Park, MD,* ☎ *301/864–1530.* ☛ *Free.* ☉ *Wed.–Fri. 11–3, weekends 11–5.*

Eastern Market. Built in 1873, Eastern Market has always been a bustling center of activity on Capitol Hill. It was designed by Adolph

Cluss, the architect of the Smithsonian Arts and Industries Museum. Inside are shops, restaurants, and galleries. There is a flea market outside on weekends. *7th and C Sts. SE. Metro: Eastern Market.*

Firearms Museum. The National Rifle Association museum moved from downtown Washington to suburban Virginia in 1994 and is scheduled to open in 1996 a museum five times larger than that at its old location. Exhibits explore the role firearms have played in the history of America. Hundreds of guns are on display here, from muzzle-loading flintlocks used in the Revolutionary War to high-tech pistols used by Olympic shooting teams. Also on display are weapons that once belonged to presidents, such as Teddy Roosevelt's .32-caliber Browning pistol and a Winchester rifle used by Dwight Eisenhower. *National Rifle Association, 11250 Waples Mill Rd., Fairfax, VA,* ☎ *703/267–1600.* ☛ *Free.* ☉ *Weekdays 10–4; closed major holidays.*

Flying Circus Airshow. This show bills itself as the only remaining barnstorming show in the country. Operating out of a Virginia aerodrome about 90 minutes outside Washington, the Flying Circus features stunt flying, wing walking, and open cockpit biplane rides for the public, on Sunday from May through October. *On Rte. 17 in Bealeton, VA, between Fredericksburg and Warrenton,* ☎ *703/439–8661. Gates open at 11 AM, show at 2:30 PM.* ☛ *$9 adults, $3 children 3–12.*

Frederick Douglass National Historic Site. Cedar Hill, the Anacostia home of noted abolitionist Frederick Douglass, was the first place designated by Congress as a Black National Historic Site. Douglass, an ex-slave who delivered fiery abolitionist speeches at home and abroad, resided here from 1877 until his death in 1895. The house has a wonderful view of the Federal City, across the Anacostia, and contains many of Douglass's personal belongings. A short film on Douglass's life is shown at a nearby visitor center. *1411 W St. SE,* ☎ *202/426–5961.* ☛ *Free.* ☉ *Mid-Oct.–mid-Apr., daily 9–4; mid-Apr.–mid-Oct., daily 9–5. Tours given on the hr. Metro: Anacostia; or catch Bus B2.*

Goddard Space Flight Center. Space flight is brought down to earth at this NASA museum in the suburban Maryland complex where scientists and technicians monitor spaceships circling the Earth, the solar system, and beyond. Local model rocket clubs send their handiwork skyward the first and third Sundays of each month. *Baltimore–Washington Pkwy. and Greenbelt Rd., Greenbelt, MD,* ☎ *301/286–8981.* ☛ *Free.* ☉ *Daily 10–4. Tours Mon.–Sat. at 11:30 and 2:30.*

Hillwood Museum. Hillwood House, the 40-room Georgian mansion of cereal heiress Marjorie Merriweather Post, contains a large collection of 18th- and 19th-century French and Russian decorative art that includes gold and silver work, icons, lace, tapestries, china, and Fabergé eggs. Also on the estate are a dacha filled with Russian objects and an Adirondacks-style cabin that houses an assortment of Native American artifacts. The grounds are composed of lawns, formal French and Japanese gardens, and paths that wind through plantings of azaleas, laurels, and rhododendrons. *4155 Linnean Ave. NW,* ☎ *202/686–5807.* ☛ *To house and grounds: $10, children under 12 not admitted on house tour.* ☛ *To grounds only: $2. House open Tues.–Sat. 11–3; grounds open Tues.–Sat. 11–4:30. House and grounds closed Feb. Make reservations well in advance to tour the house. Metro: Van Ness/UDC.*

Intelsat. This international satellite cooperative, has its headquarters in a striking glass building that looks as though it, too, had come down from space. The 45-minute tour includes a brief film about the work of the organization and a look at rocket and satellite models in the high-tech visitor center. You can also look down upon control rooms where satellite traffic is monitored. Space buffs will enjoy the visit. *3400 International Dr. NW, 1 block west of Connecticut Ave. and Van Ness St. NW, ☎ 202/944–7500. Free tours given weekdays by appointment. Metro: Van Ness/UDC.*

Maine Avenue Seafood Market is a reminder that Washington isn't far from the Chesapeake Bay, the Atlantic Ocean beyond that, and the bounty of both. The market bustles with activity as more than a dozen vendors sell fresh crabs, fish, shrimp, squid, clams, and other types of seafood. If you work up an appetite there are seven restaurants stretched out along Maine Avenue, including local seafood powerhouse **Phillips Flagship.** All have terraces overlooking the Washington Channel and the motorboats, houseboats, and sailboats that are moored there. *Maine Ave. SW. Metro: Waterfront.*

Marine Corps Barracks. Each Friday evening at 8:45 from May to September the Marine Corps Drum and Bugle Corps, the Marine Band, and the Silent Drill Team present a dress parade filled with martial music and precision marching. *8th and I Sts. SE, ☎ 202/433–6060. ☛ Free. Reservations required. Call 3 wks in advance. Metro: Eastern Market.*

Marine Corps Museum. This museum tells the story of the corps from its inception in 1775 to its role in Desert Storm. A variety of artifacts—uniforms, weapons, documents, photographs—outline the growth of the corps, including its embrace of amphibious assault and the strategy of "vertical envelopment" (helicopters, to you and me). *9th and M Sts. SE, Bldg. 58, ☎ 202/433–3534. ☛ Free. ☼ Fall–spring, Mon.–Sat. 10–4, Sun. noon–5; summer, Mon.–Thurs. and Sat. 10–4, Fri. 10–8, Sun. noon–5; closed Dec. 25 and Jan. 1.*

Meridian House and the White-Meyer House. Meridian International Center, a nonprofit institution promoting international understanding, now owns these two handsome mansions designed by John Russell Pope. The 30-room Meridian House was built in 1920 by Irwin Boyle Laughlin, scion of a Pittsburgh steel family and former ambassador to Spain. The Louis XVI–style home features parquet floors, ornamental iron grillwork, handsome moldings, period furniture, tapestries, and a garden planted with European linden trees. Next door is the Georgian-style house built for Henry White (former ambassador to France) that was later the home of the Meyer family, publishers of the *Washington Post.* The first floors of both houses are open to the public and are the scene of periodic art exhibits with an international flavor. *1630 and 1624 Crescent Pl. NW, ☎ 202/667–6670. ☛ Free. ☼ Wed.–Sun. 2–5.*

Mexican Cultural Institute. This museum is in a glorious 1911 Italianate house that was once the Embassy of Mexico. Inside are highlights of 19th- and 20th-century Mexican art, including the works of Diego Rivera, José Clemente Orozco, David Alfaro, Sigueiros, and Juan O'Gorman. *2829 16th St. NW, ☎ 202/728–1628. ☛ Free. ☼ Tues.–Fri. 9–6, Sat. 11–6.*

National Capital Trolley Museum. Some of the capital's historic trolleys have been rescued and restored and are now on display at this suburban Maryland museum, along with streetcars from Europe and elsewhere in America. For a nominal fare you can go on a 2-mile ride through the country. *Bonifant Rd. between Layhill Rd. and New Hampshire Ave., Wheaton, MD, ☎ 301/384–6088. Trolley-ride fare: $2 adults, $1.50 children 2–18. ☼ Jan.–Nov., weekends and Memo-*

rial Day, July 4, and Labor Day noon–5; Dec., weekends 5–9 PM for "Holly Trolley Illuminations"; July and Aug., Wed. noon–4.

National Cryptologic Museum. This new Maryland museum is a surprise, telling in a public way the anything but public story of "sigint" (stands for "signals Intelligence"), the government's gleaning of intelligence data from radio signals, messages, radar, and such by cracking other governments' secret codes. Connected to the super-secret National Security Agency, the museum recounts the history of intelligence from 1526 to the present. Displays include rare cryptographic books from the 16th century, items used in the Civil War, a World War II cipher machine, and a Cray supercomputer of the sort that does the code work today. *Colony Seven Rd., near Fort Meade, MD,* ☎ *301/688–5849. Take Baltimore–Washington Pkwy. north to Route 32 E.* ⊘ *Weekdays 9–3, Sat. 10–2.*

National Museum of Health and Medicine. Opened more than 125 years ago, the medical museum features exhibits that illustrate medicine's fight against injury and disease. Included are displays on the Lincoln and Garfield assassinations and one of the world's largest collections of microscopes. Because some exhibits are fairly graphic (the wax surgical models and various organs floating in alcohol, for example), the museum may not be suitable for young children or the squeamish. *Walter Reed Army Medical Center, 6825 16th St. NW,* ☎ *202/782-2200.* ☛ *Free.* ⊘ *Daily 10–5:30. Closed Dec. 25.*

National Weather Service Science and History Center. Opened in 1990 in suburban Maryland, this museum displays the tools of the National Oceanic and Atmospheric Administration, including remote data collectors, weather satellites, and "TOTO," a robotlike Totable Tornado Observatory used to study twisters. There's also the actual 1891 Cairo, Illinois, U.S. Weather Bureau office, complete with the original furniture, record books, and meteorological instruments. *1325 East-West Hwy., Silver Spring, MD,* ☎ *301/713-0622.* ☛ *Free.* ⊘ *Weekdays 8:30–5. Metro: Silver Spring.*

Navy Art Gallery. This one-room gallery hosts rotating exhibits of Navy-related paintings, sketches, and drawings, many created during combat by Navy artists. The bulk of the collection illustrates World War II. *9th and M Sts. SE, Bldg. 67,* ☎ *202/433–3815.* ☛ *Free.* ⊘ *Labor Day–Memorial Day, Wed.–Fri. 9–4, weekends 10–4; Memorial Day–Labor Day, Wed.–Fri. 9–5, weekends 10–5; closed federal holidays.*

Navy Museum. In a former weapons factory, this museum chronicles the history of the U.S. Navy from the Revolution to the present. Exhibits range from the fully rigged foremast of the USS *Constitution* (better known as "Old Ironsides") to a U.S. Navy Corsair fighter plane dangling from the ceiling. All around are models of fighting ships, displays on battles, and portraits of the sailors who fought them. Children especially enjoy peering through the operating periscopes and pretending to launch torpedoes at the display ship *Barry* floating a few hundred yards away in the Anacostia River. In front of the museum is a collection of guns, cannons, and missiles. An annex is full of unusual submarines. *9th and M Sts. SE, Bldg. 76,* ☎ *202/433–4882.* ☛ *Free.* ⊘ *Weekdays 9–4 (Memorial Day–Labor Day 9–5), weekends and holidays 10–5. Call ahead to schedule free weekday highlights tour.*

Paul E. Garber Facility. This collection of Smithsonian warehouses in suburban Maryland is where flight-related artifacts are stored and restored prior to their display at the National Air and Space Museum on the Mall. Among the 160 objects on view here are such historic craft as a Soviet MiG-15 from the Korean War and a Battle of Britain–era Hawker Hurricane IIC, as well as model satellites and assorted engines and propellers. A behind-the-scenes look at how the artifacts are preserved is included on the three-hour walking tour. Note: The tour is for ages 14 and up, and there is no heating or air-conditioning at the facility, so plan accordingly. *Old Silver Rd. at St. Barnabas Rd., Suitland, MD,* ☎ *202/357–1400. Free tours weekdays at 10 AM, weekends at 10 AM and 1 PM. Reservations required at least 3–8 wks in advance.*

Sasakawa Peace Foundation. This odd little gallery in D.C.'s downtown business district is bankrolled by a Japanese industrialist whose stated aim is to increase understanding between the United States and Japan. Contemporary Japanese and American artists show such work as ceramics, enamels, sculpture, and photographs. Visitors can also browse through a library of Japanese literature. Free videotapes on Japanese life are shown Thursday from noon to 2. *1819 L St. NW,* ☎ *202/296–6694.* ☛ *Free.* ☉ *Weekdays 10–6. Metro: Farragut North.*

Washington Dolls' House and Toy Museum. Founded in 1975 by a dollhouse historian, this compact museum contains a collection of American and imported dolls, dollhouses, toys, and games, most from the Victorian period. Miniature accessories, dollhouse kits, and antique toys and games are on sale in the museum's shops. *5236 44th St. NW,* ☎ *202/244–0024.* ☛ *$3 adults, $2 senior citizens, $1 children under 14.* ☉ *Tues.–Sat. 10–5, Sun. noon–5. Metro: Friendship Heights.*

Washington Navy Yard. The yard is the Navy's oldest shore establishment, authorized in 1799. The facility is now a supply and administrative center, but attractions you can tour, such as two military museums and a destroyer, make it a must-see for anyone interested in military history. *Metro: Eastern Market.*

Moored in the Anacostia River nearby and on permanent display is the *Barry,* a decommissioned U.S. Navy destroyer open for tours. ☎ *202/433–3377.* ☛ *Free.* ☉ *Mar.–Aug., daily 10–5; Sept.–Feb., daily 10–4.*

From June through August the Navy and Marines put on a multimedia Summer Pageant at an amphitheater across from the Navy Museum. For free reservations, call 202/433–2218.

SIGHTSEEING CHECKLISTS

Historic Buildings and Sites

This is a list of the principal buildings and sites mentioned in the Exploring section. For other attractions not listed here, *see* Off the Beaten Track, *above.*

American Red Cross (Tour 3). The neoclassical headquarters of the Red Cross. *Metro: Farragut West.*

Arlington National Cemetery (Tour 11). Among the notable people buried here are several Kennedys.

Anderson House (Tour 7). The headquarters of the Society of the Cincinnati, filled with trompe l'oeil paintings, Asian art, and military miniatures. *Metro: Dupont Circle.*

Blair House (Tour 3). Foreign dignitaries stay here when visiting the president. *Metro: McPherson Square.*

Bureau of Engraving and Printing (Tour 1). Visitors can take a self-guided tour through this huge building, where all the paper currency in the United States is printed.

Charles Sumner School (Tour 7). The Adolph Cluss–designed school, now home to administrative offices and galleries, was built for the education of black children. *Metro: Farragut North.*

Cox's Row (Tour 6). Fine examples of Federal architecture.

Customs House (Tour 6). Renaissance Revival–style Customs House is now a post office.

Decatur House (Tour 3). Federal- and Victorian-style home of naval hero Stephen Decatur. *Metro: McPherson Square.*

District (of Columbia) Building (Tour 5). Washington's mayor and city council toil in this beaux arts building. *Metro: Federal Triangle.*

Dumbarton House. (Tour 6). The Georgian headquarters of the National Society of Colonial Dames of America.

Evermay (Tour 6). An 1800 Georgian private manor house.

Folger Shakespeare Library (Tour 4). Items from the library's vast collection are often on display. *Metro: Capitol South.*

Ford's Theatre (Tour 5). The scene of Lincoln's assassination is still a working theater. *Metro: Metro Center.*

Heurich Mansion/Historical Society of Washington, D.C. (Tour 7). Beer baron's mansion houses a collection of Washingtoniana. *Metro: Dupont Circle.*

House of the Americas/Organization of American States (Tour 3). The United Nations of this hemisphere features a cooling interior fountain and atrium. *Metro: Farragut West.*

J. Edgar Hoover FBI Building (Tour 5). Exhibits on how agents solved cases and a live-ammo demonstration are part of this building's popular tour. *Metro: Federal Triangle.*

John F. Kennedy Center for the Performing Arts (Tour 8). The city's premier cultural center. *Metro: Foggy Bottom.*

Library of Congress, Jefferson Building (Tour 4). Holds some 90 million items in one of the most ornate spaces in town. *Metro: Capitol South.*

Martin Luther King Memorial Library (Tour 5). The only Ludwig Mies van der Rohe–designed building in the city and its largest public library. *Metro: Gallery Place.*

National Archives (Tour 5). The Declaration of Independence, Bill of Rights, and Constitution are displayed here. *Metro: Archives/Navy Memorial.*

Octagon House (Tour 3). The treaty ending the War of 1812 was signed here; now used for architectural exhibitions. *Metro: Farragut West.*

Old Executive Office Building (Tour 3). Executive branch offices in a building patterned after the Louvre. *Metro: Farragut West.*

Old Post Office Building (Tour 5). A pavilion of shops and restaurants with a scenic view from the clock tower. *Metro: Federal Triangle.*

Old Stone House (Tour 6). The oldest house in the city, with some parts dating from 1764.

Pentagon (Tour 11). The headquarters of the Department of Defense can be visited on a 75-minute tour.

Sewall-Belmont House (Tour 4). The early days of the women's movement are chronicled in this 1800 house. *Metro: Union Station.*

Supreme Court of the United States (Tour 4). The highest court in the land meets here October through June. *Metro: Capitol South.*

Treasury Building (Tour 3). Treasury Department headquarters. *Metro: McPherson Square.*

Union Station (Tour 4). Trains, shops, and restaurants are in this beautifully restored beaux arts station. *Metro: Union Station.*

United States Capitol (Tour 4). Congress meets here, surrounded by some of the city's finest art. *Metro: Capitol South or Union Station.*

White House (Tour 3). The most famous home in the country. *Metro: McPherson Square.*

Willard Hotel (Tour 5). An elegant 1901 hostelry. *Metro: Federal Triangle or Metro Center.*

Woodrow Wilson House (Tour 7). The 28th president retired here; today it's a museum to his accomplishments. *Metro: Dupont Circle.*

Museums and Galleries

The Smithsonian dominates the public museum and gallery scene in Washington, but there are also many private art galleries that show and sell the work of local, national, and international artists. These galleries are concentrated near Dupont Circle, in Georgetown, and on 7th Street north of Pennsylvania Avenue. For an overview of the day's events at Smithsonian museums, call **Dial-a-Museum** (☎ 202/357–2020).

Art Museum of the Americas (Tour 3). The work of contemporary Latin American artists is shown in this gallery behind the Organization of American States. *Metro: Farragut West.*

Arts and Industries Building (Tour 1). This Smithsonian museum features a re-creation of an 1876 Centennial exhibition. *Metro: Smithsonian.*

Australian Embassy (Tour 7). Aboriginal and antipodean art are on display. *Metro: Dupont Circle.*

B'nai B'rith Klutznick Museum (Tour 7). Works by Jewish artists are on display. *Metro: Farragut North.*

Canadian Embassy (Tour 5). The embassy hosts concerts and exhibits of Canadian art. *Metro: Archives/Navy Memorial.*

Corcoran Gallery of Art (Tour 3). This venerable Washington institution boasts a strong collection of European and American art and photography. *Metro: Farragut West.*

Daughters of the American Revolution Museum (Tour 3). America's Colonial past is explored at this museum. *Metro: Farragut West.*

Department of the Interior Museum (Tour 3). A quaint museum outlines the accomplishments of this agency. *Metro: Farragut West.*

Dumbarton Oaks (Tour 6). Harvard University administers two world-class museums of Byzantine art and pre-Columbian artifacts.

Explorers Hall/National Geographic Society (Tour 7). Geography and the natural world are the focus of the famous magazine's museum. *Metro: Farragut North.*

Freer Gallery of Art (Tour 1). Asian art and James McNeill Whistler's stunning *Peacock Room* highlight this Smithsonian museum. *Metro: Smithsonian.*

Joseph H. Hirshhorn Museum and Sculpture Garden (Tour 1). Modern art is housed in this circular building; the sculpture garden holds one of the largest public collections of works by Henry Moore. *Metro: Smithsonian.*

National Air and Space Museum (Tour 1). The city's most popular museum has everything from the Wright Brothers' *Flyer* to a model of the USS *Enterprise* from "Star Trek." *Metro: Smithsonian.*

National Aquarium (Tour 5). The oldest public aquarium in the country. *Metro: Federal Triangle.*

National Building Museum (Tour 5). Museum on architecture and the building arts. *Metro: Judiciary Square.*

National Gallery of Art (Tour 1). One of the world's best collections of art. *Metro: Archives.*

National Museum of African Art (Tour 1). Carvings, textile, and jewelry from sub-Saharan Africa are on display. *Metro: Smithsonian.*

National Museum of American Art (Tour 5). The collection stretches from the earliest days of American art through such lights of modernism as Jasper Johns and Robert Rauschenberg. *Metro: Gallery Place.*

National Museum of American History (Tour 1). The history of the country is traced in this Smithsonian museum. *Metro: Smithsonian.*

National Museum of American Jewish History (Tour 7). A collection of mostly military memorabilia. *Metro: Dupont Circle.*

National Museum of Natural History (Tour 1). The Hope Diamond is just one of the attractions at this most diverse Smithsonian museum. *Metro: Smithsonian.*

National Museum of Women in the Arts (Tour 5). Just what the name implies, in a beautifully restored building. *Metro: Metro Center.*

National Portrait Gallery (Tour 5). Likenesses of famous Americans and portraits of every U.S. president are on display here. *Metro: Gallery Place.*

National Postal Museum (Tour 4). The newest Smithsonian museum in Washington celebrates stamps and more. *Metro: Union Station.*

Phillips Collection (Tour 7). The collection includes works by Cézanne and O'Keeffe and Renoir's *Luncheon of the Boating Party. Metro: Dupont Circle.*

Renwick Gallery (Tour 3). This Smithsonian museum is devoted to American arts and crafts. *Metro: McPherson Square.*

Sackler Gallery (Tour 1). Treasures from the Orient are part of this Smithsonian museum's collection. *Metro: Smithsonian.*

Smithsonian Institution Castle (Tour 1). The Smithsonian's information center. *Metro: Smithsonian.*

Textile Museum (Tour 7). Oriental rugs, Coptic textiles, pre-Columbian weavings, and modern fiber art are on display here. *Metro: Dupont Circle.*

United States Holocaust Memorial Museum (Tour 1). The story of the Holocaust is told at this new museum. *Metro: Smithsonian.*

Washington Project for the Arts (Tour 5). The works of area artists are shown at this gallery. The bookstore is a favorite with local bohemians. *Metro stops: National Archives or Gallery Place.*

Churches, Temples, and Mosques

All Souls' Unitarian Church. The design of this church, erected in 1924, is based on that of St. Martin-in-the-Fields in London. *16th and Harvard Sts. NW,* ☎ *202/332–5266.*

Franciscan Monastery and Gardens. Not far from the **Shrine of the Immaculate Conception,** this Byzantine-style monastery contains facsimiles of such Holy-land shrines as the Grotto of Bethlehem and the Holy Sepulcher. Underground are reproductions of the catacombs of Rome. The gardens are especially beautiful, planted with roses that bloom in the summer. *14th and Quincy Sts. NE,* ☎ *202/526–6800.* ☉ *Daily 9–5. Tours of catacombs on the hr (except noon) Mon.–Sat. 9–4, Sun. 1–4. Metro: Brookland–Catholic University.*

Grace Episcopal Church (Tour 6).

Islamic Mosque and Cultural Center. The Muslim faithful are called to prayer five times a day from atop this mosque's 162-foot-high minaret. Each May, the Muslim Women's Association sponsors a bazaar, with crafts, clothing, and food for sale. *2551 Massachusetts Ave. NW,* ☎ *202/332–8343. Center open daily 10–5; mosque open for all 5 prayers, dawn–past sunset. Shorts are not permitted and women must wear scarves to cover their heads.*

Metropolitan African Methodist Episcopal Church. Completed in 1886, this Gothic-style church became one of the most influential black churches in the city. Abolitionist orator Frederick Douglass worshiped here and Bill Clinton chose the church as the setting for his inaugural prayer service. *1518 M St. NW,* ☎ *202/331–1426. Metro: Farragut North.*

Mt. Zion United Methodist Church (Tour 6).

National Shrine of the Immaculate Conception. This is the largest Catholic church in the United States, begun in 1920 and built with funds contributed by every parish in the country. Dedicated in 1959, the shrine is a blend of Romanesque and Byzantine styles, with a bell tower that reminds many of St. Mark's in Venice. *Michigan Ave. and 4th St. NE,* ☎ *202/526–8300.* ☉ *Apr.–Oct., daily 7–7; Nov.–Mar., daily 7–6. Sunday mass at 7:30, 9, 10:30, noon, 1:30 (in Latin), and 4:30. Metro: Brookland–Catholic University.*

Old Adas Israel Synagogue (Tour 5).

St. John's Episcopal Church (Tour 3). *Metro: McPherson Square.*

St. Matthew's Cathedral (Tour 7). *Metro: Farragut North.*

St. Sophia Cathedral. This Greek Orthodox cathedral is noted for the handsome mosaic work on the interior of its dome. Saint Sophia holds a festival of Greek food and crafts each May and October. *Massachusetts Ave. and 36th St. NW,* ☎ *202/333–4730.*

Scottish Rite Temple. This dramatic Masonic shrine is patterned after the Mausoleum of Halicarnassus. Tours available weekdays 8–2. *1733 16th St. NW, ☎ 202/232–3579.*

★ **Washington National Cathedral.** Construction of this stunning Gothic church—the sixth-largest cathedral in the world—started in 1907 and was finished on September 30, 1990, when the cathedral was consecrated. Like its 14th-century counterparts, the National Cathedral (officially Washington's Cathedral Church of St. Peter and St. Paul) has a nave, flying buttresses, transepts, and vaults that were built stone by stone. It is adorned with fanciful gargoyles created by skilled stone carvers. The tomb of Woodrow Wilson, the only president buried in Washington, is on the south side of the nave. The expansive view of the city from the Pilgrim Gallery is exceptional. The cathedral is under the governance of the Episcopal church but has played host to services of many denominations. *Wisconsin and Massachusetts Aves. NW, ☎ 202/537–6200. ☉ Fall, winter, and spring, daily 10–4:30; May 1–Labor Day, weekdays 10–9, weekends 10–4:30. Sun. services at 8, 9, 10, 11, 6:30; evensong at 4 PM. Tours Mon.–Sat. 10–3:15, Sun. 12:30–2:45; suggested donation $2 adults, $1 children. Tour information: ☎ 202/537–6207.*

Temple of the Church of Jesus Christ of Latter-Day Saints. This striking Mormon temple in suburban Maryland—one of its white towers is topped with a golden statue of the Mormon angel and prophet, Moroni—has become a Washington landmark. It is closed to non-Mormons, but a visitor center offers a lovely view of the white-marble church and has a film about the temple and what takes place inside. Tulips, dogwoods, and azaleas bloom in the 57-acre grounds each spring. In December, Washingtonians enjoy the Festival of Lights—300,000 of them—and a live nativity. *9900 Stoneybrook Dr., Kensington, MD, ☎ 301/587–0144. Grounds and visitor center open daily 10–9.*

Statues and Monuments

Washington, perhaps more than any other city in the United States, is filled with allegorical outdoor art. Examples can be found in the middle of traffic circles and on dozens of neoclassical public buildings. *The Outdoor Sculpture of Washington, DC,* by architectural historian James M. Goode, provides readable histories of the well-known and little-known works to be found in the nation's capital.

Albert Einstein (Tour 8). *Metro: Foggy Bottom.*

Alexander Hamilton (Tour 3). *Metro: Federal Triangle.*

Andrew Jackson (Tour 3). *Metro: McPherson Square.*

The Awakening. Children love this giant sculpture of a bearded man emerging from the ground near Hains Point. Adults are captivated, too. *Hains Point, East Potomac Park.*

Baron von Steuben (Tour 3). *Metro: McPherson Square.*

Bartholdi Fountain (Tour 4). *Metro: Federal Center SW.*

Boy Scouts Memorial. Just east of the Ellipse stands this group of heroic statuary: a uniformed Boy Scout flanked by a male figure representing patriotism and a female figure who holds the light of faith. *East of the Ellipse, near 15th St. NW. Metro: McPherson Square.*

Columbus Memorial Fountain (Tour 4). *Metro: Union Station.*

Confederate Statue (Tour 12).

Count de Rochambeau (Tour 3). *Metro: McPherson Square.*

Dumbarton Bridge (Tour 7). *Metro: Dupont Circle.*

Dupont Circle/Fountain (Tour 7). *Metro: Dupont Circle.*

Franklin Delano Roosevelt Memorial (Tour 5). *Metro: Archives.*

Freedmen's Memorial. This bronze statue of Abraham Lincoln standing above a newly freed slave who has just broken his chains was dedicated on April 14, 1876, the 11th anniversary of the president's assassination. Money for its construction was donated by hundreds of ex-slaves. *Lincoln Park, Massachusetts Ave. between 11th and 13th Sts. NE.*

General Casimir Pulaski (Tour 5). *Metro: Federal Triangle.*

General William Tecumseh Sherman Monument (Tour 3). *Metro: Federal Triangle.*

General Winfield Scott (Tour 5), *Metro: Archives/Navy Memorial;* (Tour 7), *Metro: Dupont Circle.*

Grand Army of the Republic (Tour 5). *Metro: Archives/Navy Memorial.*

Grant Memorial (Tour 4). *Metro: Federal Center SW.*

James Garfield Memorial (Tour 4). *Metro: Capitol South.*

Jefferson Memorial (Tour 2).

John F. Kennedy (Tour 8). *Metro: Foggy Bottom.*

Lincoln Memorial (Tour 2).

Marine Corps War Memorial (Tour 11). *Metro: Arlington Cemetery.*

Marquis de Lafayette (Tour 3). *Metro: McPherson Square.*

National Law Enforcement Officers Memorial (Tour 5). *Metro: Judiciary Square.*

Navy Memorial (Tour 5). *Metro: Archives.*

Peace Monument (Tour 4). *Metro: Union Station.*

The Peace of God that Passeth Understanding. Henry Adams commissioned Augustus Saint-Gaudens to create this memorial to Adams's wife, who had committed suicide. Known by the nickname "Grief," this figure of a shroud-draped woman is thought by many to be the most moving sculpture in the city. *In Rock Creek Cemetery, Rock Creek Rd. and Webster St. NW.*

Temperance Fountain (Tour 5). *Metro: Archives/Navy Memorial.*

Thaddeus Kosciuszko (Tour 3). *Metro: McPherson Square.*

Vietnam Veterans Memorial (Tour 2). *Metro: Foggy Bottom.*

Vietnam Women's Memorial (Tour 2). *Metro: Foggy Bottom.*

Washington Monument (Tour 2). *Metro: Federal Triangle or Smithsonian.*

Zoos

National Aquarium (Tour 5). Housed in the Department of Commerce Building and featuring tropical and freshwater fish, this is the nation's oldest public aquarium. *Metro: Federal Triangle.*

National Zoological Park (Tour 9). One of the foremost zoos in the world, the 160-acre zoo is known for its giant panda, Hsing-Hsing, and its ambitious Amazonian ecosystem. Many animals are shown in naturalistic settings. *Metro: Cleveland Park or Woodley Park/Zoo.*

3 Washington for Children

By John F. Kelly

Updated by
Mary Case

IT'S EASY TO PIGEONHOLE WASHINGTON as the archetypal grown-up place. After all, running the government of the most important country in the world is serious stuff. But the city that has the White House, the Capitol, and the Supreme Court also has the National Museum of Natural History, the Capital Children's Museum, and the National Zoo, three places children especially love. And while not every kid is wowed by the Jefferson Memorial, there hasn't been one born yet who won't enjoy a ride to the top of the Washington Monument. What's more, history that seems dry and dusty in the classroom comes alive for children in Washington, as they visit the landmarks they've seen on the evening news. And in this age of belt-tightening, the capital has one more thing going for it: most of the attractions are free.

Despite its kid-friendliness, Washington isn't bursting at the seams with hotels and restaurants that cater to families. It's not that they don't like kids; it's just that they're more accustomed to catering to their parents. Most hotels can help find a baby-sitter though, and at some time during your stay you'll probably want to take advantage of the sitting services, because for Washingtonians a night out at a fashionable eatery is usually a night away from the kids—their own and other peoples'.

Even adults can get tired traipsing around the large Smithsonian museums, so a stroller is a good idea for younger kids who may wear out easily (and the parents who'd then have to carry them). Keep in mind, though, that you'll have to leave your stroller at the entrances to the White House and the Washington Monument.

For kid-oriented fare, consult the Friday *Washington Post* "Weekend" section. Its "Carousel" listings include information on plays, puppet shows, concerts, story-telling sessions, nature programs, and other events for families. And if you find yourself stuck in traffic in a rental car, tune to WKDL, 1050 AM. The first radio station just for families in the Washington area, WKDL has music and features of interest to children and their parents.

Exploring

Pierre L'Enfant didn't design Washington's Mall with children in mind, but his central monumental core couldn't be better for them. With most of the Smithsonian museums arranged around it, and the Washington Monument and Tidal Basin a few steps away, it should be every family's base camp. Even its name can help parents coax reluctant children out for a day of sightseeing: Just tell them you're going "to the Mall."

Many of Washington's museums have exhibits designed especially for—or appealing especially to—children. On the Mall are the **Discovery Room, Dinosaur Hall,** and **O. Orkin Insect Zoo** at the **National Museum of Natural History** and the **Hands On History Room** and **Hands On Science Room** at the **National Museum of American History.** Just about everything at the **National Air and Space Museum** is cool to kids. There's an old-time carousel in front of the **Arts and Industries Building.** You know when there are kids at the **Navy Museum** because the sound of the submarine dive Klaxon reverberates through its halls. (Children love to push it and look through the museum's operating periscopes.) The **Touch Tank** at the **National Aquarium** is usually thronged by future ichthyologists, and the **National Geographic Explorers**

Hall is an interactive museum that tests youngsters' knowledge of Planet Earth.

Many Washington museums have special printed children's guides to their collections, allowing kids to, for example, take pencil in hand and go on "scavenger hunts" to pick out the shapes and patterns in a work of modern art. Ask at the information desks.

The following Smithsonian museums have **diaper-changing facilities** in both men's and women's rooms: the Smithsonian Castle, the Freer Gallery, the Hirshhorn Museum, the National Museum of Natural History, the National Museum of American History, the National Air and Space Museum, the Renwick Gallery, and the National Museum of American Art. Metro stations have no rest rooms at all.

Here are some other attractions tailor-made for family visits.

Museums, Monuments, and Exhibits

Bureau of Engraving and Printing (*see* Tour 1 *in* Chapter 2, Exploring Washington). Any kid who gets an allowance will enjoy watching money roll off the presses here. *Metro: Smithsonian.*

Capital Children's Museum. A former convent three blocks from Union Station is the site of this sprawling, decidedly hands-on museum. Everything is at kid level and just about everything is meant to be touched. That means children may take apart old typewriters, make Mexican hot chocolate, create their own old-time animations, weave their way through a maze, and fill a room with huge soap bubbles. Volunteer docents guide children and parents to different activity areas and oversee their young charges as they engage in such play as cooking tortillas or making paper flowers. The museum strives to show how people in other cultures live, so there is an international flavor to many of the exhibits. Unlike the glitzier Smithsonian offerings, this museum seems a bit frayed around the edges. But it's a comfortable sort of wear and tear, achieved through the inquisitive hands of countless young visitors, and it makes the Capital Children's Museum seem like one huge playroom. *800 3rd St. NE,* ☎ *202/543–8600.* ☛ *$6, children under 2 free.* ☉ *Daily 10–5. Closed Thanksgiving, Dec. 25, Jan. 1, Easter. Metro: Union Station.*

DAR Museum (*see* Tour 3 *in* Chapter 2, Exploring Washington). Exhibits frequently explore how families lived in Colonial times. Youngsters may not be entranced by all the displays, but they'll love the free "Colonial Adventure" tours that are usually held the first and third Sundays of the month. Costumed docents lead children ages five to seven through the museum, explaining the exhibits and describing life in Colonial America. Make reservations at least 10 days in advance by calling 202/879–3239. *Metro: Farragut West.*

The National Zoo (*see* Tour 9 *in* Chapter 2, Exploring Washington). One of the nation's best zoos is a must-see for families. Rental strollers are available for when little legs wear out. *Metro: Cleveland Park, Woodley Park/National Zoo.*

Washington Dolls' House and Toy Museum (*see* Off the Beaten Track *in* Chapter 2, Exploring Washington). Antique toys and doll houses are on display, and accessories and kits are available for purchase. Most of the collection is behind glass, disappointing younger visitors; older kids will enjoy it more. *Metro: Friendship Heights.*

The Washington Monument (*see* Tour 2 *in* Chapter 2, Exploring Washington). You can't really say you've been to Washington until you've taken in the view from atop this 555-foot-tall obelisk. *Metro: Federal Triangle, Smithsonian.*

Shopping

Young visitors to Washington can leave with a lot more than they came with, from souvenir T-shirts to paper models of the White House. Shoppers shouldn't overlook the merchandise on the Mall. The Smithsonian museums have creatively stocked shops, and many of the items have the benefit of actually being educational.

Favorite Smithsonian shops include those in the **National Museum of American History** (books, games), the **National Museum of Natural History** (dinosaur models, stuffed animals), and the **National Air and Space Museum.** The last is where you'll find something kids seem incapable of resisting: astronauts' freeze-dried ice cream sandwiches in foil pouches. (Warning to grown-ups: They're messy and not particularly tasty.)

As for more traditional finds, there's **F.A.O. Schwarz,** the upscale toy store; the **Kid's Closet,** a children's clothing store in downtown D.C.; and the **Cheshire Cat,** a bookstore just for children (*see* Chapter 4, Shopping). The Cheshire Cat also has occasional reading and story-telling sessions, and well-known children's book authors sometimes stop by to meet their readers.

The Great Train Store (Union Station, 40 Massachusetts Ave. NE, ☎ 202/371–2881) has all manner of train sets, engineers' hats, and other choo-choo-related toys and memorabilia. **Al's Magic Shop** (1012 Vermont Ave. NW, ☎ 202/789–2800) has been catering to both magicians and pranksters for more than 50 years. **All Wound-Up** (Pavilion at Old Post Office, 1100 Pennsylvania Ave. NW, ☎ 202/842–0635) sells scores of wind-up toys, model cars, and stuffed animals. Right next door, **Juggling Capitol** (☎ 202/789–1799) has everything juggling klutzes and experienced clowns might need. At the **ReUse** store (418 S. Washington St., Alexandria, VA, ☎ 703/549–0111) you'll find scraps of wood, old egg cartons, empty coffee cans, bits of yarn, bags of bottle caps, and other cast-off items designed to be recycled into children's art projects. Kids who want to pretend they're famous can get their likeness computer-superimposed on the cover of *National Geographic* (at **National Geographic Explorers Hall,** 17th and M Sts. NW, ☎ 202/857–7689) or on a postage stamp, a $100 bill, or Mount Rushmore (at the **National Museum of American History,** 12th St. and Constitution Ave. NW, ☎ 202/357–2700).

Parks and Playgrounds

Washington prides itself on the trees that line its streets, and that green thumb extends to the city's parks. You won't need to venture far to find a patch of grass for running on or a pool of water for dipping hot feet into.

The biggest stretch of parkland is Rock Creek Park (*see* The Outdoors *in* Chapter 5, Sports and the Outdoors). Start at the **Nature Center** (5200 Glover Rd. NW, ☎ 202/426–6829), where easily hiked trails lead off in all directions. There's a small room filled with pelts, bones, feathers, and shells for naturalists-in-training to handle, and another with stuffed animals representative of the mid-Atlantic. On weekends, rangers lead nature walks, show and discuss live animals, and present films. The center's 70-seat planetarium introduces young visitors to the night sky at 1 PM, with a show for ages four and up, and at 4 PM, with a show for ages seven and up. Children also like the falling water of **Pierce Mill** (Tilden St. and Park Rd. NW), where rangers grind grain into flour.

Running parallel to the Potomac is the Chesapeake & Ohio (C&O) Canal, a favorite spot for jogging and bicycling. Kids especially like the **mule-drawn barge rides,** which depart spring through early autumn from Georgetown, and the Great Falls Tavern Visitors Center on the Maryland side of the C&O Canal National Historic Park (*see* The Outdoors *in* Chapter 5, Sports and the Outdoors).

There's a small play area close to the Capitol: The **judicial office building beside Union Station** (2nd and E Sts. NE) has a modest but choice selection of play equipment behind it. The new type of playground—with lots of tubes and bridges—hasn't found its way into Washington yet, but there are two in suburban Maryland worth a trip. Both **Cabin John Regional Park** (7400 Tuckerman La., Rockville, MD, ☎ 301/299–4555) and **Wheaton Regional Park** (2000 Shorefield Rd., Wheaton, MD, ☎ 301/946–7033) boast modern, terraced playgrounds with corkscrewing plastic slides, bouncing wooden bridges, sandboxes, and mazes. A bonus: Both have ice rinks and trains that operate seasonally, and there's even a carousel at Wheaton. Several members of the **Discovery Zone** franchise family have recently opened in the Maryland and Virginia suburbs. These indoor fitness centers are loaded with tunnels, ball bins, padded cubes and mats, and much more, all designed to let kids under 12 climb, jump, run, and basically go wild in their stocking feet. The cost is about $7 for two hours of play. Those closest to downtown D.C.—about 10 miles—are at White Flint Mall (3rd Floor, 11301 Rockville Pike, North Bethesda, MD, ☎ 301/231–0505) and Skyline Mall (5195-A Leesburg Pike, Falls Church, VA, ☎ 703/379–6900).

Kite fliers can be found most windy weekends near the Washington Monument grounds. (Buy a kite at the National Air and Space Museum if you want to join them.) One of the oldest **miniature golf courses** in the country operates during the summer in East Potomac Park (see The Outdoors *in* Chapter 5, Sports and the Outdoors). **City Golf** is an indoor course at the Old Post Office Pavilion (1100 Pennsylvania Ave. NW, ☎ 202/898–7888). A good way to tire out rambunctious offspring is to set them adrift in the **Tidal Basin** (*see* Tour 2 *in* Chapter 2, Exploring Washington) at the helm of a paddleboat.

Young Paul Wylies and Nancy Kerrigans can practice their moves at two **ice rinks** close to the Mall: **The Sculpture Garden Outdoor Rink** (Constitution Ave. between 7th and 9th Sts. NW, ☎ 202/371–5340) and the **Pershing Park Ice Rink** (Pennsylvania Ave. between 14th and 15th Sts. NW, ☎ 202/737–6938). Rental skates are available. Both rinks operate seasonally.

There are no beaches in Washington, but **Wild World** (13710 Central Ave., Largo, MD, ☎ 301/249–1500) is a 115-acre water theme park in suburban Maryland that operates late May through August. It has a wave pool, a roller coaster, children's rides, and water slides.

Dining

When Washingtonians go out for a nice meal at a trendy downtown restaurant they usually leave the kids at home. That doesn't mean you need to check your children at the door, just that you shouldn't be surprised if you're one of the few obvious parents in attendance, especially in such neighborhoods as Adams-Morgan and Dupont Circle, where the restaurants cater to a young, single crowd. Most restaurants, however, stock booster seats and high chairs for kids who need a lift, and well-behaved babies are generally fawned upon wherever they go.

Inside the Beltway

For your own peace of mind you might want to eat somewhere with a loud dining room (the well-reviewed **Red Sage** and **Primi Piatti** have noisy atmospheres) or at just about any Chinese restaurant (whose staffs seem especially tolerant of children).

Some other suggestions: **The American Cafe** chain, with many locations in the Washington area (*see* Chapter 6, Dining), has been keeping parents sane since it opened in 1979, with a children's menu kids can draw on (crayons provided). **Hamburger Hamlet** (5225 Wisconsin Ave. NW, ☎ 202/244–2037) also lets kids express themselves on place mats. **T. G. I. Friday's** (2100 Pennsylvania Ave. NW, ☎ 202/872–4344) is a down-to-earth restaurant offering hearty American fare; children's portions are available. **Geppetto** (2917 M St. NW, ☎ 202/333–2602) is an Italian restaurant with irresistible carved marionettes as part of the decor. **Swensen's** (4200 Wisconsin Ave. NW, ☎ 202/244–5544) prides itself on being a family restaurant and scoops up its own brand of ice cream for dessert. Teens and teens-in-training might enjoy the music and memorabilia of the **Hard Rock Cafe** (999 E St. NW, ☎ 202/737–7625) and the movie costumes and set pieces of **Planet Hollywood** (1101 Pennsylvania Ave. NW, ☎ 202/783–7827). For fast food a shade more interesting than hamburgers and fries, check out the food courts at Washington's three main malls: **Union Station** (50 Massachusetts Ave. NW), **The Shops at National Place** (13th and F Sts. NW), and **The Pavilion at the Old Post Office** (12th St. and Pennsylvania Ave. NW).

Suburban Washington

Restaurants in the suburbs are generally kid friendlier, with a few standouts. **The Calvert Grille** (3106 Mount Vernon Ave., Alexandria, VA, ☎ 703/836–8425), specializing in barbecued baby-back ribs, seats families in a back room that's equipped with toys and butcher paper so kids can draw on the tables. The often crowded '50s-style, meat-and-potatoes **Silver Diner** (11806 Rockville Pike, Rockville, MD, ☎ 301/770–2828) has a basket of crayons and a pile of connect-the-dot place mats at the cash register. Travelers on a budget should check out **Chili's** (11428-A Rockville Pike, Rockville, MD, ☎ 301/881–8588), where anything on the children's menu is $1 on weekends. And for interactive dining for the Nintendo generation, there's **Chuck E. Cheese** (several locations, including 6303 Richmond Hwy., Alexandria, VA, ☎ 703/660–6800).

Lodging

Washington has hotels for everyone, from the sightseer on a budget to the big spender on a junket. Luckily for families, children under 16 stay free in most hotels. Here are some things to keep in mind when deciding on lodging with the little ones: Staying at an all-suite hotel will allow you to spread out and, if you prepare your meals in a kitchenette, keep costs down. A pool may be essential for a stay with kids; game rooms are a plus. Major convention hotels, and those on Capitol Hill and the waterfront, don't see as many families as those downtown, in Foggy Bottom, uptown, or in the Maryland and Virginia suburbs. The closer you are to a Metro stop, the quicker you'll be able to hit the sightseeing trail.

Hotels that families should consider include the **Omni Shoreham**, which features a weekend matinee cabaret for children, and the **Sher-**

aton Washington; both are within walking distance of the National Zoo. The **Days Inn Connecticut Avenue** is away from the bustle of downtown, but only one Metro stop from the zoo. Several all-suite hotels are clustered in Foggy Bottom, including the **Embassy Suites** and two **Guest Quarters** hotels. In Georgetown, **Georgetown Suites** is spacious and reasonably priced.

Baby-Sitting Services

Most larger hotels and those with concierges can arrange baby-sitting with one of Washington's licensed, bonded child-care agencies. Rates are usually per hour, with a four-hour minimum, and you may need to pay the sitter's transportation costs. The average cost is around $10 an hour for one child, with additional children about $1 more per hour; some agencies charge more to sit for additional nonrelated children. Most agencies are happy to provide references, and some sitters will even take kids sightseeing. A tip: Though most agencies can arrange last-minute child care, they appreciate as much notice as you can give them.

WeeSit (10681 Oak Thrust Ct., Burke, VA 22015, ☎ 703/764–1542) works with many of the city's largest hotels. **Chevy Chase Babysitters** (10771 Middleboro Dr., Damascus, MD 20872, ☎ 301/942–2931) has been in business since 1960. **Mothers' Aides Inc.** (Box 7088, Fairfax Station, VA 22039, ☎ 703/250–0700) counts schoolteachers among its sitters. **Helpers Plus Inc.** (4700 Auth Pl., Suite 401, Camp Springs, MD 20746, ☎ 301/894–7200) employs certified nursing assistants.

The Arts

Washington has a lively arts scene for young and old alike. The museum community and the Kennedy Center serve as a mecca for traveling troupes, and the home-grown talent isn't bad either, with children's concerts and plays staple entertainment for many a Washington family. Museums often host programs related to their exhibitions—African trickster stories at the National Museum of African Art, for example—and "serious" groups such as the National Symphony Orchestra and the Washington Chamber Symphony have special programs to woo young fans.

Check the "Carousel" listings in the *Washington Post* "Weekend" section for special events that crop up during the year. For example, the **Ringling Bros. and Barnum & Bailey Circus** usually moves into the D.C. Armory for two weeks each April, and Wolf Trap Farm Park hosts the three-day **International Children's Festival,** with performers from around the world, each Labor Day weekend.

The **Kennedy Center** (☎ 202/467–4600) is the setting for more than 80 family events each year, including the two-day **Imagination Celebration** each April. Year-round offerings include dance, music, storytelling, plays, and concerts for prekindergarten to eighth-grade kids. It's also the home base of the **National Symphony Orchestra,** whose Family Concerts are for children as young as three. Other concerts, which include "instrument petting zoos," are for youngsters six and up.

The **Hirshhorn Museum** (7th St. and Independence Ave. SW, ☎ 202/357–2700) screens free children's movies and cartoons most Saturday mornings at 11.

Adventure Theater (7300 MacArthur Blvd., Glen Echo, MD, ☎ 301/320–5331) produces such traditional plays and musicals as *Charlotte's Web, Robin Hood,* and *Aesop's Fables* weekends year-round at Glen Echo Park. Plays are aimed at children ages 4 to 12 and are presented in a 192-seat theater. The audience sits on carpeted steps, perfect for sprawling families. Reservations are suggested.

Discovery Theater (900 Jefferson Dr. SW, ☎ 202/357–1500), in the west hall of the Smithsonian's Arts and Industries Building, is the setting for plays, puppet shows, and storytellers October through June. Most presentations are for those in preschool through second grade, but some offerings are for children as old as 12.

Now This! (Omni Shoreham Hotel, Marquee Lounge, 2500 Calvert St. NW, ☎ 202/745–1023) is a musical-comedy improvisation group that brings things down to kid level for Saturday matinees. Children shout out suggestions to help the actors keep the show rolling.

At the **Puppet Co. Playhouse** (7300 MacArthur Blvd., Glen Echo, MD, ☎ 301/320–6668) in Glen Echo Park, skilled puppeteers manipulate marionettes in classic plays and stories.

Saturday Morning at the National (1321 Pennsylvania Ave. NW, ☎ 202/783–3372) is a performance series for youngsters that has featured such acts as mimes, puppet shows, dance troupes, magicians, and children's theater groups. The performances are free, on a first-come, first-seated basis, at the National Theatre, Saturdays at 9:30 AM and 11 AM from October through March.

The **Washington Chamber Symphony** (☎ 202/452–1321) turns children on to classical music by providing workbooks, bringing kids on stage, marching the orchestra down the aisles, or having kids sing along with the proceedings. Its "Family Series" programs are for children as young as four; "Concerts for Young People" are for ages six and up. Most performances are at the Kennedy Center.

A few suburban dinner theaters have children's weekend matinees to supplement their nighttime adult offerings. The plays—such favorites as *Jack and the Beanstalk, Little Red Riding Hood,* and *Beauty and the Beast*—usually include lunch or a snack. Among the theaters: **West End Dinner Theatre** (4615 Duke St., Alexandria, VA, ☎ 703/370–2500) and **Burn Brae Dinner Theatre** (U.S. 29 at Blackburn Rd., Burtonsville, MD, ☎ 301/384–5800).

4 Shopping

By Deborah
Papier

Updated by
Mary Case

ONCE A SHOPPING TRIP in the Washington area really was a trip—a long trek to one of the suburban shopping malls, which offered far more than could be found in town. It is still true that some major national retailers have bypassed the city, so that a visitor wanting to check out Bloomingdale's, Nordstrom, or Macy's has to venture to Montgomery Mall or White Flint Mall in Bethesda, Maryland (the latter near the White Flint Metro), the twin megamalls in Tysons Corner, Virginia (reachable by bus but not by subway), or the Fashion Centre mall at Pentagon City (Metro: Pentagon City). In recent years, however, the city's own shopping scene has been revitalized. Although some longtime retailers have gone bankrupt, Filene's Basement (the Boston-based upscale fashion discounter) has moved in to fill the gap left by Raleighs' departure, and the remaining department stores have upgraded both their facilities and their merchandise. Many of the smaller one-of-a-kind shops have managed to survive urban renewal, designer boutiques are increasing, and interesting specialty shops and minimalls are popping up all over town. Weekdays downtown, street vendors offer a funky mix of jewelry, brightly patterned ties, buyer-beware watches, sunglasses, and African-inspired clothing, accessories, and art. Of course, T-shirts and Capital City souvenirs are always in plentiful supply, especially on the streets ringing *the* Mall.

On the discount scene, several major outlet centers are within 45 minutes of the city (including Potomac Mills, the mile-long mall off I–95 that bills itself as Virginia's leading tourist attraction); closer to the District, the off-price Nordstrom Rack and other discount shops are clustered in City Place mall, which opened in 1992 in downtown Silver Spring, Maryland (Metro: Silver Spring).

Store hours vary greatly, so it is safest to call ahead. In general, Georgetown stores are open late and on Sunday; stores downtown that cater to office workers close at 6 PM and may not be open at all on Saturday or Sunday. Some stores extend their hours on Thursday.

Sales tax is 6%, and the major credit cards are accepted virtually everywhere.

Shopping Districts

Georgetown remains Washington's favorite shopping area. Though it is not on a subway line, and parking is impossible, people still flock here. The attraction (aside from the lively street scene) is the profusion of specialty shops in a charming, historic neighborhood. In addition to tony antiques, elegant crafts, and high-style shoe and clothing boutiques, the area offers wares that attract students and other less-well-heeled shoppers: books, music, and fashions from popular chain stores, such as the Gap and Benetton.

The hub of Georgetown is the intersection of Wisconsin Avenue and M Street, with most of the stores lying to the east and west on M Street and to the north on Wisconsin. Near that intersection, at 3222 M Street NW, is **Georgetown Park** (☎ 202/298–5577), a three-level mall that looks like a Victorian ice-cream parlor inside. The pricey clothing and accessory boutiques and ubiquitous chain stores (Victoria's Secret) in the posh mall draw international tourists in droves. Next door to the mall, New York City's premier gourmet food store, Dean & Deluca (3276 M St. NW, ☎ 202/342–2500), attracts visitors and residents alike.

Dupont Circle has some of the same flavor as Georgetown. Here, too, there is a lively mix of shops and restaurants, with most of the action on the major artery of Connecticut Avenue. There are many book and record stores in the neighborhood, as well as stores selling coffees, stationery, and bric-a-brac. The street scene here is grittier than Georgetown's, with fewer teens and older shoppers and more twentysomethings and thirtysomethings.

In **Adams-Morgan,** scattered among the dozens of Latin, Ethiopian, and Caribbean restaurants in this most bohemian of Washington neighborhoods, are a score of the city's most eccentric shops. It's a minefield of quality, but great fun for the bargain hunter. A word of caution—call ahead to verify hours. Adams-Morganites are often not clock-watchers, but you can be sure a weekend afternoon stroll will find a good representation of the shops open and a great few hours of browsing. Most of the shops are on 18th Street NW, between Columbia Road and California Avenue.

The city's department stores can be found in the "new" downtown. Its fulcrum is **Metro Center,** which spans 11th and 12th streets NW along G Street. The Metro Center subway stop takes you directly into the basements of downtown's two major department stores, Woodward & Lothrop, familiarly called "Woodies," and Hecht's. Take the 11th and G streets exit to Woodies; for Hecht's, follow the signs to the 12th or 13th street exits.

The Shops at National Place (by Metro Center, 13th and F Sts. NW, ☎ 202/783–9090), takes up three levels, one of which is devoted to food stands. The Shops is oriented primarily to younger consumers. This is a good place to drop off teenagers weary of the Smithsonian and more in the mood to buy T-shirts. Banana Republic, Victoria's Secret, and The Sharper Image are three of the catalogue stores that have outlets here.

Although Washington doesn't have anything on the order of Boston's Faneuil Hall, it does have the **Pavilion at the Old Post Office** (12th St. NW and Pennsylvania Ave., ☎ 202/289–4224), a renovated building dating from the last century. There's an atrium with 29 specialty stores along with more than 30 other small shops, such as Caswell & Massey (for toiletries and perfumes) and Juggling Capitol (for beginner to expert jugglers), but the tourist-oriented shops have had a hard time attracting local clientele. The observation deck in the building's clock tower offers an excellent view of the city, and there's even an indoor miniature golf course featuring Washington monuments (City Golf, ☎ 202/898–7888).

One of the most delightful shopping enclaves in the city is **Union Station** (☎ 202/371–9441; Metro: Union Station), at Massachusetts Avenue NE near North Capitol Street. Resplendent with marble floors and gilded, vaulted ceilings, it's now both a working train station and a mall with three levels of stores—one with food stands and a cinema multiplex—and, appropriately, the Great Train Store, which offers train memorabilia and toy versions from the inexpensive to four-digit Swiss models. The east hall, reminiscent of London's Covent Garden, is filled with vendors of expensive and ethnic wares in open stalls. Christmas is an especially pleasant time to shop here.

As the **Capitol Hill** area has become gentrified, additional unique shops and boutiques have sprung up here. Many are clustered around the 1873 building known as **Eastern Market** (7th and C Sts. SE, one block north of Eastern Market Metro). Inside are produce and meat counters, plus

Washington Shopping

Amadi's Place, **12**
Ann Taylor, **3, 48**
Appalachian
Spring, **63**
Beadazzled, **23**
Betsy Fisher, **33**
Britches of
Georgetown, **30**
Britches Great
Outdoors, **36**
Brooks Brothers, **8, 45**
Burberrys, **38**
Chanel Boutique, **53**

Chapters, **49**
Charles Schwartz
& Son, **3**
Chenonceau
Antiques, **13**
Cherishables, **22**
Cheshire Cat, **9**
Chevy Chase Pavilion
(shopping center), **4**
Church's, **46**
Curious Kids, **4**
Earl Allen, **51**
Eastern Market, **66**

Fahrney's, **54**
Filene's
Basement, **3, 43**
Forecast, **67**
Georgetown Leather
Design, **39**
Hecht's, **56**
Hugo Boss, **5, 37**
Indian Craft
Shop, **52**
J. Press, **42**
Joan and David, **4**
John B. Adler, **55**

Kemp Mill Music, **6,
18, 25, 44**
Khismet Wearable
Art, **15**
The Kid's Closet, **35**
Kitchen Bazaar, **10**
Kobos, **14**
Kramerbooks, **24**
La Bottega Fine
Papers, **4**
Lammas Books, **26**
Laura Ashley
Home, **3**

Georgetown Shopping

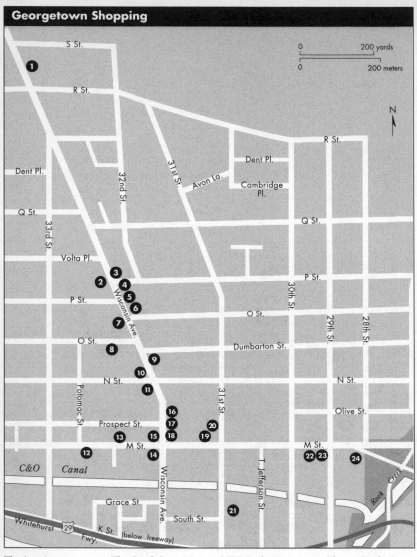

The American
Hand, **23**

Ann Taylor, **14**

Appalachian
Spring, **6**

Betsey Johnson, **9**

Britches Great
Outdoors, **18**

Britches of
Georgetown, **17**

The Coach Store, **15**

Commander
Salamander, **7**

Dean & Deluca, **12**

Earl Allen, **19**

F.A.O. Schwarz, **14**

Georgetown Antiques
Center, **22**

Georgetown
Park (mall), **14**

G.K.S. Bush, **24**

Hugo Boss, **3**

Indian Craft Shop, **14**

Kemp Mill Music, **11**

Little Caledonia, **5**

Martin's, **10**

Miller & Arney
Antiques, **1**

Old Print Gallery, **20**

Olsson's Books &
Records, **16**

Opportunity Shop, **4**

Orpheus Records, **13**

The Phoenix, **2**

Susquehanna, **8**

Yes!, **21**

the Market Five art gallery; outside are a farmer's market (on Saturdays) and a flea market (on weekends). Across 7th Street are Mission Traders, Antiques on the Hill, and Forecast, a clothing store for women.

The final major shopping district is on upper Wisconsin Avenue straddling the Maryland border. Here is the **Mazza Gallerie** (5300 Wisconsin Ave. NW, ☎ 202/966–6114; Metro: Friendship Heights), a four-level mall anchored by the ritzy Neiman Marcus department store and a Filene's Basement. Its other stores include Williams-Sonoma's kitchenware and Laura Ashley Home. Three other department stores are close by: Lord & Taylor, Woodward & Lothrop, and Saks Fifth Avenue (*see* Department Stores, *below*).

Across from Mazza Gallerie is the newer, similarly upmarket **Chevy Chase Pavilion** (5335 Wisconsin Ave. NW, ☎ 202/686–5335). Its exclusive women's clothing stores include Joan & David and Steilmann European Selection (which carries Karl Lagerfeld's sportier KL line). Other specialty shops of note here are La Bottega Fine Papers, Curious Kids toys, and Rock Creek, a two-store chain that sells high-quality, fashionable men's and women's athletic clothing and shoes.

Department Stores

Filene's Basement (1133 Connecticut Ave. NW, ☎ 202/872–8430; 5300 Wisconsin Ave. NW, ☎ 202/966–0208) steeply discounts Christian Dior, Hugo Boss, Burberrys, and other designer men's and women's clothing labels in addition to offering off-price apparel, shoes, perfume, and accessories. Although the bargains may not be as stunning as those at the original store in Boston, neither branch reeks of bargain-basement atmosphere. The downtown one is especially well-appointed in wood and brass, with a handsome elevator to take you to the upper level.

Hecht's (12th and G Sts. NW, ☎ 202/628–6661) main downtown store is bright and spacious, and its sensible groupings and attractive displays of merchandise make shopping relatively easy on the feet and the eyes. The clothes sold here are a mix of conservative and trendy lines, with the men's department assuming increasing importance. Cosmetics, lingerie, and housewares are also strong departments.

Lord & Taylor (5255 Western Ave. NW, ☎ 202/362–9600) lets other stores be all things to all people while it focuses on nonutilitarian housewares and classic clothing by such designers as Anne Klein and Ralph Lauren. All of the clothing is American designed and manufactured.

Neiman Marcus (Mazza Gallerie, ☎ 202/966–9700) is not for shoppers who looks at price tags; this Dallas-headquartered store caters to customers who value quality above all. The carefully selected merchandise includes couture clothes, furs, precious jewelry, crystal, and silver.

Saks Fifth Avenue (5555 Wisconsin Ave., ☎ 301/657–9000), though not technically a Washington department store since it is just over the Maryland line, is nonetheless a Washington institution. The major draw is the wide selection of European and American couture clothes; other attractions are the shoe, jewelry, fur, and lingerie departments.

Woodward & Lothrop (11th and F Sts. NW, ☎ 202/347–5300), the largest of several downtown stores, this Woodies has eight floors of merchandise that can accommodate just about any need or whim. There are two floors of women's clothing in a variety of styles and price ranges, another floor for juniors, one floor for men, and a large children's department. In addition, just about anything you could need for the home can be found here, including gourmet food. There is also a branch across the Maryland border (Wisconsin and Western Aves., ☎ 301/654–7600; Metro: Friendship Heights).

Specialty Stores

Antiques and Collectibles

Chenonceau Antiques (2314 18th St. NW, ☎ 202/667–1651) has two floors of mostly American 19th- and 20th-century pieces selected by a buyer with an exquisite eye. Merchandise includes beautiful 19th-century paisley scarves from India and from Scotland, and 1920s glass lamps. Closed Monday–Thursday.

Cherishables (1608 20th St. NW, ☎ 202/785–4087) spotlights American 18th- and 19th-century furniture and decorative arts, with emphasis on the Federal period.

Georgetown Antiques Center (2918 M St. NW, ☎ 202/338–3811), in a Victorian town house, has two dealers who share space: Cherub Gallery (☎ 202/337–2224) specializes in Art Nouveau and Art Deco, and **Michael Getz Antiques** (☎ 202/338–3811) sells fireplace equipment and silverware.

G. K. S. Bush (2828 Pennsylvania Ave. NW, ☎ 202/965–0653) offers formal American furniture from the 18th and early 19th centuries, plus related American antiques and works of art.

Marston Luce (1314 21st St. NW, ☎ 202/775–9460) specializes in American folk art, including quilts, weather vanes, and hooked rugs. There are also home and garden furnishings, primarily American, but some English and French as well.

Miller & Arney Antiques (1737 Wisconsin Ave. NW, ☎ 202/338–2369) sells English, American, and European furniture and accessories from the 18th and early 19th centuries, plus Oriental porcelain.

Old Print Gallery (1220 31st St. NW, ☎ 202/965–1818) houses the area's largest collection of old prints and maps, including Washingtoniana.

Opportunity Shop of the Christ Child Society (1427 Wisconsin Ave. NW, ☎ 202/333–6635), a Georgetown thrift shop, sells vintage clothing and good-quality household goods. Consigned fine antiques at moderate prices are available on the second floor.

Retrospective (2324 18th St. NW, ☎ 202/483–8112) is a small shop crammed with high-quality furniture and accessories, mostly from the '40s and '50s. Here you can still buy the princess phone that lit up your nightstand in 1962 and the plates your mother served her meat loaf on.

Susquehanna (3216 O St. NW, ☎ 202/333–1511) is the largest antiques shop in Georgetown, specializing in American furniture and paintings.

Uniform (2318 18th St. NW, ☎ 202/483–4577) is the best of the vintage clothing and household accessories shops in Adams-Morgan—it has an assortment from the '50s and '60s that makes it seem like the entire country transferred to the moon for 20 years. The mix varies, but in addition to the obligatory lava lamps you'll find three-button suits and pillbox hats, feathered mules with Lucite heels, and plates, lamps, and dishes that could have been props for the Jetsons.

Books

Chapters (1512 K St. NW, ☎ 202/347–5495), a "literary bookstore," eschews cartoon collections and diet guides, filling its shelves instead with serious contemporary fiction, classics, and poetry.

No matter where you go, travel is easier when you know the code.^{SM}

dial **1 8 0 0**
C A L L
A T T®

Dial 1 800 CALL ATT and you'll always get through from any phone with any card* and you'll always get AT&T's best deal.** It's the one number to remember when calling away from home.

*Other long distance company calling cards excluded.
**Additional discounts available.

AT&T
Your True Choice

Cheshire Cat (5512 Connecticut Ave. NW, ☎ 202/244–3956), a bookstore for children, carries a selection of records, cassettes, posters, and books on parenting.

Kramerbooks (1517 Connecticut Ave. NW, ☎ 202/387–1400), open 24 hours on weekends, shares space with a café that has late-night dining and weekend entertainment. The stock is small but well-selected.

Lammas Books (1426 21st St. NW, ☎ 202/775–8218) includes a selection of music by women as well as women's and lesbian literature.

Mystery Books (1715 Connecticut Ave. NW, ☎ 202/483–1600) has Washington's largest collection of detective, crime, suspense, and spy fiction. They deliver "Crime and Nourishment" gift baskets anywhere in the USA (☎ 800/955–2279).

Olsson's Books & Records (1239 Wisconsin Ave. NW, ☎ 202/338–9544; 1307 19th St. NW, ☎ 202/785–1133; 1200 F St. NW, ☎ 202/347–3686; 418 7th St. NW, ☎ 202/638–7610) carries a large and varied collection. Hours vary significantly from store to store.

Second Story Books (2000 P St. NW, ☎ 202/659–8884) encourages hours of browsing in this used-books (and records) emporium on Dupont Circle.

Trover Books (221 Pennsylvania Ave. SE, 202/547–2665) specializes in the latest political volumes and out-of-town newspapers.

Vertigo Books (1337 Connecticut Ave. NW, ☎ 202/429–9272), just south of Dupont Circle, emphasizes international politics, world literature, and African-American studies.

Yawa (2206 18th St. NW, ☎ 202/483–6805) features a large collection of African and African-American fiction and nonfiction, magazines, and children's books; it also sells ethnic jewelry, crafts, and greeting cards.

Yes! (1035 31st St. NW, ☎ 202/338–7874) is a bookstore geared to self-development. It has an unusual stock of volumes on philosophies of the world, meditative disciplines, and mental, physical, and spiritual health.

Children's Clothing and Toys

Amadi's Place (1800 Belmont St. NW, ☎ 202/332–4751) offers children's clothing, locally designed and sewn, in eye-catching African fabrics. The styles, in sizes 0 to 12, are a mix of Western and African-inspired, such as black velvet dresses with a *kente* cloth ruffle. Closed Monday–Wednesday (except by appointment).

F.A.O. Schwarz (in Georgetown Park, 3222 M St. NW, ☎ 202/342–2285) is the most upscale of toy stores, carrying such items as a toy car (a Mercedes, of course) that costs almost as much as the real thing. Among the other imports are stuffed animals (many larger than life), dolls, and children's perfumes.

The Kid's Closet (1226 Connecticut Ave. NW, ☎ 202/429–9247) is the downtown choice for baby clothes and shower gifts; there are also some togs for older children.

Crafts and Gifts

The American Hand (2906 M St. NW, ☎ 202/965–3273) furnishes one-of-a-kind functional and nonfunctional pieces from America's foremost ceramic artists, plus limited edition objects for home and office, such as architect-designed dinnerware.

Appalachian Spring (1415 Wisconsin Ave. NW, ☎ 202/337–5780, and Union Station, ☎ 202/682–0505) sells traditional and contemporary crafts, including quilts, jewelry, weavings, pottery, and blown glass.

Beadazzled (1522 Connecticut Ave. NW, ☎ 202/265–2323) supplies a truly dazzling array of ready-to-string beads, jewelry, and books on craft history and techniques.

Fahrney's (1430 G St. NW, ☎ 202/628–9525) started out as a pen bar in the Willard Hotel, a place to fill your fountain pen before embarking on the day's business. Today it sells pens in silver, gold, and lacquer by the world's leading manufacturers.

Indian Craft Shop (in Georgetown Park, 3222 M St. NW, ☎ 202/342–3918; Dept. of Interior, 1849 C St. NW, Room 1023, ☎ 202/208–4056) sells handicrafts, including jewelry, pottery, sand paintings, weavings, and baskets, from a dozen Native American tribes.

Martin's (1304 Wisconsin Ave. NW, ☎ 202/338–6144) is a long-established Georgetown purveyor of china, crystal, and silver.

Moon, Blossoms and Snow (225 Pennsylvania Ave. SE, ☎ 202/543–8181) specializes in wearable art. In addition to hand-painted, hand-woven garments, the store sells contemporary American ceramics, glass, jewelry, and wood.

Music Box Center (918 F St. NW, ☎ 202/783–9399), an exquisite specialty store, provides listening opportunities via more than 1500 music boxes that play 500 melodies.

Nomad (2407 18th St. NW, ☎ 202/332–2998) offers reasonably priced clothing, artifacts, and jewelry with an ethnic flair.

The Phoenix (1514 Wisconsin Ave. NW, ☎ 202/338–4404) sells Mexican crafts, including folk art, silver jewelry, fabrics, and native and contemporary clothing in natural fibers.

Skynear and Company (2122 18th St. NW, 202/797-7160; Mazza Gallerie, 202/362-7541) has owners, an Egyptian husband and a Native American wife, who travel the world for the unusual. The result is an extravagant assortment of rich textiles, furniture, and home accessories for the art of living.

Jewelry
Charles Schwartz & Son (Mazza Gallerie, ☎ 202/363–5432) is a full-service jeweler that specializes in precious stones in traditional and modern settings. Fine watches are also offered.

Pampillonia Jewelers (Mazza Gallerie, ☎ 202/363–6305; 1213 Connecticut Ave. NW, ☎ 202/628–6305) provides traditional designs in 18-karat gold and platinum, including many pieces for men.

The Tiny Jewel Box (1147 Connecticut Ave. NW, ☎ 202/393–2747) sells well-chosen estate jewelry, contemporary jewelry, and unique gifts.

Kitchenware
Kitchen Bazaar (4401 Connecticut Ave. NW, ☎ 202/244–1550), the flagship store of a local chain, carries everything one could possibly need to equip a kitchen.

Little Caledonia (1419 Wisconsin Ave. NW, ☎ 202/333–4700), a "Tom Thumb department store" for the home, has nine rooms crammed with thousands of unusual and imported items; candles, cards, fabrics, and lamps round out the stock of decorative kitchenware.

Leather Goods

The Coach Store (1214 Wisconsin Ave. NW, ☎ 202/342–1772) carries a complete (and expensive) line of well-made handbags, briefcases, belts, and wallets.

Georgetown Leather Design (1150 Connecticut Ave. NW, ☎ 202/223–1855) sells a full line of leather goods, most of them made for the store, including jackets, briefcases, wallets, gloves, and handbags.

Men's Clothing

Britches of Georgetown (1219 Connecticut Ave. NW, ☎ 202/347–8994; 1247 Wisconsin Ave. NW, ☎ 202/338–3330) carries an extensive selection of traditional but trend-conscious designs in natural fibers.

Brooks Brothers (1840 L St. NW, ☎ 202/659–4650; 5500 Wisconsin Ave., ☎ 301/654–8202), the oldest men's store in America, has sold traditional formal and casual clothing since 1818. It is the largest men's specialty store in the area and has a small women's department as well.

Hugo Boss (1201 Connecticut Ave. NW, ☎ 202/887–5081; 1517 Wisconsin Ave. NW, ☎ 202/338–0120; 5454 Wisconsin Ave., ☎ 301/907–7806) sells clothes from this German designer and manufacturer, noted for his classic fabrics and unique silhouettes.

J. Press (1801 L St. NW, ☎ 202/857–0120) was founded in 1902 as a custom shop for Yale University. It is a stalwartly traditional clothier; Shetland wool sport coats are a specialty.

Men's and Women's Clothing

Britches Great Outdoors (1225 Wisconsin Ave. NW, ☎ 202/333–3666; 1801 M St. NW, ☎ 202/775–8983) the casual version of Britches of Georgetown, has filled many Washington closets with rugby shirts and other sportswear.

Burberrys (1155 Connecticut Ave. NW, ☎ 202/463–3000) made its reputation with the trench coat, but this British company also manufactures traditional men's and women's apparel.

Commander Salamander (1420 Wisconsin Ave. NW, ☎ 202/333–9599) is about as funky as Washington gets—leather, chains, silver skulls. As much entertainment as shopping, it's open until 11 on weekends.

Forecast (218 7th St. SE, ☎ 202/547–7337) is for women who want a classic, contemporary look.

John B. Adler (901 15th St. NW, ☎ 202/842–4432), a longtime Washington clothier, offers what used to be called the Ivy League look in suits, sport coats, and formal and casual wear.

Kobos (2444 18th St. NW, ☎ 202/332–9580) provides a rainbow of clothing and accessories imported from West Africa, plus a small selection of African music.

Music

Kemp Mill Music (1254 Wisconsin Ave. NW, ☎ 202/333–1392; 1518 Connecticut Ave. NW, ☎ 202/332–8247; 2459 18th St. NW, ☎ 202/387–1011; 1900 L St. NW, ☎ 202/223–5310; 4000 Wisconsin Ave. NW, ☎ 202/364–9704) is local chain store, with even more suburban locations; it sells popular-music CDs and cassettes at low prices.

Olsson's Books & Records (*see* Books, *above*) carries a full line of compact discs and cassettes, with a good classical and folk music selection.

Orpheus Records (3249 M St. NW, 202/337–7970) specializes in new and used jazz and blues records.

Serenade Record Shop (1800 M St. NW, ☎ 202/452–0075) is a full-catalogue music store with a strong classical collection.

Tower Records (2000 Pennsylvania Ave. NW, ☎ 202/331–2400 and suburban branches in Rockville, MD, ☎ 301/468–8901, and Vienna, VA, ☎ 703/893–6627), with 16,000 square feet of selling space, offers the area's best selection of music in all categories, plus videos and laser discs. ☉ Daily until midnight.

Shoes

Church's (1820 L St. NW, ☎ 202/296–3366) is an English company whose handmade men's shoes are noted for their comfort and durability.

Shoe Scene (1330 Connecticut Ave. NW, ☎ 202/659–2194) directly imports fashionable, moderately priced shoes for women.

Women's Clothing

Ann Taylor (1720 K St. NW, ☎ 202/466–3544; 3222 M St. NW, ☎ 202/338–5290; 5300 Wisconsin Ave. NW, ☎ 202/244–1940; Union Station, ☎ 202/371–8010) sells sophisticated fashions for the woman who has broken out of the dress-for-success mold. Ann Taylor also has an excellent shoe department.

Betsey Johnson (1319 Wisconsin Ave. NW, ☎ 202/338–4090) sells fanciful frocks for the young and restless.

Betsy Fisher (1224 Connecticut Ave. NW, ☎ 202/785–1975) focuses on tasteful, rather than conservative, clothing that appeals to women of all ages.

Chanel Boutique (1455 Pennsylvania Ave. NW, ☎ 202/638–5055), in the Willard Hotel annex, sells goodies from the legendary house of fashion.

Earl Allen (3109 M St. NW, ☎ 202/338–1678; 1825 I St. NW, ☎ 202/466–3437) caters to the professional woman, offering conservative but distinctive dresses and sportswear, much of it made exclusively for this shop.

Khismet Wearable Art (1800 Belmont Rd. NW, ☎ 202/234–7778) has original fashions and traditional garments designed by Millée Spears, who lived in Ghana. She uses ethnic textiles both for garments suitable for the office and for an evening out. Closed Monday–Tuesday.

Rizik Bros. (1100 Connecticut Ave. NW, ☎ 202/223–4050), a Washington institution, combines designer clothing and accessories with expert service. The sales staff is trained to find styles—from the large inventory—and prices that meet customers' desires. Take the elevator up from the northwest corner of Connecticut and L streets.

5 Sports and the Outdoors

SPORTS

By John F. Kelly

Updated by
Bruce Walker

WHEN CONVERSATION turns to America's great sports towns, Washington isn't often high on the list. The honors usually go to New York, Los Angeles, or Boston. Nevertheless, Washington is home to an impressive variety of opportunities for both spectators and participants. According to national surveys, the residents of metropolitan Washington are more active than the nation as a whole. Washingtonians jog, cycle, swim, fish, lift weights, play tennis, and sail more than the residents of any other major city in the United States. One reason may be that Washington's climate is generally mild year-round. Another reason is the plenitude of parks, trails, and athletic facilities throughout the area.

Whether you're coming to Washington for a few days of sightseeing or a few days of business, bring your sweats. There is more to the District than national monuments and boardrooms.

Participant Sports and Fitness

Bicycling

Bicycling is one of Washington's most popular activities for both locals and visitors. The numerous trails in the District and its surrounding areas are well maintained and clearly marked. Most of the paths described below in the section on jogging—the Mall, the Mount Vernon Trail, and Rock Creek Park—are also suitable for bikers.

ROUTES AND TRAILS

For scenery, you can't beat the towpath that starts in Georgetown and runs along the **C&O Canal** into Maryland (*see* Parks and Woodlands *in* The Outdoors, *below*). You could pedal to the end of the canal, 184 miles away in Cumberland, Maryland, but most cyclists are content to roll to Great Falls, 15 miles from where the canal starts. The towpath, a gravel-and-packed surface, is occasionally bumpy, but along the way you'll pass through wooded areas and see abundant flora and fauna and 19th-century locks from the canal's working days.

Cyclists interested in serious training might want to try the 3-mile loop around the golf course in **East Potomac Park,** Hains Point (entry is near the Jefferson Memorial). This is a favorite training course for dedicated local racers and would-be triathletes. A note of caution, though: Restrict your workouts to the daytime; the area is not safe after dark.

RENTALS

Bicycles can be rented at the following locations:

Bicycle Exchange (1506-C Belle View Blvd., Alexandria, VA, ☎ 703/768–3444), near the Mount Vernon Trail.

Big Wheel Bikes (1034 33rd St. NW, Georgetown, ☎ 202/337–0254, near the C&O Canal Towpath; 315 7th St. SE, ☎ 202/543–1600, near Capitol Hill; 2 Prince St., Alexandria, VA, ☎ 703/739–2300), near the Mount Vernon Trail.

City Bikes (2501 Champlain St. NW, ☎ 202/265–1564), near the Rock Creek bike path.

Fletcher's Boat House (4740 Canal Rd. at Reservoir Rd., ☎ 202/244–0461).

Metropolis Bike & Scooter (709 8th St. SE, ☎ 202/543–8900) also rents Rollerblades.

Proteus Bicycle Shop (2422 18th St. NW, ☎ 202/332–6666; 7945 MacArthur Blvd., Cabin John, MD, ☎ 301/229–5900, near the C&O Canal).

Thompson's Boat Center (Virginia Ave. and Rock Creek Park, behind Kennedy Center, ☎ 202/333–4861).

Tow Path Cycle (823 S. Washington St., Alexandria, VA, ☎ 703/549–5368).

INFORMATION AND ORGANIZATIONS

The **Washington Area Bicyclist Association** (1819 H St. NW, Suite 640, Washington, DC, 20006, ☎ 202/872–9830, FAX 202/862–9762) offers information and publications on cycling in the nation's capital. Two invaluable local cycling guides are *The Greater Washington Area Bicycle Atlas,* published with the American Youth Hostels Association, and Michael Leccese's *Short Bike Rides in and Around Washington, D.C.*

Boating

Canoeing, sailing, and powerboating are all popular in the region. There are several places to rent boats along the **Potomac River** north and south of the city. You can dip your oars just about anywhere along the Potomac for canoeing in the C&O Canal, sailing in the widening river south of Alexandria, even kayaking in the raging rapids at Great Falls. Washington is home to some of the best white-water kayakers and white-water canoeists in the country; on weekends they practice below Great Falls in **Mather Gorge,** a canyon carved by the Potomac River just north of the city, above Chain Bridge. The water is deceptive and dangerous, and only top-level kayakers should consider a run there. It is, however, safe to watch the experts at play from a post above the gorge. For information, call the ranger stations at Great Falls, Virginia (☎ 703/285–2966), or Great Falls, Maryland (☎ 301/299–3613).

BOAT RENTALS

The two boathouses listed here are convenient for tourists.

Fletcher's Boat House (*see* Bicycling, *above*), rents rowboats and canoes.

Thompson's Boat Center (*see* Bicycling, *above*), rents canoes, rowboats, rowing shells, and sailboards.

Paddleboats are available during the summer on the east side of the **Tidal Basin** (☎ 202/484–0206) in front of the Jefferson Memorial. The **Washington Sailing Marina** (☎ 703/548–9027), just south of National Airport on the George Washington Parkway, and the **Belle Haven Marina** (☎ 703/768–0018), just south of Old Town Alexandria on the George Washington Parkway, rent Sunfish, Windsurfers, and larger boats to those qualified to charter.

SAILING

If you're really interested in sailing, consider taking a day trip to Annapolis, Maryland (about an hour's drive from the District). Annapolis is one of the best sailing centers on the East Coast, and the Chesapeake Bay is one of the great sailing basins of the world. The **Annapolis Sailing School** (☎ 410/267–7205) is a world-renowned school and charter company.

Fishing

The Potomac River is something of an environmental success story. Once dangerously polluted, it has rebounded in recent years, to the benefit of local fish and, therefore, local fisherman. Largemouth bass, striped bass, shad, and white and yellow perch are all down there somewhere, willing to take your bait.

FISHING SPOTS

A 5-mile stretch of the Potomac River—roughly from the Wilson Memorial Bridge in Alexandria south to Ft. Washington National Park—is one of the country's best spots for largemouth bass fishing. It has, in fact, become something of an East Coast mecca for anglers in search of this particular fish. The area around Fletcher's Boat House on the C&O Canal is one of the best spots for perch.

FISHING GUIDES AND TACKLE SHOPS

The simple act of renting a boat and going fishing in Washington is complicated by the fact that this stretch of the Potomac is divided among three jurisdictions: Virginia, Maryland, and the District of Columbia. It's not always easy to determine in whose water you're fishing or which licenses you should have. The best solution is to hire a guide. **Life Outdoors Unlimited** (☎ 301/937–0010), run by nationally known fisherman and conservationist Ken Penrod, is an umbrella group of area freshwater fishing guides. A dozen of the area's best guides are listed with Penrod, and for about $250 a day a guide will take care of all your needs, from tackle to boats, and advise you on which licenses are required. Penrod's guides are all professionals and will teach novices and guide experts.

Two of the best tackle shops in the area are **Delta Tackle** (1435 Powhatan St., Alexandria, VA, ☎ 703/549–5729) and **Angler & Archer** (16069 Frederick Rd., Rockville, MD, ☎ 301/330–3474).

INFORMATION

Gene Mueller, a nationally known hunting and fishing writer, has a column three times a week (Monday, Wednesday, and Friday) in the *Washington Times*. He takes readers' telephone calls Thursday mornings at 202/636–3268. The "Fish Lines" column in Friday's *Washington Post* "Weekend" outlines where the fish are biting, from the Potomac to the Chesapeake Bay.

Golf

Serious golfers must resign themselves to driving out of the District to find a worthwhile course. None of the three public courses in town could be considered first-rate. Still, people line up to play here and at other local public courses, sometimes arriving as early as 2 AM to snare a tee time. (Some courses allow you to call ahead to reserve a tee time; call for details.)

PUBLIC COURSES WITHIN THE DISTRICT

All three of the public courses in the District have the same greens fees: $13.50 for 18 holes on weekdays, $9 for nine; weekends it's $17 and $10.50, respectively.

The **Hains Point course** (☎ 202/863–9007) in East Potomac Park near the Jefferson Memorial is a flat, wide, featureless, 6,303-yard, par-72 course. Its greatest claim to fame is that professional golfer and Washington resident Lee Elder got his start there. It also has two nine-hole courses and a driving range. One of the country's oldest miniature golf courses operates here during the summer.

Langston Golf Course (26th St. and Benning Rd. NE, ☎ 202/397–8638) is a par-72, 6,300-yard course. It's popular, although its greens and fairways are poorly maintained; holes 8 and 9, by the Anacostia River, are challenging.

Rock Creek Park Golf Course (16th and Rittenhouse Sts. NW, ☎ 202/882–7332) is a 4,798-yard, par-65 course with an easy front nine but challenging back. Its tight, rolling, well-treed back nine make it the most attractive public course in the city of Washington.

PUBLIC COURSES IN NEARBY SUBURBS

There are several excellent suburban public courses within a half hour of downtown.

Reston National (11875 Sunrise Valley Dr., Reston, VA, ☎ 703/620–9333) is a four-star, 6,480-yard, par-71 course widely considered the best public course in the metropolitan area. Well maintained, it is heavily wooded but not too difficult for the average player. The fee is $32 on weekdays and $40 weekends.

Also 30 minutes from town is **Northwest Park** (15701 Layhill Rd., Wheaton, MD, ☎ 301/598–6100). This 6,732-yard, par-72 course is extremely long and windy, making for slow play, but it is immaculately groomed and fair. It also has a short-nine course. The fee for 18 holes is $17 weekdays, $18.50 weekends; the short-nine course is $9 and $10.

Maryland's 6,209-yard, par-72 **Enterprise** (2802 Enterprise Rd., Mitchellville, MD, ☎ 301/249–2040), near the Beltway in Prince George's County, has a reputation as the best-manicured public course in the area. Its well-landscaped layout gives it a country-club feel. The fee for 18 holes is $17 weekdays, $22 weekends.

If you are flying into or out of Dulles Airport and want to fit in a round of golf, try **Penderbrook** (West Ox Rd. and I–66, ☎ 703/385–3700). A short but imaginative 5,927-yard, par-72 course, it is one of the best public greens in the area. The 5th, 11th, 12th, and 15th holes are exceptional. The weekday fee is $29 and the weekend fee is $39 for 18 holes.

Health Clubs

The number of health clubs in the area has been on the increase in recent years. All of the clubs in Washington require that you be a member—or at least a member of an affiliated club—in order to use their facilities. Some hotels, however, have made private arrangements with neighboring health clubs to enable hotel guests to use the club's facilities (in some cases guests pay a daily fee). Check with your hotel when making reservations.

A number of downtown hotels are associated with the **fitness center at the ANA Hotel.** All you need to do is show your hotel room key to the center's employees and pay a $20 daily fee ($10 for ANA guests). One of the fanciest fitness centers in Washington, the ANA is the place where celebrities like Cybill Shepherd, Holly Hunter, and Arnold Schwarzenegger come to sweat (ANA Hotel, 2401 M St. NW, ☎ 202/457–5070).

Card-carrying members of the **International Racquet Sports Association (IRSA)** can use the facilities at one of the many member clubs in Washington for a daily fee. You must present your membership card from your home club. The IRSA "Passport" lists member clubs.

The **National Capital YMCA** (1711 Rhode Island Ave. NW, ☎ 202/862–9622) offers just about everything a body could want, from basketball, weights, racquetball, squash, and swimming to exercise equipment. Some downtown hotels offer their guests free one-day passes to the YMCA—check with your concierge. Members of an out-of-town Y must show their membership card and pay a usage fee ranging from $5 to $15 per visit, depending on the time of day.

Horseback Riding

Rock Creek Park Horse Center (Military Rd. and Glover Rd. NW, ☎ 202/362–0117) is open all year offering lessons and trail rides. The guided trail rides, for beginning riders 12 and up, are an hour long; the hours vary according to season.

Ice Skating

The **Sculpture Garden Outdoor Rink** (Constitution Ave. between 7th and 9th Sts. NW, ☎ 202/371–5340) appears each winter with the cold weather. **Pershing Park Ice Rink** (Pennsylvania Ave. between 14th and 15th Sts. NW, ☎ 202/737–6938) is also popular. Skates can be rented at both locations. **Ft. Dupont Park** (37th and Ely Pl. SE, ☎ 202/581–0199) has a beautiful rink; the park itself, though, is in a less-than-wonderful section of town. Two indoor, year-round suburban rinks you might try are at **Mount Vernon Recreation Center** (2017 Belle View Blvd., Alexandria, VA, ☎ 703/768–3222) and **Cabin John Regional Park** (10610 Westlake Dr., Rockville, MD, ☎ 301/365–0585). They, too, have rentals.

Jogging

If you really want to see the people who run Washington, go for a jog. Members of Congress, senators, and Supreme Court justices can often be spotted on the Mall, running loops around the monuments. Georgetown power brokers hoof it along the towpaths of the C&O Canal or on the meandering trails in Rock Creek Park. At lunchtime in Arlington, the Pentagon empties out along the Mount Vernon Trail. Even Mr. Clinton jogs, though it's usually on the White House's custom-built jogging track.

ROUTES, TRAILS, AND TRACKS

Downtown Washington and nearby northern Virginia offer some of the most scenic running trails in the country, and running is one of the best ways to take in the vistas of the city. The most popular paths are presented below. Joggers unfamiliar with the city should not go out at night, and, even in daylight, it's best to run in pairs if you venture beyond the most public areas and the more heavily used sections of the trails.

The Mall. The loop around the Capitol and past the Smithsonian museums, the Washington Monument, the Reflecting Pool, and the Lincoln Memorial is the most popular of all Washington running trails. At any time of day, hundreds of joggers, speed walkers, bicyclists, and tourists can be seen making their way along the gravel pathways of this 4½-mile loop. If you're looking for a longer run, you can veer south of the Mall on either side of the Tidal Basin and head for the Jefferson Memorial and East Potomac Park, the site of many races. Monday, Wednesday, and Thursday evenings at 6:30 the **Capitol Hill Runners** (☎ 301/283–0821) set off on a 4- to 8-mile run from the 1st Street SW garage entrance of the Rayburn House Office Building.

Mount Vernon Trail. Just across the Potomac in Virginia, this trail is another favorite with Washington runners. The northern (shorter) section begins near the pedestrian causeway leading to Theodore Roosevelt Island (directly across the river from the Kennedy Center) and goes past National Airport and on to Old Town Alexandria. This stretch is approximately 3½ miles one way. You can get to the trail from the District by crossing either the Theodore Roosevelt Bridge (at the Lincoln Memorial) or the Rochambeau Memorial Bridge (also known as the 14th Street Bridge, at the Jefferson Memorial). South of National Airport, the trail runs down to the Washington Marina. The final mile of the trail's northern section meanders through protected wetlands before ending in the heart of Old Town Alexandria. The longer, southern section of the trail (approximately 9 miles) takes you along the banks of the Potomac from Alexandria all the way to George Washington's home, Mount Vernon.

Rock Creek Park. A miraculously preserved bit of wilderness in the middle of Washington, Rock Creek Park has 15 miles of trails, a bicycle path, a bridle path, picnic groves, playgrounds, and a boulder-strewn rolling stream, from which it gets its name (the creek is not safe or pleasant for swimming). Starting at P Street on the edge of Georgetown, Rock Creek Park runs all the way to Montgomery County, Maryland. The most popular run in the park is a trail along the creek extending from Georgetown to the National Zoo (about a 4-mile loop). In summer, there is considerable shade, and there are water fountains at an exercise station along the way. The roadway is closed to traffic on weekends. On Sunday mornings, the **Fleet Feet Sports Shop** (☎ 202/387–3888), in Adams-Morgan near the National Zoo, sponsors 5-mile runs in Rock Creek Park.

C&O Canal. Now maintained by the National Park Service, the towpath is a favorite spot with both runners and cyclists. The most popular loop is from a point just north of Key Bridge in Georgetown to Fletcher's Boat House (approximately 4 miles round-trip).

INFORMATION AND ORGANIZATIONS

For information on group runs and weekend races, check the calendar in the "Weekend" sections in the Friday *Washington Post* and Thursday *Washington Times*. For general information about running and races in the area, call the **Gatorade/Road Runners Club of America Hotline** (☎ 703/683–7722). For a list of running clubs in the Washington area, contact the **Road Runners Club of America** (1150 S. Washington St., Suite 250, Alexandria, VA 22314, ☎ 703/836–0558).

Swimming

There are no beaches in the Washington area. If you want to swim during your visit, it's best to stay at a hotel that has a pool. A few years ago it was possible to gain entry to some hotel pools for a small fee, but that practice has by and large been discontinued. Health-club pools, too, are open only to members, though the downtown YMCA has a pool and welcomes members of out-of-town Ys—for a fee. The District of Columbia maintains eight public indoor pools, 20 large outdoor pools, and another 15 outdoor pools, which are smaller but still fun for children. For more information and a list of public facilities, contact the **Aquatic Department** of the **D.C. Department of Recreation** (1230 Taylor St. NW, Washington, DC, 20011, ☎ 202/576–6436).

Tennis

It comes as no surprise that tennis, the sport of the rich, famous, and powerful, is extremely popular in Washington. The District of Columbia maintains 144 outdoor courts, but since some of them are in rather seedy parts of town, it is best to check on the neighborhood in question before heading out. Free permits, required at all public courts, are issued by the Department of Recreation. Send a SASE for a permit and a list of all city-run courts. You can also call for information on specific courts (Department of Recreation, 3149 16th St. NW, Washington, DC, 20010, ☎ 202/673–7646).

The best courts in the area are at two locations: **Hains Point** (East Potomac Park, ☎ 202/554–5962) has outdoor courts as well as courts under a bubble for wintertime play. Fees run from $15 to $24 an hour depending on the time and season. The **Washington Tennis Center**

(16th and Kennedy Sts. NW, ☎ 202/722–5949) has clay and hard courts. Fees range from $15 to $24 an hour, depending on the time. Both locations will take court reservations up to one week in advance.

Spectator Sports

Tickets for all USAir Arena, Patriot Center, and Baltimore Arena events can be purchased through **TicketMaster** (☎ 202/432–7328 in DC, ☎ 410/481–7328 in Baltimore, or ☎ 800/551–7328 in other areas).

Baseball

Because the District doesn't have its own professional baseball team, resident baseball fans go to Baltimore to root for the **Orioles.** Their beautiful new ballpark, Oriole Park at Camden Yards (333 W. Camden St., Baltimore, MD, ☎ 202/432–7328 for tickets), seats 48,000, with tickets ranging from $5 for bleacher seats to $25 for club level seats.

If you prefer your baseball à la *Bull Durham,* head south of the Beltway to the G. Richard Pfitzner Stadium in Woodbridge, Virginia, where you can watch the **Prince William Cannons** (☎ 703/590–2311), the Class A affiliate of the New York Yankees. Tickets range from $4.50 to $6.50. Or travel north up I–270 in Maryland to either the Oriole Class A **Frederick Keys** (☎ 301/662–0013) or the Toronto Blue Jay Class A **Hagerstown Suns** (☎ 301/791–6266). Tickets range from $3 to $7, and children under 14 wearing Little League uniforms get in to Keys games free. In 1994, the **Bowie Baysox** (☎ 301/805–6000), the Orioles' Class AA farm team, opened a brand-new, 10,000-seat stadium in suburban Prince George's County, Maryland.

Basketball

The **Washington Bullets'** home games are held at the USAir Arena in Landover, Maryland, just outside the Beltway. Their schedule runs from September to April. For tickets, call TicketMaster, ☎ 202/432–7328 or 800/551–7328; call 301/622–3865 for detailed schedule information. Tickets range from $11 to $33.

Among the Division I **college basketball** teams in the area, former NCAA national champion Georgetown University's Hoyas are the best known. Their home games are played at the USAir Arena (☎ 301/350–3400). Other Division I schools include the University of Maryland (☎ 301/314–7070), George Mason University (☎ 703/993–3000), George Washington University (☎ 202/994–3865), American University (☎ 202/885–3267), the U.S. Naval Academy (☎ 410/268–6060), and Howard University (☎ 202/806–7198).

Football

Washington is a football-crazy town—never, *never* say anything bad about the **Redskins.** Unfortunately, unless you're a close relative of the team's owner you can pretty much forget about getting tickets to a home game. Since 1966, all Redskins games at the 55,750-seat Robert F. Kennedy Stadium on the eastern edge of Capitol Hill have been sold out to season-ticket holders. Tickets are occasionally advertised in the classified section of the *Post,* but expect to pay considerably more than face value. You might have better luck trying to get tickets to one of the Skins' preseason games in August. For years, team owner Jack Kent Cooke has been fighting to build a new 78,000-seat stadium. First he settled on a deal with Virginia, then with the District, and most recently with Maryland.

The area **colleges** offer an excellent alternative for frustrated football fans. Teams from the University of Maryland (☎ 301/314–7070), the

U.S. Naval Academy (☎ 410/268–6060) in Annapolis, and Howard University (☎ 202/806–7198) all play a full schedule of football.

Horse Racing

Maryland has a long-standing affection for the ponies. You can watch and wager on thoroughbreds at **Laurel Race Course** (Rte. 198 and Race Track Rd., Laurel, MD, ☎ 301/725–0400) during a season that runs January to mid-March, June through July, and October through December. On the third Saturday in May the Preakness Stakes is run at Baltimore's **Pimlico Race Course** (Hayward and Winner Aves., Baltimore, MD, ☎ 410/542–9400). The course has additional thoroughbred racing from April through June, and July through the beginning of October. Race days at both Laurel and Pimlico are usually Tuesday and Thursday through Sunday. You'll find harness racing just outside the Beltway at **Rosecroft Raceway** (6336 Rosecroft Dr., Fort Washington, MD, ☎ 301/567–4000). Race days are usually Tuesday through Saturday in a season that runs from February to mid-December.

Ice Hockey

The **Washington Capitals'** season runs from October through April. In recent years the team has come close to greatness, but it has always choked at playoff time. Washingtonians love the Capitals, nonetheless. Home games are played at the USAir Arena. Tickets range from $12 to $45. Call 301/350–3400 or TicketMaster at 202/432–7328 or 800/551–7328.

THE OUTDOORS

Washington is a green and leafy city, with some neighborhoods a full 10 degrees cooler than the rest of town on hot summer days. Of course some of the capital's best parks are monuments, meaning much of Washington's parkland is dotted with inscribed slabs of stone. Washington does have a few wild streaks, though: Rock Creek Park, the 1,800-acre swath of green that snakes through the city (*see* Jogging *in* Sports, *above*), is home to native woodland, meadows, and all manner of fauna, from deer to shrews. The area along the C&O Canal west of Georgetown is an explosion of wildflowers, complete with songbirds and the occasional beaver colony. Theodore Roosevelt Island, an 88-acre nature preserve in the Potomac across from the Kennedy Center, features 2½ miles of trails through marshland, swampland, and upland forests.

Parks and Woodlands

Audubon Naturalist Society. A self-guided nature trail winds its way through this estate and around the local Audubon Society's suburban Maryland headquarters (in a mansion known as Woodend, designed in the 1920s by Jefferson Memorial architect John Russell Pope). You're never very far from the trill of birdsong here, as the Audubon Society has turned the 40-acre grounds into something of a nature preserve, forbidding the use of toxic chemicals and leaving some areas in a wild, natural state. The bookstore stocks titles on conservation, ecology, and birding, as well as bird feeders and birdhouses. *8940 Jones Mill Rd., Chevy Chase, MD,* ☎ *301/652–9188.* ☛ *Free. Grounds open daily sunrise–sunset. Bookstore open Mon.–Wed. and Fri. 10–6, Thurs. 10–8, Sat. 9–5.*

C&O Canal National Historical Park. Started in 1828, the C&O Canal was designed to link a growing capital with an expanding America. It stretched 184 miles to the west, with canal boats carrying loads of coal, timber, and wheat. Today, the canal is a long, skinny park, with one end in Georgetown and the other in Cumberland, Maryland. Canoeists paddle the canal's "watered" sections while hikers and bikers use the 12-foot-wide towpath that runs alongside it. In warmer months you can hop a mule-drawn canal boat for a brief trip. The Great Falls Tavern Visitors Center in Maryland serves as a museum and headquarters for the rangers who manage the C&O Canal. You can walk over a series of bridges to Olmsted Island in the middle of the Potomac for a spectacular view of the falls. Great Falls also offers mule-drawn boat rides. (*See also* Tour 6 *in* Chapter 2, Exploring Washington.) *Georgetown: 1057 Thomas Jefferson St. NW,* ☎ *202/653–5190. Great Falls: Terminus of MacArthur Blvd., Potomac, MD,* ☎ *301/299–2026.* ☛ *$4 per vehicle. Great Falls open daily sunrise–sunset. Closed Thanksgiving and Dec. 25.*

East Potomac Park. This 328-acre tongue of land hangs down from the Tidal Basin between the Washington Channel to the east and the Potomac River to the west. Facilities include playgrounds, picnic tables, tennis courts, swimming pools, a driving range, two nine-hole golf courses, and an 18-hole golf course. The park's miniature golf course, built during the "midget golf" craze of the '20s, is the oldest in the area; its art deco-ish architecture is a welcome contrast to the artificial, theme-park design of most subsequent courses. Double-blossoming cherry trees line Ohio Drive and bloom about two weeks after the single-blossoming variety that attracts throngs to the Tidal Basin each spring. *The Awakening,* a huge, fantastical sculpture of a man emerging from the ground, sits on Hains Point, at the tip of the park. There are plans to build a "peace garden" here that will have plantings resembling a giant olive branch. *Approach park via Maine Ave. SW, heading west; or from Ohio Dr., heading south (follow signs carefully).* ☎ *202/619–7222. In summer, Ohio Dr. closed to traffic weekends and holidays 3 PM–6 AM. Metro: Smithsonian, L'Enfant Plaza.*

Ft. Washington Park. Built to protect the city from enemies sailing up the Potomac, this 1808 fort was burned by the British during the War of 1812. Rebuilt, it served as an Army post until 1945. The National Park Service maintains it now and holds historical programs there every weekend. *From the Capital Beltway (Rte. 95) take the Indian Head Hwy. exit (Rte. 210) and drive 4½ mi south; look for sign on right.* ☎ *301/763–4600. Entrance fee: $4 per vehicle, $2 per person without vehicle. Park open daily 8–sunset. Visitor center open Feb.–Nov. daily 9–5; Dec. and Jan. daily 9–4:30. Fort open daily 9–5. Closed Dec. 25 and Jan. 1.*

Glen Echo Park. This park was once the site of the Chautauqua Assembly, built in 1891 to promote liberal and practical education among the masses. It served a stint as an amusement park and is now run by the National Park Service, which offers space to a variety of artists, who conduct classes year-round. Monthly exhibits of artists' work are shown in a stone tower left over from the Chautauqua period. An antique carousel is open in the summer, and there are big-band and square dancing in the Spanish ballroom. On weekends, Adventure Theater presents shows for children. (*See also* Tour 1 *in* Chapter 9, Excursions.) *7300 MacArthur Blvd., Glen Echo, MD,* ☎ *301/492–6282. Call for information on events, tours, performances, and carousel hrs.*

Glover-Archbold Park. Groves of beeches, elms, and oaks dot stretches of grassland at this 183-acre park, part of the Rock Creek system. A 3.6-mile nature trail runs the length of Glover-Archbold, a gift to the city in 1924. *Garfield St. and New Mexico Ave. NW.*

Great Falls Park. The waters of the Potomac River cascade dramatically over a steep, jagged gorge, creating the spectacle that gives this 800-acre Virginia park its name. Climbers scale the rock faces leading down to the water while experienced kayakers shoot the rapids. You can watch both from the park's observation deck. The more athletic can follow blazed trails through the park, some of which offer views of the river. A visitor center offers information on the park and on the ruins from two previous endeavors: George Washington's unsuccessful Patowmack Canal, designed to skirt unnavigable portions of the river, and Matildaville, a town founded by Henry "Light Horse Harry" Lee. Across the rapids is the C&O Canal National Historical Park (*see above*). Note: Although the area is ideal for hiking, picnicking, climbing, and fishing, the rocks and the river are extremely dangerous here. The Park Service urges caution. (*See also* Tour 1 *in* Chapter 9, Excursions.) *Route 193 (Georgetown Pike) and Old Dominion Dr., Great Falls, VA,* ☎ *703/285–2966.* ☛ *Mar.–Nov. $4 per vehicle, $2 per person without vehicle. Park open daily 8–dark. Visitor center open Mar.–Nov. 10–5; Dec.–Feb. 10–4. Park closed Dec. 25.*

Huntley Meadows. This 1,200-acre Alexandria, Virginia, refuge has a reputation as a birder's delight. More than 200 species of fowl—from ospreys to owls, egrets to ibis—can be spotted here. Much of the park is wetlands, making it a favorite of aquatic species. Fur can be found as well as feathers: A boardwalk circles through a marsh, putting visitors in sight of beaver lodges, and 3 miles of trails wend through the park, making it likely you'll spot deer, muskrats, and river otters. *3701 Lockheed Blvd., Alexandria, VA,* ☎ *703/768–2525.* ☛ *Free. Park open daily dawn–dusk. Visitor center open Mar.–Dec., Mon. and Wed.–Fri. 9–5, weekends noon–5; Jan. and Feb., weekends noon–5.*

Rock Creek Park. The 1,800 acres of park on either side of Rock Creek have provided a cool oasis for Washington residents since Congress set them aside in 1890. Thirty picnic areas are scattered throughout the park. Bicycle routes and hiking and equestrian trails wind through the groves of dogwoods, beeches, oaks, and cedar. Rangers at the **Nature Center and Planetarium** (south of Military Rd. at 5000 Glover Rd. NW, ☎ 202/426–6829; open Wed.–Sun. 9–5, closed federal holidays and Sun. preceding a Mon. holiday) will acquaint you with the park and inform you of scheduled activities. Guided nature walks leave from the center weekends at 3. A highlight of the park is **Pierce Mill,** a restored 19th-century gristmill powered by the falling water of Rock Creek. National Park Service employees grind grain into flour and sell it to visitors (Rock Creek Park at Tilden St. and Beach Dr., ☎ 202/426–6908; open Wed.–Sun. 9–5; Metro: Van Ness/UDC). Other park features include **Ft. Reno, Ft. Bayard,** and **Ft. DeRussy,** remnants of the original ring of forts that guarded Washington during the Civil War, and the **Rock Creek Park Golf Course,** (*see* Golf, *above*) an 18-hole public course. *Between 16th St. and Connecticut Ave. NW,* ☎ *202/426–6829 for park activities, 202/882–7332 for golf course. Park open daylight hrs only; hrs for individual sites vary.*

Theodore Roosevelt Island. This 88-acre island wilderness-preserve in the Potomac River is a living tribute to the conservation-minded 26th president. It features 2½ miles of nature trails through marshland, swampland, and upland forest. Cattails, arrowarum, pickerelweed, willow, ash, maple, and oak all grow on the island, providing a habitat for frogs, raccoons, birds, squirrels, and the occasional red or gray fox. There is also a 17-foot bronze statue of Roosevelt, executed by Paul Manship. *A pedestrian bridge connects the island to a parking lot on* *the Virginia shore, which is accessible from the northbound lanes of the GW Memorial Pkwy. From downtown, take Constitution Ave. west across the Theodore Roosevelt Bridge to GW Memorial Pkwy. north and follow signs.* ☎ *703/285–2598.* ☛ *Free. Island open dawn–dusk.*

Gardens

Bishop's Garden. This compact, traditional English-style garden is on the grounds of the Washington Cathedral. Boxwoods, ivy, tea roses, yew trees, and an assortment of arches, bas-reliefs, and stonework from European ruins provide a restful counterpoint to the cathedral's Gothic towers. *Wisconsin and Massachusetts Aves. NW,* ☎ *202/537–6200.* ☛ *Free.* ☼ *Daily 10–4:30. Metro: Woodley Park/Zoo.*

Brookside Gardens. At this rolling 50-acre display garden in suburban Maryland, formal seasonal displays of bulbs, annuals, and perennials and a sprawling azalea garden flourish. Inside, the two conservatories house—depending on the time of year—Easter lilies, tropicals, Japanese chrysanthemums, or poinsettia trees. *1500 Glenallan Ave., Wheaton, MD,* ☎ *301/949–8230, TTY 301/929–6509.* ☛ *Free. Grounds open daily 9–sunset; conservatories open weekdays 10–5, weekends and holidays 10:30–4. Closed Dec. 25.*

Constitution Gardens (*see* Tour 2 *in* Chapter 2, Exploring Washington). The area south of Constitution Avenue between 17th and 23rd streets NW features paths winding through groves of trees, a lake, a memorial to signers of the Declaration of Independence, and the sobering Vietnam Veterans Memorial. *Metro: Foggy Bottom.*

Dumbarton Oaks (*see* Tour 6 *in* Chapter 2, Exploring Washington). These 10 acres of formal gardens, in a variety of styles, are some of the loveliest in the city.

Hillwood Museum (*see* Tour 12, *in* Chapter 2, Exploring Washington.) The grounds of Marjorie Merriweather Post's Georgian-style Hillwood House have a French-style parterre, a rose garden, a Japanese garden, paths that wind through azaleas and rhododendrons, and a greenhouse in which 5,000 orchids bloom.

Kahlil Gibran Memorial Garden. Dedicated in 1991, this tiny urban park combining Western and Arabian symbols is perfect for quiet contemplation. Limestone benches engraved with sayings from Gibran curve around a fountain and a bust of the Lebanese-born poet. *3100 block of Massachusetts Ave. NW.*

Kenilworth Aquatic Gardens. Exotic water lilies, lotuses, hyacinths, and other water-loving plants thrive in this 12-acre sanctuary of quiet pools and marshy flats. In a pool near the visitor center bloom East Indian lotus plants grown from 350-year-old seeds recovered from a dry Manchurian lake-bed. The gardens are home to a variety of wetland animals, including turtles, frogs, muskrats, and some 40 species of birds. Early morning is the best time to visit, when day-bloomers are just opening and night-bloomers have yet to close. July is the best month to visit, as nearly everything is in bloom. *Kenilworth Ave. and Douglas St. NE,* ☎ *202/426–6905.* ☛ *Free. Gardens open daily 7–4, visitor center open daily 8:30–4. Garden walks held on summer weekends at 9, 11, and 1.*

Lafayette Square (*see* Tour 3 *in* Chapter 2, Exploring Washington). The White House faces this park and its five statues honoring heroes of the American Revolution and the War of 1812. *Metro: McPherson Square.*

Meridian Hill Park. Landscape architect Horace Peaslee created this often-overlooked park after a 1917 study of the parks of Europe. It contains elements of France (a long, straight mall bordered with plants), Italy (terraces and wall fountains), and Switzerland (a lower-level reflecting pool based on one in Zurich). It's also known as Malcolm X Park. Drug activity makes it unwise to visit this park alone, even in daylight hours. Steer clear after dark. *16th and Euclid Sts. NW,* ☎ *202/426–6851.*

Pershing Park (*see* Tour 3 *in* Chapter 2, Exploring Washington). Inscribed granite slabs in this downtown park recount battles of World War I. There's ice skating here in winter. *Metro: Federal Triangle.*

United States Botanic Gardens (*see* Tour 4 *in* Chapter 2, Exploring Washington). This conservatory houses all manner of plants, from cacti to orchids. *Metro: Federal Center SW.*

United States National Arboretum. During the azalea season, from the middle of April to the end of May, this 444-acre oasis is a blaze of color. In the summer, clematis, ferns, peonies, rhododendrons, and roses bloom. The arboretum is an ideal place to visit for either a relaxing stroll or a scenic drive. Also popular are the National Herb Garden and the National Bonsai Collection. *3501 New York Ave. NE,* ☎ *202/ 245–2726.* ☛ *Free.* ☉ *Weekdays 8–5, weekends and holidays 10–5. Bonsai Collection open daily 10–3:30. Closed Dec. 25.*

West Potomac Park (*see* Tour 2 *in* Chapter 2, Exploring Washington). This park between the Potomac and the Tidal Basin is best known for its flowering cherry trees. *Metro: Smithsonian.*

Zoos

National Aquarium (*see* Tour 5 *in* Chapter 2, Exploring Washington). Housed in the Department of Commerce Building and featuring tropical and freshwater fish, this is the nation's oldest public aquarium. *Metro: Federal Triangle.*

National Zoological Park (*see* Tour 9 *in* Chapter 2, Exploring Washington). One of the foremost zoos in the world, the 160-acre zoo is known for its giant panda, Hsing-Hsing, and ambitious Amazonia ecosystem. Many animals are shown in naturalistic settings. *Metro: Cleveland Park, Woodley Park/Zoo.*

Cemeteries

No jogging is allowed, nor picnicking, and you have to be careful where you walk. Still, cemeteries have an appeal unlike any other park. There's the history of those buried there and the art of the tombstones and memorials that mark their graves. Washington has its share of politicians' graves, but more fascinating are the surprises you'll discover in its cemeteries.

Arlington National Cemetery (*see* Tour 11 *in* Chapter 2, Exploring Washington). Once the estate of Robert E. Lee and his family, Arlington's 612 acres are a veritable Who's Who of the American military and politics. Buried here are several Kennedys, Audie Murphy, Joe Louis, Lee Marvin, Dashiell Hammett, and 200,000 other veterans.

Congressional Cemetery (1801 E St. SE, ☎ 202/543–0539) dates from 1807 and was the first national cemetery created by the government. Notables buried here include William Thornton, architect of the U.S. Capitol; John Philip Sousa, composer of the Marine Corps march; Civil War photographer Mathew Brady; and FBI director J. Edgar Hoover.

There are also 76 members of Congress, many of them buried under ponderous markers. A brochure for a self-guided walking tour is available at the office.

Glenwood Cemetery (2219 Lincoln Rd. NE, ☎ 202/667–1016), not far from Catholic University, has its share of notable residents, including the artists Constantino Brumidi, responsible for much of the U.S. Capitol's beauty, and Emanuel Leutze, the painter of *Washington Crossing the Delaware*. More striking are the tombstones of two more obscure citizens. Benjamin Greenup was the first firefighter killed on duty in Washington, and he's honored with an obelisk carved with his death scene. Teresina Vasco, a child who died at age 2 after playing with matches, is immortalized sitting in her favorite rocking chair.

Oak Hill Cemetery (*see* Tour 6 *in* Chapter 2, Exploring Washington), set on terraces stepping down to Rock Creek, may be the most beautiful in Washington. Among those buried here are John H. Payne, who penned "Home Sweet Home," William Corcoran, founder of the Corcoran Gallery of Art, and Edwin M. Stanton, Lincoln's secretary of war.

Rock Creek Cemetery (Rock Creek Church Rd. and Webster St. NW, ☎ 202/829–0585), the city's oldest cemetery, is administered by the city's oldest church, St. Paul's Episcopal, which built its first building in 1775 (though all that remains of that one are its brick walls). There are many beautiful and imposing monuments in the cemetery, but the best known and most moving is the one honoring Marion Hooper "Clover" Adams. The wife of historian Henry Adams committed suicide in 1885, and sculptor Augustus Saint-Gaudens created the enigmatic figure of a seated, shroud-draped figure. Saint-Gaudens called it *The Peace of God that Passeth Understanding,* though it's best known by a more descriptive nickname: "Grief."

Organizations

Hikes and nature walks are listed in the *Washington Post's* Friday "Weekend" section. Outings are sponsored by the following organizations:

Audubon Naturalist Society (8940 Jones Mill Rd., Chevy Chase, MD 20815, ☎ 301/652–9188, ext. 3006) offers wildlife identification walks, environmental education programs, and—in the spring—a weekly Saturday "bird walk" at its suburban Maryland headquarters. Birders interested in new local avian sightings will want to call the Audubon Society's Voice of the Naturalist tape (☎ 301/652–1088).

Potomac-Appalachian Trail Club (118 Park St. SE, Vienna, VA 22180, ☎ 703/242–0965) sponsors hikes—usually free—on trails from Pennsylvania to Virginia, including the C&O Canal and the Appalachian Trail.

Sierra Club (☎ 202/547–2326 and 202/547–5551) offers regional outings for about $1.

6   Dining

By Deborah
Papier

Updated by
Bruce Walker

ALTHOUGH PARTICULAR RESTAURANTS may falter or fall, in general, Washington's restaurants are getting better and better. (And sometimes, cheaper and cheaper: The sluggish economy of the early '90s has meant more reasonably priced fare and fixed-price specials in many of the city's top dining rooms.) In the 1980s, Italian restaurants came to rival French establishments, which had for a long time set the standard in fine dining. Now many French-trained chefs are turning to health-conscious New American cuisine, spicy Southwestern recipes, or tapas for new inspiration.

Despite the dearth of ethnic neighborhoods in Washington and the corresponding lack of the kinds of restaurant districts found in many cities, you *can* find almost any type of food here, from Nepalese to Salvadoran to Ethiopian. In the city's one officially recognized ethnic enclave, **Chinatown** (centered on G and H streets NW between 6th and 8th, with its own Metro station at Gallery Place), innovations such as Mongolian barbecue and hot pot are starting to enliven the menus of the area's plentiful but unexceptional traditional Chinese restaurants. (First-rate Thai restaurants, however, are common throughout the city.)

Aside from Chinatown, there are seven areas of the city where restaurants are concentrated:

Most of the deluxe restaurants are **downtown** near K Street NW, also the location of many of the city's blue-chip law firms. These are the restaurants that feed off expense-account diners and provide the most elegant atmosphere, most attentive service, and often the best food. Thanks to the early '90s recession, the exorbitant prices have either come down or at least not gone up; President Clinton's edicts on government ethics have led to $20 lunch "specials" aimed at lobbyists.

In the old downtown district, remodeling and new construction has slowed. Those restaurants that opened during the building boom, however, continue to thrive, especially if they're along redeveloped Pennsylvania Avenue. Visitors with children can take advantage of the many sandwich shops geared to office workers but will find far fewer choices evenings and weekends. One exception is the Foggy Bottom neighborhood around 20th Street and Pennsylvania Avenue NW, where the presence of George Washington University has attracted family-oriented chains such as T. G. I. Friday's and Mick's.

The other area of town long known as a restaurant district is **Georgetown,** whose central intersection is Wisconsin Avenue and M Street. Georgetown contains some of the city's priciest houses as well as some of its cheesiest businesses, and its restaurants are similarly diverse, with white-tablecloth dining places next door to hole-in-the-wall joints. The closest Metro stop for all Georgetown restaurants is Foggy Bottom/GWU. Keep an eye out, also, for restaurants in the adjacent **West End.** This area, bounded roughly by Rock Creek Park to the west, N Street to the north, 20th Street to the east, and K Street to the south, is increasingly bridging the gap between Georgetown and downtown restaurant zones.

A youthful culinary competitor to Georgetown is **Adams-Morgan.** Eighteenth Street NW extending south from Columbia Road is wall-to-wall restaurants, with new ones opening so fast it's almost impossible to track them. Although the area has retained some of its Hispanic identity, the new eating establishments tend to be Asian, New American, Ethiopian, or Caribbean. The nearest Metro stop—Woodley Park/Zoo—is a 10- to 20-minute walk, and parking can be impossible, so it's better to take a cab here at night. **Woodley Park,** however, has its own lineup of popular ethnic restaurants right by the Metro.

South from Adams-Morgan and north from K Street is **Dupont Circle,** around which a number of restaurants are clustered. Some of the city's best Italian places can be found here, as can a variety of cafés, most boasting outdoor seating. Espresso bars, nurtured here before popping up all over Washington in 1992, are a good source for breakfast and light or late fare. Those on 17th Street NW are especially popular with young adults.

Capitol Hill has a number of bar-eateries that cater to congressional types in need of fortification after a day spent running the country. The dining possibilities on Capitol Hill are boosted by Union Station, which contains some decent, if high-price, restaurants and a large food court with fast food ranging from barbecue to sushi.

The restaurants in many of the city's luxury hotels are another source of fine dining: the Willard Hotel's formal dining room, the Mayflower's Nicholas, the Ritz-Carlton's Jockey Club, and the Morrison-Clark Inn's dining room. These are noted only in the Lodging chapter (with the exception of Jean-Louis Palladin's two establishments at the Watergate, described in this chapter). One caveat: Although their cuisine may be artful and fresh, these hotel restaurants may also have notably high prices and slow service.

Outside the city limits are some thriving restaurant districts. Downtown **Bethesda, Maryland,** offers a wealth of possibilities; some even think that Georgetown is losing business to Bethesda's bistros. Virginia has its Georgetown equivalent in **Old Town Alexandria,** as well as some of the area's best Asian restaurants, in Arlington. Wilson Boulevard in **Arlington** has many popular Vietnamese establishments and branches of other D.C. restaurants. The Bethesda, King Street, and Clarendon Metro stations make these gourmet "ghettos" accessible to visitors.

What to Wear

Gentlemen may be more comfortable wearing jackets and/or ties in $$$ and $$$$ restaurants, even when there is no formal dress code.

CATEGORY	COST*
$$$$	over $35
$$$	$25–$35
$$	$15–$25
$	under $15

per person for a three-course meal, excluding drinks, service, and sales tax (10% in D.C., 4.5%–9% in VA, 5% in MD)

Adams-Morgan/Woodley Park

African

$$ Bukom Cafe. Sunny African pop music, a palm-frond-and-*kente*-cloth decor, and a spicy West African menu brighten this narrow two-story dining room. Appetizers include *kose* (deep-fried balls of black-eyed peas and onions), gizzard kebabs (for the adventurous), and *nklakla* (tomato soup with goat). Entrées range from lamb with melon seeds and whole chicken in cassava leaves to vegetarian dishes such as ratatouille with fried plantains, rice, and peas. Live music nightly and late hours (until 2 AM Wednesday, Thursday, and Sunday; until 3 AM Friday–Saturday) keep this place hopping, even by Adams-Morgan stan-

SEE
ADAMS-MO
WOODLEY PAR
DETAIL M

1 - 9

15 - 24

Theodore
Roosevelt
Island

Theodore
Roosevelt Bridge

California St.
S St.
Decatur Pl.
R St.
Sheridan
Circle Mass. Ave.
Q St.
Rock Creek
P St.
O St.
N St.
M St.
L St.
Pennsylvania Washington
Circle
K St.
Washington
H St.
G St.
F St.
E St.
Virginia Ave.

DUPONT
CIRCLE
Dupont
Circle
FARRAC
W

FOGGY
BOTTOM-GWU

S St.
R St.
34th St.
32nd St.
31st St.
Wisconsin Ave.
31st St.
30th St.
29th St.
28th St.
27th St.
N St.
R St.
P St.
O St.

C&O Canal
K St. (under freeway)
Whitehurst Fwy.
Francis Scott
Key Bridge
George Washington
Memorial Pkwy.

Massachusetts Ave.
Florida Ave.
18th St.
New H
New Hampshire Ave.
Connecticut Ave.
19th St.
20th St.
21st St.
18th St.

22nd St.
25th St.
24th St.
23rd St.
22nd St.
26th St.

Aditi, **13**	Crepizza, **9, 27**	Jean-Louis at the	Madurai, **12**
America, **73**	Galileo, **42**	Watergate Hotel , **33**	Maison Blanche, **55**
American Café, **8,**	Georgia Brown's, **57**	Kinkead's, **43**	Marrakesh, **67**
21, 63, 75	Gerard's Place, **58**	La Brasserie, **76**	The Monocle, **77**
Andalucia, **1**	Hard Rock Cafe, **68**	La Chaumière, **32**	Morton's of
Bistro Français, **29**	Hard Times	La Colline, **79**	Chicago, **22, 26**
Bombay Club, **56**	Cafe, **3, 15**	Las Pampas, **11**	Nora, **36**
Cafe Asia, **45**	Hibiscus Cafe, **14**	Lauriol Plaza, **38**	Notte Luna, **59**
Café Atlántico, **65**	i Ricchi, **50**	Le Lion D'Or, **53**	Obelisk, **39**
Coco Loco, **66**	Jaleo, **70**	Little Viet Garden, **16**	Occidental Grill, **61**
Cottonwood Cafe, **2**		Madeo, **34**	Old Ebbitt Grill, **60**

Old Glory, **30**
Palladin by Jean-Louis, **33**
The Palm, **49**
Panjshir, **17**
Paolo's, **4, 18, 28**
Peasant Restaurant & Bar, **69**
Phillips Flagship, **72**
Pizzeria Paradiso, **40**

Planet Hollywood, **64**
Primi Piatti, **23, 44**
Red, Hot and Blue, **5, 19, 46**
Red Sage, **62**
Rio Grande Cafe, **6, 20**
River Club, **25**
Sala Thai, **41**
Sam and Harry's, **48**

Sarinah Satay House, **10**
Sea Catch, **31**
701 Pennsylvania Avenue, **71**
Sfuzzi, **74**
Skewers, **52**
Star of Siam, **24, 47**
Tabard Inn, **51**
Taberna del Alabardero, **54**

Tastee Diner, **7**
Trattoria al Sole, **35**
Two Quail, **78**
Zorba's Cafe, **37**

dards. ✕ *2442 18th St. NW,* ☎ *202/265–4600. Reservations advised weekends. AE, D, MC, V. Closed Mon. No lunch Sun. Metro: Woodley Park/Zoo.*

Brazilian

$$ The Grill from Ipanema. The Grill focuses on Brazilian cuisine, from spicy seafood stews to grilled steak and other hearty meat dishes. Appetizers include clams baked with hot peppers and cilantro and fried alligator. The traditional *feijoada,* a stew of black beans, pork, and smoked meat, is served Wednesday and Saturday. ✕ *1858 Columbia Rd. NW,* ☎ *202/986–0757. AE, DC, MC, V. No lunch weekdays. Metro: Woodley Park/Zoo.*

Ethiopian

$ Fasika's. Overlooked by some American diners in favor of Meskerem, Fasika's nevertheless attracts plenty of Ethiopian expatriates and Washingtonians with its version of Adams-Morgan's most ubiquitous cuisine. There is no silverware here; instead, the food is scooped up with *injera,* a spongy flat bread that also does duty as the platter on which the meal is presented. The country's main dish is the *watt,* or stew, which may be made with chicken, lamb, beef, or shrimp in a spicy sauce; mild versions are called *alicha.* Several vegetarian watts and alichas are also available. Ethiopian musicians entertain Thursday through Sunday nights. ✕ *2447 18th St. NW,* ☎ *202/797–7673. Reservations advised. AE, DC, MC, V. Metro: Woodley Park/Zoo.*

$ Meskerem. Distinctive for its bright, appealingly decorated dining
★ room, Meskerem has another attractive feature: a balcony where you can eat Ethiopian-style—seated on the floor on leather cushions, with large woven baskets for tables. The specialties here are *fitfit* dishes, in which the injera is served in pieces already soaked in the watt stews; *kitfo,* a buttery raw beef dish like steak tartare that can also be served very rare; and the green chili–spiked potato salad. Meat and vegetarian combination platters are also available. ✕ *2434 18th St. NW,* ☎ *202/462–4100. Reservations advised. AE, DC, MC, V. Metro: Woodley Park/Zoo.*

French

$$ La Fourchette. On a block in Adams-Morgan where new restaurants are opening almost weekly and closing just as fast, La Fourchette has stayed in business since 1978 by offering good bistro food at reasonable prices. Most of the menu consists of daily specials and an early-bird fixed-price menu, but you can pretty much count on finding bouillabaisse and rabbit on the list. The most popular entrées on the regular menu are the hearty veal and lamb shanks. La Fourchette also looks the way a bistro should, with an exposed brick wall, a tin ceiling, bentwood chairs, and quasi-post-Impressionist murals. ✕ *2429 18th St. NW,* ☎ *202/332–3077. Reservations advised for groups. AE, DC, MC, V. No lunch weekends. Metro: Woodley Park/Zoo.*

Italian

$$ i Matti. Owned by chef Roberto Donna of the highly praised Galileo, i Matti is a much less formal but just as popular restaurant. The stark modern setting and the crowds of well-dressed young people somehow encapsulate Adams-Morgan chic. It's possible to order anything from a pizza to polenta to a multicourse meal from the large menu. The breads, including six types of *bruschetta* (grilled bread with olive oil and garlic), and the pizzas are delicious. Osso buco is a good bet in winter. ✕ *2436 18th St. NW,* ☎ *202/462–8844. Reservations advised. AE, DC, MC, V. No lunch Sun. Metro: Woodley Park/Zoo.*

Bukom Cafe, **6**
Fasika's, **5**
The Grill from
Ipanema, **3**
i Matti, **7**
La Fourchette, **9**
Meskerem, **8**
New Heights, **2**
Peyote Café, **10**
Saigon
Gourmet, **1**
Star of Siam, **4**

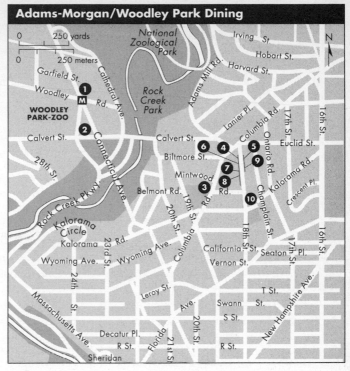

New American

$$$ **New Heights.** With its precise geometrical design softened by pastel colors, New Heights is one of Washington's most attractive restaurants. (Robert De Niro booked it for a private lunch during Clinton's inauguration week.) The menu varies seasonally but always includes a vegetarian entrée, such as Thai-style ravioli. Salmon, a frequent offering, might be grilled with vegetables, swiss chard, and horseradish beurre blanc. The restaurant is a good choice for Sunday brunch. ✕ 2317 Calvert St. NW, ☎ 202/234–4110. Reservations advised. AE, D, DC, MC, V. No lunch Mon.–Sat. Metro: Woodley Park/Zoo.

Southwestern/Tex-Mex

$ **Peyote Café.** Located downstairs from Roxanne Restaurant (from whose Southwestern menu you may also order), this pub takes cheeky liberties with its decor and food, and wins with both. Twinkling lights, tables with bar stools, and a swinging jukebox attract a young crowd of primarily students and singles. The eclectic menu aims to please everyone: Meat eaters can choose from such dishes as *carne asada* (grilled rib-eye steak), grilled salmon, "gringo-killer" fried chicken, and "sweat hot fire" shrimp. Vegetarians look for the cactus sign on the menu, which indicates meatless dishes. ✕ 2319 18th St. NW, ☎ 202/462–8330. No reservations. AE, DC, MC, V. No lunch weekdays. Metro: Woodley Park/Zoo.

Thai

$$ **Star of Siam.** This three-restaurant chain doesn't offer the hottest or most elaborately presented Thai cuisine, but its dishes are among the most reliable in the city. Spicy-food lovers can try the squid salad or boneless roast duck appetizers and an entrée such as beef curry with coconut milk, eggplant, potato, and peanut. Vegetarians should skip the blander rice and egg noodle plates and opt for *pad pik pak*, a stir-fry of mixed vegetables with hot pepper. Soups are fragrant and on the tangy side. ✗ *2446 18th St. NW (upstairs; Metro: Woodley Park/Zoo),* ☎ *202/986–4133; also 1136 19th St. NW (Metro: Dupont Circle),* ☎ *202/785–2839; and 1735 N. Lynn St. in Arlington, VA (Metro: Rosslyn),* ☎ *703/524–1208. Weekend reservations advised. AE, D, DC, MC, V. Adams-Morgan: no lunch weekdays; downtown: no lunch Sun.; Rosslyn: no lunch weekends.*

Vietnamese

$$ **Saigon Gourmet.** Service is brisk and friendly at this popular, French-influenced dining room. The upscale neighborhood patrons return for the ultracrisp *cha-gio* (spring rolls), the savory *pho* (beef broth), and seafood soups, and the delicately seasoned and richly sauced entrées. Shrimp Saigon mixes prawns and pork in a peppery marinade, and another Saigon dish—grilled pork with rice crepes—is a Vietnamese variation on Chinese *moo shu*. Bananas flambé are an entertaining way to end a meal, as the waiter seems to pour flames from one plate to the other. ✗ *2635 Connecticut Ave. NW,* ☎ *202/265–1360. Reservations advised. AE, D, DC, MC, V. Metro: Woodley Park/Zoo.*

Capitol Hill

American

$$$ **America.** A Washington outpost of owner Michael Weinstein's America in New York, Union Station's America is installed in the west front, with a two-story section in the center and a seasonal outdoor café. The high ceilings of the renovated station amplify the din of this lively bar and restaurant. The menu is enormous, with nearly four square feet of regular offerings ranging from Kansas City steaks and Minnesota scrambled eggs to New Orleans *muffuletta* sandwiches, New Mexico–style pasta, Jersey pork chops, and San Diego fish tacos. The kitchen has its successes and failures—a good general rule is "the simpler the better." Desserts are good, and service is pleasant though chaotic. ✗ *Union Station, 50 Massachusetts Ave. NE,* ☎ *202/682–9555. Reservations advised. AE, DC, MC, V. Metro: Union Station.*

$$$ **The Monocle.** Separated in both location and ambience from the younger, more bustling Capitol Hill scene, the Monocle is still probably the best place for spotting senators at lunch and dinner; management keeps members of Congress informed on when it's time to vote. The cooking, American cuisine with a Continental touch, is adequate if unexciting, but it's the old-style Capitol Hill atmosphere, not the food, that's the real draw here. Seafood is a specialty; try the crab cakes, and take advantage of the fresh fish specials. The fireplaces and political portraits in this former pair of town houses add to the aura of cozy tradition. ✗ *107 D St. NE,* ☎ *202/546–4488. Reservations advised. AE, DC, MC, V. Closed Sun. No lunch Sat. Metro: Union Station.*

$$ **Two Quail.** A welcome respite from the men's club atmosphere of traditional Capitol Hill eateries, this cute, floral-pattern tearoom is tops among women for both romantic and power dining. The smallish menu has both rich fare—apricot-stuffed pork chop, chicken stuffed with cornbread and pecans, or filet mignon—and lighter, seafood pastas and meal-size salads. Service can be leisurely. ✗ *320 Massachusetts Ave. NE,* ☎ *202/543–8030. Reservations advised. AE, DC, MC, V. No lunch weekends. Metro: Union Station.*

French

$$$ **La Brasserie.** La Brasserie is one of Capitol Hill's most pleasant, most satisfying restaurants. The dining rooms are on two floors of adjoining town houses, with outdoor dining in season. The basically French menu changes daily, a good indication of the cuisine's character. The crème brûlée, served cold or hot with fruit, is superb. For breakfast, this small spot is charming. ✗ *239 Massachusetts Ave. NE,* ☎ *202/546– 9154. Reservations advised. AE, DC, MC, V. Metro: Union Station.*

$$$ **La Colline.** Chef Robert Gréault has worked to make La Colline into
★ one of the city's best French restaurants and the best of any type on Capitol Hill. The menu, which changes daily, places an emphasis on seafood, with offerings ranging from simple grilled preparations to fricassées and gratins with imaginative sauces. The nonseafood menu usually offers duck with an orange or cassis sauce and veal with chanterelles. The dessert selection is plentiful, as is the wine list. Capitol Hill power brokers also favor La Colline, with its in-house bakery, for weekday breakfast. ✗ *400 N. Capitol St.,* ☎ *202/737–0400. Reservations advised. AE, DC, MC, V. Closed Sun. No lunch Sat. Metro: Union Station.*

Italian

$$$ **Sfuzzi.** Its prime location in the southeast corner of Union Station, Capitol view upstairs, and trompe l'oeil classical-Italian interior attract a young, noisy crowd of Hill staffers. Although more elaborate American-Italian concoctions are available, the best items on the menu are the pizzas, which may be ordered as an appetizer to be shared or as a main course. The crust is crisp, yeasty, and flavorful, and the toppings immaculately fresh and varied. Its bistro features lighter, inexpensive fare such as salads and sandwiches. ✗ *Union Station, 50 Massachusetts Ave. NE,* ☎ *202/842–4141. Reservations advised. AE, DC, MC, V. Metro: Union Station.*

Seafood

$$ **Phillips Flagship.** This enormous seafood restaurant draws people by the hundreds; the Waterman's Harvest buffet (available with lobster in season) and Sunday brunch are perennially popular. Its cavernous rooms and capacious decks overlook the Capitol Yacht Club's marina; there's a sushi bar (Mon.–Sat.), a party room with its own deck, catering rooms, and space for 1,400. Despite its size, a large, amiable staff serves the excellent seafood with dispatch. The succulent soft crabs, large crab cakes, and special blackened catfish are accompanied by chunky fresh vegetables, perfectly cooked. There's parking across the street and underground, and the restaurant is accessible to people using wheelchairs. ✗ *900 Water St. SW,* ☎ *202/488–8515. AE, D, DC, MC, V. Metro: l'Enfant Plaza.*

Downtown

American

$$$$ **The Palm.** Food trends come and go, but the Palm pays no attention; it offers the same hearty food it always has—gargantuan steaks and Nova Scotia lobsters, several kinds of potatoes, New York cheesecake. The staff's been packing them in since the mid-'70s with this kind of fare, and they're not about to let the calorie- and cholesterol-counters spoil the party. Its plain decor is patterned after the New York original, and the businesslike air is matched by the clientele. The Palm also offers a bargain lunch menu that includes shrimp, veal, and chicken salad. ✗ *1225 19th St. NW,* ☎ *202/293–9091. Reservations advised. AE, DC, MC, V. No lunch weekends. Metro: Dupont Circle.*

$$$$ **Sam and Harry's.** The surroundings are understated and genteel, the Evening Star jazz bar is a popular downtown gathering place, and the dining room is packed at lunch and dinner. Although the miniature crab cakes are a good way to begin, the main attractions are the porterhouse steak, the prime rib, and the signature strip steak. For those who've sworn off beef, Sam and Harry's also has daily fish specials and Maine lobster. Desserts are all made in its kitchen. ✗ *1200 19th St. NW,* ☎ *202/296–4333. Reservations advised. AE, DC, MC, V. Closed Sun. No lunch Sat. Metro: Dupont Circle.*

$$$ **Peasant Restaurant & Bar.** The Atlanta-based Peasant Corporation also owns the Pleasant Peasant (☎ 202/364–2500) in Mazza Gallerie (Metro: Friendship Heights) and the inexpensive, family-oriented Mick's (2401 Pennsylvania Ave. NW, ☎ 202/331–9613; 1220 19th St. NW, ☎ 202/785–2866). The company made its downtown location traditional and clubby, with dark-wood paneling and crisp white tablecloths. Its proximity to Capitol Hill makes it a popular spot for lobbying lunches. The daily menu is in the New American melting-pot style and likely to include pasta selections, grilled fish, and steaks. The signature desserts are enormous and rich. ✗ *801 Pennsylvania Ave. NW,* ☎ *202/638–2140. Reservations advised. AE, D, DC, MC, V. No lunch weekends. Metro: Archives/Navy Memorial.*

$$ **Old Ebbitt Grill.** This reincarnation of Washington's longest-lived restaurant is obviously doing something right—it does more business than almost any other eating place in town. People flock here to drink at the several bars, which seem to go on for miles, and to enjoy the oyster bar and carefully prepared bar food that includes buffalo chicken wings, hamburgers, and Reuben sandwiches. But this is not just a place for casual nibbling; the Old Ebbitt offers serious diners homemade pastas and a list of daily specials, with the emphasis on fish dishes and steak. Despite the crowds, the restaurant never feels cramped, thanks to its well-spaced, comfortable booths. Service can be slow at lunch. ✗ *675 15th St. NW,* ☎ *202/347–4800. Reservations advised. AE, DC, MC, V. Metro: Metro Center.*

$ **American Café.** In 1980 someone had the bright idea of opening a restaurant that would serve fresh, healthful food—but not health food—at affordable prices in a casual environment. And so the American Café empire was born. Sandwiches, such as the namesake roast beef on a humongous croissant, are still the mainstay of the café, with salads and nibbles rounding off the regular menu. But specials, which change every two weeks, are often intriguing: a fresh fish, a seafood pie, a chicken dish, and barbecued ribs. Weekend brunches offer temptations such as strawberry-banana-nut waffles and stuffed French toast. Service can be slow, but families and downtown diners on a budget find the American Cafés a lifesaver. ✗ *The Shops at National Place,* ☎ *202/626–0770; 227 Massachusetts Ave. NE,* ☎ *202/547–8500; 5252 Wisconsin Ave. NW,* ☎ *202/363–5400; 4238 Wilson Blvd., Arlington, VA,* ☎ *703/522–2236; 8601 Westward Center Dr., Vienna, VA,* ☎ *703/848–9488. AE, MC, V.*

$ **Hard Rock Cafe.** If you can stand the loud music—and the tourist-season line to get in—you'll find respectable American fare at one of the few downtown restaurants open daily for lunch *and* dinner. A fruit and veggie sandwich and a veggie burger are two alternatives to the heartier offerings, such as the pulled-pork "pig sandwich," predictable burgers, and a New York strip steak. Sweets include shakes, sundaes, and a banana split. ✗ *999 E St. NW,* ☎ *202/737–7625. No reservations. AE, MC, V. Metro: Metro Center.*

$ **Planet Hollywood.** This celebrity-owned chain restaurant serves California "new classic" cuisine, with the accent on healthful dishes. Burgers come in beef, turkey, and veggie versions. You also get meat, poultry, and veggie choices in pizza and pasta. From the dessert menu, try some of Arnold Schwarzenegger's mother's apple strudel with cinnamon, sour cream sauce, and nutmeg ice cream. There's plenty of memorabilia—from Marlene Dietrich's "Blonde Venus" costume to a Luke Perry–autographed surfboard. Also, check out the handprint wall, with plaster palm prints of Harrison Ford, Wesley Snipes, Lauren Bacall, Clint Eastwood, and others. ✕ *1101 Pennsylvania Ave. NW,* ☎ *202/783–7827. No reservations. AE, D, MC, V. Metro: Federal Triangle.*

Asian

$ **Cafe Asia.** One of the rare pan-Asian restaurants with few weak spots, Cafe Asia presents Japanese, Chinese, Thai, Singaporean, Indonesian, and Vietnamese variations on succulent themes. Highlights include grilled shrimp paste on sugarcane, moist *satays* (skewered meats), spicy fish in banana leaves, and a sushi bar. Vegetarians can choose from several tofu dishes, curries, and salads. The decor is spartan and the staff small, but the low prices and multiple cuisines make waits worthwhile. At dinnertime the patrons are more the young Dupont Circle crowd than suited downtowners. ✕ *1134 19th St. NW,* ☎ *202/659–2696. AE, MC, V. Closed Sun. Metro: Dupont Circle.*

Caribbean

$$ **Café Atlántico.** Formerly one of the liveliest spots in Adams-Morgan,
★ Café Atlántico in 1995 moved to the booming "Pennsylvania Quarter" in search of a bigger home. Appetizers include conch or cod fritters, shrimp and potato croquettes, and yuca fritters, all beautifully fried. Pork loin, jerk chicken, a vegetarian plate, and lamb curry are among the main courses. Service is friendly and helpful. ✕ *8th and E Sts. NW,* ☎ *202/328–5844. No reservations. AE, DC, MC, V. Closed lunch. Metro: Gallery Place/Chinatown.*

French

$$$$ **Jean-Louis at the Watergate Hotel.** A showcase for the cooking of Jean-
★ Louis Palladin, this small restaurant is often cited as one of the best in the United States. The contemporary French fare is based on regional American ingredients—crawfish from Louisiana, wild mushrooms from Oregon, game from Texas—combined in innovative ways. There are two limited choice, fixed-price dinners: one with five courses for $85 per person, the other with six courses (the additional course is a foie gras dish), for $95. There is also a pretheater menu of four courses for $45, designed for, but not limited to, those attending the nearby Kennedy Center. In 1993 Palladin opened a less formal restaurant upstairs offering simpler, markedly less expensive concoctions such as pot-au-feu, steak, sausage, and attractively presented salads. Palladin by Jean-Louis, as it's called, is open daily for breakfast, lunch, and dinner; reservations are suggested (☎ *202/298–4455; $$$*). ✕ *2650 Virginia Ave. NW (downstairs in Watergate Hotel, which can be entered from Virginia or New Hampshire Aves.),* ☎ *202/298–4488. Reservations required. Jacket and tie. AE, DC, MC, V. Dinner only. Closed Sun., Mon., and Aug. Metro: Foggy Bottom.*

$$$$ **Le Lion D'Or.** Other French restaurants may flirt with fads, but this one
★ sticks to the classics—or at any rate the neoclassics—and does them so well that its popularity remains undiminished year after year. This is the sort of food that makes the French posture of cultural superiority almost defensible: lobster soufflé, crepes with oysters and caviar, ravioli with foie gras, salmon with crayfish, and roast pigeon with mushrooms. The long list of daily specials can get rather confusing unless you take notes while the waiter recites them. But don't forget to place an order for a dessert soufflé. ✕ *1150 Connecticut Ave. NW (entrance on 18th St. NW),* ☎ *202/296–7972. Reservations advised. Jacket and tie. AE, DC, MC, V. Closed Sun. No lunch Sat. Metro: Farragut North.*

$$$$ **Maison Blanche.** This perennial power-broker favorite owes its bipartisan popularity not only to its location near the White House and executive office buildings but also to its Old World elegance, the friendliness of the family that runs it, and its large repertoire of classic and modern French dishes. The menu, which changes four times a year, is supplemented by a large number of daily specials, primarily fish. Maison Blanche goes to great lengths to obtain Dover sole, which it serves simply grilled. This is perhaps the restaurant's most popular dish, but also exceptional are the rack of lamb and the pasta dishes. The pastry chef has a proper reverence for chocolate, and the wine list is extensive, with California wines well represented. ✕ *1725 F St. NW,* ☎ *202/842–0070. Reservations advised. AE, DC, MC, V. Closed Sun. No lunch Sat. Metro: Farragut West.*

Indian

$$$ **Bombay Club.** Just a block from the White House, the Bombay Club
★ tries to re-create for tired Executive Office bureaucrats, power lawyers, and journalists the kind of solace they might have found in a private club had they been 19th-century British colonials in India rather than late-20th-century Washingtonians. It's a beautiful restaurant. The bar, which serves hot hors d'oeuvres at cocktail hour, is furnished with rattan chairs and paneled with dark wood. The dining room, with potted palms and a bright blue ceiling above white plaster moldings, is elegant and decorous. The menu includes unusual seafood specialties and a large number of vegetarian dishes, but the real standouts are the breads and the seafood appetizers. ✕ *815 Connecticut Ave. NW,* ☎ *202/659–3727. Reservations advised. AE, DC, MC, V. No lunch Sat. Metro: Farragut West.*

International

$$$ **Coco Loco.** One of the hot spots in the "Pennsylvania Quarter" area, Coco Loco serves Mexican tapas, such as shrimp stuffed with white cheese and wrapped in bacon, red snapper with coconut milk and plantains, and *chiles rellenos* (stuffed chilis) in a tomato-cream puree, at the tapas bar and in the front dining area. If you're into serious meat-eating, try the Brazilian-style *churrasqueria*—a parade of skewered grilled meats that are brought to your table and sliced right onto your plate. Wednesday through Saturday night, half the restaurant becomes an upscale nightclub. ✕ *810 7th St. NW,* ☎ *202/289–2626. Reservations advised. AE, DC, MC, V. No lunch weekends. Metro: Gallery Place/Chinatown.*

$$$ **Gerard's Place.** Gerard Pangaud left the Ritz-Carlton Pentagon City
★ to come downtown. He left excesses behind, concentrating on fresh, intriguingly prepared entrées like poached lobster with a ginger, lime, and Sauternes sauce; venison served with dried fruits and pumpkin and beetroot purees; and seared tuna with black olives and roasted red peppers. Desserts are exquisite; like the chocolate tear (a teardrop-shape flourless chocolate cake veined with raspberry), they usually float on an equally delicious coulis. The main dining room is strikingly colored in gray and burnt umber. A private dining room was added in 1995. ✕ *915 15th St. NW,* ☎ *202/737–4445. Reservations advised. AE, MC, V. Closed Sun. No lunch Sat. Metro: McPherson Square.*

$$$ **701 Pennsylvania Avenue.** This sleek restaurant features an eclectic cuisine drawn from Italy, France, Asia, and the Americas. You might start your meal with tuna tartar topped with caviar, progress to a Moroccan-style grilled tuna with herbed couscous, and finish with an Italian cappuccino cake. The restaurant's Caviar Lounge offers choices ranging from beluga to Alaskan keta and 18 types of vodka. The fixed-price pretheater dinner ($21.50) is popular; diners include Shakespeare Theatre patrons and well-dressed political power brokers. ✕ *701 Pennsylvania Ave. NW,* ☎ *202/393–0701. Reservations advised. AE, DC, MC, V. No lunch weekends. Metro: Archives/Navy Memorial.*

Italian

$$$$ **Galileo.** Chef Roberto Donna's more formal companion to i Matti (*see*
★ *above*), this spacious, popular restaurant boasts homemade everything, from bread sticks to mozzarella. And it all tastes terrific. The menu changes twice daily, but there is always risotto; a long list of grilled fish; a game bird, such as quail, guinea hen, or woodcock; and one or two beef or veal dishes. Preparations are generally simple. For example, the veal chop might be served with mushroom-and-rosemary sauce, the beef with black-olive sauce and polenta. ✕ *1110 21st St. NW,* ☎ *202/293–7191. Reservations advised. AE, DC, MC, V. No lunch weekends. Metro: Foggy Bottom.*

$$$ **i Ricchi.** Priced for expense accounts, i Ricchi remains a favorite of crit-
★ ics and crowds for its earthy Tuscan cuisine. There are two menus, one for spring and summer, one for fall and winter. The spring list includes such offerings as rolled pork and rabbit roasted in wine and fresh herbs, and skewered shrimp; winter brings grilled lamb chops, thick soups, and sautéed beef fillet. But whatever the calendar says, it always feels like spring in this airy dining room, which is decorated with terra-cotta tiles, cream-color archways, and floral frescoes. ✕ *1220 19th St. NW,* ☎ *202/835–0459. Reservations advised. AE, DC, MC, V. Closed Sun. No lunch Sat. Metro: Dupont Circle.*

$$ **Notte Luna.** This glitzy, power-lunch spot features a dramatic black-and-neon dining room, an open kitchen with a wood-burning pizza oven, and informal, ambitious cuisine. The menu offers the Italian-restaurant staples of pasta, pizza, and veal dishes, but with unexpected twists. You can order your cracker-thin pizza topped with lamb sausage or your pasta with grilled salmon. All meals start with crisp bread, cheese spread, and olives. Desserts, such as fresh berries or *tiramisù*, are always a treat. ✕ *809 15th St. NW,* ☎ *202/408–9500. Reservations advised. AE, DC, MC, V. No lunch weekends. Metro: McPherson Square.*

$$ **Primi Piatti.** A meal here—at the D.C. branch, at least—is like a taxi ride in Rome at rush hour: The crowds and the noise are overwhelming, but you'll never forget the trip. The restaurant makes a point of serving dishes that are both authentically Italian and light and healthful. There's a wood-burning grill, on which several kinds of fish are cooked each day—tuna with raisins and pine nuts is one preparation—as well as lamb and veal chops. Meat is also done to a succulent turn on the rotisserie. Pastas are made in house and are quite good, as are the pizzas. The wine list is unusually descriptive. ✕ *2013 I St. NW,* ☎ *202/223–3600; 8045 Leesburg Pike, Vienna, VA,* ☎ *703/893–0300. Reservations advised. AE, DC, MC, V. No lunch weekends. Metro: Farragut West or Foggy Bottom (Virginia location is about 2 mi from West Falls Church Metro stop).*

Moroccan

$$ **Marrakesh.** This is one of Washington's happy surprises: a bit of Morocco in a part of the city better known for auto-supply shops. The menu is a fixed-price ($22) feast shared by everyone at your table and eaten without silverware. The first course is a platter of three salads; the second, *b'stella*—a chicken version of Morocco's traditional pigeon pie. For the first main course, you choose among several chicken preparations; the second main course consists of beef or lamb. These are followed by vegetable couscous, fresh fruit, mint tea, and pastries. Belly dancers put on a nightly show. Alcoholic drinks can really drive up the tab here. ✕ *617 New York Ave. NW,* ☎ *202/393–9393. Reservations required. No credit cards (checks accepted). Dinner only. Metro: Mount Vernon Square.*

New American

$$$ Occidental Grill. In the stately Willard Hotel complex, this popular restaurant used to be two establishments: the formal Occidental upstairs and the clubby Occidental Grill downstairs. But in keeping with the economizing sensibility of today's city, the two merged and now offer innovative and artful dishes, attentive service, and lots of photos of politicians and other power brokers past and present. The menu changes frequently, but you can count on poultry, fish, and steak as grilled options—tuna might be marinated in fresh herbs and garlic and served with a tomato *tapenade* (a condiment made with capers, anchovies, and olives)—plus salads and sandwiches. ✕ *1475 Pennsylvania Ave. NW,* ☎ *202/783–1475. Reservations advised. AE, DC, MC, V. Metro: Metro Center.*

$$–$$$ Kinkead's. When chef Bob Kinkead's glossy, formal Twenty-One Federal restaurant closed in 1992, some saw it as the belated end of the '80s. The emphasis in his new establishment is on the kitchen, not your checkbook; the multichambered dining room even includes a downstairs pub with American-style tapas (a '90s buzzword) and other inexpensive fare. Upstairs, you can watch Kinkead and company turn out grilled dishes (such as squid) with garden salsas, Southwestern-inspired seafood soups and appetizers, and a few savory meat and fowl dishes. A fresh sorbet finishes your meal with a light tang. Sunday brunch is an engaging choice. ✕ *2000 Pennsylvania Ave. NW,* ☎ *202/296–7700. Reservations advised. AE, DC, MC, V. No dinner upstairs Sun. Metro: Foggy Bottom.*

$$ Madeo. Each month the adventurous chef here offers a different three-course fixed-price dinner ($18.95) to tempt large appetites. The creative American dishes, which emphasize seafood, now share the plate with Southwestern-inspired fare. Be prepared for hefty portions of desserts like bread pudding and cannoli. The long, narrow shape of this pretty room is mitigated by an airy atrium ceiling. ✕ *1113 23rd St. NW,* ☎ *202/457–0057. Reservations advised. AE, DC, MC, V. Metro: Foggy Bottom.*

Southern

$$$ Georgia Brown's. Opened in 1993 in the space of the much-beloved McPherson Grill, this elegant New Southern establishment quickly won over the old clientele of government officials, lobbyists, and *Washington Post* journalists. Chef Terrell Danley serves shrimp head on, Carolina style; braised rabbit with hoppin' John and smoked bacon green beans; and beef tenderloin medallions with a bourbon-pecan sauce and fried-grits cake. Fried green tomatoes are given the gourmet treatment, while vegetarians can enjoy a nutty roasted eggplant soup or a salad of poached pears, goat cheese, and mesclun greens followed by a vegetable plate of roasted corn, delicately crunchy lima and green beans, and mushroom rice. The airy, curving dining room has white honeycomb windows and an unusual ceiling ornamentation of bronze ribbons. ✕ *950 15th St. NW,* ☎ *202/393–4499. Reservations advised. AE, DC, MC, V. No lunch Sat. Metro: McPherson Square.*

Southwestern/Tex-Mex

$$$
★   Red Sage. Within lassoing distance of the White House, this upscale rancher's delight has pulled in both George Bush and Bill Clinton since its opening in 1992. Millions were spent on the decor, which includes a barbed-wire-and-lizard theme, and a pseudo-adobe warren of

dining rooms. Upstairs is the chili bar and café, where thrifty trend-setters can enjoy the comparatively inexpensive sandwiches and ap-petizers. Downstairs, chef Mark Miller's Berkeley-Santa Fe background surfaces in elaborate, artful presentations, such as grilled duck breast with *habanero* pepper and fig sausage, spicy lamb chops with wild-mushroom tamale, red chili risotto, and even a vegetarian plate. Chilis are everywhere, but the limited selection of entrées includes lighter op-tions now. That's good, because you'll want to save room for homey desserts like plum cobbler with cinnamon ice cream. An in-house mar-ket sells baked goods. ✕ *605 14th St. NW,* ☎ *202/638–4444. Reser-vations advised. AE, D, DC, MC, V. No lunch Sun. Metro: Metro Center.*

Spanish

$$$ **Taberna del Alabardero.** Spanish is spoken here—a regal Castilian that matches the formal dining room and high-class service. You can start with tapas ranging from a hefty gazpacho to fried calamari and ven-ture on to authentic paella, seafood casseroles, and elegant Spanish "country" dishes. The plush Old World decor and handsome bar cre-ate a romantic atmosphere. The clientele is similarly well-heeled and cosmopolitan. ✕ *1776 I St. NW (entrance on 18th St.),* ☎ *202/429–2200. Reservations advised. AE, DC, MC, V. Closed Sun. No lunch Sat. Metro: Farragut West.*

$$ **Jaleo.** This lively Spanish bistro encourages you to make a meal out
★ of its long list of hot and cold tapas, although such entrées as paella, seafood stew, and grilled fish are perfectly respectable (and equally fill-ing). Highlights of the appetizer-sized tapas are *gambas al ajillo* (sautéed garlic shrimp), fried potatoes with spicy tomato sauce, *pinchitos* (a skewer of grilled chorizo) with garlic mashed potatoes, and from the cold menu, a salad of black beans and garbanzos with oranges, and roasted veg-etables tossed with oil and sherry vinegar. The gazpacho is substantial and garlicky, and you can offset all that garlic with apple flan or a fruit and nut tart. ✕ *480 7th St. NW,* ☎ *202/628–7949. AE, D, MC, V. Metro: Archives/Navy Memorial.*

Dupont Circle

Greek

$ **Zorba's Cafe.** A family of four can eat heartily—and tastily—for less than $25 at this popular Greek eatery. Two inside levels and outdoor seating in season accommodate fans of Zorba's grilled meat and homey vegetable dishes. The half chicken marinated in oregano is a winner, but be sure to check out the specials. Vegetarians and light eaters will find much to choose from. Pizza, subs, and sandwiches are available for non-Greek palates. The grill is open until 11 PM (10 PM Sundays). ✕ *1612 20th St. NW,* ☎ *202/387–8555. No reservations. No credit cards. Metro: Dupont Circle.*

Italian

$$$ **Obelisk.** Here you can find eclectic Italian cuisine and a small, fixed-price menu ($38) that includes both traditional dishes and chef Peter Pastan's imaginative innovations. The list, which changes daily, usu-ally offers one meat, one fish, and one poultry entrée. The meat is likely to be lamb, with garlic and sage or perhaps anchovies; fish might be a pompano stuffed with bay leaves; a typical poultry selection is the hardly typical pigeon with chanterelles. The minimally decorated din-ing room is tiny, with tables so closely spaced that even whispers can be overheard. ✕ *2029 P St. NW,* ☎ *202/872–1180. Reservations ad-vised. MC, V. Dinner only. Closed Sun. Metro: Dupont Circle.*

$$$ **Trattoria al Sole.** Formerly called Vincenzo, al Sole changed its name
★ and lowered its prices but continues to offer many of the same dishes
with no change in quality. The emphasis is on simply prepared seafood
dishes such as *tiella di pesce* (seafood and potato casserole) and *branzino
al salmoriglio* (grilled rockfish with oregano). The menu also includes
meat and game dishes such as roast duck with polenta. Part of the din-
ing room is in an airy, glass-roof courtyard. ✕ *1606 20th St. NW,* ☎
*202/667–0047. Reservations advised. AE, DC, MC, V. Closed Sun.
No lunch Sat. Metro: Dupont Circle.*

$ **Pizzeria Paradiso.** Sharing a kitchen with elite Obelisk, this petite
pizzeria sticks to crowd-pleasing basics: pizzas, *panini* (sandwiches),
a few salads, and desserts. Although the standard pizza is satisfying,
you can enliven things by ordering it with fresh buffalo mozzarella or
unusual toppings such as potatoes, capers, and mussels. The sandwiches
are assembled with homemade focaccia; gelato is also a house specialty.
The trompe l'oeil ceiling adds space and light to a simple interior. ✕
2029 P St. NW, ☎ *202/223–1245. No reservations. DC, MC, V.
Metro: Dupont Circle.*

Middle Eastern

$$ **Skewers.** As the name implies, the focus is on kebabs, served with al-
mond-flaked rice or pasta. The lamb with eggplant and the chicken
with roasted pepper are the most popular, but filet mignon and shrimp
are equally tasty. The vegetable kebabs and the array of appetizers, such
as hummus with *fool* (fava beans), make this ideal for vegetarians.
Minikebabs are served either with pita bread or in a salad. If the
restaurant is too crowded, you can enjoy the cheap California eats downstairs at Café Luna (☎ 202/387–4005) or the reading room-coffee-
house upstairs at Luna Books (☎ 202/332–2543). ✕ *1633 P St. NW,*
☎ *202/387–7400. Weekend reservations advised. AE, DC, MC, V.
Metro: Dupont Circle.*

New American

$$$ **Nora.** Although it bills itself as an "organic restaurant," Nora is no col-
lective-run juice bar. The food is sophisticated and attractive, like the
quilt-decorated dining room. The menu changes daily; starters have in-
cluded a mango and brie quesadilla with sun-dried cherry salsa and a
Dungeness crab and shiitake cake. Entrées such as fish or loin lamb chops
may be grilled, and a vegetarian plate balances such hearty dishes as
veal scaloppine and Indonesian beef on skewers. Desserts are listed with
recommended wines and brandies: pear and blueberry cobbler and pra-
line ice cream, for example, with calvados. Patrons may want to try chef
Nora Pouillon's Asia Nora in the West End (2213 M St. NW, ☎
202/797–4860; $$–$$$$). ✕ *2132 Florida Ave. NW,* ☎ *202/462–5143.
Reservations advised. MC, V. Dinner only. Closed Sun. Metro: Dupont
Circle.*

$$$ **Tabard Inn.** With its artfully artless decor and quasi-health-food menu,
the Tabard is an idiosyncratic restaurant in a town-house hotel that
has a devoted clientele of baby boomers with '60s values and '80s in-
comes. The lounge looks like a garage sale waiting to happen, and the
two dining rooms are likewise somewhat shabby. But the courtyard
may be Washington's prettiest outdoor eatery, and the Tabard's New
American cuisine, although it doesn't always quite come off, is fresh
and interesting. The produce that the Inn uses is grown without the
use of pesticides; meat is hormone-free and naturally raised. Most of
the menu changes daily; complicated preparations of fish and vegetarian
platters are specialties. Breakfast and brunch here are a treat. ✕ *1739
N St. NW,* ☎ *202/833–2668. Reservations advised. MC, V. Metro:
Dupont Circle.*

South American/Spanish

$$ Lauriol Plaza. Located in upper Dupont Circle, halfway to Adams-Morgan, this charming corner enclave flirted briefly with Tex-Mex before popular demand restored Spanish dishes to prominence. Tortilla chips and other Mexican/Latin American standards are still available, but sangria, seviche, and rustic entrées like tongue are specialties. The simply decorated dining room, with white tablecloths and white walls enlivened by gilt-framed paintings, can get noisy; the terrace is preferable in good weather. ✕ *1801 18th St. NW,* ☎ *202/387–0035. No reservations. AE, DC, MC, V.*

Thai

$$ Sala Thai. This is not the sort of Thai restaurant where you go for the burn; Sala Thai will make the food as spicy as you wish, but the chef is interested in flavor, not fire. Among the subtly seasoned offerings are *panang goong* (shrimp in curry-peanut sauce), chicken sautéed with ginger and pineapple, and flounder with a choice of four sauces. Mirrored walls and soft lights soften the ambience of this small downstairs dining room. ✕ *2016 P St. NW,* ☎ *202/872–1144. AE, DC, MC, V. Metro: Dupont Circle.*

Georgetown/West End

American

$$$$ Morton's of Chicago. This national steak house chain claims to serve the country's best beef, and it's certainly not the vinyl-boothed dining room that keeps it busy. In the classic steak house tradition, Morton's emphasizes quantity as well as quality. The New York strip and porterhouse steaks, two of the most popular offerings, are well over a pound each. For diners with even larger appetites (or those sharing), there's a 3-pound porterhouse. Morton's also includes lamb, veal, chicken, lobster, and grilled fish on its menu—which for some reason is not printed but instead recited by a waiter who displays the raw ingredients on a cart. ✕ *3251 Prospect St.,* ☎ *202/342–6258; 8075 Leesburg Pike, Vienna, VA,* ☎ *703/883–0800. Reservations advised. AE, DC, MC, V. Georgetown branch: dinner only; Virginia branch: no lunch weekends.*

Argentine

$$ Las Pampas. Grilled fresh fish and a smattering of Tex-Mex staples now supplement the traditional Argentine menu, which reflects that country's love of beef and its Continental heritage. The beef, which is fresh, not aged, is cooked over a special grill that simulates charcoal heat; the result is a firm-texture steak with a crusty surface and a juicy interior. The familiar New York strip and filet mignon are available from the grill, but the preferred choice is the *churrasco*, a special Argentine cut. The wine list includes a preponderance of Argentine vintages. Upstairs, a colorful Southwestern cantina comes alive weekend nights, although the diners in general are a conservative, international lot. ✕ *3291 M St. NW,* ☎ *202/333–5151. Reservations advised. AE, DC, MC, V.*

Barbecue

$$ Old Glory. Always teeming with visiting Texans, Georgetown students, and closet Elvis fans, the flag-waving Old Glory sticks to barbecue basics: sandwiches and platters of pulled and sliced pork, beef brisket, grilled and pulled chicken, ribs, and sausage. The open pit will also roast vegetables, but they're an unusual choice here. Side dishes include succotash, hoppin' John, and Silver Queen corn on the cob in season. Desserts are also Southern influenced: tin roof sundae, coconut-cherry cobbler, and fresh fruit pies. ✕ *3139 M St. NW,* ☎ *202/337–3406. AE, D, DC, MC, V.*

Caribbean

$$ Hibiscus Cafe. Jamaican chef Sharon Banks and her Panamanian husband, Jimmie Banks, opened this tropical Georgetown hideaway in 1993. The modishly designed restaurant, with its mixture of vibrant tableware and eclectic seating, draws weekend crowds with its spicy jerk chicken and quail dishes, shrimp curry, and Caribbean-seasoned vegetable medleys. Outdoor seating was added in 1995. The Hibiscus Kafe opened in 1995 at 2000 Pennsylvania Avenue NW, serving breakfast and lunch (Caribbean style, of course). ✕ *3401 K St. NW,* ☎ *202/338– 0408. Reservations advised. AE. Closed Sun. and Mon. No lunch Sat.*

French

$$$ La Chaumière. A longtime favorite of Washingtonians seeking an escape from the hurly-burly of Georgetown, La Chaumière has the rustic charm of a French country inn, particularly during the winter, when its central stone fireplace warms the room. The food is country French, with an emphasis on seafood—fish stew, mussels, and scallops are on the regular menu, and there is usually a grilled fish special. The restaurant also has a devoted following for its meat dishes, which include such hard-to-find entrées as venison and calves' brains. Many local diners plan their meals around La Chaumière's rotating specials, particularly the couscous on Wednesday and the cassoulet on Thursday. ✕ *2813 M St. NW,* ☎ *202/338–1784. Reservations required. AE, DC, MC, V. Closed Sun. No lunch Sat.*

$$ Bistro Français. This French country restaurant is a favorite among the city's chefs. What do the professionals order when they want to eat someone else's cooking? The minute steak maître d'hôtel, a sirloin with herb butter, accompanied by french fries. Among amateur eaters, the big draw is the rotisserie chicken. The extensive list of daily specials may include *suprême* of salmon with broccoli mousse and beurre blanc. The restaurant is divided into two parts—the café side and the more formal dining room; the café menu includes sandwiches and omelets in addition to the entrées. The Bistro also offers $11.95 fixed-price lunches and $16.95 early and late-night dinner specials and stays open until 3 AM Sunday–Thursday, 4 AM Friday and Saturday. ✕ *3128 M St. NW,* ☎ *202/338–3830. Reservations advised. AE, DC, MC, V.*

Indian

$$ Aditi. At first glance this two-story dining room seems to be too elegant for a moderately priced Indian restaurant. The dim interior features burgundy carpets and chairs and pale mint-color walls with brass sconces. There's a small first floor, with a dramatic staircase leading to a larger room with windows that overlook the busy street. But the decor is not the only draw: Tandoori and curry dishes, although not aggressively spiced, are expertly prepared. The rice *biryani* entrées are good for lighter appetites, and $4.95 will get you a delicious bread sampler. ✕ *3299 M St. NW,* ☎ *202/625–6825. AE, DC, MC, V.*

Indonesian

$$ **Sarinah Satay House.** All you can see of this delightful restaurant
★ from busy Wisconsin Avenue is its wooden sign above a green door; open it, follow the stairs down and up again, and you're in a lush, enclosed garden with real trees growing through the ceiling. Carved monkeys, parrots, and puppets add to the setting, where batik-clad waiters offer serenely unrushed service. The food is exquisite. Potato croquettes and the traditional *loempia* and *resoles* (crisp and soft spring

rolls) come with a tangy, chili-spiked peanut dipping sauce, while the perfectly grilled chicken satay is accompanied by a smoky-sweet peanut dip. A bargain is the combination *nasi rames:* chicken in coconut sauce, beef skewers, and spicy green beans with rice ($8.95). Vegetarians may order well-seasoned noodle, rice, and vegetable dishes. Cool your palate afterward with an *es teler,* a shaved-ice dessert with exotic fruits. ✕ *1338 Wisconsin Ave. NW,* ☎ *202/337–2955. Reservations advised. AE, D, DC, MC, V. Closed Mon. No lunch Sun.*

Mediterranean

$$–$$$ **Crepizza.** Owned, operated, and patronized by a smart international set, this airy restaurant has a high ceiling and outdoor seating in warm weather. In addition to its many variations of crepes (try the Norwegian—slices of salmon and shallots served in a cream sauce) and pizzas (from a wood-burning oven), Crepizza serves a host of salads, carpaccio, pastas, and roasted meats. Those who immediately flip to the back of a menu to peek at dessert offerings will be saved the trouble: Sweet crepes are highlighted on the menu's cover; the Saint-Tropez (hot Belgian chocolate and sliced bananas topped with a scoop of vanilla ice cream) is the most popular. A lively late-night crowd comes to dine and, on Tuesday night, to dance to popular European records under the watchful eyes of such film goddesses as Birgitte Bardot and Sophia Loren, whose movie posters adorn the walls. This Crepizza opened in late 1994 just north of Georgetown's hub at the intersection of Wisconsin Avenue and M Street; Crepizza's mall location is much less trendy and has an abbreviated menu. ✕ *3206 N St. NW,* ☎ *202/ 337–1275; Mazza Gallerie, 5300 Wisconsin Ave. NW,* ☎ *202/363– 1991. AE, MC, V.*

New American

$$$ **River Club.** Until someone invents a time machine, there is no better way to experience the Big Band era than to take a trip to the River Club, an art deco extravaganza in an out-of-the-way part of Georgetown. Decorated in ebony, silver, neon, and marble, the River Club is in fact a nightclub, with a disc jockey who plays everything from '30s and '40s music to contemporary dance music; there's live music Tuesday through Thursday. Start your meal with Chinese smoked lobster, then finish it off with layered white and dark chocolate mousse. You can also stick with caviar and champagne. ✕ *3223 K St. NW,* ☎ *202/333– 8118. Reservations advised. Jacket and tie. AE, DC, MC, V. Dinner only. Closed Sun. and Mon.*

Seafood

$$$ **Sea Catch.** Despite the proximity of Chesapeake Bay, Washington isn't known for casual seafood restaurants or crab houses the way nearby Baltimore is. At this formal establishment, hidden in a courtyard overlooking the C&O Canal, the standards at least match the high prices. A gleaming raw bar offers huge shrimp and farm-raised clams and oysters. The jumbo crab cakes have little filler. The entrées come ungarnished; a side order of potatoes, mushrooms with pecans, or sautéed spinach can be shared. The staff is likely to bring you a complimentary aperitif. ✕ *1054 31st St. NW,* ☎ *202/337–8855. Reservations advised. AE, D, DC, MC, V. Closed Sun.*

Vegetarian

$ **Madurai.** Although some vegetarians may be upset that this longtime Georgetown favorite now shares quarters with Tandoor (☎ 202/337– 3376), a meat-serving establishment, few will miss the dingy interior of its previous residence a few doors down M Street. Diners can order from both the Tandoor and Madurai menus in the comfortably furnished room with burgundy and brown accents. The curries range from the familiar—a very spicy *aloo gobi* (potato and cauliflower)—to the exotic (lotus root), and portions are very large. The potato- and pea-stuffed *samosas* make a hearty appetizer in addition to the fried lentil-flour *pappadums* brought to your table. The all-you-can-eat Sunday brunch is famous for sustaining Georgetown students and vegetarians. ✕ *3316 M St. NW,* ☎ *202/333–0997. AE, D, MC, V.*

Maryland/Virginia Suburbs

Afghani

$$ **Panjshir.** The Falls Church location favors a plush red and dark wood decor, the Vienna branch is more into pinks, but both serve succulent kebabs of beef, lamb, and chicken and fragrant stews (with and without meat) over impeccably cooked rice. Sautéed pumpkin is surprisingly fresh-tasting and not too sweet. All entrées come with Afghan salad (a Green Goddess–like dressing) and hearty bread. ✕ *924 W. Broad St., Falls Church, VA,* ☎ *703/536–4566; 224 Maple Ave. W, Vienna, VA,* ☎ *703/281–4183. Weekend reservations advised. AE, MC, V. No lunch Sun.*

American

$ **Hard Times Cafe.** Country-western music is always playing on the jukebox, good microbrew beers are on the bar list, and the chili, for which this restaurant is known, comes three main ways. Texas-style is mostly ground beef; Cincinnati-style is slightly sweet and cinnamony and is often ordered over spaghetti; and the vegetarian version is the hottest, with a blend of peanuts, mushrooms, bell peppers, and vegetable protein that's amazingly "meaty." ✕ *1404 King St., Alexandria, VA,* ☎ *703/683–5340; 3028 Wilson Blvd., Arlington, VA,* ☎ *703/528–2233; 394 Elden St., Herndon, VA,* ☎ *703/318–8941; 1117 Nelson St., Rockville, MD,* ☎ *301/294–9720. No reservations. AE, MC, V.*

$ **Tastee Diner.** These diners are the real thing, open 24 hours with a menu that hasn't changed in years (and pretty stagnant prices, too). Where else is meat loaf on special, or a sandwich, coffee, and pie available for under $5? Students and others on low budgets (or little sleep) ignore the dust. ✕ *7731 Woodmont Ave., Bethesda, MD,* ☎ *301/652–3970; 8516 Georgia Ave., Silver Spring, MD,* ☎ *301/589–8171. No reservations. MC, V (Bethesda only).*

Barbecue

$ **Red, Hot and Blue.** A Memphis offshoot with three D.C.-area locations, this barbecue joint is known for its ribs. They come "wet"—with sauce—or, when simply smoked, "dry." The pulled-meat sandwiches and low prices mean Red, Hot and Blue is also known for its crowds. ✕ *1120 19th St. NW,* ☎ *202/466–6731 (AE, MC, V); 1600 Wilson Blvd., Arlington, VA,* ☎ *703/276–7427 (AE, MC, V); 16811 Crabbs Branch Way, Gaithersburg, MD,* ☎ *301/948–7333 (MC, V). No reservations at any location.*

Italian

$$ **Paolo's.** Complimentary house-made bread sticks start the meals here; wise choices to follow might be the "beggar's purse" filled with wild mushrooms, spinach, and Taleggio cheese, or the grilled sea scallops. Then two of you can split a pizza from the wood-burning oven, with toppings that range from roasted vegetables to grilled chicken to duck confit. Grilled meat entrées and a variety of pasta dishes (some low-fat) are also available. The Georgetown location is the noisiest. ✕ *1801 Rockville Pike, Rockville, MD,* ☎ *301/984–2211; 11898 Market St.,*

Reston, VA, ☎ 703/318–8920; 1303 Wisconsin Ave. NW, ☎ 202/333–7353. AE, DC, MC, V.

Southwestern

$$ Cottonwood Cafe. This stylish restaurant, also found in Boston, offers an innovative blend of Santa Fe, Texas, and New American dishes. The blue-cornmeal calamari appetizer is a must. Entrées are generously sized; try the "fire and spice" pasta with andouille sausage and shrimp, or the "Barbacoa" (grilled chicken and shrimp marinated in barbecue sauce with baked banana, cheese, and *pico de gallo*). ✕ *4844 Cordell Ave., Bethesda, MD, ☎ 301/656–4844. Reservations advised. AE, MC, V. No lunch Sun.*

$$ Rio Grande Cafe. The grilled quail, goat dishes (on Thursday), and other upscale Tex-Mex fare are worth braving the crowds. The margaritas help the wait go faster. Crates of Mexican beer stacked against the walls add atmosphere, as does a perpetual-motion tortilla machine. ✕ *4919 Fairmont Ave., Bethesda, MD, ☎ 301/656–2981; 4301 N. Fairfax Dr., Arlington, VA, ☎ 703/528–3131; 1827 Library St., Reston, VA, ☎ 703/904–0703. No reservations. AE, D, DC, MC, V.*

Spanish

$$ Andalucia. *Zarzuela,* a seafood stew, is one special of this traditional Spanish restaurant. The spartan Rockville location (hidden in an office-and-shopping strip) was popular enough to spawn the more formally furnished Bethesda branch, which features a full tapas bar and a tempting dessert cart. Classical Spanish guitarists can be heard at both locations on weeknights. ✕ *12300 Wilkins Ave., Rockville, MD, ☎ 301/770–1880; 4931 Elm St., Bethesda, MD, ☎ 301/907–0052. AE, MC, V. Closed Mon.*

Vietnamese

$ Little Viet Garden. Although nearby Queen Bee (3181 Wilson Blvd., ☎ 703/527–3444) has longer lines, patrons here swear by the crisp cha-gio, homey pho soups with glass noodles, stuffed crisp crepes, and a signature steak. There's also terrace dining in season. ✕ *3012 Wilson Blvd., Arlington, VA, ☎ 703/522–9686. AE, D, MC, V.*

7 Lodging

By Jan Ziegler

Updated by
Bruce Walker

ALTHOUGH THE NATION'S CAPITAL rode a hotel boom in the 1980s, the emphasis these days is on renovation rather than new construction. Still, visitors who plan to spend the night, a week, or a month in D.C. will find a large variety of accommodations from which to choose. Hostelries include grand hotels with glorious histories, quiet Victorian inns, the hotel and motel chains common to every American city, and small independently operated hotels that offer little more than good location, a smile, and a comfortable, clean place to lay your head.

Because Washington is an international city, nearly all hotel staffs are multilingual. All hotels in the $$$ and $$$$ categories have concierges; some in the $$ group do, too. All the hotels we list are air-conditioned. All the large hotels and many of the smaller ones offer meeting facilities and special features for business travelers, ranging from state-of-the-art teleconferencing equipment to modest conference rooms with outside catering. Nearly all the finer hotels have superb restaurants whose traditionally high prices are almost completely justified.

Not all the city's hotels are included here; there are simply too many to list. Most of the major chains have properties in desirable locations throughout town and in the near suburbs. For a complete listing of hotels in the area, contact the Washington, D.C., Convention and Visitors Association (1212 New York Ave. NW, Washington, DC 20005, ☎ 202/789–7000). **Capitol Reservations** books rooms at more than 70 better hotels in good locations at rates 20%–40% off; call 202/452–1270 or 800/847–4832 from 9 to 6 weekdays; the company also sells packages with tours and meals. **Washington D.C. Accommodations** will book rooms in any hotel in town, with discounts of 20%–40% at about 40 locations; call 202/289–2220 or 800/554–2220 from 9 to 5 weekdays.

A word about reservations: They are crucial. Hotels are often full of conventioneers, politicians in transit, or families and school groups in search of cherry blossoms and monuments. If you're interested in visiting Washington at a calmer time—and if you can stand tropical weather—come in July or August, during the congressional recess. You may not spot many VIPs, but hotels will have more rooms to offer at lower rates, and you'll be able to relax. (August, however, is the busiest season for the Washington International Youth Hostel, so budget travelers should seek alternatives at this time). Rates often drop in late December and January, too. Keep in mind also that rates can be significantly lower if they are part of a group, corporate, or weekend package. Also, some of the older hotels have a few smaller rooms that rent for prices in a lower category. It's always worth a call to check for special rates.

The hotel reviews here are grouped within neighborhoods according to price. Hotels' parking fees range from $5 to $15 a night, depending on how close to downtown you are.

CATEGORY	COST*
$$$$	over $190
$$$	$145–$190
$$	$100–$145
$	under $100

*All prices are for a standard double room, excluding room tax (13% in DC, 12% in MD, and 9.75% in VA) and $1.50 per night occupancy tax.

Washington Lodging

American Inn of Bethesda, **2**

ANA Hotel, **32**

Bellevue Hotel, **65**

Best Western Rosslyn Westpark, **12**

Capital Hilton, **48**

Capitol Hill Suites, **67**

Carlton Hotel, **49**

Crystal City Marriott, **16**

Days Inn Connecticut Avenue, **5**

Doubletree, **33, 38**

Embassy Row Hotel, **27**

Embassy Suites, **30**

Four Seasons Hotel, **22**

Georgetown Dutch Inn, **19**

Georgetown Inn, **10**

Georgetown Suites, **21**

Governor's House Hotel, **41**

Grand Hyatt, **55**

Hay-Adams Hotel, **50**

Henley Park Hotel, **57**

Holiday Inn Capitol Hill, **63**

Holiday Inn Central, **44**

Holiday Inn Chevy Chase, **3**

Holiday Inn Conference Center at College Park, **60**

Hotel Anthony, **39**

Hotel Sofitel Washington, **26**

Hotel Tabard Inn, **42**

Hotel Washington, **51**

Howard Johnson's Kennedy Center, **36**

Howard Johnson's National Airport, **14**

Hyatt Regency Bethesda, **1**

Hyatt Regency on Capitol Hill, **62**

Jefferson Hotel, **45**

J.W. Marriott, **53**

Kalorama Guest House, **23**

Key Bridge Marriott, **11**

Latham Hotel, **20**

Loews L'Enfant Plaza, **61**

Madison Hotel, **47**

Marriott at Metro Center, **54**

Morrison House, **17**

Morrison-Clark Inn Hotel, **59**

Normandy Inn, **9**

Omni Shoreham Hotel, **7**

Park Hyatt, **31**

Phoenix Park Hotel, **66**

Quality Hotel Silver Spring, **43**

Quality Inn Iwo Jima, **15**

Radisson Barceló Hotel, **29**

Ramada Inn-Rockville, **4**

Ritz-Carlton, **28**

Ritz-Carlton, Pentagon City, **18**

River Inn, **35**

Sheraton Washington Hotel, **6**

Stouffer Renaissance Mayflower, **40**

Vienna Wolf Trap Motel, **13**

Washington Court, **64**

Washington Courtyard by Marriot, **24**

Washington Hilton and Towers, **25**

Washington International AYH-Hostel, **58**

Washington Renaissance Hotel, **56**

Washington Vista Hotel, **46**

Watergate Hotel, **37**

Willard Inter-Continental, **52**

Windsor Park Hotel, **8**

Wyndham Bristol Hotel, **34**

Bed-and-Breakfasts

To find reasonably priced accommodations in small guest houses and private homes, contact either of the following B&B services: **Bed 'n' Breakfast Accommodations Ltd. of Washington, D.C.** (Box 12011, Washington, DC 20005, ☎ 202/328–3510) or **Bed and Breakfast League, Ltd.** (Box 9490, Washington, DC 20016-9490).

To reserve a room in any property in this chapter, you can contact **Fodor's new toll-free lodging reservations hot line** (1–800–FODORS–1 or 1–800/363–6771; 0800–89–1030 in Great Britain; 0014/800–12–8271 in Australia; 1800–55–9101 in Ireland).

Capitol Hill

$$$$ **Hyatt Regency on Capitol Hill.** This hotel has the typical Hyatt garden atrium, but with high-tech edges. Close to Union Station and the Mall, this is a mecca for families and for businesspeople with dealings on the Hill. Suites on the south side have a view of the Capitol dome, which is just a few blocks away, as does the 11th-floor Capitol View Club restaurant. ⌧ *400 New Jersey Ave. NW, 20001,* ☎ *202/737–1234 or 800/233–1234,* ⌧ *202/393–7927. 803 rooms, 31 suites. 2 restaurants, 2 bars, room service, pool, health club, parking (fee). AE, DC, MC, V.*

$$$$ **Washington Court.** This luxury hotel is one of the few hostelries in D.C. where it is possible to make a truly grand entrance. Three terraced tiers of polished steps lead to an atrium surmounted by a skylight. It shares its view of the Capitol with the Hyatt and others on the same street. Rooms were renovated in 1993, with a phone and TV in every bathroom. ⌧ *525 New Jersey Ave. NW, 20001,* ☎ *202/628–2100 or 800/321–3010,* ⌧ *202/737–2641. 250 rooms, 15 suites. Restaurant, piano bar, room service, health club, parking (fee). AE, DC, MC, V.*

$$$ **Phoenix Park Hotel.** Just steps from Union Station and only four blocks from the Capitol, this high-rise hotel has an Irish club theme and is the home of the Dubliner, one of Washington's best bars. Leather, wood paneling, and leaded glass abound in the bar's re-creation of the decor in the houses of 18th-century Irish gentry. Guest rooms (renovated in 1994) are bright, traditionally furnished, and quiet; penthouse suites have fireplaces. A new wing was built in 1995, adding 61 rooms and suites, three meeting rooms, and a ballroom. The Powerscourt Restaurant is named after an Irish castle and imports chefs from the Emerald Isle annually to enhance its already popular Celtic-Continental fare. The hotel has special services for hearing-impaired guests. ⌧ *520 N. Capitol St. NW, 20001,* ☎ *202/638–6900 or 800/824–5419,* ⌧ *202/638–4025. 136 rooms, 15 suites. 2 restaurants, access to health club, laundry service, parking (fee). AE, DC, MC, V.*

$$ **Bellevue Hotel.** This charming hotel has been in business since 1929. The public rooms on the main floor have balconies and are modeled after great halls in manor houses of yore. Accommodations here are standard modest-hotel fare—some in need of refurbishment—but the staff is friendly. The location is convenient, near Union Station and major Metro stations and within six blocks of the Supreme Court and the Smithsonian museums. ⌧ *15 E St. NW, 20001,* ☎ *202/638–0900 or 800/327–6667,* ⌧ *202/638–5132. 138 rooms, 2 suites. Restaurant, bar, room service, library, free parking. AE, DC, MC, V.*

$$ **Capitol Hill Suites.** Tucked away on a quiet street behind the Madison Building of the Library of Congress, this former apartment building has been converted into an all-suite hotel. Its proximity to the House office buildings means that it is often filled with visiting lobbyists when Congress is in session, and its location near Capitol South Metro makes it an ideal spot to get a feel for both residential and official Wash-

ington. New TVs, furniture, and sprinklers were installed in 1994; all rooms have kitchens and are attractively furnished in Queen Anne style with a blue-and-rose color scheme. ▦ *200 C St. SF., 20003,* ☎ *202/543–6000 or 800/424–9165,* ℻ *202/547–2608. 152 suites. Kitchens, access to health club, parking (fee). AE, DC, MC, V.*

$ **Holiday Inn Capitol Hill.** A good value for the budget-minded traveler (some rooms are as low as $79), this hotel shares the block with the Hyatt and offers the same views and convenient location. Children under age 18 stay free. A renovation of the entire hotel was completed in 1995. ▦ *415 New Jersey Ave. NW, 20001,* ☎ *202/638–1616 or 800/638–1116,* ℻ *202/347–1813. 341 rooms, 5 suites. Restaurant, bar, room service, pool, parking (fee). AE, DC, MC, V.*

Downtown

$$$$ **Capital Hilton.** There are three advantages here: location, location, and location. The busy Capital Hilton is not only just up the street from official Washington, including the White House and many monuments, but also smack in the middle of the K Street business corridor. Built in 1943 as a Statler Hotel, the building underwent a $55 million renovation in 1990 that enlarged the rooms by a third. They were refurbished in 1994 and are sleekly furnished in shades of emerald green and salmon. The Towers section on the top four floors offers VIP accommodations. The Twigs restaurant has better food and service than the on-site Trader Vic's; still, the ticky-tacky tropical theme room is a tradition with some businesspeople. ▦ *1001 16th St. NW, 20036,* ☎ *202/393–1000 or 800/445–8667,* ℻ *202/639–5726. 515 rooms, 36 suites. 2 restaurants, room service, beauty salon, health club, laundry service and dry cleaning, parking (fee). AE, DC, MC, V.*

$$$$ **Carlton Hotel.** Entering the Carlton is like stepping into an updated Italian Renaissance mansion: Gilt, carved wood, stone, plaster, and 19th-century details abound. This hotel is in a bustling business sector near the White House, yet the rooms are quiet and service is cordial and dignified. Built in 1926, the hotel completed a $27 million face-lift in the early 1990s, in which all rooms were renovated. They are done in pastel colors and are furnished with antiques and reproductions. The ornate Allegro dining room serves New American cuisine. All rooms have three telephones with voice mail and call waiting; some rooms have faxes. ▦ *923 16th St. NW, 20006,* ☎ *202/638–2626 or 800/325–3535,* ℻ *202/347–1806. 184 rooms, 13 suites. Restaurant, bar, room service, exercise room, parking (fee). AE, DC, MC, V.*

$$$$ **Grand Hyatt.** Imagine a 1930s movie-musical set. Studio-built walls of a Mediterranean hillside village rise around a courtyard; a gazebo and curved lounge and dining areas surround a blue lagoon fed by waterfalls. On a small island in the lagoon is a man in black tie playing Cole Porter tunes on a white grand piano. The Grand Hyatt has created just such a fanciful interior in this bustling high-rise hotel that successfully compensates for the relative drabness of the neighborhood. The Grand Hyatt is across the street from the Washington Convention Center and just steps away from downtown shopping and theaters. Quiet, contemporary rooms (renovated in 1994) are reached by glass-walled elevators. Some suites have whirlpools or saunas; others have large desks, fax machines, and computer hookups. The Zephyr Deli is a popular lunch spot, and the Grand Cafe serves country breakfasts on weekends. Via Pacifica, the latest addition, prepares Italian-American fare. ▦ *1000 H St. NW, 20001,* ☎ *202/582–1234 or 800/233–1234,* ℻ *202/637–4718. 889 rooms, 58 suites. 4 restaurants, 2 bars, room service, health club. AE, DC, MC, V.*

$$$$ **Hay-Adams Hotel.** Built in 1927, the Hay-Adams sits upon the site of
★ houses owned by John Hay and Henry Adams, a prominent diplomat
and historian of turn-of-the-century Washington. Italian Renaissance
in design, the hotel looks like a mansion in disguise. The John Hay lounge
seems to belong to an English Tudor residence. The guest rooms are
the most brightly colored in the city, decorated in 23 different English-
country-house schemes. Rooms on the south side have a picture-postcard view of the White House, as does the Lafayette restaurant. Some
rooms have kitchenettes, but the guests here are unlikely to cook for
themselves. The hotel's afternoon tea is renowned. The staff is dignified and friendly. ⌑ *1 Lafayette Sq. NW, 20006,* ☎ *202/638–6600
or 800/424–5054,* ℻ *202/638–2716. 125 rooms, 18 suites. 2 restaurants, bar, room service, laundry service and dry cleaning, parking (fee).
AE, DC, MC, V.*

$$$$ **Jefferson Hotel.** Incoming and outgoing administration officials have stayed
★ at the Jefferson since it opened. The undistinguished exterior of this 1923
building is deceiving; past the stately foyer the atmosphere is classically
elegant and is reminiscent of the 18th and early 19th centuries. Rooms
are furnished with antiques and reproductions as well as original art.
Double-glazed windows ensure quiet on a busy intersection. The restaurant has a fine menu of American cuisine. The staff of this small hotel
remembers who you are and greets you by name; laundry is hand ironed
and delivered in wicker baskets. ⌑ *1200 16th St. NW, 20036,* ☎
202/347–2200 or 800/368–5966, ℻ *202/785–1505. 68 rooms, 32 suites.
Restaurant, bar, room service, in-room VCRs, access to health club, laundry service, concierge, parking (fee). AE, DC, MC, V.*

$$$$ **J. W. Marriott.** This large, glossy hotel is in a prime location on Pennsylvania Avenue, close to the White House and next door to the National
Theatre. Rooms (renovated in 1994) are furnished in quiet colors. Ask
for a room on the Pennsylvania Avenue side, or you may end up looking across a courtyard at the blank windows of another section of the
complex. Guests have indoor access to the National Press Building and
the shops and restaurants of National Place. The signature dessert at the
Continental Celadon restaurant is Painter's Palette, made of chocolate
topped with fruit sorbets. ⌑ *1331 Pennsylvania Ave. NW, 20004,* ☎
202/393–2000 or 800/228–9290, ℻ *202/626–6991. 738 rooms, 34
suites. 4 restaurants, bar, room service, indoor pool, exercise room,
laundry service and dry cleaning, parking (fee). AE, DC, MC, V.*

$$$$ **Madison Hotel.** Elegance and fine service are the hallmarks of the Madison, where guests may be visiting heads of state or the subjects of in-
terviews in the *Washington Post,* whose office is across the street.
Deceivingly contemporary on the outside, the 14-story Madison houses
a world-class collection of antiques, Oriental rugs, and fine art. Even
the front lobby is graced by a rare antique Chinese altar table. The guest
rooms are also furnished with antiques and reproductions, and the Madison's suites are among the most opulent and unhotel-like in Washington. Renovated in 1992, the rooms and suites are decorated in peach
or blue tones and Oriental touches. The elegant Montpelier restaurant
will give you many reasons to use it. ⌑ *15th and M Sts. NW, 20005,*
☎ *202/862–1600 or 800/424–8577,* ℻ *202/785–1255. 318 rooms,
35 suites. 2 restaurants, bar, room service, exercise room, parking
(fee). AE, DC, MC, V.*

$$$$ **Stouffer Renaissance Mayflower.** The Stouffer Renaissance Mayflower
was opened in 1925 for Calvin Coolidge's inauguration and continues to be a central part of Washington life. The ornate lobby gleams
with gilded trim and electrified candelabra. Renovated in 1992, the rooms
feature custom-designed furniture, warmly colored fabrics, full marble bathrooms (with mini TVs), and indirect lighting. Afternoon tea

is popular, and the Nicholas restaurant serves contemporary seafood. The Mayflower is steps from the K Street business corridor, the White House, and Dupont Circle. ⌖ *1127 Connecticut Ave. NW, 20036,* ☎ *202/347–3000 or 800/468–3571,* FAX *202/466–9083. 659 rooms, 78 suites. 2 restaurants, bar, room service, sauna, exercise room, shops, parking (fee). AE, DC, MC, V.*

$$$$ **Washington Renaissance Hotel.** This 15-story hotel opened in 1989 as part of Washington's World Technology Trade Center, just across from the Washington Convention Center and near the "Pennsylvania Quarter," a slowly gentrifying area of restaurants and clubs. A completely equipped convention hotel, even including a "secure" auditorium for top-secret meetings, the Renaissance is primed for business travelers. The hotel's spacious rooms are decorated in teal and cinnamon, with mahogany furniture and floral upholstery. The Renaissance Club Tower, a hotel within a hotel served by private elevators and a full-time concierge, pampers business travelers. The lobby's Chinese rock garden and fountain remind guests of their proximity to Washington's Chinatown, and the Techworld complex brings more than 50 shops, including a bank, a florist, a car-rental agency, and a travel agency, close to the hotel. All public areas were renovated in 1994. ⌖ *999 9th St. NW, 20001,* ☎ *202/898–9000 or 800/228–9898,* FAX *202/789–4213. 779 rooms, 21 suites. 3 restaurants, bar, deli, room service, indoor pool, health club, parking (fee). AE, DC, MC, V.*

$$$$ **Willard Inter-Continental.** "This hotel, in fact, may be much more
★ justly called the center of Washington and the Union than either the Capitol, the White House, or the State Department," Nathaniel Hawthorne wrote while covering the Civil War. Indeed, the Willard, whose present building dates from 1901, welcomed every American president from Franklin Pierce in 1853 to Dwight Eisenhower in the 1950s. But the huge building fell on hard times and closed in 1968. When renovation began in 1984, grass was growing in the rooms and a tree had sprouted in one of the restaurants. The new Willard is a faithful renovation, presenting an opulent, beaux arts feast to the eye. Rooms are furnished with Queen Anne reproductions; all have a minibar. The sixth floor, which was designed with the help of the Secret Service and the State Department, has lodged numerous heads of state. One of the restaurants here, the Willard Room, has won nationwide acclaim, and the "Willard Collection" of shops includes Chanel and other designer boutiques. ⌖ *1401 Pennsylvania Ave. NW, 20004,* ☎ *202/628–9100 or 800/327–0200,* FAX *202/637–7326. 303 rooms, 38 suites. 2 restaurants, 2 bars, minibars, room service, health club, laundry service and dry cleaning, shops, meeting rooms, parking (fee). AE, DC, MC, V.*

$$$ **Henley Park Hotel.** Constructed as an apartment building in 1918 and
★ converted to a small hotel in 1983, the Henley Park offers a bit of Britain in the still-dodgy neighborhood near the Washington Convention Center. It's now one of the National Trust for Historic Preservation's designated Historic Hotels. Though the architecture is Tudor style, the decor is Edwardian; a cozy sitting room with working fireplace could well have been transplanted from an English country house. Afternoon tea here is renowned, and the Coeur de Lion serves traditional regional American and Continental meals. Guest rooms are warmly furnished with chintz and Oriental porcelain lamps. The hotel is in an iffy area that's only a short ride on public transportation to the major sights, but it's best to take a cab if you're returning after dark. Limo service is available. ⌖ *926 Massachusetts Ave. NW, 20001,* ☎ *202/638–5200 or 800/222–8474,* FAX *202/638–6740. 78 rooms, 18 suites. Restaurant, bar, room service, access to health club, parking (fee). AE, DC, MC, V.*

$$$ **Marriott at Metro Center.** Marriott bought this former Holiday Inn and did a $2.5 million renovation, including marbling of the entire lobby. The hotel is decorated throughout with art commissioned from Washington artists. The hotel's restaurant and bar—Metro Grille and Bar— is a handsome two-level facility decorated in mahogany, oak, brass, and marble. The New American cuisine of executive chef Dennis Marcinik has made the restaurant a popular downtown lunch and dinner spot for locals as well as guests. The larger-than-average rooms (renovated in 1994), decorated in mauve and soft blue, are more comfortable than luxurious. Each has a desk and two easy chairs. Two executive floors offer a complimentary Continental breakfast, a courtesy bar, and a private lounge. ▦ *775 12th St. NW, 20005,* ☎ *202/737–2200,* ℻ *202/347–0860. 456 rooms, 12 suites. Restaurant, bar, room service, indoor pool, health club, laundry service and dry cleaning, parking (fee). AE, DC, MC, V.*

$$$ **Washington Vista Hotel.** This 14-story member of the Hilton International family is a few blocks from the White House, the Washington Convention Center, and the K Street business corridor. Designed to look like an urban town square, the Vista has a garden-courtyard lobby that is flooded by light from a 130-foot window facing M Street. Guest rooms and restaurants are in the surrounding towerlike structures. Opened in 1983, the hotel has been host to Elizabeth Taylor, Kirk Douglas, and countless business travelers from the United States and abroad; it gained undeserved notoriety as the site of then Mayor Marion Barry's arrest in 1990. Rooms are contemporary in design and decorated in earth tones, burgundy, and green; each has three phones. The Presidential Suite and six other suites were designed by Hubert de Givenchy; these have whirlpools, French silk and cotton-blend wall coverings, and original art from France. The buffet lunch at the Verandah is a bargain at $9.95. ▦ *1400 M St. NW, 20005,* ☎ *202/429–1700 or 800/847–8232,* ℻ *202/728–0530. 386 rooms, 14 suites. 2 restaurants, 2 bars, room service, health club, baby-sitting, parking (fee). AE, DC, MC, V.*

$$ **Governor's House Hotel.** This hotel, formerly a Holiday Inn, is only two blocks from Dupont Circle. All guest rooms were refurbished in 1990, the lobby and halls in 1994. The staff is friendly. Herb's Restaurant draws a lively professional and arty crowd. Families can take advantage of the 24 rooms with kitchenettes. ▦ *1615 Rhode Island Ave. NW, 20036,* ☎ *202/296–2100 or 800/821–4367,* ℻ *202/331–0227. 152 rooms, 9 suites. Restaurant, bar, room service, pool, access to health club, parking (fee). AE, DC, MC, V.*

$$ **Hotel Anthony.** This small hotel with a courteous staff offers the basics in the midst of the K and L streets business district, close to the White House. Some rooms have a full kitchen, some a wet bar; king, queen, or extra-long double beds are available. Weekend rates are almost half price. ▦ *1823 L St. NW, 20036,* ☎ *202/223–4320 or 800/424–2970,* ℻ *202/223–8546. 99 rooms. Restaurant, room service, access to health club, parking (fee). AE, DC, MC, V.*

$$ **Hotel Washington.** Since its opening in 1918, this hostelry has been
★ known as the hotel with a view. Washingtonians bring visitors to the outdoor rooftop bar for cocktails and a view of the White House grounds and the Washington Monument. The oldest continuously operating hostelry in the city and now a national landmark, the Hotel Washington sprang from the drawing boards of John Carrère and Thomas Hastings, who designed the New York Public Library. Renovated in 1987, the hotel has retained its Edwardian character. The guest rooms, some of which look directly onto the White House grounds, are furnished with antique reproductions; the windows are festooned with swags, heavy draperies, and lace. Antique beiges predominate. Suite

506 is where Elvis Presley stayed on his trips to D.C. Rates border on the expensive. ⚉ *515 15th St. NW, 20004,* ☎ *202/638–5900,* FAX *202/638–1594. 344 rooms, 16 suites. Restaurant, bar, deli, lobby lounge, room service, exercise room, laundry service and dry cleaning, business services. AE, DC, MC, V.*

$$ **Morrison-Clark Inn Hotel.** Victorian with an airy, modern twist, this
★ unusual historic inn, created by merging two 1864 town houses, is now one of the National Trust for Historic Preservation's designated Historic Hotels. Appended to one of the houses is a 1917 Chinese Chippendale porch; Oriental touches echo throughout the public rooms, which also boast marble fireplaces and 14-foot-high mirrors with original gilding. Antique-filled rooms—some with bay windows, fireplaces, or access to a porch—have different personalities; one is called the "deer and bunny room" because of its decorative trim. A new addition contains 40 rooms in the neoclassical style. Country rooms are plainly furnished with pine, wicker, and rattan. The restaurant, with its New American–Southern cuisine, has been roundly praised; a complimentary Continental breakfast is served. Take a cab to the hotel after dark. ⚉ *Massachusetts Ave. and 11th St. NW, 20001,* ☎ *202/898–1200 or 800/332–7898,* FAX *202/289–8576. 54 rooms. CP. Restaurant, room service, exercise room, laundry service and dry cleaning, parking (fee). AE, D, DC, MC, V.*

$ **Holiday Inn Central.** This Holiday Inn overlooking Scott Circle has a fresh approach to elegance on a budget. The rooms, a mix of parlor suites and deluxe rooms, are generally spacious. There are five no-smoking floors. Teal predominates in the bright, attractive lobby, which hosts a bar and the Avenue Café and Lounge. The rooftop pool is open in summer. The Dupont Circle Metro is three blocks away, although a cab is advised at night. ⚉ *1501 Rhode Island Ave. NW, 20005,* ☎ *202/483–2000 or 800/465–4329,* FAX *202/797–1078. 183 rooms, 30 suites. Restaurant, bar, no-smoking floors, room service, pool, exercise room, shop, recreation room, laundry service, parking (fee). AE, DC, MC, V.*

$ **Washington International AYH-Hostel.** This well-kept hostel offers clean dormitory rooms with 250 bunk beds and a kitchen, laundry room, and living room. Single men and women are in separate rooms; families are given their own room if the hostel is not full. The hostel also sponsors tours, movies, and other programs. You can register 24 hours a day, but exercise caution in this downtown neighborhood if you arrive here at night. The price for American Youth Hostels members is $17 ($20 for nonmembers); the maximum stay is 15 days. Naturally, youthful European travelers predominate, and July–September is the busiest period. ⚉ *1009 11th St. NW, 20001,* ☎ *202/737–2333,* FAX *202/737–1508. 250 beds. Kitchen, shop, coin laundry. MC, V.*

Dupont Circle

$$$$ **Ritz-Carlton.** Just off Dupont Circle, the Ritz-Carlton is popular with Washington politicos and celebrities. The childhood home of Al Gore, this intimate hotel has an English hunt-club theme; rooms have views of Embassy Row or Georgetown and the National Cathedral. The pricey Jockey Club restaurant, with its half-timber ceilings, dark wood paneling, and red-checker tablecloths, draws the crowned heads of Washington. The Fairfax Bar is a cozy spot for a drink beside the fire (with piano entertainment some evenings). Guests have access to a nearby golf course, pool, and tennis courts. ⚉ *2100 Massachusetts Ave. NW, 20008,* ☎ *202/ 293–2100 or 800/241–3333,* FAX *202/466–9867. 174 rooms, 32 suites. Restaurant, bar, minibars, room service, in-room VCRs, massage, sauna, exercise room, meeting rooms. AE, DC, MC, V.*

$$$ Embassy Row Hotel. Near Dupont Circle in a neighborhood of grand houses now used mostly as embassies, museums, and galleries, this hotel is convenient for both business and leisure travelers. All rooms and public areas were renovated in 1995. The spacious rooms are decorated in neutral colors and light woods with accents of rich crimson and forest green. The bar is perhaps the coziest in Washington, and the cooking of chef Jim Papovich at Bistro Twenty-Fifteen, the hotel's restaurant, has made it a favorite of locals and tourists alike. The roof deck and pool offer fine views of the city. ☎ *2015 Massachusetts Ave. NW, 20036,* ☎ *202/265–1600 or 800/424–2400,* FAX *202/328–7526. 168 rooms, 28 suites. Restaurant, bar, room service, pool, exercise room, parking (fee). AE, DC, MC, V.*

$$$ Hotel Sofitel Washington. Built in 1906, this small hotel strives for the
★ ambience of a European luxury hotel. Decorated in warm peach tones with traditional furniture, the rooms are among the largest in any Washington hotel. All have separate work spaces and three telephones with voice mail and computer ports. The Trocadero Café serves breakfast, lunch, and dinner. Conference facilities accommodate up to 150 people. ☎ *1914 Connecticut Ave. NW, 20009,* ☎ *202/797–2000 or 800/424–2464,* FAX *202/462–0944. 108 rooms, 37 suites. Restaurant, bar, room service, access to health club, laundry service and dry cleaning, parking (fee). AE, DC, MC, V.*

$$$ Radisson Barceló Hotel. This hotel is close to Georgetown, in a convenient location on P Street near Dupont Circle. Its most striking feature is the size of the guest rooms, among the largest of any hotel in the city. Each room has a king- or two queen-size beds, a sofa and chairs, a large writing desk, a minibar, three telephones, and bathrooms equipped with hair dryers. The Spanish Barceló Hotels company, which bought it in 1992, spent $7 million renovating the rooms and lobby. The second-floor outdoor swimming pool, open only in summer, has a lovely setting—a brick courtyard enclosed by the walls of the hotel and the backs of a row of century-old town houses to the east. Chef Greggory Hill, formerly of New Heights, designed the Southwest-Mediterranean menu for the Gabriel restaurant. ☎ *2121 P St. NW, 20037,* ☎ *202/293–3100 or 800/843–6664,* FAX *202/857–0134. 235 rooms, 65 suites. Restaurant, bar, room service, pool, sauna, exercise room, parking (fee). AE, DC, MC, V.*

$$$ Washington Hilton and Towers. One of the city's busiest convention
★ hotels, this is as much an event as a place to stay. At any moment, you could run into a leading actor, a cabinet official, six busloads of teenagers from Utah, 500 visiting heart surgeons, or Supreme Court Justice Sandra Day O'Connor, who is among the notables who have played tennis here. The light-filled but compact guest rooms have marble bathrooms. The hotel is a short walk from the shops and restaurants of Dupont Circle and the Adams-Morgan neighborhood. ☎ *1919 Connecticut Ave. NW, 20009,* ☎ *202/483–3000 or 800/445–8667,* FAX *202/265–8221. 1,062 rooms, 88 suites. 3 restaurants (1 seasonal), 2 bars, room service, pool, 3 tennis courts, health club, shops, parking (fee). AE, DC, MC, V.*

$$ Washington Courtyard by Marriott. This high-rise just up the street from
★ Dupont Circle is one of the city's best values for travelers on a budget. Visitors who can't find rooms at the Washington Hilton stay here, as do international tourists and businesspeople. Guest rooms are clean, quiet, and decorated with light colors and blond wood; those on the west and south have good views. Coffee and cookies are served daily in the European-style lobby. ☎ *1900 Connecticut Ave. NW, 20009,* ☎ *202/332–9300 or 800/842–4211,* FAX *202/328–7039. 147 rooms.*

Restaurant, bar, pool, access to health club, parking (fee). AE, DC, MC, V.

$ **Hotel Tabard Inn.** Three Victorian town houses were linked in the 1920s to form an inn, one of the oldest continuously running hotels in Washington. Named after the hostelry of Chaucer's *Canterbury Tales*, the hotel is furnished throughout with broken-in Victorian and American Empire antiques. Dim lighting and a genteel shabbiness strike some as off-putting, others as charming. Rooms have a phone but no TV, and service can be uneven. There is no room service, but the Tabard Inn Restaurant serves breakfast, lunch, and dinner. On a quiet street, the hotel is a quick walk to Dupont Circle and the K Street business district. Reserve early and be aware that most rooms with private bath are moderately priced. ⌕ *1739 N St. NW, 20036,* ☎ *202/785–1277,* FAX *202/785–6173. 40 rooms, 25 with bath. Restaurant. MC, V.*

Georgetown

$$$$ **Four Seasons Hotel.** A polished staff is at your service the moment you
★ approach the doors of this contemporary hotel conveniently situated between Georgetown and Foggy Bottom. The Four Seasons is a gathering place for Washington's elite. Rooms are traditionally furnished in light colors; the quieter ones face the courtyard, others have a view of the C&O Canal. Afternoon tea is served in the Garden Terrace Lounge. The Four Seasons is also home to the private nightclub Desirée, which is open to hotel guests, and perhaps the poshest health club of any hotel in America. Guests may choose between watching movies on a VCR or listening to French lessons on a Walkman as they burn calories on their exercise bikes. ⌕ *2800 Pennsylvania Ave. NW, 20007,* ☎ *202/342–0444 or 800/332–3442,* FAX *202/342–1673. 160 rooms, 36 suites. 2 restaurants, bar, room service, pool, health club, nightclub, parking (fee). AE, DC, MC, V.*

$$$ **Georgetown Dutch Inn.** Tucked away on a side street in Georgetown, this modest all-suite hotel has a homey ambience and a few clients who stay for months at a time. The small lobby is decorated with 18th-century touches; rooms have family-room-style furnishings. All have a sofa bed in the living room and a walk in kitchen. Some bedrooms lack windows. Nine two-bedroom suites are built on two levels, with the bedrooms upstairs. Complimentary Continental breakfast is served in the lobby. ⌕ *1075 Thomas Jefferson St. NW, 20007,* ☎ *202/337–0900,* FAX *202/333–6526. 47 suites. CP. Room service, access to health club, free parking. AE, DC, MC, V.*

$$$ **Latham Hotel.** A small, colonial-style hotel in the midst of one of the city's liveliest neighborhoods, the Latham has rooms with a sleek, updated look that contrast with the redbrick, neocolonial exterior. Some rooms have minibars inside European-style armoires, while others have been remodeled for guests with mobility difficulties. Nine carriage suites offer two-level accommodations on the M Street side (courtyard views overlook the C&O Canal). The hotel is popular with Europeans, sports figures, and devotees of Georgetown. Chef Michel Richard of the trendy L.A.-based restaurant Citrus is responsible for the menu of the popular Citronelle restaurant. ⌕ *3000 M St. NW, 20007,* ☎ *202/726–5000 or 800/368–5922,* FAX *202/337–4250. 134 rooms, 9 suites. Restaurant, bar, room service, pool, access to health club, parking (fee). AE, DC, MC, V.*

$$ **Georgetown Inn.** With an atmosphere like a gentleman's sporting club of 80 years ago, the inn re-creates the intimacy and quiet of a small European hotel. The architecture is redbrick and 18th century in fla-

vor, appropriate to the hotel's setting. Renovation has brought a fresh look to interiors. The Georgetown Bar & Grill, where everyone from shorts-clad tourists to businesspeople can feel comfortable, has been brightened. Traditionally furnished rooms, in teal and mauve color schemes, are unhotel-like, with attractive wood furniture and gold-framed paintings. ▦ *1310 Wisconsin Ave. NW, 20007,* ☎ *202/333–8900 or 800/424–2979,* FAX *202/625–1744. 95 rooms, 8 suites. Restaurant, bar, room service, exercise room, parking (fee). AE, DC, MC, V.*

$$ Georgetown Suites. This all-suite hotel is a find for people who consider standard hotel rooms cramped and overpriced. Set back in a red-brick courtyard one block south of M Street in the heart of Georgetown, this unassuming property has different-size suites, all with full kitchens, iron and ironing boards, hair dryers, and voice mail. Continental breakfast is free as are local phone calls and long-distance access. There might not be someone to help with bags, and it's a 10-minute walk to the Metro, but the comfort and value Georgetown Suites delivers can't be beat. This hotel rents by the day, week, and month; close to 40% of guests are staying long term. One-bedroom suites have sofa beds; kids under 12 stay free. ▦ *1111 30th St. NW, 20007,* ☎ *202/298–7800 or 800/348–7203,* FAX *202/333–5792. 138 suites. CP. Kitchens, exercise room, laundry service and dry cleaning, parking (fee). AE, DC, MC, V.*

Southwest

$$$$ Loews L'Enfant Plaza. Loews is an oasis of velvet and chintz in L'Enfant Plaza—a concrete, fortresslike collection of office buildings with underground shops and its own Metro stop. Travelers with government business stay here, too, in proximity to several agency headquarters and just down the street from Capitol Hill. Each room has a fully stocked liquor cabinet and a refrigerator, plus a safe. All rooms were refurbished in 1995. Pets are allowed. Cafe Pierre serves an international menu at lunch and dinner. ▦ *480 L'Enfant Plaza SW, 20024,* ☎ *202/484–1000 or 800/223–0888,* FAX *202/646–4456. 348 rooms, 22 suites. 3 restaurants, 2 bars, room service, in-room VCRs, indoor pool, health club, parking (fee). AE, DC, MC, V.*

Northwest/Upper Connecticut Avenue

$$$$ Omni Shoreham Hotel. You're in good company when you check in
★   at this grand, 1930s Art Deco–Renaissance hotel. The Beatles stayed here on their first U.S. tour, and John Kennedy courted Jackie in the Blue Room cabaret, where Judy Garland, Marlene Dietrich, and Maurice Chevalier once appeared (it's now a meeting room). Resembling an old-time resort, this hotel overlooks Rock Creek Park and its jogging and bike paths and is close to the Adams-Morgan neighborhood, Dupont Circle, and the National Zoo. In back is the pool, where you can look out to a sweeping lawn and woods beyond. Some of the large, light-filled rooms have fireplaces; half overlook the park; all were renovated in 1995. Comedienne Joan Cushing frequently holds forth in the Marquee Lounge, which has a weekend matinee cabaret for children. ▦ *2500 Calvert St. NW, 20008,* ☎ *202/234–0700 or 800/834–6664,* FAX *202/332–1373. 720 rooms, 50 suites. Restaurant, bar, snack bar, room service, pool, 3 tennis courts, basketball, exercise room, horseshoes, shuffleboard, shops, cabaret, parking (fee). AE, DC, MC, V.*

$$$$ Sheraton Washington Hotel. A veritable city on a hill, this is Washington's largest hotel. It consists of an "old town"—a 1920s redbrick structure that used to be an apartment building—and the modern sprawl of the new, convention-ready, main complex. The 201 rooms and the public areas of the 10-story old section are furnished traditionally in soft colors and have large closets. Rooms in the newer section (renovated in 1995) are contemporary, with chrome and glass touches. Most rooms have a good view; some were specially designed for people with mobility problems. The courtyard is graced by a modernistic fountain; the hotel also has an airy atrium and plush, sunken-seating areas galore. Pastry chef Wolfgang Friedrich has a carry-out shop on the premises (calorie-watchers beware). The hotel is close to the National Zoo and just a few yards from the Woodley Park Metro station. There's a post office on the premises. ☎ *2660 Woodley Rd. NW, 20008,* ☎ *202/328–2000 or 800/325–3535,* FAX *202/234–0015. 1,380 rooms, 125 suites. 3 restaurants, bar, no-smoking rooms, room service, 2 pools, barbershop, exercise room, shops, baby-sitting, laundry service, meeting rooms, parking (fee). AE, DC, MC, V.*

$$ **Windsor Park Hotel.** Directly across from the Chinese Embassy, in the residential Kalorama neighborhood, the Windsor Park has small, immaculate rooms, decorated with Queen Anne–style furnishings and period art, each with a small refrigerator. Continental breakfast is free. Street parking is almost nonexistent, but there is a garage two blocks away. ☎ *2116 Kalorama Rd. NW, 20008,* ☎ *202/483–7700 or 800/247–3064,* FAX *202/332–4547. 39 rooms, 5 suites. CP. Refrigerators. AE, DC, MC, V.*

$ **Days Inn Connecticut Avenue.** An alternative for those who prefer to stay away from the downtown hustle and bustle, this Days Inn is on a wide avenue in a more residential area. The nearby Van Ness Metro stop provides quick transportation to the National Zoo. The University of the District of Columbia is next door. Rooms have standard hotel furnishings and may be small. There are several cafés nearby. ☎ *4400 Connecticut Ave. NW, 20008,* ☎ *202/244–5600 or 800/325–2525,* FAX *202/244–6794. 150 rooms, 5 suites. Restaurant, room service, shops, parking (fee). AE, DC, MC, V.*

$ **Kalorama Guest House.** Really great-grandma's house in disguise, this
★ inn consists of five separate turn-of-the-century town houses: three on a quiet street in the Adams-Morgan neighborhood and two in residential Woodley Park. The Kalorama's comfortable atmosphere is created by dark wood on the walls; hand-me-down antique oak furniture, traditional, slightly worn upholstery; brass or antique wooden bedsteads; and calico curtains at the windows. The coffeepot is always on, the staff is knowledgeable and friendly, and guests have the run of each house, its front parlor, and the areas where complimentary breakfast and afternoon aperitifs are served. Rooms range from large to tiny; none has a phone or a TV. The inn in Adams-Morgan is steps from the liveliest part of this interesting neighborhood. The Woodley Park inn is near the National Zoo. Both are a short walk to the Metro. ☎ *1854 Mintwood Place NW, 20009,* ☎ *202/667–6369,* FAX *202/319–1262. 2700 Cathedral Ave. NW, 20008,* ☎ *202/328–0860. 50 rooms, 30 with bath, 5 suites. CP. AE, DC, MC, V.*

$ **Normandy Inn.** A small, European-style hotel on a quiet street in the
★ exclusive embassy area of Connecticut Avenue, the Normandy is near restaurants and some of the most expensive residential real estate in Washington. The rooms are standard and functional, but comfortable; all have refrigerators. A Continental breakfast and afternoon tea are served. In addition, there is a wine and cheese reception for guests every Tuesday evening. ☎ *2118 Wyoming Ave. NW, 20008,* ☎ *202/483–1350 or 800/424–3729,* FAX *202/387–8241. 65 rooms, 10 suites. CP. Refrigerators, room service, parking (fee). AE, D, MC, V.*

West End/Foggy Bottom

$$$$ **ANA Hotel.** Owned by the Japanese ANA company, this establishment
★   is a stylish combination of the contemporary and the traditional. Built
in 1985 and renovated from 1991 to 1992, the ANA offers bright, airy,
traditionally furnished rooms, with maid service twice daily. About a
third of the rooms have a view of the central courtyard. The hotel's
informal restaurant, the Bistro, has the flavor of 19th-century Paris and
contains an antique mahogany bar. The Colonnade has an excellent
champagne Sunday brunch. The state-of-the-art health club includes
rowing machines, a cross-country ski simulator, treadmills, Cybex
equipment, a sauna, a steam room, and a pool. ☎ *2401 M St. NW,
20037,* ☎ *202/429–2400 or 800/228–3000,* FAX *202/457–5010. 407
rooms, 8 suites. 2 restaurants, bar, café, room service, beauty salon,
health club, parking (fee). AE, DC, MC, V.*

$$$$ **Park Hyatt.** A notable collection of modern art adorns this West End
hotel, built in 1986. The interior of its main level is constructed of stone
and polished marble, and guests walk on carpeting so thick it almost
bounces. Bronzes, chinoiserie, and a fortune teller at tea in the recently
renovated main-floor lounge are a few of the Old World touches that
offset the spareness of the hotel's design. The rooms are a blend of traditional and contemporary elements and contain reproductions of
Chinese antiques from Washington museum collections. The staff has
a "never say no" policy. ☎ *1201 24th St. NW, 20037,* ☎ *202/789–
1234 or 800/233–1234,* FAX *202/457–8823. 104 rooms, 120 suites.
Restaurant, bar, outdoor café, room service, indoor pool, beauty salon,
massage, health club, parking (fee). AE, DC, MC, V.*

$$$$ **Watergate Hotel.** The internationally famous Watergate, its distinc-
★   tive sawtooth design a landmark along the Potomac, offers guests a
taste of old-English gentility. Scenic murals and a portrait of Queen
Elizabeth contribute to the effect. Large rooms have live plants or fresh
flowers, many have balconies, and most have striking river views.
Jean-Louis Palladin runs the hotel's two superb restaurants. The hotel
is accustomed to serving the world's elite, but it also welcomes vaca-
tioning families and couples on getaway weekends. Part of the exclusive Watergate apartment and commercial complex, the hotel is next
door to the Kennedy Center and a short walk from Georgetown; complimentary limousine service to Capitol Hill or downtown is available
weekdays. ☎ *2650 Virginia Ave. NW, 20037,* ☎ *202/965–2300 or
800/424–2736,* FAX *202/337–7915. 90 rooms, 146 suites. 2 restaurants,
bar, room service, indoor pool, health club, parking (fee). AE, DC,
MC, V.*

$$$ **Embassy Suites.** The hodgepodge of decorative details and cinder-
block construction suggest the hanging gardens of Babylon recon-
structed in a suburban shopping mall. In the atrium, waterfalls gush,
tall palms loom, and plants drip over balconies. Classical columns are
mixed with plaster lions and huge Asian temple lights. Businesspeople
flock to the hotel during the week, but it is also ideal for families. Each
suite, furnished in neo–art deco, has two remote-control TVs, as well
as a refrigerator, microwave, coffeemaker, and queen-size sofa bed. Com-
plimentary cocktails and a cooked-to-order breakfast are served in the
atrium. The Italian restaurant, Panevino, has received favorable reviews.
Situated in a fairly quiet enclave in the West End, Embassy Suites is
within walking distance of Georgetown, the Kennedy Center, and
Dupont Circle. ☎ *1250 22nd St. NW, 20037,* ☎ *202/857–3388 or
800/362–2779,* FAX *202/293–3173. 318 suites. Full breakfast included.
Restaurant, room service, indoor pool, health club, shop, recreation
room, parking (fee). AE, D, DC, MC, V.*

$$$ **Wyndham Bristol Hotel.** This hotel doesn't offer much in the way of views, but the location is excellent: Midway between the White House and Georgetown, the Wyndham is a favorite place for movie and theater people because the Kennedy Center is just a few blocks away. The rooms here are quiet, although the building is bordered on two sides by major thoroughfares. The hotel looks as if it belongs to someone who collects Chinese porcelain: A whole cabinetful greets guests on arrival in the small, quiet lobby. The rest of the hotel, created in 1984 from an apartment building, is English in decor; each room has a butler's table. ☎ *2430 Pennsylvania Ave. NW, 20037, ☎ 202/955–6400, 800/996–3426, or 800/631–4200 in Canada, FAX 202/775–8489. 202 rooms, 37 suites. Restaurant, bar, room service, health club, laundry service, parking (fee). AE, DC, MC, V.*

$$ **Doubletree.** All of the units in these two all-suite hotels in Foggy Bottom, now under separate management, have a fully equipped walk-in kitchen, a minibar, a dishwasher, and a sofa sleeper. The staff is small and so are the lobbies, but the rooms, decorated in a combination of traditional and contemporary decor, are well furnished and comfortable. The two-bedroom suites have a table that seats eight, which is good for family dinners as well as business conferences. The New Hampshire Avenue location has an outdoor rooftop pool (a great spot for viewing fireworks on July 4). Both hotels are close to the Kennedy Center, Georgetown, and George Washington University. ☎ *801 New Hampshire Ave. NW, 20037, ☎ 202/785–2000 or 800/424–2900, FAX 202/ 785–9485; 2500 Pennsylvania Ave. NW, 20037, ☎ 202/333–8060 or 800/424–2900, FAX 202/338–3818. Together, 224 suites. Kitchens, room service, pool (New Hampshire Ave.), access to health club, library. AE, DC, MC, V.*

$$ **River Inn.** A member of the highly rated Potomac Hotel Group, which also operates the similar Inn at Foggy Bottom and One Washington Circle hotels nearby, this small, all-suite hotel is steps from Georgetown, George Washington University, and the Kennedy Center. On the premises is the cozy Foggy Bottom Cafe. The best views are from the 14 Potomac Suites, each of which has a full walk-in kitchen. The lobby is sleek and contemporary, but the room furnishings are homey and modest. This is a popular spot with parents of George Washington University students. ☎ *924 25th St. NW, 20037, ☎ 202/337 7600 or 800/424–2741, FAX 202/625–2618. 127 suites. Restaurant, room service, use of pool at One Washington Circle and health club at the Watergate. AE, DC, MC, V.*

$ **Howard Johnson Kennedy Center.** This eight-story lodge offers HoJo reliability in a location close to the Kennedy Center and Georgetown. Rooms are large and comfortable, and each has a refrigerator. ☎ *2601 Virginia Ave. NW, 20037, ☎ 202/965–2700 or 800/654–2000, FAX 202/ 965–2700 ext. 7910. 192 rooms. Restaurant, refrigerators, pool, laundry service, free parking. AE, DC, MC, V.*

Suburban Maryland

$$ **Holiday Inn Chevy Chase.** A short walk to the Friendship Heights Metro on the D.C. border, this very comfortable Holiday Inn is in the heart of one of the area's most upscale shopping districts. While the on-site Julian's restaurant has deli fare, the nearby Chevy Chase Pavilion and Mazza Gallerie malls have expanded family dining options; a wealth of gourmet choices are one Metro stop away in Bethesda or a 15-minute car trip down Wisconsin Avenue into Georgetown. Coffee and newspapers are complimentary. Families booking ahead can bring the rates down to the $ category and, as at all Holiday Inns, accom-

panying children under 18 stay free. ⊠ *5520 Wisconsin Ave., Chevy Chase, MD 20815,* ☎ *301/656–1500 or 800/465–4329,* ℻ *301/656– 5045. 206 rooms, 10 suites. Restaurant, room service, pool, health club. AE, DC, MC, V.*

$$ **Quality Hotel Silver Spring.** This conveniently located hotel is about three blocks north of the Silver Spring Metro station and close to the shops and restaurants in downtown Silver Spring, including the glossy new, discount-oriented City Place complex. The marble and mahogany lobby, with many places to sit, is comfortable and intimate. The rooms are done in mauve, gray, and soft pink. ⊠ *8727 Colesville Rd., Silver Spring, MD 20910,* ☎ *301/589–5200 or 800/376–7666,* ℻ *301/588– 1841. 228 rooms, 28 suites. 2 restaurants, bar, room service, indoor pool, sauna, exercise room. AE, D, DC, MC, V.*

$–$$$ **Hyatt Regency Bethesda.** The atrium lobby, with glass elevators and ferns, is reminiscent of other Hyatt Regencies. So are the attentive service and the comfortable—if unremarkable—rooms, decorated in peach or hunter green with modern furnishings and light wood accents. The hotel's restaurant is a pleasant place for breakfast before setting out to see the sights of downtown Washington, about 15 minutes away by Metro. The adjacent Metro plaza has a small ice rink, open in winter, and an indoor food court. ⊠ *1 Bethesda Metro Center, Bethesda, MD 20814,* ☎ *301/657–1234 or 800/233–1234,* ℻ *301/657–6453. 368 rooms, 13 suites. 2 restaurants, bar, room service, indoor pool, sauna, exercise room. AE, DC, MC, V.*

$ **American Inn of Bethesda.** At the less glamorous north end of downtown Bethesda, the American Inn sets no new standards for motel decor, but the rooms are clean, generally bright, and all have cable TV. The hotel offers a complimentary Continental breakfast and houses two respectable restaurants: La Posada, a Mexican eatery, and El Caribe, which serves moderately priced Spanish/Latin American fare. Many other restaurants and nightclubs are in walking distance; the Bethesda Metro stop is a 10-minute walk away. ⊠ *8130 Wisconsin Ave., Bethesda, MD 20814,* ☎ *301/656–9300 or 800/323–7081,* ℻ *301/656–2907. 75 rooms, 1 suite. CP. 2 restaurants, pool, laundry service, concierge. AE, D, DC, MC, V.*

$ **Holiday Inn Conference Center at College Park.** Close to the University of Maryland campus and NASA's Goddard Space Flight Center, this meetings-oriented Holiday Inn is also convenient for families. A complimentary shuttle takes guests to the Metro; downtown Washington is a 25-minute train ride away. An indoor pool, an exercise room, cable TV, and a game room can also keep kids (who stay free) occupied on nontouring days. ⊠ *10000 Baltimore Blvd. (Rte. 1), College Park, MD 20740,* ☎ *301/345–6700 or 800/441–4923,* ℻ *301/441–4923. 222 rooms. Restaurant, bar, indoor pool, exercise room, recreation room, laundry service, meeting rooms. AE, DC, MC, V.*

$ **Ramada Inn–Rockville.** Also known as the Ramada Inn at Congressional Park, this seven-story hotel looks like an office building with its sturdy brick facade. Once inside, though, the decor is pleasantly cheery, with celery and rose furnishings in the rooms, all of which have small refrigerators, hair dryers, and clock radios. Rooms on the executive floor also have expansive work desks and comfy recliners. Shuttle service is provided to area offices; the Twinbrook Metro stop (on the red line, about 30 minutes to downtown) is two blocks away across bustling Rockville Pike. The Ramada's Sonora Southwestern restaurant serves all three meals of the day; fast food and upscale restaurants are nearby on the Pike. ⊠ *1775 Rockville Pike, Rockville, MD 20852,*

☎ 301/881–2300 or 800/255–1775, FAX 301/881–9047. 160 rooms, 4 suites. Restaurant. AE, DC, MC, V.

Suburban Virginia

$$$$ **Morrison House.** The architecture and furnishings of the Morrison
★   House in Old Town Alexandria are so faithful to the style of the Federal period (1790–1820) that it is often thought to be a renovation of a historic building rather than a new one built in 1985. Owner Robert Morrison consulted with a curator from the Smithsonian in furnishing the hotel, and the parquet floors, crystal chandeliers and sconces, and period furnishings re-create the atmosphere of a grand American house of 200 years ago. The guest rooms are an elegant blend of early American charm, with four-poster beds and armoires, and the usual modern conveniences. The Elysium Restaurant serves Mediterranean-inspired cuisine in two separate dining rooms: the casual Grill and the more formal Dining Room. ⊞ 116 S. Alfred St., Alexandria, VA 22314, ☎ 703/838–8000 or 800/367–0800, FAX 703/684–6283. 42 rooms, 3 suites. 2 restaurants, access to health club. AE, DC, MC, V.

$$$$ **Ritz-Carlton, Pentagon City.** This 18-story hotel is in Arlington, but its
★   location at the Pentagon City Metro stop makes it more convenient to downtown Washington than many closer hotels. The decor looks to the Virginia horse country for its inspiration, and a $2 million collection of art and antiques, mostly from the 18th and 19th centuries, may be seen in the hotel's public spaces. Rooms, many with views of the monuments across the river, are decorated in rose or blue; each has an overstuffed chair with ottoman, Chippendale-style furniture, and silk bed coverings. To use the hotel's fully equipped fitness center, all you need to bring is your sneakers—a full line of workout clothing, including swimsuits, is provided. The adjacent mall has cinemas, a food court, and 150 shops. ⊞ 1250 S. Hayes St., Arlington, VA 22202, ☎ 703/415–5000 or 800/241–3333, FAX 703/415–5060. 304 rooms, 41 suites. Restaurant, bar, room service, indoor pool, health club. AE, DC, MC, V.

$$$ **Crystal City Marriott.** This business hotel is close to National Airport and the Pentagon, in a thicket of office and apartment buildings. It's a good bet for families because the sights of the Mall are just minutes away by Metro. The lobby, with its lush plantings and marble floor, is more luxurious than the rooms, which were renovated in 1994 in rich, dark colors. The atrium restaurant is light-filled and pleasant. ⊞ 1999 Jefferson Davis Hwy., Arlington, VA 22202, ☎ 703/413–5500 or 800/228–9290, FAX 703/413–0185. 336 rooms, 9 suites. Restaurant, 2 bars, room service, pool, health club, laundry service and dry cleaning, business services, meeting rooms. AE, DC, MC, V.

$$$ **Key Bridge Marriott.** This Marriott in Arlington is a short walk across the Key Bridge to Georgetown; it's also near the Rosslyn Metro station, which provides easy access to Washington's major sights. The rooms were redecorated in 1994 in contemporary decor; many of them have a view of Washington, as does the rooftop restaurant. You can swim from the indoor to the outdoor pool via an underwater connection; when it gets cold, the portal is closed, and guests can stay wet in the interior section. Air traffic from Washington National can be noisy at times. ⊞ 1401 Lee Hwy., Arlington, VA 22209, ☎ 703/524–6400 or 800/228–9290, FAX 703/243–3280. 565 rooms, 20 suites. 2 restaurants, 2 bars, room service, indoor-outdoor pool, beauty salon, health club, shops. AE, DC, MC, V.

$$ Best Western Rosslyn Westpark. This dependable budget hotel is a five-minute walk from the Rosslyn Metro and a leisurely stroll or short drive from Georgetown, but the best thing about it may be the view of the Washington monuments from the Vantage Point restaurant's panoramic windows. Although the location, near Fort Myer and adjacent to Arlington National Cemetery, is very quiet at night, you can easily get to a wide variety of dining rooms and nightclubs along the orange line in Virginia or the blue and orange lines in Washington. A nice touch: free local calls. ☎ *1900 N. Fort Myer Dr., Arlington, VA 22209, ☎ 703/527–4814 or 800/368–3408, FAX 703/522–7480. 308 rooms. 2 restaurants, indoor pool, sauna, exercise room, laundry service and dry cleaning. AE, D, DC, MC, V.*

$ Howard Johnson's National Airport. This high-rise version of the reliable family chain is only a mile from the monuments on the Mall, but you don't have to walk: There's a complimentary shuttle to the Crystal City Metro stop (where there are several miles of underground shopping centers and offices). Rooms are standard, but clean and recently renovated, with cable TV and clock radios. The Olympic-size pool, like the on-site Bob's Big Boy restaurant, is a great draw for families. ☎ *2650 Jefferson Davis Hwy. (Rte. 1), Arlington, VA 22202, ☎ 703/684–7200 or 800/278–2243, FAX 703/684–3217. 278 rooms, 1 suite. Restaurant, pool, exercise room, laundry service, airport shuttle. AE, D, DC, MC, V.*

$ Quality Inn Iwo Jima. Within walking distance of the memorial it's named after and the Rosslyn Metro, this consistently well-regarded budget hotel offers easy access to Georgetown and the Pentagon-National Airport area. Simply decorated rooms have coffeemakers and cable TV. The helpful staff can arrange sightseeing tours. Rates drop in winter; there are discounts for senior citizens; and children under 18 stay free. ☎ *1501 Arlington Blvd. (Rte. 50), Arlington, VA 22209, ☎ 703/524–5000 or 800/221–2222, FAX 703/522–5484. 141 rooms. Restaurant, bar, room service, pool, exercise room, laundry service. AE, D, DC, MC, V.*

$ Vienna Wolf Trap Motel. This three-story motel in Vienna's low-rise downtown, close to the office complexes and giant retail centers of Tysons Corner, is also just a quick bus or car ride from the Vienna Metro stop (on the orange line, 30 minutes by Metro from downtown). The prices are extremely reasonable: $38 to $45. Half of the large rooms have been renovated in attractive light colors or had their furniture upgraded in 1993; some '70s decor remains, but all rooms are clean and have coffeemakers and cable TV. Although the motel faces a busy suburban shopping artery, it is set back far enough to block most noises. Free coffee and doughnuts are available in the lobby at breakfast, and a number of restaurants are within walking distance. ☎ *430 Maple Ave. W, Vienna, VA 22180, ☎ 703/281–2330, FAX 703/281–2838. 115 rooms. Laundry service and dry cleaning. AE, DC, MC, V.*

8 The Arts and Nightlife

THE ARTS

By John F. Kelly

Updated by
Bruce Walker

WASHINGTONIANS no longer balance a chip on their shoulder when it comes time to discuss sophisticated entertainment. In the past 20 years this cultural backwater has been transformed into a cultural capital. The Kennedy Center is a world-class venue, home of the National Symphony Orchestra and host to Broadway shows, ballet, modern dance, opera, and more. Washington even has its own "off Broadway": a half dozen or so plucky theaters spread out around the city that offer new twists on both old and new works. Several art galleries present highly regarded chamber music series. The service bands from the area's numerous military bases ensure an endless supply of martial music of the John Philip Sousa variety as well as rousing renditions of more contemporary tunes. At the other end of the spectrum, Washington was the birthplace of hardcore, a socially aware form of punk rock music that has influenced young bands throughout the country. Go-go—infectious, rhythmic music that mixes elements of rap, rhythm and blues, and funk—was touted as the next big thing to come out of the capital city but seems to have confined itself largely to Washington.

Friday's *Washington Post* "Weekend" section is the best guide to events for the weekend and the coming week. The *Post's* daily "Guide to the Lively Arts" also outlines cultural events in the city. The *Washington Times* "Weekend" section comes out on Thursday. The free weekly *City Paper* hits the streets on Thursday and covers the entertainment scene well. You might also consult the "City Lights" section in the monthly *Washingtonian* magazine.

Any search for cultured entertainment should start at the **John F. Kennedy Center for the Performing Arts** (New Hampshire Ave. and Rock Creek Pkwy. NW). On any given night America's national cultural center may be hosting a symphony orchestra, a troupe of dancers, a Broadway musical, *and* a comedy whodunit. In other words, the "Ken-Cen" has a little of everything. It is actually five stages under one roof: the **Concert Hall,** home park of the National Symphony Orchestra; the 2,200-seat **Opera House,** the setting for ballet, modern dance, grand opera, and large-scale musicals; the **Eisenhower Theater,** usually used for drama; the **Terrace Theater,** a Philip Johnson–designed space that showcases chamber groups and experimental works; and the **Theater Lab,** which is home to cabaret-style performances (since 1987 the audience-participation hit mystery, **Shear Madness,** has been playing here). For information, call 202/467–4600 or 800/444–1324.

Tickets

Tickets to most events are available by calling or visiting each theater's box office.

Protix (☎ 703/218–6500) takes reservations for events at Wolf Trap and elsewhere in the city. It also has outlets in selected Woodward & Lothrop and Safeway stores.

TicketMaster (☎ 202/432–7328 or 800/551–7328) takes phone charges for events at most venues around the city. You can purchase TicketMaster tickets in person at all Hecht Company department stores. No refunds or exchanges are allowed.

TicketPlace sells half-price, day-of-performance tickets for selected shows; a "menu board" lists available performances. Only cash is accepted, and there's a 10% service charge per order. TicketPlace also is a full-price TicketMaster outlet. *Lisner Auditorium, 730 21st St. NW,* ☎ *202/842–5387.* ☉ *Tues.–Fri. noon–4, Sat. 11–5. Tickets for Sun. and Mon. performances sold on Sat.*

Theater

Commercial Theaters and Companies

Arena Stage (6th St. and Maine Ave. SW, ☎ 202/488–3300). The city's most respected resident company (established 1950), the Arena was the first theater outside New York to win a Tony award. It presents a wide-ranging season in its three theaters: the theater-in-the-round Arena, the proscenium Kreeger, and the cabaret-style Old Vat Room. The ambitious New Voices series in the Old Vat allows audiences to see plays in development at reduced prices.

Ford's Theatre (511 10th St. NW, ☎ 202/347–4833). Looking much the way it did when President Lincoln was shot at a performance of *Our American Cousin,* Ford's is host mainly to musicals, many with family appeal. Dickens's *A Christmas Carol* is presented each holiday season.

Lincoln Theatre (1215 U St. NW, ☎ 202/328–9177). From the 1920s to the 1940s, the Lincoln hosted the same performers as the Cotton Club and the Apollo Theatre in New York City: Cab Calloway, Lena Horne, Duke Ellington. The recently renovated 1,240-seater shows films and welcomes such acts as the Count Basie Orchestra and the Harlem Boys and Girls choir.

National Theatre (1321 E St. NW, ☎ 202/628–6161). Destroyed by fire and rebuilt four times, the National Theatre has operated in the same location since 1835. It presents pre- and post-Broadway shows.

Shakespeare Theatre (450 7th St. NW, ☎ 202/393–2700). Four plays—three by the Bard and another classic from his era—are presented each year by the acclaimed Shakespeare Theatre troupe. In 1992 it moved from its former home in the Folger Library to a new, state-of-the-art, 447-seat space. For two weeks each June the company has its own version of New York's Shakespeare in the Park: a free play presented under the stars at Carter Barron Amphitheatre (*see below*).

Warner Theatre (13th and E Sts. NW, ☎ 202/783–4000). One of Washington's grand theaters, the 1924 building received a complete face-lift in 1992. The renovated space now hosts road shows, dance recitals, and the occasional pop music act.

Small Theaters and Companies

Washington's small theaters and companies long labored in obscurity. They are spread out over the District, often performing in churches and other less-than-ideal settings. But fans of independent theater have enjoyed a veritable explosion of new companies in the last few years, many of which tackle difficult, controversial, and specialized subject matter. All compete quite fiercely for the Helen Hayes Award, Washington's version of the Tony. (Several acclaimed alternative stages are on 14th Street NW and near Dupont Circle. Note: Take a cab here after dark.)

Gala Hispanic Theatre (1625 Park Rd. NW, ☎ 202/234–7174). Established in 1976, this company produces Spanish classics as well as contemporary and modern Latin American plays in both Spanish and English.

Olney Theatre (2001 Rte. 108, Olney, MD, ☎ 301/924–3400). Musicals, comedies, and summer stock are presented in this converted barn, an hour from downtown in the Maryland countryside.

Signature Theatre (3806 S. Four Mile Run Dr., Arlington, VA, ☎ 703/820–9771). This plucky group burst upon the scene in 1990 with critically acclaimed productions of Stephen Sondheim musicals. In 1993 it moved from rented space to a 126-seat theater in a converted bumper-plating facility in suburban Virginia. Sondheim is still a favorite with Signature and Signature is said to be a favorite of Sondheim.

Source Theatre (1835 14th St. NW, ☎ 202/462–1073). The 107-seat Source Theatre presents established plays with a sharp satirical edge and modern interpretations of classics. Each July and August, Source hosts the Washington Theater Festival, a celebration of new plays, many by local playwrights.

Studio Theatre (1333 P St. NW, ☎ 202/332–3300). An eclectic season of classic and offbeat plays is presented in this 200-seat theater, one of the nicest among Washington's small, independent companies. The upstairs, 50-seat Secondstage is home to particularly experimental works.

Washington Stage Guild (924 G St. NW, ☎ 202/529–2084). Founded in 1985 and performing in historic Carroll Hall, Washington Stage Guild tackles the classics as well as more contemporary fare. Shaw is a specialty.

Woolly Mammoth (1401 Church St. NW, ☎ 202/393–3939). Unusual, imaginatively produced shows have earned this company good reviews and favorable comparisons to Chicago's Steppenwolf.

Music

Orchestra
The **National Symphony Orchestra** (☎ 202/416–8100). The season at the Kennedy Center extends from September to June. During the summer, the NSO performs at Wolf Trap and presents concerts on the West Lawn of the Capitol on Memorial Day and Labor Day weekends and on July 4. One of the cheapest ways to hear—if not necessarily see—the NSO perform in the Kennedy Center Concert Hall is to get a $10 "obstructed view" ticket.

Concert Halls
DAR Constitution Hall (18th and C Sts. NW, ☎ 202/638–2661). Constitution Hall was the home of the National Symphony Orchestra before the Kennedy Center was built. The 3,700-seat hall still hosts visiting performers, from jazz to pop to rap.

George Mason University (Rte. 123 and Braddock Rd., Fairfax, VA). The GMU campus in suburban Virginia is home to the ambitious Center for the Arts, a glittering complex that opened in 1990 and hosts a full range of performing arts events, from music to ballet to drama. There is a 1,900-seat concert hall, the 500-seat proscenium Harris Theatre, and the intimate 200-seat Black Box Theatre (☎ 703/993–8888 for center events). Also on campus is the 9,500-seat Patriot Center, site of pop acts and sporting events (☎ 703/993–3000 for recorded calendar or 202/432–7328 for ticket information).

John F. Kennedy Center for the Performing Arts (New Hampshire Ave. and Rock Creek Pkwy. NW; *see above.*)

Lisner Auditorium (21st and H Sts. NW, ☎ 202/994–6800). This 1,500-seat theater on the campus of George Washington University is the setting for pop, classical, and choral music.

Merriweather Post Pavilion (☎ 301/982–1800 or 301/596–0660 off-season). An hour north of Washington, in Columbia, Maryland, Merriweather Post is an outdoor pavilion with some covered seating. It plays host in warmer months to big-name pop acts.

National Gallery of Art (6th St. and Constitution Ave. NW, ☎ 202/842–6941 or 202/842–6698). Free concerts by the National Gallery Orchestra, conducted by George Manos, as well as performances by outside recitalists and ensembles, are held in the venerable West Building's West Garden Court on Sunday evenings from October to June. Most performances highlight classical music, though April's American Music Festival often features jazz. Entry is on a first-come, first-served basis.

Nissan Pavilion at Stone Ridge (7800 Cellar Door Dr., Gainesville, VA, ☎ 703/549–7625 or 202/432–7328). Cellar Door Productions, the country's largest concert promoter, built its own 25,000-seat venue in 1995. In rural Virginia, about an hour from downtown Washington, the pavilion hosts all types of music.

Smithsonian Institution (☎ 202/357–2700). An amazing assortment of music—both free and ticketed—is presented by the Smithsonian. Some highlights: American jazz, musical theater, and popular standards are performed in the National Museum of American History's Palm Court. In the third-floor Hall of Musical Instruments, musicians periodically perform on historic instruments from the museum's collection. The Smithsonian Associates Program (☎ 202/357–3030) offers everything from a cappella groups to Cajun zydeco bands, many of which perform in the National Museum of Natural History's Baird Auditorium. In warm weather performances are held in the courtyard between the National Portrait Gallery and the National Museum of American Art.

USAir Arena (1 Harry S. Truman Dr., Landover, MD, ☎ 301/350–3400 or 202/432–7328). The home stadium for the Washington Capitals hockey and Washington Bullets basketball teams is also the area's top venue for big-name pop, rock, and rap acts. Formerly known as the Capital Centre, it seats 20,000.

Wolf Trap Farm Park (1551 Trap Rd., Vienna, VA, ☎ 703/255–1900). Just off the Dulles Toll Road, about a half hour from downtown, Wolf Trap is the only national park dedicated to the performing arts. On its grounds is the **Filene Center,** an outdoor theater that is the scene of pop, jazz, opera, ballet, and dance performances each June through September. The rest of the year, the intimate, indoor **Barns at Wolf Trap** (☎ 703/938–2404) hosts folk, jazz, rock, chamber, opera, and other music. For tickets, call ProTix (☎ 703/218–6500). On summer performance nights, Metrorail operates a $3.50 round-trip shuttle bus between the West Falls Church Metro station and the Filene Center. The fare is exact change only and the bus leaves 20 minutes after the show, or no later than 11 PM, whether the show is over or not.

Choral Music
Choral Arts Society (☎ 202/244–3669). Founded in 1965, this 180-voice choir performs a varied selection of classical pieces at the Kennedy Center from September to April. Three Christmas sing-alongs are scheduled each December.

Choral and church groups frequently perform in the impressive settings of the **Washington National Cathedral** (☎ 202/537–6200) and the **National Shrine of the Immaculate Conception** (☎ 202/526–8300).

Chamber Music

Corcoran Gallery of Art (17th St. and New York Ave. NW, ☎ 202/638–3211). Hungary's Takacs String Quartet and the Cleveland Quartet are among the chamber groups that appear in the Corcoran's Musical Evening Series, one Friday each month from October to May, with some summer offerings. Concerts are followed by a reception with the artists.

Folger Shakespeare Library (201 E. Capitol St. SE, ☎ 202/544–7077). The Folger Shakespeare Library's internationally acclaimed resident chamber music ensemble, the Folger Consort, regularly presents a selection of instrumental and vocal pieces from the medieval, Renaissance, and Baroque periods, during a season that runs from October to May.

National Academy of Sciences (2101 Constitution Ave. NW, ☎ 202/334–2436). Free performances by such groups as the Juilliard String Quartet and the Beaux Arts Trio are given October through May in the academy's acoustically nearly perfect 670-seat auditorium.

Phillips Collection (1600 21st St. NW, ☎ 202/387–2151). The long, paneled music room of gallery founder Duncan Phillips's home is the setting for Sunday afternoon recitals from September through May. Chamber groups from around the world perform; May is devoted to performing artists from the Washington area. Arrive early for the 5 PM concerts.

Performance Series

Armed Forces Concert Series. From June to August, service bands from all four branches of the military perform Monday, Tuesday, Thursday, and Friday evenings, on the East Terrace of the Capitol and several nights a week at the Sylvan Theater (*see below*) on the Washington Monument grounds. The traditional band concerts include marches, patriotic numbers, and some classical music. The bands often perform at other locations throughout the year. *For information: Air Force,* ☎ *202/767–5658; Army,* ☎ *703/696–3718; Navy,* ☎ *202/433–2525; Marines,* ☎ *202/433–4011.*

Carter Barron Amphitheater (16th St. and Colorado Ave. NW, ☎ 202/426–6837 or 202/426–6893 off-season). On Saturday and Sunday nights from mid-June to August this lovely, 4,250-seat outdoor theater in Rock Creek Park plays host to pop, jazz, gospel, and rhythm and blues artists, such as Chick Corea, Nancy Wilson, and Tito Puente. The National Symphony Orchestra also performs, and for two weeks in June the Shakespeare Theatre presents a free play by the Bard.

District Curators (☎ 202/783–0360). An independent, nonprofit organization, this group presents adventurous contemporary performers from around the world in spaces around the city. Past artists have included Laurie Anderson, Philip Glass, the World Saxophone Quartet, and the Japanese dance troupe Sankai Juku.

Ft. Dupont Summer Theater (Minnesota Ave. and F St. SE, ☎ 202/426–7723 or 202/619–7222). The National Park Service presents national and international jazz artists at 8:30 on Friday and Saturday evenings from mid-June to August at this outdoor theater. Past performers at the free concerts have included Wynton Marsalis, Betty Carter, and Ramsey Lewis.

Sylvan Theater (Washington Monument grounds, ☎ 202/619–7225 or 202/619–7222). Service bands from the four branches of the military perform at this outdoor theater from mid-June to August, Tuesday, Thursday, Friday, and Sunday nights.

Washington Performing Arts Society (☎ 202/833–9800). An independent nonprofit organization, WPAS books high-quality classical music, ballet, modern dance, and some drama into halls around the city. Most of the shows—ranging from the Harlem Boys Choir to the Vienna Philharmonic—are held at the Kennedy Center. The **Parade of the Arts** series features shows with family appeal.

Opera

Mount Vernon College (2100 Foxhall Rd. NW, ☎ 202/625–4655). The college's intimate Hand Chapel is the setting for rarely produced chamber operas each winter and spring.

Opera Theater of Northern Virginia (☎ 703/549–5039). The three operas produced during this company's season are sung in English and staged at an Arlington, Virginia, community theater. Each December the company presents a one-act opera especially for young audiences.

Summer Opera Theater Company (Hartke Theater, Catholic University, ☎ 202/526–1669). This independent professional company mounts two fully staged productions each summer, one in June and one in July.

Washington Opera (☎ 202/416–7800 or 800/876–7372). Seven operas—presented in their original languages with English supertitles—are performed each season (November–March) in the Kennedy Center's Opera House and Eisenhower Theater. Performances are often sold out to subscribers, but returned tickets can be purchased an hour before curtain time. Standing room tickets go on sale at the Kennedy Center box office each Saturday at 10 AM for the following week's performances.

Dance

Dance Place (3225 8th St. NE, ☎ 202/269–1600). This studio theater, which presented its first performance in 1980, hosts a wide assortment of modern and ethnic dance most weekends.

Joy of Motion (1643 Connecticut Ave. NW, ☎ 202/387–0911). A dance studio by day, Joy of Motion is the home of several area troupes, including Michelle Ava and Company (modern dance), the Dupont Alley Dance Company (jazz), and TAPestry (you guessed it—tap).

Mount Vernon College (2100 Foxhall Rd. NW, ☎ 202/625–4655). An emerging center for dance in Washington, this women's liberal arts college presents dance companies in the fall and spring. Past participants in the dance series have included the troupes of Robert Small, Nancy Meehan, and Gus Solomons, Jr.

Smithsonian Associates Program (☎ 202/357–3030). National and international dance groups often perform at various Smithsonian museums.

Washington Ballet (☎ 202/362–3606). In October, February, and May this company presents classical and contemporary ballets from the works of such choreographers as George Balanchine, Marius Petipa, and Choo-San Goh, mainly at the Kennedy Center and the Warner Theatre. Each December the Washington Ballet presents *The Nutcracker*.

Film

Washington has a wealth of first-run movie theaters, in the city and in nearby suburbs:

AMC Union Station 9 (Union Station, ☎ 202/842–3757) on Capitol Hill features nine screens and validated, three-hour parking at an adjacent parking lot. Closer to downtown are **Cineplex Odeon's West End 1–4** (23rd and L Sts. NW, ☎ 202/293–3152) and **West End 5, 6, 7** (23rd and M Sts. NW, ☎ 202/452–9020). The art deco **Cineplex Odeon Uptown** (3426 Connecticut Ave. NW, ☎ 202/966–5400) boasts a single huge screen, Dolby sound, and a wonderful balcony. Other first-run movie theaters are clustered near Dupont Circle, in Georgetown, and around upper Wisconsin Avenue.

If you find movie-theater seats a little too confining or the choice of soft drinks a little too soft, there are two locations in the suburbs where films are shown in a dinner-theater-like setting: Patrons sit at tables, and waiters and waitresses take orders for (and then deliver) pizza, hot dogs, nachos, and beer. You must be 21 or over or with a parent to attend the **Bethesda Theatre Cafe** (7719 Wisconsin Ave., Bethesda, MD, ☎ 301/656–3337) and the **Arlington Cinema 'N' Drafthouse** (2903 Columbia Pike, Arlington, VA, ☎ 703/486–2345).

Several Washington theaters screen revivals and foreign, independent, and avant-garde films.

American Film Institute (Kennedy Center, ☎ 202/785–4600). More than 700 different movies—including contemporary and classic foreign and American films—are shown each year at the American Film Institute's theater in the Kennedy Center. Filmmakers and actors are often present to discuss their work.

Biograph (2819 M St. NW, ☎ 202/333–2696). Washington's home for alternative cinema, the Biograph presents a mixture of first-run and repertory domestic and foreign films that have in common "their position out of the mainstream."

Filmfest DC, an annual citywide festival of international cinema, takes place in late April and early May. For information, write to Box 21396, Washington, D.C. 20009, or call 202/274–6810.

Hirshhorn Museum (☎ 202/357–2700), **National Gallery of Art East Building** (☎ 202/737–4215), and **National Archives** (☎ 202/501–5000). These museums on the Mall often show historical, unusual, or experimental films.

The Key (1222 Wisconsin Ave. NW, ☎ 202/333–5100). This four-screen theater specializes in foreign films and presents an annual animation festival.

Mary Pickford Theater (Jefferson Bldg. of the Library of Congress, 1st St. and Independence Ave. SE, ☎ 202/707–5677). This 64-seat theater shows classic and historically important films for free.

National Geographic Society (17th and M Sts. NW, ☎ 202/857–7588). Educational films with a scientific, geographic, or anthropological focus are shown here weekly.

NIGHTLIFE

Washington's nightlife scene has contracted a bit in the last few years; locals have seen some favorite spots close their doors for good. But the city still boasts a range of choices. Its bars and nightclubs cater to a wide spectrum of customers, from proper political appointees to blue-collar regulars in from the suburbs. Many nightspots are clustered in a few key areas, simplifying things for the visitor who enjoys bar-hopping. Georgetown, in northwest Washington, leads the pack with an explosion of bars, nightclubs, and restaurants on M Street east and west of Wisconsin Avenue and on Wisconsin Avenue north of M Street. A half dozen Capitol Hill bars can be found on a stretch of Pennsylvania Avenue between 2nd and 4th streets SE. There is another high-density nightlife area around the intersection of 19th and M streets NW. Near the city's lawyer- and lobbyist-filled downtown, this neighborhood is especially active during happy hour.

As for music, Washington audiences are catholic in their tastes and so are Washington's music promoters. That means you can hear funk at a rock club, blues at a jazz club, and calypso at a reggae club. And it means big-name acts often perform at venues that also book Broadway shows and other nonmusical forms of entertainment. The music listings below are an attempt to impose order on this chaos. Your best bet is to consult Friday's "Weekend" section in the *Washington Post* and the free weekly *City Paper*. It's also a good idea to call clubs ahead of time to find out who's on that night and what sort of music will be played.

Bars and Lounges

Bardo Rodeo. A Plymouth Fury crashing through the window of a converted car dealership sets the tone of this new suburban Virginia brew pub, which bills itself as the largest on the East Coast. It's a frenetic place—with loud music, mismatched furniture, and a sometimes lackadaisical approach to service—but it brews a changing assortment of stouts, ales, and bitters, and it has a wonderful approach to naming the food: Items on the menu have included "Honey, Where's the Keys to the Ducati?" (a pizza) and "She Was So Fine I'd Eat the Corn Out of Her Daddy's Garden" (a quesadilla). *2000 Wilson Blvd., Arlington, VA, ☎ 703/527–9399. ☉ Sat.–Wed. 4:30 PM–2 AM, Thurs. and Fri. 11:30 AM–2 AM. MC, V.*

Brickskeller. A beer lover's mecca, this is the place to go when you want something more exotic than a Bud Lite. More than 500 brands of beer are for sale—from Central American lagers to U.S. microbrewed ales. Bartenders oblige beer-can collectors by opening the containers from the bottom. *1523 22nd St. NW, ☎ 202/293–1885. ☉ Mon.–Thurs. 11:30 AM–2 AM, Fri. 11:30 AM–3 AM, Sat. 6 PM–3 AM, Sun. 6 PM–2 AM. AE, D, DC, MC, V.*

Capitol City Brewing Company. Capitalizing on the microbrewery trend so popular elsewhere, Capitol City is the first brewery to operate in the District since Prohibition. A gleaming copper bar dominates the airy room, with metal steps leading up to where the brews are actually made. Capitol City makes everything from a bitter to a bock, though not all types are available at all times. As at a restaurant with a constantly changing menu, consult the brewmaster's chalkboard to see what's on tap. *1100 New York Ave. NW, ☎ 202/628–2222. ☉ Mon.–Sat. 11 AM–2 AM, Sun. 11 AM–midnight. AE, DC, MC, V.*

Champions. Walls covered with jerseys, pucks, bats, and balls, and the evening's big game on the big-screen TV, leave little doubt that this popular Georgetown establishment is a sports lover's bar. Ballpark-style food enhances the mood. *1206 Wisconsin Ave. NW, ☎ 202/965–4005. ☉*

Mon.–Thurs. 5 PM–2 AM, Fri. 5 PM–3 AM, Sat. 11:30 AM–3 AM, Sun. 11:30 AM–2 AM. 1-drink minimum Fri. and Sat. after 10 PM. AE, DC, MC, V.

Dubliner. Snug, paneled rooms; thick, tasty Guinness; and nightly live entertainment are the main attractions at Washington's premier Irish pub frequented by Capitol Hill staffers. *520 North Capitol St. NW, ☎ 202/737–3773. ⊙ Sun.–Thurs. 11 AM–1:30 AM, Fri.–Sat. 11 AM–2:30 AM. AE, DC, MC, V.*

15 Mins. A college-age clientele ventures downtown to enjoy the funky decorations, tiny dance floor, progressive music, and black lights that bathe the back room in an eerie, purplish glow. Blues bands, local new music bands, and obscure alternative music heroes such as Eugene Chadbourne and Marc Ribot play at the club or in the adjacent Rothschild's Cafeteria. The front room attracts after-work drinking types. The name? It's how much fame Andy Warhol said we'd each have. *1030 15th St. NW, ☎ 202/408–1855. ⊙ Mon.–Tues. 5 PM–2 AM, Wed.–Thurs. noon–2 AM, Fri. noon–3 AM, Sat. 8 PM–3 AM. Cover charge. AE, MC, V.*

Fishmarket. There's something different in just about every room of this multilevel, multiroom space in Old Town Alexandria, from piano bar crooner to ragtime piano shouter to guitar strummer. The operative word here is boisterous. Order the largest size if you like your beer in massive quantities; it comes in a glass big enough to wash your face in. *105 King St., Alexandria, VA, ☎ 703/836–5676. ⊙ Mon.–Sat. 11:15 AM–1 AM, Sun. 11:15 AM–midnight. AE, DC, MC, V.*

Food for Thought. Lots of Birkenstock sandals, natural fibers, and activist conversation give this Dupont Circle lounge and restaurant (vegetarian and organic meat) a '60s coffeehouse feel. Nightly folk music completes the picture. *1738 Connecticut Ave. NW, ☎ 202/797–1095. ⊙ Mon.–Thurs. 11:30 AM–12:30 AM (closed Mon. 3–5), Fri. 11:30 AM–1:30 AM, Sat. noon–1:30 AM, Sun. 4 PM–12:30 AM. AE, DC, MC, V.*

Hawk 'n' Dove. A friendly neighborhood bar in a neighborhood coincidentally dominated by the Capitol building. Regulars include political types, lobbyists, and well-behaved Marines (from a nearby barracks). *329 Pennsylvania Ave. SE, ☎ 202/543–3300. ⊙ Sun.–Thurs. 10 AM–2 AM, Fri. and Sat. 10 AM–3 AM. AE, D, DC, MC, V.*

Sign of the Whale. The best hamburger in town is available at the bar in this well-known post-Preppie/neo-Yuppie haven. *1825 M St. NW, ☎ 202/785–1110. ⊙ Sun.–Thurs. 11:30 AM–2 AM, Fri. and Sat. 11:30 AM–3 AM. AE, D, DC, MC, V.*

Yacht Club. Enormously popular with well-dressed, middle-age singles, this suburban Maryland lounge is the brainchild of irrepressible entrepreneur and matchmaker Tommy Curtis, who measures his success by the number of engagements and marriages spawned aboard the Yacht Club. At last count it was approaching 70. *8111 Woodmont Ave., Bethesda, MD, ☎ 301/654–2396. Jacket and tie (casual Wed.). ⊙ Tues.–Thurs. 5 PM–1 AM, Fri. 5 PM–2 AM, Sat. 8 PM–2 AM. AE, D, DC, MC, V.*

Cabarets

Capitol Steps. The musical political satire of the Capitol Steps, a group of current and former Hill staffers, is presented on Friday and Saturday at Chelsea's, a Georgetown nightclub, and occasionally at other spots around town. (The troupe's name comes from a purported trysting spot of politician John Jenrette and his wife, Rita.) *1055 Thomas Jefferson St. NW, ☎ 202/298–8222 (Chelsea's) or 703/683–8330* *(the Capitol Steps). Shows Fri. at 8 PM and Sat. at 7:30 PM most weeks. Ticket charge. Reservations required. AE, MC, V.*

Gross National Product. After years of spoofing Republican administrations with such shows as *BushCapades* and *Man Without a Contra,* then aiming its barbs at the Democrats in *Clintoons,* this irreverent comedy troupe was most recently performing *A Newt World Order.* GNP stages its shows at Arena Stage's Old Vat Theater and at the Bayou in Georgetown. *Call 202/783–7212 (GNP) for location and reservations. Shows Fri. 8 PM and Sat. 8 and 10 PM. Ticket charge. Reservations suggested. MC, V.*

Marquee Lounge. This cabaret in the Omni Shoreham Hotel is where Mark Russell was ensconced for many years. Today funnywoman Joan Cushing assumes the character of quintessential Washington insider "Mrs. Foggy-bottom" and, with a small cast, pokes fun at well-known political figures in satirical skit and song. Now This!, a musical-comedy improv troupe, acts out audience suggestions every Thursday night, and various other cabaret offerings round out the schedule. *2500 Calvert St. NW, ☎ 202/745–1023. Joan Cushing: shows Fri. and Sat. 8 PM. Now This!: Thurs. 8 PM. Ticket charge. Reservations required. AE, D, DC, MC, V.*

Comedy Clubs

In the past few years the number of comedy groups in Washington that welcome, indeed rely on, the zany suggestions of audience members has mushroomed. These improvisation groups pop up at various venues, performing in the laughs-at-any-cost style of Chicago's Second City troupe, but many disappear as quickly as they appeared. Among those with some stability are **ComedySportz** (Thurs.–Sat. at their new club, The Fun Factory, 3112 Mt. Vernon Ave., Alexandria, VA, ☎ 703/471–5212) and **Dropping the Cow** (Sat. at Square One Theatre, Wisconsin Ave. and Q St. NW, ☎ 202/829–0529).

Comedy Cafe. Local and national comics appear at this club in the heart of downtown. Wednesday is open-mike night; Thursday is local talent; on Friday and Saturday, name comedians headline. *1520 K St. NW, ☎ 202/638–5653. Shows Thurs. 8:30 PM, Fri. 8:30 and 10:30 PM, Sat. 7, 9, and 11 PM. Cover charge. AE, D, DC, MC, V.*

Comedy Connection. This suburban Maryland club hosts comics six nights a week. Black comedians, such as Franklin Ajaye, Sherman Hemsley, and Jimmie Walker, call the Connection home when in town. *312 Main St., Laurel, MD, ☎ 301/490–1993 (shows Thurs. 9 PM, Fri. and Sat. 8:30 and 10:45 PM, Sun. 9 PM); 1401 University Blvd., Hyattsville, MD, ☎ 301/445–6700 (shows Wed.–Fri. and Sun. 8:30). Cover charge and 2-drink minimum. No tennis shoes. Reservations advised. AE, D, DC, MC, V.*

Garvin's Comedy Clubs. Garvin's is one of the oldest names in comedy in Washington and pioneered the practice of organizing comedy nights in suburban hotels. *☎ 202/872–8880 for information and reservations for both locations: Westpark Hotel, 8401 Westpark Dr., Tysons Corner, VA (shows Fri. 9 PM, Sat. 8 and 10 PM); Augie's Restaurant, I–395 and S. Glebe Rd., Arlington, VA (shows Fri. and Sat. 9 PM). Cover charge and drink minimum. Reservations required. MC, V.*

Headliners. In 1994 this club moved from one bigger hotel space to two smaller ones. Now more intimate, the rooms are host to local and regional acts on weekdays and national talent on the weekends. *Hol-*

iday Inn, 2460 Eisenhower Ave., Alexandria, VA, ☎ 703/379–4242 (shows Fri. 9 PM, Sat. 8:30 and 10:30 PM); Holiday Inn, 8120 Wisconsin Ave., Bethesda, MD, ☎ 301/942–4242 (shows Tues.–Thurs. 8:30 PM, Fri.–Sat. 8:30 and 10:30 PM. Cover charge. Reservations required. AE, D, DC, MC, V.

The Improv. A new heavyweight on the Washington comedy scene, the Improv is descended from the club that sparked the stand-up boomlet in New York City and across the country. Name headliners are common. *1140 Connecticut Ave. NW, ☎ 202/296–7008. Sun.–Thurs. 8:30 PM, Fri. and Sat. 8:30 and 10:30 PM. Cover charge and 2-item (not necessarily drinks) minimum. AE, MC, V.*

Acoustic/Folk/Country Clubs

Perhaps surprisingly, Washington has a very active local folk scene. For information on different folk events—from contra (a form of folk) dancing to storytelling to open sings—call the recorded information line of the **Folklore Society of Greater Washington** (☎ 202/546–2228).

Afterwords. This place could just as easily be called Beforewords or Duringwords, shoehorned as it is in a bookshop near Dupont Circle. Folkish acts entertain browsing bohemian bookworms as well as patrons seated at a cozy in-store café. *1517 Connecticut Ave. NW, ☎ 202/ 387–1462. ⊗ Mon.–Thurs. 7:30 AM–1 AM and Fri. 7:30 AM–Mon. 1 AM. AE, D, MC, V.*

Birchmere. The best place in the area to hear acoustic folk and bluegrass acts is in an unpretentious suburban strip shopping center. Favorite sons the Seldom Scene are Thursday-night regulars. Audiences come to listen, and the management politely insists on no distracting chatter. *3901 Mt. Vernon Ave., Alexandria, VA, ☎ 703/549–5919. ⊗ Sun.–Thurs. 6:30 PM–11 PM, Fri.–Sat. 7 PM–12:30 AM. MC, V.*

Junction. On the site of a former dinner theater, the Junction has two hardwood dance floors totaling more than 4,000 square feet. Local C&W fans consider it one of the best places to learn a two-step, and then practice it. *1330 E. Gude Dr., Rockville, MD, ☎ 301/217–5820. ⊗ Daily 11 AM–2 AM. Cover charge Fri. and Sat. AE, D, MC, V.*

Zed Restaurant. Can cowboy hats and boots exist in a city of Brooks Brothers suits? A visit to Zed proves that they can. Each evening, bands in this suburban Virginia night spot play hits from Nashville and other points south and west. Two-stepping is encouraged. *6151 Richmond Hwy., Alexandria, VA, ☎ 703/768–5558. ⊗ Daily 11 AM–2 AM. AE, MC, V.*

Dance Clubs

Washington's dance clubs have taken a hint from their New York counterparts, transforming themselves nearly every night into different incarnations. Club owners rent their spaces to entrepreneurs who tailor the music and ambience to a certain type of crowd. Thus, a club might offer heavy "industrial" music on a Wednesday, host a largely gay clientele on a Thursday, and thump to the sounds of '70s disco on a Friday. It's best to call ahead or consult the often intriguing ads in the free weekly *City Paper.*

Chelsea's. Should a dance like the *lambada* ever again bubble up from South America, you'll find it at this elegant Georgetown club near the C&O Canal. On Monday, there is Ethiopian music; Wednesday is world music night; hot Latin acts appear Thursday through Saturday; and, for a change of pace, it's Persian music on Wednesday and Sunday. *1055 Thomas Jefferson St. NW,* ☎ *202/298–8222.* ☉ *Wed., Thurs., and Sun. 9:30 PM–2 AM, Fri. and Sat. 9:30 PM–4 AM. Cover charge Fri. and Sat. AE, MC, V.*

Dancers. The name describes this suburban Maryland club's clientele. They're attracted to the 1,200-square-foot dance floor and the club's no-smoking, no-alcohol policy. Generally it's big bands on alternate Mondays, rhythm-and-blues bands on alternate Thursdays, swing dancing on Friday, and Latin sounds on Saturday. Good old (vintage '70s) disco finds its way into the mix, too. Dance lessons are usually offered early in the evening. *4609 Willow La., Bethesda, MD,* ☎ *301/ 656–0595.* ☉ *Thurs.–Sat. 8 PM–12:30 AM; classes start at 7 PM. Cover charge. No credit cards.*

Fifth Column. A trendy, well-dressed crowd waits in line to dance to the latest releases from London and Europe on three floors of this converted bank. Avant-garde art installations change every six months. *915 F St. NW,* ☎ *202/393–3632.* ☉ *Mon. 9 PM–2 AM, Wed. and Thurs. 10 PM–2 AM, Fri. and Sat. 10 PM–3 AM. Cover charge. AE, MC, V.*

Kilimanjaro. Deep in ethnically diverse Adams-Morgan, Kilimanjaro specializes in "international" music from the Caribbean and Africa. Every Thursday there's a local reggae band, and there are occasional weekend shows. *1724 California St. NW,* ☎ *202/328–3838.* ☉ *Wed.– Thurs. 5 PM–2 AM, Fri. 5 PM–4:30 AM, Sat. 8 PM–4 AM, Sun. 6 PM–2 AM. Cover charge. D, MC, V.*

Ritz. This downtown nightclub, near the J. Edgar Hoover FBI Building, is popular with the black professional crowd. It has five separate rooms of music, with DJs spinning everything, from Top 40 and reggae in "Club Matisse" to house music in the upstairs "Freezone." *919 E St. NW,* ☎ *202/638–2582.* ☉ *Wed. 9 PM–2 AM, Fri. 5 PM–3 AM, Sat. 9 PM–3 AM, Sun. 9 PM–2 AM. Cover charge. Jacket and tie Fri. and Sat. AE, MC, V.*

River Club. If you own a pair of spats, they wouldn't look out of place at this elegant Georgetown supper club. Its art deco decor, like an Erté print come to life, serves as a backdrop for big band music from Doc Scantlin, Washington's answer to Cab Calloway on Thursday nights. On Wednesday nights, enjoy the sounds of the Admirals. On weekends a DJ spins everything from Motown to big band. This is the perfect place for starring in your own Astaire and Rogers movie. *3223 K St. NW,* ☎ *202/333–8118.* ☉ *Tues.–Thurs. 7 PM–2 AM, Fri. and Sat. 7 PM–3 AM. Cover charge. Jacket and tie. AE, DC, MC, V.*

Tracks. A gay club with a large contingent of straight regulars, this warehouse-district disco has one of the largest dance floors in town and stays open late. *1111 1st St. SE,* ☎ *202/488–3320.* ☉ *Thurs. 9 PM–4 AM, Fri. 8 PM–5 AM, Sat. 8 PM–6 AM, Sun. 4 PM–8 PM (tea dance) and 8 PM–4 AM. Cover charge.*

Zei. The latest entry in Washington's competition to be as hip as the Big Apple, Zei (pronounced "zee") is a New York–style dance club in a former electric power substation. It wants to attract "young, upscale politically aware women and men" with the relentless thump of Euro-Pop dance music and a design that includes a wall of television sets peering down on the proceedings. *1415 Zei Alley NW (14th St. between H and I Sts. NW),* ☎ *202/842–2445.* ☉ *Wed. and Thurs. 10*

PM–2 AM, *Fri. and Sat. 10* PM–3 AM *(call for occasional weeknight events). No tennis shoes. Cover charge. AE, D, DC, MC, V.*

Jazz Clubs

Blues Alley. The restaurant turns out Creole cooking, while cooking on stage are such nationally known performers as Charlie Byrd and Ramsey Lewis. You can come for just the show, but those who come for a meal get better seats. *Rear 1073 Wisconsin Ave. NW,* ☎ *202/337– 4141.* ⊘ *Sun.–Thurs. 6* PM–*midnight, Fri. and Sat. 6* PM–2 AM. *Shows at 8 and 10, plus occasional midnight shows Fri. and Sat. Cover charge and $7 food/drink minimum. AE, DC, MC, V.*

Cafe Lautrec. The Toulouse-Lautrec decor, French food, and Gallic atmosphere are almost enough to convince you you're on the Left Bank of the Seine rather than the right bank of the Potomac. Cool cats play cool jazz nightly with tap-dancing fixture Johne Forges hoofing atop tables most Fridays and Saturdays. *2431 18th St. NW,* ☎ *202/265– 6436.* ⊘ *Sun.–Thurs. 5* PM–2 AM, *Fri. and Sat. 5* PM–3 AM. *$6 minimum Tues. and Thurs.–Sun. AE, DC, MC, V.*

One Step Down. Low-ceilinged, intimate, and boasting the best jazz jukebox in town, this small club books talented local artists and the occasional national act. The venue of choice for many New York jazz masters, the place is frayed and smoky, as a jazz club should be. Live music is presented Thursday–Monday. *2517 Pennsylvania Ave. NW,* ☎ *202/331–8863.* ⊘ *Mon.–Thurs. 10* AM–2 AM, *Fri. 10* AM–3 AM, *Sat. noon–3* AM, *Sun. noon–2* AM. *Cover charge and minimum. AE, DC, MC, V.*

Takoma Station Tavern. In the shadow of the Metro stop that lends its name, this club hosts local favorites such as Marshall Keys and Keith Killgo, with the occasional nationally known artist stopping by to jam. The jazz happy hours starting at 6:30 Wednesday through Friday pack the joint. There's reggae on Sundays. *6914 4th St. NW,* ☎ *202/829–1999.* ⊘ *Sun.–Thurs. 4* PM–2 AM, *Fri. and Sat. 4* PM–3 AM. *No sneakers or athletic wear. AE, DC, MC, V.*

219 Basin Street Lounge. Across the Potomac in Old Town Alexandria above the 219 Restaurant, jazz combos perform Thursday through Saturday in an attractive Victorian-style bar. Musicians from local service bands often stop by to sit in. *219 King St., Alexandria, VA,* ☎ *703/ 549–1141.* ⊘ *Sun. 10* AM–10 PM, *Mon.–Thurs. 11* AM–10:30 PM, *Fri. 11* AM–11 PM, *Sat. 8* AM–11 PM. *Cover charge. AE, D, DC, MC, V.*

Rock, Pop, and Rhythm and Blues Clubs

The Bayou. In Georgetown, underneath the Whitehurst Freeway, the Bayou is a Washington fixture that showcases national acts on weeknights and local talent on weekends. Bands cover rock in all its permutations: pop rock, hard rock, soft rock, new rock, and classic rock. Tickets are available at the door or through TicketMaster. Occasional no-alcohol, all-ages shows allow those under 18 a chance to dance. *3135 K St. NW,* ☎ *202/333–2897. Generally open daily 8* PM–2 AM. *Cover charge. No credit cards.*

Grog and Tankard. A college-age crowd downs cheap pitchers of beer while listening to exuberant local bands in this small, comfortably disheveled night spot. *2408 Wisconsin Ave. NW,* ☎ *202/333–3114.* ⊘ *Sun.–Thurs. 5* PM–2 AM, *Fri.–Sat. 5* PM–3 AM. *Cover charge after 9* PM. *AE, MC, V.*

9:30 Club. This trendy club in the center of Washington's old downtown books an eclectic mix of local, national, and international artists, most of whom play what used to be known as "new wave" music. The regulars dress to be seen, but visitors won't feel out of place. Get tickets at the door or through TicketMaster. *930 F St. NW,* ☎ *202/393-0930. Hrs vary according to shows but generally open Sun.–Thurs. 7:30 PM–midnight, Fri.–Sat. 9 PM–2 AM. Cover charge. MC, V.*

Tornado Alley. Owner Mark Gretschel is a great booster of "roots" music, such as blues, Cajun, zydeco, and anything else that swirls in like the eponymous wind from America's heartland. This suburban Maryland club resembling a high school gym hosts such national cult favorites as Koko Taylor, Wayne Toups and Zydecajun, Junior Wells, and Clarence "Gatemouth" Brown, as well as local heroes, such as ex-Commander Cody guitarist Bill Kirchen. *11319 Elkin St., Wheaton, MD,* ☎ *301/929–0795. Hrs vary according to shows but generally open Tues.–Thurs. 5 PM–1 AM, Fri. and Sat. 5 PM–2 AM, Sun. 5 PM–1 AM. Cover charge. D, MC, V.*

9 Excursions

TOUR 1: THE C&O CANAL AND GREAT FALLS

By Michael Dolan

Updated by Bruce Walker

IN THE 18TH AND EARLY 19TH CENTURIES, the Potomac River was the main transport route between Cumberland, Maryland, one of the most important ports on the nation's frontier, and the seaports of the Chesapeake Bay. Tobacco, grain, whiskey, furs, iron ore, timber, and other commodities were sent down the Potomac from Cumberland to the ports of Georgetown and Alexandria, which served as major distribution points for both domestic and international markets.

Although it served as a vital link with the country's western territories, the Potomac did have some drawbacks as a commercial waterway: Rapids and waterfalls along the 190 miles between Cumberland and Washington made it impossible for traders to navigate the entire distance by boat. Just a few miles upstream from Washington, the Potomac cascaded through two such barriers—the breathtakingly beautiful Great Falls and the less dramatic but no less impassable Little Falls.

To help traders move goods between the eastern markets and the western frontier more efficiently, 18th-century engineers proposed that a canal with a series of elevator locks be built parallel to the river. The first such canal was built at the urging of George Washington, who actually helped found a company just for this purpose. In 1802, after 17 years of work, his firm opened the Patowmack Canal on the Virginia side of the river.

In 1828 Washington's canal was replaced by the **Chesapeake & Ohio (C&O) Canal,** which had been dug along the opposite shore. The C&O stretched from the heart of Washington to Cumberland. Starting near what is now the intersection of 17th Street and Constitution Avenue NW (the public rest room there was originally a lock house), the C&O moved barges through 75 locks.

Ironically, the C&O Canal began operation the same day as the Baltimore & Ohio Railroad, the concern that eventually put the canal out of business. The C&O route to the west nevertheless did prove to be a viable alternative for traders interested in moving goods through the Washington area and to the lower Chesapeake. During the mid-19th century, the canal boats carried as many as a million tons of merchandise a year. The C&O Canal stopped turning a profit in 1890 but remained in business until 1924, when a disastrous storm left it in ruins. Ownership then shifted to the B&O Railroad, which sold the canal to the federal government in 1938 for $2 million. In 1939 the canal became part of the National Capital Parks System.

In the 1950s a proposal to build a highway over the canal near Washington was defeated by residents of the Palisades, a neighborhood that overlooks the waterway. Since 1971 the canal has been a national park, providing Washingtonians and visitors with a window into the past and a marvelous place to pursue recreational activities.

The twin parks of **Great Falls**—on either side of the river 13 miles northwest of Georgetown—are also now part of the National Park system. The 800-acre park on the Virginia side is a favorite place for outings for local residents and is easily accessible by tourists. The steep, jagged falls roar into a narrow gorge, providing one of the most spectacular scenic attractions in the East.

Exploring

Numbers in the margin correspond to points of interest on the C&O Canal and Great Falls map.

This tour moves from Georgetown northwest along the Potomac to Great Falls Park. The canal itself is worth a day's stroll or ride.

① The towpath along the canal in **Georgetown** passes traces of that area's industrial past, such as the Godey Lime Kilns near the mouth of Rock Creek, as well as the fronts of numerous houses that date from 1810. From April through early November mule-drawn barges leave for 90-minute trips from the Foundry Mall on Thomas Jefferson Street NW, half a block south of M Street. No reservations are required for the public trips. *For information, ☎ 202/653–5190 or 301/299–2026. For group reservations and rates, ☎ 301/299–3613. Cost: $5 adults, $3.50 senior citizens and children under 13.*

② **Fletcher's Boat House** rents canoes and bicycles and sells fishing tackle and D.C. fishing licenses. Fishermen often congregate here to try their luck with shad, perch, catfish, striped bass, and other freshwater species. *4740 Canal Rd. at Reservoir Rd., ☎ 202/244–0461. Spring, 5:30 AM–5 PM; summer, weekdays 7:30 AM–7:30 PM, weekends 5:30 AM–7:30 PM; closed winter.*

③ **Chain Bridge**—named for the chains that held up the original structure—links the District with Virginia. The bridge was built to enable cattlemen to bring Virginia herds to the slaughterhouses along the Potomac on the Maryland side. During the Civil War the bridge was guarded by Union troops stationed at earthen fortifications along what is now Potomac Avenue NW. The Virginia side of the river in the area around Chain Bridge is known for its good fishing and narrow, treacherous channel.

Glen Echo is a charming village of Victorian houses that was founded in 1891 when brothers Edwin and Edward Baltzley fell under the spell of the Chautauqua movement, an organization that promoted liberal and practical education among the masses. The brothers sold land and houses to further their dream, but the Glen Echo Chautauqua lasted only one season. Their compound served a stint as an amusement park and is now run by the National Park Service as an arts and cultural cen-

④ ter. **Glen Echo Park** (7300 MacArthur Blvd., ☎ 301/492–6282) is noted not only for its whimsical architecture, including a stone tower left from the Chautauqua period, but also for its splendid 1921 Dentzel carousel. From late spring to early fall you can buy a cheap trip into the past, complete with music from a real calliope. The park is also the site of frequent folk festivals, and dances are held in the ornate Spanish Ballroom. For scheduling information, check the "Weekend" section in Friday's *Washington Post* or the free weekly *City Paper*.

The nearby **Clara Barton House,** one of the most striking Victorian structures in Glen Echo, has been preserved as a monument to the founder of the American Red Cross. Barton moved here toward the end of her life, using the place for a while to store Red Cross supplies and as the organization's headquarters. Today the building is furnished with original period artifacts. *5801 Oxford Rd., Glen Echo, MD, ☎ 301/492–6245.* ☛ *Free.* ☺ *Daily 10–5; guided tours hourly on the ½ hr.*

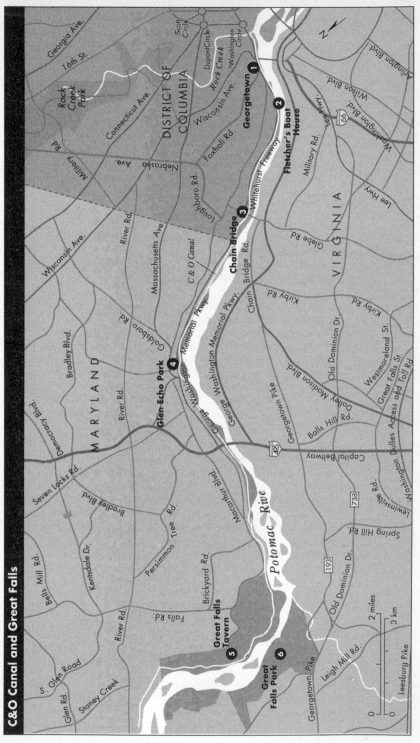

⑤ **Great Falls Tavern,** on the Maryland side of Great Falls Park, features displays of canal history and a platform from which to look at the falls. Better yet, walk over the Olmsted Bridges out to a small island in the middle of the river for a spectacular view. On the canal walls are "rope burns" caused by decade upon decade of friction from barge lines. Half a mile west a flood marker shows how high the Potomac can go—after a hurricane in 1972 the river crested far above the ground where visitors stand. Canal barge trips start here between April and October. The tavern ceased being a hostelry long ago, so if you're hungry head for the snack bar a few paces north of the tavern. *Park,* ☎ *301/299– 2026.* ☛ *$4 per vehicle, $2 per person without vehicle, good for 7 days for MD and VA sides of the park.* ☉ *Daily sunrise–sunset. Closed Thanksgiving and Dec. 25. Tavern and museum,* ☎ *301/299–3613.* ☉ *Daily 9–5.*

⑥ The Virginia side of **Great Falls Park,** which is not accessible from the Maryland side, offers the best views of the Potomac, as well as trails leading past the old Patowmack Canal and among the boulders and forests lining the edge of the falls. Horseback riding is permitted—maps are available at the visitor center—but you can't rent horses in the park. Swimming and wading are prohibited, but there are fine opportunities for fishing (a Virginia, Maryland, or D.C. license is required for anglers 16 and older), rock climbing (climbers must register at the visitor center beforehand), and white-water kayaking (*below* the falls only, and only by experienced boaters). From peaks beside the river and from several artificial platforms you can watch helmeted kayakers and climbers test their skills against the river and the rocks. As is true all along this stretch of the river, the currents are deadly. Despite frequent signs and warnings, each year some visitors dare the water and lose. It's best to keep away from even the most benign-looking ripple. ☎ *703/285–2966.* ☛ *$4 per vehicle, $2 per person without vehicle, good for 7 days for MD and VA sides of the park.* ☉ *Daily 8 AM until dark. Closed Dec. 25.*

Getting Around

By Car

To reach the Virginia side of Great Falls Park, take the scenic and winding Route 193 (Exit 13 off Route 495, the Capitol Beltway) to Route 738, and follow the signs. It takes about 25 minutes to drive to the park from the Beltway. You can get to the Maryland side of the park by following MacArthur Boulevard from Georgetown or by taking Exit 41 off the Beltway, following the signs to Carderock.

By Foot, Canoe, or Bicycle

The C&O Canal Park and its towpath are favorite destinations for joggers, bikers, and canoeists. The towpath has only a slight grade, which makes for a leisurely ride or hike. Most recreational bikers consider the 13 miles from Georgetown to Great Falls an easy ride; there's only one short stretch of rocky ground near Great Falls where bikers need to carry their cycles. You can also take a bike path that parallels MacArthur Boulevard for much of the distance to the Maryland side of the park. Storm damage has left parts of the canal dry, but many segments remain intact and navigable by canoe. You can rent canoes or bicycles at **Fletcher's Boat House,** just upriver from Georgetown (*see* Exploring, *above*). In winter the canal sometimes freezes solid enough to allow for ice skating; during particularly hard freezes it's possible to skate great distances along it, occasionally interrupting your stride for short clambers around the locks.

Guided Tours

A tour of the visitor center and museum at **Great Falls Park** (☏ 703/ 285–2966) in Virginia takes 30 minutes. Staff members conduct special tours and walks year-round. Visitors are encouraged to take self-guided tours along well-marked trails, including one that follows the route of the old Patowmack Canal.

On the Maryland side, the old **Great Falls Tavern** (☏ 301/299–2026) serves as a museum and a headquarters for the rangers who manage the C&O Canal. During warm weather, replicas of the old mule-drawn boats carry visitors along this stretch of the canal; similar trips also begin in Georgetown. History books and canal guides are on sale at both parks as well as at many bookstores in the District.

TOUR 2: ANNAPOLIS

Although it has long since been overtaken by Baltimore as the major Chesapeake port, **Annapolis** is still a popular destination for oyster catchers and yachting aficionados, and on warm sunny days the City Dock is thronged with billowing sails set strikingly against a background of redbrick waterfront buildings, mostly shops and restaurants. Annapolis's enduring nautical reputation derives largely from the presence of the United States Naval Academy, whose handsomely uniformed students grace the city streets in their summer whites and winter navy-blues (the *real* navy blue, which is practically black). October sailboat and powerboat shows attract national attention, keeping local hotels and restaurants full even after the summer tourist season has ended.

In 1649 a group of Puritan settlers relocated from Virginia to a spot at the mouth of the Severn River; the community that they called Providence is now an upscale residential area. Lord Baltimore—who held the Royal charter to settle Maryland—named the area around the new town Anne Arundel County, after his wife; in 1684 Anne Arundel Town was established, across from Providence, on the south side of the Severn. Ten years later, Anne Arundel Town became the capital of Maryland and was renamed Annapolis—for Princess Anne, who later became queen. Annapolis received its city charter in 1708.

Annapolis—not the better-known Baltimore—is the state capital. One of the country's largest assemblages of 18th-century architecture (including 50 pre-Revolutionary buildings) recalls the city's days as a major port, particularly for the export of tobacco. In fact, in 1774 local patriots matched their Boston counterparts (who had thrown their famous tea party the previous year) by burning the *Peggy Sue,* a ship loaded with taxed tea. A decade later, in 1783 and 1784, Annapolis served as the nation's first peacetime capital. Annapolis's waterfront orientation makes it possible for visitors to do the city justice in a single well-planned day.

Exploring

Numbers in the margin correspond to points of interest on the Annapolis map.

❶ Start your tour at the redbrick **Information Booth** operated by the **Annapolis–Anne Arundel County Conference and Visitors Bureau,** where you can pick up maps and brochures. The booth is on the city dock, adjacent to the harbormaster's office (☏ 410/268–8687; open Apr.–Oct., daily 10–5; information also is available year-round daily 9–5 at 26 West St.). Outside, both motor- and sail-craft dozens of feet long moor

204

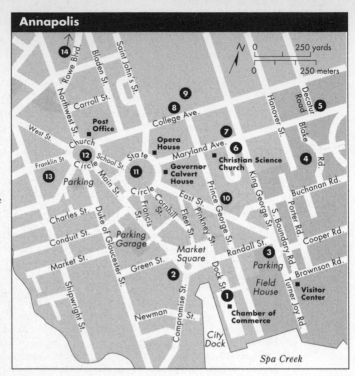

at the edges of Dock Street and Market Place. A variety of shops, restaurants, and bars populate the dock area.

TIME OUT   The **reconstructed Market House** pavilion—originally a collection of mid-19th-century market stalls in the center of Market Square—now sells baked goods, fast food, and fish (prepared or to cook at home). The building offers no seating, but you've got the entire dock on which to set up your picnic.

② On Main Street by the dock, the **Maritime Museum** occupies a warehouse that stored supplies for the Revolutionary Army during the War of Independence, when the city was a vital link in the supply chain. Exhibits pertain to the history of maritime commerce in Annapolis and include artifacts of Colonial-era trade and a diorama of the city's waterfront in the 18th century. *77 Main St.,* ☎ *410/268–5576.* ☛ *Free.* ⊙ *Apr.–Oct., daily 9–5, Nov.–Mar., daily 10–4. Closed Thanksgiving and Dec. 24, 25.*

★ **③** Cross the square and follow Randall Street a few blocks to reach the **United States Naval Academy.** By the gate at King George Street you'll find Ricketts Hall, where you can join a guided tour or pick up information for your own excursion. The academy, established in 1845 on the site of a U.S. Army fort, occupies 329 scenic riverside acres, earning the dubious title of "country club on the Severn" from its West Point rivals. In the center of campus the bronze-dome, interdenominational **④** **U.S. Naval Chapel** contains the crypt of the Revolutionary War hero John Paul Jones, who, in an engagement with a British ship, uttered **⑤** the famous declaration, "I have not yet begun to fight!" The **museum in Preble Hall** tells the story of the U.S. Navy, with displays of miniature ships and flags from the original vessels. Periodic full-dress parades and (in warmer months) daily noontime musters of the midshipmen take place at various spots around campus, but the most remarkable sight may be the sample student quarters open to the public—they're quite a bit neater than the typical college dorm! ☎ *410/ 263–6933. Visitor center open daily 9–4.* ☞ *Free. Cost of tour: $5 adults, $4 senior citizens, $3 children grades 1–12. 1-hr tours depart June–Aug., every ½ hr, Mon.–Sat. 9:30–3:30, Sun. 12:30–3:30; Mar.–May and Sept.–Nov., hourly, Mon.–Sat. 10–3, Sun. 12:30–3; Dec.–Feb., Mon.–Sat. 11 and 1, Sun. 12:30 and 2:30. Closed Thanksgiving, Dec. 25, and Jan. 1.*

⑥ Leave the Academy via Maryland Avenue and you will pass the three-story redbrick **Hammond-Harwood House.** The house is the only verifiable full-scale example of the work of William Buckland, the most prominent Colonial architect at the time of his death, in 1774—the year in which the house was completed. Buckland was famous for his interior woodwork, which may also be seen in the Chase-Lloyd House across the street and in George Mason's Gunston Hall in Lorton, Virginia. Exquisite moldings, cornices, and other carvings appear throughout, including garlands of roses above the front doorway. These were meant to be part of the manorial wedding present from Matthias Hammond, a lawyer and revolutionary, to his fiancée, who jilted him before the project was finished. Hammond never married, and he died in 1784. The Harwoods took over the house toward the turn of the century. Today the house is furnished with 18th-century pieces, and the garden is tended with regard to period authenticity. *19 Maryland Ave.,* ☎ *410/269–1714.* ☺ *Mon.–Sat. 10–4, Sun. noon–4.* ☞ *$4 adults, $3 children 6–18 (combination ticket with Paca House, see below, is $9 adults, $4.50 children 6–18). Closed Thanksgiving, Dec. 25, and Jan. 1. Call for group rates.*

⑦ Across the street is the gracefully massive facade—sheer except for a center third beneath a pediment—of the **Chase-Lloyd House.** In 1774 the tobacco planter and revolutionary Edward Lloyd IV completed work begun five years earlier by Samuel Chase, a Supreme Court justice and future signer of the Declaration of Independence. The first floor is open to the public and contains more of Buckland's handiwork, including a parlor mantelpiece with tobacco leaves carved into the marble. The house is furnished with a mixture of 18th-, 19th-, and 20th-century pieces. The staircase parts dramatically around a Palladian window (an arched, triple window whose center segment is taller than its flanks). For more than 100 years the house has served as a home for elderly Episcopalian women. *22 Maryland Ave.,* ☎ *410/263–2723.* ☞ *$2.* ☺ *Mar.–Dec., Tues.–Sat. 2–4.; Jan. and Feb., Tues., Fri., and Sat. 2–4.*

⑧ A left on King George Street will take you to College Avenue and **St. John's College,** alma mater of Francis Scott Key, lyricist of *The Star Spangled Banner.* The college has been best known since 1937, however, for its Great Books curriculum—a four-year program of math, science, music, languages, and the works of great authors from Homer to Freud. Climb the gradual slope of the long, brick-paved path to the **⑨** impressive golden cupola of **McDowell Hall,** the third-oldest academic building in the country, just as St. John's is the third-oldest college in the country (after Harvard and William and Mary). Founded as King William's School in 1696, the school was chartered under its current name in 1784. The enormous tulip poplar called the **Liberty Tree,** on the lawn fronted by College Avenue, is possibly 600 years old. In its shade colonists and Indians made treaties in the 17th century, revolutionaries rallied in the 18th century, Union troops encamped in the 19th century, and commencement takes place every spring. The **Elizabeth Myers Mitchell Art Gallery** (☎ 410/626–2556; open Tues.–Sun. noon–5, Fri. noon–5 and 7–8 PM), on the east side of Mellon Hall, presents a variety of exhibits and special programs related to the fine arts. Down King George Street toward the water is the **Carroll-Barrister House,** now the college admissions office. The house was built in 1722 at Main and Conduit streets and was moved onto campus in 1957. Charles Carroll—not the signer of the Declaration, but his cousin—who helped draft Maryland's Declaration of Rights, was born here. ☎ *410/263– 2371. Free tours available by appointment.*

Head south on King George Street and make a right on College Avenue and a left on Prince George Street. Cross Maryland Avenue, and ⑩ a block farther down on your left you'll come to the **William Paca House and Garden**—the house built in 1765 and the garden originally finished in 1772 and gradually restored in this century. These comprise the estate of William Paca, a signer of the Declaration of Independence and governor of Maryland from 1782 to 1785. Inside, the main floor (furnished with 18th-century antiques) retains its original Prussian-blue and soft-gray color scheme. The second floor contains a mixture of 18th- and 19th-century pieces. The adjacent 2-acre garden provides a longer perspective on the back of the house, plus worthwhile sights of its own: a Chinese Chippendale bridge, a pond, a wilderness area, and formal arrangements. *186 Prince George St.,* ☎ *410/263–5553.* ☛ *House and garden, $6 adults, $3 children 6–18; house only, $4 adults, $2 children 6–18; garden only, $3 adults, $1.50 children 6–18. A combination ticket is offered for the Paca House and garden and the Hammond-Harwood House (see above) at $9 adults, $4.50 children 6–18. House and garden open Jan.–Feb., Fri.–Sat. 10–4, Sun. noon–4; Mar.–Dec., Mon.–Sat. 10–4, Sun. noon–4. Closed Thanksgiving, Dec. 24, and Dec. 25.*

Return on Prince George Street to Maryland Avenue and turn left. The ⑪ domed **Maryland State House,** completed in 1780, is the oldest state capitol in continuous legislative use and the only one where the U.S. Congress has sat. During 1783 and 1784 when Congress convened here, it accepted the resignation of General George Washington as commander in chief of the Continental Army, and it ratified the Treaty of Paris with the king, concluding the War of Independence. Both of these matters were determined in the Old Senate Chamber, which is filled with intricate woodwork (featuring the ubiquitous tobacco motif) that's also attributed to Buckland. Also decorating this room is Charles Willson Peale's painting *Washington at the Battle of Yorktown,* considered to be the masterpiece of the Revolutionary War period's finest portrait artist. The state Senate and House now hold their sessions in two other chambers in the building. Also on the grounds is the oldest public building in Maryland, the minuscule redbrick **Treasury,** built in 1735. *State Circle,* ☎ *410/974–3400.* ☛ *Free.* ☉ *Daily 9–5. Visitor center open weekends 10–4. ½-hr tours daily at 11 and 3. Closed Thanksgiving, Dec. 25, and Jan. 1.*

School Street leads you to the center of Church Circle, where you'll ⑫ see the Episcopal **St. Anne's Church**—the third church of that name on that spot. The first, built in 1704, was torn down in 1775. The second, built in 1792, burned down in 1858; however, parts of the walls survived and were incorporated into the present structure, which was built in 1859. The parish was founded in 1692, and King William III donated the communion silver. The churchyard contains the grave of the last Colonial governor, Sir Robert Eden. *Church Circle,* ☎ *410/267–9333.* ☛ *Free.* ⊙ *Daily 7:30–6.*

TIME OUT   **Ram's Head Tavern** (33 West Street, ☎ 410/268-4545), serves award-winning chili, sandwiches, and salads, as well as bottled beer from more than two dozen countries.

One block west on Franklin Street brings you to the ivy-covered red-brick former church that houses the **Banneker-Douglass Museum of Afro-American Life.** Changing exhibits, lectures, films, and literature are brought together here to give a picture of the African-American experience in Maryland. *84 Franklin St.,* ☎ *410/974–2894.* ☛ *Free.* ⊙ *Tues.–Fri. 10–3, Sat. noon–4.*

Return to Church Circle and follow Northwest Street in the direction you might expect to Rowe Boulevard. A 10-minute walk on Rowe Boulevard brings you to the 6-acre **Helen Avalynne Tawes Garden.** This botanical garden, across from the Navy–Marine Corps Stadium parking lot, next to the Tawes State Office Building Complex, is planted with flora representative of different regions of the state. Western Maryland's mountain forests and the marshland along the Chesapeake are evoked by rhododendrons and reeds, respectively; the ponds host various fish, fowl, and amphibians. Naturally, the state flower, the black-eyed Susan, is well represented. *580 Taylor Ave.,* ☎ *410/974–3717.* ☛ *Free.* ⊙ *Daily dawn–dusk. Call for information on weekday tours.*

Getting Around

There is no regular train or bus service from Washington to Annapolis. The drive from Washington (east on U.S. Route 50, to the Rowe Boulevard exit) normally takes 35–45 minutes, but if you travel between 3:30 and 6:30 PM you could be stuck in traffic for as long as two hours.

Parking spots on Annapolis's historic downtown streets are rare, but there's a free lot at the Navy–Marine Corps Stadium (to the right of Rowe Boulevard as you enter town from Route 50), from which a shuttle (☎ 410/263–7964) heads to downtown for 75¢.

Guided Tours

"Acoustiguide" walking tours of the city's historic district, prepared by the **Historic Annapolis Foundation** (☎ 410/267–7619) and narrated by Walter Cronkite, are available at the **Maritime Museum** (*see below*). The rental is $7 adults, $2.50 children under 13. Guides from **Three Centuries Tours** (☎ 410/263–5401) wear colonial dress and take visitors to the State House, St. John's College, and the Naval Academy. The fee is $7 adults, $3 children 6–18.

Cruises offered by **Chesapeake Marine Tours, Inc.** (☎ 410/268–7600 or 301/261–2719 in Washington, DC) depart from the city dock in good weather. Tours range from 40 minutes to 7½ hours, extending as far as St. Michael's, a preserved 18th-century fishing village and yachting mecca on the eastern shore of the bay. Prices range from $6 to $35.

TOUR 3: MOUNT VERNON, WOODLAWN, AND GUNSTON HALL

Long before the capital city was planned, the shores of the Potomac had been divided into plantations by wealthy traders and gentleman farmers. Even though most traces of the Colonial era were obliterated as the capital grew in the 19th century, several splendid examples of plantation architecture remain on the Virginia side of the Potomac just 15 miles or so south of the District. The three mansions described in this section can easily be visited in a single day: **Mount Vernon,** one of the most popular sites in the area, was the home of George Washington; **Woodlawn,** the estate of Washington's granddaughter; and **Gunston Hall,** the home of George Mason—patriot and author of the document on which the Bill of Rights was based. Spread out on hillsides overlooking the river, these estates offer a look into a way of life long gone.

Exploring

Numbers in the margin correspond to points of interest on the Mount Vernon, Woodlawn, and Gunston Hall map.

Mount Vernon

★ ❶ **Mount Vernon** and the surrounding lands had been in the Washington family for nearly 90 years by the time George inherited it all in 1761. Before taking over command of the Continental Army, Washington was a yeoman farmer, directing the management of the 8,000-acre plantation, of which more than 3,000 acres were under cultivation. He also oversaw the transformation of the main house from an ordinary farm dwelling into what was for the time a grand mansion.

The main house, with its red roof, is elegant though understated. The exterior is made of yellow pine painted and coated with layers of sand— "rusticated," in the language of the day—to resemble white-stone blocks.

The inside of the building is more ornate, especially the formal receiving room with its molded ceiling decorated with agricultural motifs. Throughout the house you'll find other, smaller symbols of the owner's eminence, such as a key to the main portal of the Bastille, presented to Washington by the Marquis de Lafayette, and Washington's presidential chair. Small groups of visitors are ushered from room to room, each of which is staffed by a guide who describes the furnishings and answers questions.

The real (often overlooked) treasure of Mount Vernon is the view from around back: Beneath a 90-foot portico (George Washington's contribution to the language of architecture), the home's dramatic riverside porch looks out on an expanse of lawn that slopes down to the Potomac. In springtime the view of the river (a mile wide at the point at which it passes the plantation) is framed by the blossoms of wild plum and dogwood. Ships of the U.S. and foreign navies always salute when passing the house.

Tours of the sprawling grounds are self-guided. Visitors are free to visit the plantation workshops, the kitchen, the carriage house, the gardens, reconstructions of the slave quarters, and, down the hill toward the boat landing, the tomb of George and Martha Washington. Among the souvenirs sold at the plantation are stripling boxwoods that began life as clippings from bushes planted in 1798, the year before Washington died. *8 mi south of Alexandria, at the southern end of the George Washington Parkway.* ☎ *703/780–2000. General* ☛ *$7 adults, $6 senior citizens 62 and older, $3 children 6–11 accompanied by adult. A limited number of wheelchairs is available at the main gate.* ☼ *Mar., daily 9–5; Apr.–Aug., daily 8–5; Sept.–Oct., daily 9–5; Nov.–Feb., daily 9–4. Tour of house and grounds takes about 2 hrs.*

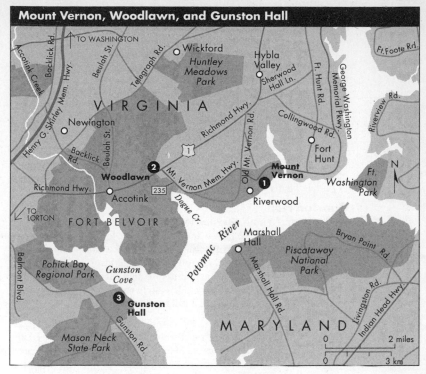

Mount Vernon, Woodlawn, and Gunston Hall

Woodlawn

2 Three miles from Mount Vernon on Route 1, **Woodlawn** Plantation occupies a piece of ground that was originally part of the Mount Vernon estate; even today you can see the red roof of Washington's home from Woodlawn. The house at Woodlawn was built for Washington's step-granddaughter, Nellie Custis, who married his favorite nephew, Lawrence Lewis. (Lewis had come to Mount Vernon from Fredericksburg to help the general manage his five farms.)

The Lewises' home, completed in 1805, is noteworthy from an architectural standpoint. It was designed by William Thornton, who drew up the original plans for the Capitol. Like Mount Vernon, the Woodlawn house is made wholly of native materials, including the clay for its bricks and the yellow pine used throughout the interior.

In the tradition of Southern riverfront mansions, Woodlawn has a central hallway that provides a cool refuge during the summer. At one corner of the passage is a bust of George Washington, set on a pedestal so that the crown of the head is at 6'2"—Washington's actual height. Elsewhere is a music room with a ceiling two feet higher than any other in the building, built that way to improve the acoustics for the harp and clavichord recitals that the Lewises and their children enjoyed.

After Woodlawn passed out of the Lewis family's hands it was owned by a Quaker community, which established there a meetinghouse and the first integrated school in Virginia. Subsequent owners included the playwright Paul Kester and Senator and Mrs. Oscar Underwood of Alabama. The property was acquired by the National Trust for Historic Preservation in 1957.

Also on the grounds of Woodlawn is the **Pope-Leighey House,** designed by Frank Lloyd Wright and built in 1940. The structure originally stood in nearby Falls Church, Virginia; it was rescued from the path of a highway and moved to the Woodlawn grounds in 1964. Wright's modernist design in cypress, brick, and glass offers a peculiar counterpoint to the Georgian stylings of Woodlawn. It is not to every taste, but it *is* an architectural education. *Woodlawn, 3 mi west on Rte. 235 from Mount Vernon,* ☎ *703/780–4000.* ☛ *$6 adults, $4 students and senior citizens.* ☺ *Jan.–Feb., weekends 9:30–4; Mar.–Dec., daily 9:30–4:30. Tours every ½ hr. Last tour at 4. Pope-Leighey House* ☛ *$5 adults, $3.50 students and senior citizens.* ☺ *Jan.–Feb., weekends 9:30–4; Mar.–Dec., daily 9:30–4:30. Tours every ½ hr. Last tour at 4. A $10 combination ticket ($7 students and senior citizens) covers entry to Woodlawn and Pope-Leighey House. Closed Thanksgiving, Dec. 25, and Jan. 1.*

Gunston Hall

❸ Unlike Mount Vernon, **Gunston Hall,** 15 miles away in Lorton, is rarely crowded with visitors. This was the home of a lesser-known George: George Mason—gentleman farmer, captain of the Fairfax militia, and author of the Virginia Declaration of Rights. Mason was one of the framers of the Constitution but refused to sign the final document because it did not prohibit slavery, adequately restrain the powers of the federal government, or include a bill of rights.

Completed in 1759, Gunston Hall is built of native brick, black walnut, and yellow pine. The architectural style of the time demanded absolute balance in all structures. Hence the "robber" window on a second-floor storage room and the fake door set into one side of the center hallway. The house's interior, with its carved woodwork in styles from Chinese to Gothic, has been meticulously restored, with paints made from the original recipes and with carefully carved replacements for the intricate mahogany medallions in the moldings.

The formal gardens are famous for their boxwoods, some of which were planted in the 1760s and have now grown to be 12 and 14 feet high. In Mason's day boxwood was used as a garden border because its acrid smell repelled deer.

To reach Gunston Hall, turn south on Route 1 from Woodlawn and follow the highway 7 miles, then turn left and follow the signs. The tour takes 30 minutes. ☎ *703/550–9220.* ☛ *$5 adults, $4 senior citizens, $1.50 grades 1–12.* ☺ *Daily 9:30–5. Last tour at 4:30. Closed Thanksgiving, Dec. 25, and Jan. 1.*

Getting Around

By Car

To get to Mount Vernon from the Capitol Beltway (Route 495), take exit 1 onto the George Washington Memorial Parkway, and follow the signs. From downtown Washington, cross into Arlington on either Key Bridge, Memorial Bridge, or the 14th Street bridge, and drive south on the George Washington Memorial Parkway toward National Airport. Proceed past the airport and through Alexandria straight to Mount Vernon. The trip from Washington takes about a half hour.

To reach Woodlawn and Gunston Hall you need a car. From Mount Vernon, continue south on the George Washington Parkway to Route 1. The entrance to Woodlawn is straight across from the exit; to reach Gunston Hall, turn left and follow the signs.

By Subway and Bus

You can get to Mount Vernon from the District by using the Metro and bus service. From downtown, take the yellow line train to Huntington ($1.50–$2.05, depending on the time of day). Then catch Fairfax County Connector Bus 101/Ft. Hunt to Mt. Vernon (50¢). Bus 101 leaves Huntington once an hour and operates Monday–Sunday 6:30 AM–8:15 PM, Saturday 7:20 AM–7:30 PM, Sunday 9:30–6. Returning to Huntington from Mt. Vernon, the bus will be labeled 101/Huntington. (Call 703/339–7200 for specific schedule information.)

By Boat

An especially pleasant way to travel down the Potomac is to cruise on the **Potomac Spirit,** which makes the 4½-hour trip from Washington to Mount Vernon Tuesday–Sunday, twice daily from mid-June through August and once daily from September through October and late March to mid-June. *Boats leave from Pier 4, 6th and Water Sts. SW,* ☎ *202/554–8000. Round-trip fare: $22 adults, $19.75 senior citizens, $13.25 children 6–11.*

By Bicycle

An asphalt bicycle path leads from the Virginia side of Memorial Bridge (adjacent to the Lincoln Memorial), past National Airport, and through Alexandria all the way to Mount Vernon. The trail is steep in places, but a biker in moderately good condition can make the 16-mile trip in less than two hours. Bicycles can be rented at several locations in Washington (*see* Bicycling *in* Chapter 5, Sports and the Outdoors).

Guided Tours

Tourmobile offers trips to and from Mount Vernon. Tours depart from April through October, daily at 10 AM, noon, and 2 PM from Arlington Cemetery and the Washington Monument. Reservations must be made in person one hour before departure. ☎ *202/554–5100. Cost: $16.50 adults, $8 children 3–11. 2-day combo tickets good for Mount Vernon and several sites in Washington: $25.50 adults, $12.50 children.*

Gray Line Tours runs half-day trips to Mount Vernon and Old Town Alexandria. Buses depart daily at 8:30 AM from Union Station. ☎ *301/ 386–8300. Cost: $22 adults, $12 children 3–11; 15% discount for AARP members. No tours on Thanksgiving, Dec. 25, and Jan. 1.*

TOUR 4: FREDERICKSBURG, VIRGINIA

On land once favored by Indian tribes as fishing and hunting ground, this compact city near the falls of the Rappahannock River figured prominently at crucial points in the nation's history, particularly during the Revolutionary and Civil wars. Just 50 miles south of Washington on I-95, Fredericksburg is today a popular day-trip destination for history buffs. The town's 40-block **National Historic District** contains more than 350 original 18th- and 19th-century buildings, including the house George Washington bought for his mother, Mary Washington, James Monroe's law office, the Rising Sun Tavern, and Kenmore, the magnificent 1752 plantation home of George Washington's sister. The town is a favorite with antiques collectors, who enjoy cruising the dealers' shops along Caroline Street.

Although its site was visited by explorer Captain John Smith as early as 1608, the town of Fredericksburg wasn't founded until 1728. Established as a frontier port to serve nearby tobacco farmers and iron miners, Fredericksburg took its name from England's crown prince at the time, and the streets still bear names of members of his family: George, Caroline, Sophia, Princess Anne, Hanover, William, and Amelia.

George Washington knew Fredericksburg well, having grown up just across the Rappahannock on Ferry Farm. He lived there from age 6 to 16, and the legends about chopping down a cherry tree and throwing a coin across the Rappahannock—later mythologized as the Potomac—go back to this period of his life. In later years Washington often returned to visit his mother here on Charles Street.

Fredericksburg prospered in the decades after independence, benefiting from its location midway along the 100-mile path between Washington and Richmond, an important intersection of railroad lines and waterways. When the Civil War broke out in 1861, Fredericksburg became the linchpin of the Confederate defense of Richmond and, as such, the inevitable target of Union assaults. In December 1862, Union forces attacked Fredericksburg in what was to be the first of four major battles fought in and around the town. In the battle of Sunken Road, Confederate defenders sheltered by a stone wall at the base of Marye's Heights mowed down Union soldiers by the thousands as they charged across the fields on foot and on horseback.

By war's end, the fighting in Fredericksburg and in battles at nearby Chancellorsville, the Wilderness, and Spotsylvania Court House had claimed more than 100,000 dead or wounded. Fredericksburg's cemeteries hold the remains of 17,000 soldiers from both sides. Despite heavy bombardment and house-to-house fighting, however, much of the city remained intact.

A walking tour through the town proper takes three to four hours; battlefield tours each can take that long. The short hop across the Rappahannock to Chatham Manor is well worth it, if for no other reason than that the site offers a splendid view of all of Fredericksburg.

Exploring

Numbers in the margin correspond to points of interest on the Fredericksburg map.

❶ Stop by the **Fredericksburg Visitor Center** for booklets and pamphlets on local history, information on restaurants and lodging, and an orientation slide show. You can get parking passes here, good for a whole day in what would normally be two-hour zones. Also available are money-saving Hospitality Passes to city attractions. A pass to seven sites costs $16 for adults, $6 for those 6–18; the costs of any four sites are $11.50 and $4, respectively. The center is in a structure that was built in 1824 as a residence and confectionery; during the Civil War it was used to hold prisoners. *706 Caroline St.,* ☎ *703/373–1776 or 800/678–4748.* ☉ *Mid-June–Labor Day, daily 9–7; Sept. 2–mid-June, daily 9–5. Closed Thanksgiving, Dec. 25, and Jan. 1.*

★ ❷ At the **Fredericksburg Battlefield Visitor Center** you can learn about Fredericksburg's role in the Civil War by attending the succinct slide show and then moving on to displays of soldiers' art and battlefield relics. Park rangers lead frequent walking tours of the area. The center offers tape-recorded tour cassettes ($2.75 rental, $4.25 purchase) and maps showing how to reach hiking trails at the nearby Wilderness, Chancellorsville, and Spotsylvania Court House battlefields (all within 15 miles of Fredericksburg). Just outside is Sunken Road, where from December 11 to 13, 1862, General Robert E. Lee led his troops to a bloody

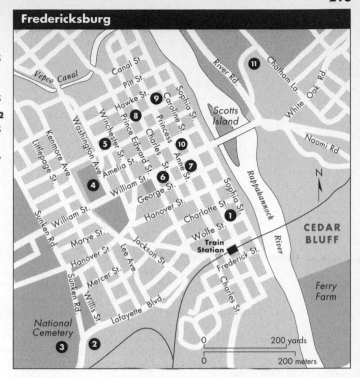

but resounding victory over Union forces attacking across the Rappahannock; 18,000 men from both sides died in the clash. Much of the stone wall that hid Lee's sharpshooters has been rebuilt, but 100 yards from the visitor center part of the original wall looks out on the statue *The Angel of Marye's Heights,* by Felix de Weldon. This memorial honors Sergeant Richard Kirkland, a South Carolinian who risked his life to bring water to wounded foes; he later died at the Battle of Chickamauga. *Lafayette Blvd. at Sunken Rd.,* ☎ *703/373-6122.* ⊙ *Mid-June–Labor Day, daily 8:30–6:30; Sept. 3–mid-June, weekdays 9–5, weekends 9–6. Closed Dec. 25 and Jan. 1.*

❸ The **National Cemetery** is the final resting place of 15,000 Union casualties, most of whom were never identified. *Lafayette Blvd. at Sunken Rd.,* ☎ *703/373-6122.* ⊙ *Daily sunrise–sunset.*

❹ The **Confederate Cemetery** contains the remains of more than 2,000 soldiers (most of them unknown) as well as the graves of generals Dabney Maury, Seth Barton, Carter Stevenson, Daniel Ruggles, Henry Sibley, and Abner Perrin. *Entrance at 1100 Washington Ave., near the corner of Washington Ave. and Amelia St., no* ☎. ⊙ *Dawn–dusk.*

★ ❺ **Kenmore** was the home of Fielding Lewis, a patriot, plantation owner, and brother-in-law of George Washington. (Lewis sacrificed much of his fortune to operate a gun factory that supplied the American forces during the Revolution.) Kenmore's plain exterior belies the lavish interior; these have been called some of the most beautiful rooms in America. The plaster moldings in the ceilings are outstanding and even more ornate than Mount Vernon's. Of equal elegance are the furnishings, which include a large standing clock that belonged to Mary Washington. Across the street are fine examples of Victorian architecture and a monument to Mary Washington, as well as the entrance to the Confederate cemetery. After the 60-minute tour visitors to Kenmore are served tea and gingerbread made according to a Washington family recipe. *1201 Washington Ave.,* ☎ *703/373–3381.* ☛ *$5 adults, $2.50 students 6–18, 20% discount to groups of 10 or more, $10 "family ticket."* ☉ *Mar.–Nov., daily 9–5; Dec., daily 10–4; Jan.–Feb., Sat. 10– 4, Sun. 12–4. Closed Thanksgiving, Dec. 24, 25, 31, and Jan. 1.*

6 The **James Monroe Museum and Memorial Library** is the tiny one-story building where the man who was to be the fifth president of the United States practiced law from 1787 to 1789. In this building are many of Monroe's possessions, collected and preserved by his family until this century, including a mahogany dispatch-box used during the negotiation of the Louisiana Purchase and the desk on which Monroe signed the doctrine named for him. *908 Charles St.,* ☎ *703/899–4559.* ☛ *$3 adults, $1 children 6–18, $2.40 group adult, 80¢ group student.* ☉ *Mar.–Nov., daily 9–5; Dec.–Feb., daily 10–4. Closed Thanksgiving, Dec. 24, 25, 31, and Jan. 1.*

7 A block away is the **Fredericksburg Area Museum and Cultural Center.** Housed in an 1816 building once used as a market and town hall, the museum's six permanent exhibit galleries tell the story of the area from prehistoric times, through the Revolutionary and Civil wars, to the present. Displays include dinosaur prints from a nearby quarry, Native American artifacts, an 18th-century plantation account book with an inventory of slaves, and Confederate memorabilia. *907 Princess Anne St.,* ☎ *703/371–3037.* ☛ *$3 adults, $1 children 6–18.* ☉ *Mar.–Nov., Mon.–Sat. 9–5, Sun. 1–5; Dec.–Feb., Mon.–Sat. 10–4, Sun. 1–4. Closed Thanksgiving, Dec. 24, 25, and Jan. 1.*

TIME OUT Stop for a gourmet sandwich or a slice of quiche at the **Made in Virginia Store Deli** (101 William St., ☎ 703/371-2233). Do not skip the rich desserts.

8 On Charles Street is the modest white **home of Mary Washington.** George purchased it for her in 1772, and she spent the last 17 years of her life there, tending the charming garden, where her boxwood still flourishes and where many a bride and groom now exchange their vows. Displays include many of Mrs. Washington's personal effects, as well as period furniture and, in the garden, plants she herself started. *1200 Charles St.,* ☎ *703/373–1569.* ☛ *$3 adults, $1 students, $2.50 group adult, 75¢ group student.* ☉ *Mar.–Nov., daily 9–5; Dec.–Feb., daily 10–4. Closed Thanksgiving, Dec. 24, 25, 31, and Jan. 1.*

9 In 1760 George Washington's brother Charles built as his home what became the **Rising Sun Tavern,** a watering hole for such pre-Revolutionary patriots as the Lee brothers, Patrick Henry, Washington, and Jefferson. A "wench" in period costume leads the tour without stepping out of character. From her perspective you watch the activity— day and night, upstairs and down—at this busy institution. In the taproom you are served spiced tea. *1304 Caroline St.,* ☎ *703/371– 1494.* ☛ *$3 adults, $1 students, $2.50 group adult, 75¢ group student.* ☉ *Mar.–Nov., daily 9–5; Dec.–Feb., daily 10–4. Closed Thanksgiving, Dec. 24, 25, and Jan. 1.*

10 The **Hugh Mercer Apothecary Shop** offers a close-up view of 18th- and 19th-century medicine. It was established in 1771 by Dr. Mercer, a Scotsman who served as a brigadier general of the Revolutionary Army (he was killed at the Battle of Princeton). General George S. Patton of World War II fame was one of Mercer's great-great-great-grandsons. Dr. Mercer might have been more careful than most other Colonial physicians, yet his methods will make you cringe. A costumed hostess will explicitly describe amputations and cataract operations. You will also hear about therapeutic bleeding and see the gruesome devices used in Colonial dentistry. *1020 Caroline St. at Amelia St.,* ☎ *703/373–3362.* ☛ *$3 adults, $1 students 6–18, $2.50 group adult, 75¢ group student.* ☉ *Mar.–Nov., daily 9–5; Dec.–Feb., daily 10–4. Closed Thanksgiving, Dec. 24, 25, 31, and Jan. 1.*

⑪ **Chatham Manor** is a fine example of Georgian architecture, built between 1768 and 1771 by William Fitzhugh on a site overlooking the Rappahannock and the town of Fredericksburg. Fitzhugh, a noted plantation owner, frequently hosted such luminaries of his day as George Washington and Thomas Jefferson. During the Civil War, Union forces commandeered the house and converted it into a headquarters and hospital. President Abraham Lincoln visited to confer with his generals; Clara Barton and the poet Walt Whitman tended the wounded. After the war the house and gardens were restored by private owners and eventually donated to the National Park Service. Concerts often are held here during the summer. *Chatham La., Stafford County (take William St. across the bridge and follow signs approximately ½ mi),* ☎ *703/373–4461.* ☛ *Free.* ☉ *Daily 9–5. Closed Dec. 25 and Jan. 1.*

Getting Around

By Car
To get to Fredericksburg from the District, take I–95 south to Route 3, turn left, and follow the signs. The drive takes about an hour one way, except during rush hour.

By Train
Amtrak trains bound for Fredericksburg depart six times daily from Washington's Union Station and take about an hour (☎ 202/484–7540 or 800/872–7245). The Fredericksburg railroad station is near the historic district (Caroline St. and Lafayette Blvd). A round-trip ticket from Washington costs $20.

By Bus
Greyhound Lines (☎ 202/289–5160 or 800/231–2222) departs several times a day from Washington to Fredericksburg. A round-trip ticket is $29. Buses stop at a station on alternate Route 1, about 2 miles from the center of town; cabs are available there.

Guided Tours

Contact the tour coordinator at the **Fredericksburg Visitor Center** (*see* Exploring, *above*) to arrange a group tour of the city as well as of battlefields and other historic sites in the area. Reservations are required. The **Fredericksburg Department of Tourism** (in the Visitor Center) publishes a booklet that includes a short history of Fredericksburg and a self-guided tour covering 29 sights.

10 Portraits of Washington

HISTORY AT A GLANCE

1608 Captain John Smith sails from Jamestown up the Potomac River. Colonization follows.

1775–83 American Revolutionary War.

1788 U.S. Constitution ratified.

1789 New York is the capital. George Washington becomes the first U.S. president.

1790 Philadelphia is now the capital; but in return for the South's assumption of the North's Revolutionary War debt, George Washington will select a Southern capital site.

1792 White House construction begins.

1793 Capitol Building construction begins.

1800 Congress relocates from Philadelphia; John Adams, elected in **1797,** moves into an unfinished White House.

1803 The city's population is 3,000.

1812–15 War of 1812. In **1814,** British burn Washington, including such landmarks as the White House and the Capitol; storms save the city from total destruction.

1846 Smithsonian Institution established.

1861–65 Civil War. Lincoln assassinated in **1865.**

1900 The city's population is 300,000.

1912 Cherry trees, gifts from Japan, are planted.

1914–18 World War I (United States enters in **1917**).

1929–39 Great Depression.

1939–45 World War II (United States enters in **1941**).

1943 Pentagon completed.

1963 President Kennedy assassinated in Dallas.

1972 Watergate break-in.

1976 Metrorail service begins.

1994 The city's population is 570,000.

PRESIDENTS

George Washington	(1789–97)
John Adams	(1797–1801)
Thomas Jefferson	(1801–09)
James Madison	(1809–17)
James Monroe	(1817–25)
John Quincy Adams	(1825–29)
Andrew Jackson	(1829–37)
Martin Van Buren	(1837–41)
William Henry Harrison	(1841)
John Tyler	(1841–45)
James Knox Polk	(1845–49)
Zachary Taylor	(1849–50)
Millard Fillmore	(1850–53)

Franklin Pierce	(1853–57)
James Buchanan	(1857–61)
Abraham Lincoln	(1861–65)
Andrew Johnson	(1865–69)
Ulysses Simpson Grant	(1869–77)
Rutherford Birchard Hayes	(1877–81)
James Abram Garfield	(1881)
Chester Alan Arthur	(1881–85)
(Stephen) Grover Cleveland	(1885–89)
Benjamin Harrison	(1889–93)
(Stephen) Grover Cleveland	(1893–97)
William McKinley	(1897–1901)
Theodore Roosevelt	(1901–1909)
William Howard Taft	(1909–13)
(Thomas) Woodrow Wilson	(1913–21)
Warren Gamaliel Harding	(1921–23)
(John) Calvin Coolidge	(1923–29)
Herbert Clark Hoover	(1929–33)
Franklin Delano Roosevelt	(1933–45)
Harry S. Truman	(1945–53)
Dwight David Eisenhower	(1953–61)
John Fitzgerald Kennedy	(1961–63)
Lyndon Baines Johnson	(1963–69)
Richard Milhous Nixon	(1969–74)
Gerald Rudolph Ford	(1974–77)
James Earl (Jimmy) Carter	(1977–81)
Ronald Wilson Reagan	(1981–89)
George Herbert Walker Bush	(1989–93)
William Jefferson (Bill) Clinton	(1993–)

SPEAKING OF WASHINGTON

Compiled by John F. Kelly

WASHINGTON, D.C., is a bit like the weather: Everybody likes to talk about it. Unlike the weather though, we can do something about Washington. Every few years Americans are invited to throw the bums out and usher a new crop of bums in. And there's no doubt these politicians will form some opinion of their new home.

Politicians, poets, presidents, First Ladies, humorists, foreign visitors—they've all put pen to paper in expressing their opinion of the city that literally rose from the swamp.

"That Indian swamp in the wilderness."— Thomas Jefferson, circa 1789

"A century hence, if this country keeps united, it will produce a city though not so large as London, yet of magnitude inferior to few others in Europe."—George Washington, 1789

"May the spirit which animated the great founder of this city, descend to future generations."—John Adams, 1800

"I had much rather live in the house at Philadelphia. Not one room or chamber is finished of the whole. It is habitable by fires in every part, 13 of which we are required to keep daily or sleep in wet or damp places."—Abigail Adams, 1800 (after moving into the White House)

"This boasted [Pennsylvania] Avenue is as much a wilderness as Kentucky. Some half-starved cattle browsing among the bushes present a melancholy spectacle to the stranger . . . . So very thinly is the city peopled that quails and other birds are constantly shot within a hundred yards of the Capitol."—Charles W. Jansen, 1806

"This embryo capital, where Fancy sees / Squares in morasses, obelisks in trees; / Which second-sighted seers, ev'n now, adorn / With shrines unbuilt, and heroes yet unborn. / Though nought but woods, and Jefferson they see, / Where streets should run, and sages *ought* to be."— Thomas Moore, 1806

"Washington has certainly an air of more magnificence than any other American town. It is mean in detail, but the outline has a certain grandeur about it."—James Fenimore Cooper, 1838

"In democratic communities the imagination is compressed when men consider themselves; it expands indefinitely when they think of the state. Hence it is that the same men who live on a small scale in cramped dwellings frequently aspire to gigantic splendor in the erection of their public monuments. The Americans have traced out the circuit of an immense city on the site which they intend to make their capital, but which up to the present time is hardly more densely peopled than Pontoise, though, according to them, it will one day contain a million inhabitants. They have already rooted up trees for 10 miles around lest they should interfere with the future citizens of this imaginary metropolis. They have erected a magnificent palace for Congress in the center of the city and have given it the pompous name of the Capitol."—Alexis de Tocqueville, 1840

"This town looks like a large straggling village reared in a drained swamp."— George Combe, 1842

"It is sometimes called the City of Magnificent Distances but it might with greater propriety be termed the City of Magnificent Intentions . . . . Spacious avenues that begin in nothing and lead nowhere; streets, a mile long, that only want houses, roads, and inhabitants; public meetings that need but a public to be complete; and ornaments of great thoroughfares, which only lack great thoroughfares to ornament—are its leading features. One might fancy the season over and most of the houses gone out of town forever with their masters."—Charles Dickens, 1842

"I . . . found the capital still under the empire of King Mud . . . . Were I to say that it was intended to be typical of the condition of the government, I might be considered cynical."—Anthony Trollope, 1862

"Washington is the paradise of gamblers, and contains many handsome and elegantly-fitted-up establishments. It is said at least one hundred of these 'hells' were in full blast during the war."—Dr. John B. Ellis, 1870

"Why, when I think of those multitudes of clerks and congressmen—whole families of them—down there slaving away and keeping the country together, why then I know in my heart there is something so good and motherly about Washington, that grand old benevolent National Asylum for the Helpless."—Mark Twain, 1873

"One of these days this will be a very great city if nothing happens to it."—Henry Adams, 1877

"Wherever the American citizen may be a stranger, he is at home here."—Frederick Douglass, 1877

"Washington is no place in which to carry out inventions."—Alexander Graham Bell, 1887

"But taking it all in all and after all, Negro life in Washington is a promise rather than a fulfillment. But it is worthy of note for the really excellent things which are promised."—Paul Laurence Dunbar, 1900

"In Washington there is no life apart from government and politics: it is our daily bread; it is the thread which runs through the woof and warp of our lives; it colors everything."—A. Maurice Low, 1900

"What you want is to have a city which every one who comes from Maine, Texas, Florida, Arkansas, or Oregon can admire as being something finer and more beautiful than he had ever dreamed of before."— James Bryce, 1913

"Things get very lonely in Washington sometimes. The real voice of the great people of America sometimes sounds faint and distant in that strange city. You hear politics until you wish that both parties were smothered in their own gas."—Woodrow Wilson, 1919

"Congress has been writing my material for years and I am not ashamed of what I have had. Why should I pay some famous Author, or even myself, to sit down all day

trying to dope out something funny to say on the Stage? . . . No, sir, I have found that there is nothing as funny as things that have happened . . . Nothing is so funny as something done in all seriousness . . . Each state elects the most serious man it has in the District . . . He is impressed with the fact that he is leaving Home with the idea that he is to rescue his District from Certain Destruction, and to see that it receives its just amount of Rivers and Harbors, Postoffices and Pumpkin Seeds. Naturally, you have put a pretty big load on that man . . . It's no joking matter to be grabbed up bodily from the Leading Lawyer's Office of Main Street and have the entire populace tell you what is depending on you when you get to Washington."—Will Rogers, 1924

"Washington . . . is the symbol of America. By its dignity and architectural inspiration . . . we encourage that elevation of thought and character which comes from great architecture."—Herbert Hoover, 1929

"Of my first trip to the top of the Washington Monument, which must have been made soon after it was opened in 1888, I recall only the fact that we descended by walking down the long, dark steps, and it seemed a journey without end. There was in those days a bitter debate as to whether a baseball thrown from the top of the monument could be caught by a catcher on the ground, and my father was much interested and full of mathematical proofs that it couldn't be done. Some time later it was tried, and turned out to be very easy."—H. L. Mencken, 1936

"Living in contemporary Washington, caught literally and physically in L'Enfant's dream, and encountering on every hand the brave mementos of Washington, Jefferson, Jackson, Lincoln and Roosevelt, is to live as close as possible to both the source and the climax of the major sequences of the human story."—George Sessions Perry, 1946

"Washington isn't a city, it's an abstraction."—Dylan Thomas, 1950

"There are a number of things wrong with Washington. One of them is that everyone has been too long away from home."—Dwight D. Eisenhower, 1955

"Whatever we are looking for, we come to Washington in millions to stand in silence and try to find it."—Bruce Catton, 1959

"Washington is a literal cesspool of crime and violence."—Sen. James O. Eastland, 1960

"A city of southern efficiency and northern charm."—John F. Kennedy, 1960

"Every dedicated American could be proud that a dynamic experience of democracy in his nation's capital had been made visible to the world."—Martin Luther King, Jr., 1963

"Washington is several miles square and about as tall, say, as the Washington Monument, give or take a little. It is surrounded on all four sides by reality."—Arthur Hoppe, 1975

"One of my earliest recollections of Washington is of a tragicomic speech by Michigan Congressman Fred Bradley, protesting that all the wining and dining was getting him down. 'Banquet life is a physical and mental strain on us hardly imaginable to the folks back home,' said the distraught Bradley. 'The strain is terrific.' He was dragooned into attending altogether too many parties, he complained; but his appeal for fewer invitations was greeted with guffaws. Three weeks later Representative Bradley, age forty-nine, dropped dead. The official diagnosis was heart failure."—Jack Anderson, 1979

"As we quietly approached our new home, I told Rosalyn with a smile that it was a nice-looking place. She said, 'I believe we're going to be happy in the White House.' We were silent for a moment, and then I replied, 'I just hope that we never disappoint the people who made it possible for us to live here.' Rosalyn's prediction proved to be correct, and I did my utmost for four solid years to make my own hope come true."—Jimmy Carter, 1982, from *Keeping Faith: Memoirs of a President*

"The first thing that struck me about the White House was how cold it was. The country was still suffering from the energy crisis, and President Carter had ordered that the White House thermostats be turned down."—Nancy Reagan, 1989, from *My Turn*

"I think all of us are beginning to understand Washington better and get a more realistic sense of how it works. I have a clearer idea in my own mind what it will take to make the arguments that will change the government's direction. The problems are not quite as overwhelming and undefined as when we started off our 'Agenda for Change'—I feel liberated."—Hillary Rodham Clinton, 1993, from *Hillary Rodham Clinton: A First Lady for Our Time*

EDIFICE TREKS

By John F. Kelly

WASHINGTON PROBA-bly produces more words than any other city in the world. Politicians orate, pundits speculate, and commentators narrate. But Washington's words have a peculiarly fleeting quality. They're copied into notebooks, transferred to computer screens, then set into type and bound into reports that are filed on shelves and forgotten. They're printed in newspapers that yellow and turn to dust. Words are spat out in sound bytes on the evening news, then released into the ether, lost forever. In the wordy war of politics, a paper trail is something best avoided.

But there is a stone trail in Washington, too: The words someone felt were important enough not just to commit to parchment, paper, or videotape, but to engrave in sandstone, marble, or granite. On the buildings of Washington are noble sentiments and self-serving ones, moving odes and contemplative ones.

A reading tour of Washington's inscriptions amounts to a classical education. The inscriptions, lofty in position and tone, are taken from the Bible, from the Greeks and Romans, from poets and playwrights, from presidents and politicians. When viewing Washington's inscriptions, soaking up what is in most cases a perfect union of poesy and architecture, it's easy to see why the words "edifice" and "edify" spring from the same root.

Lesson one starts in Union Station, that great Beaux Arts bathhouse on Capitol Hill. Architect Daniel Burnham's 1908 train station is encrusted with carvings that do everything from romantically outline the development of the railroad to offer lessons in both humility and hospitality.

On the western end of the shining white Vermont granite structure, above the entrance to the Metro, is written (in all capital letters, as most inscriptions are):

He that would bring home the wealth of the Indies must carry the wealth of the Indies with him. So it is in travelling. A man must carry knowledge with him if he would bring home knowledge.

A bit heavy to digest when dashing for the Metroliner on a rainy Monday morning, but worth mulling over once a seat is found.

At the other end of the station is the perfect sentiment for the returning hero:

Welcome the coming, speed the parting guest. Virtue alone is sweet society. It keeps the key to all heroic hearts and opens you a welcome in them all.

These are just two of the half dozen inscriptions on Union Station. Above allegorical statues by Louis Saint-Gaudens that stand over the main entrance are inscriptions celebrating the forces that created the railroads, including this set singing the praises of fire and electricity:

Fire: greatest of discoveries, enabling man to live in various climates, use many foods, and compel the forces of nature to do his work. Electricity: carrier of light and power, devourer of time and space, bearer of human speech over land and sea, greatest servant of man, itself unknown. Thou has put all things under his feet.

So inspirational were these and the other Union Station inscriptions thought that the Washington Terminal Company, operators of the station, once distributed free pamphlets imprinted with them. This probably saved more than a few sore necks.

Union Station's inscriptions were selected by Charles William Eliot, who was president of Harvard University. According to John L. Andriot's "Guide to the Inscriptions of the Nation's Capital," Eliot borrowed from such sources as the Bible, Shakespeare, Alexander Pope, and Ralph Waldo Emerson. Eliot also penned his own epigrams, a seemingly modest skill until you start to wonder what you'd come up with when confronted with a big blank wall that will bear your words forever.

Eliot wrote the two inscriptions on the City Post Office right next to the station. The inscriptions, facing Massachusetts Avenue, describe the humble letter carrier as a:

Carrier of news and knowledge, instrument of trade and industry, promoter of mutual acquaintance of peace and of goodwill among men and nations . . . and a . . . Messenger of sympathy and love, servant of parted friends, consoler of the lonely, bond of scattered family, enlarger of the common life.

It's said that President Woodrow Wilson edited these inscriptions, unaware that the Ivy League wordsmith Eliot had written them. Like all good editors, Wilson improved them.

Rocks and Hard Places

Behind every inscription in Washington is the person who carved it, the man or woman who put chisel or pneumatic drill to stone and, with a sharp eye and a steady hand, made the most lasting of impressions.

Ann Hawkins is one such carver. (You can admire her chisel work throughout the National Gallery of Art. She did the names on the Patrons' Permanent Fund in the east building, a roll call of philanthropists.)

"There are two comments I get from people who watch me carve and they make perfect symmetry," says Hawkins. "Half the people say 'Oh, that looks so tedious. You must have a lot of patience.' But I also get 'That looks *fun.*' And they wish they could do it."

Hawkins studied four years before she could carve well enough to take her first paying commission. She's been carving professionally since 1982, and in that time she's decided that stones are "living, breathing things." And each one is different. Sandstone is soft. Slates can be brittle and hard, with knots in them almost like wood. White Vermont marble feels sugary and crumbles a bit at the first stroke. Tennessee pink marble is chunky and firm.

There are a lot of things a stone carver has to take into account before striking the first blow, Hawkins says. "The nature of the stone, the light the inscription will receive, the weathering of the stone, how large the letters will be, what distance they'll be viewed from."

The most important part of carving, she says, is the layout of the inscription. The letters must be spaced correctly, not bunched too tightly together as if they were typeset, but spread comfortably and handsomely. The inscription must look as if it is *of* the stone, not *on* the stone.

Hawkins draws the letters on paper that— "after being measured from every direction" to make sure it's straight—is taped to the stone over sheets of typewriter carbon paper. She then outlines the inscription, transferring it to the stone. With a tungsten-carbide-tip chisel she starts hammering, sometimes working her way around the edges of the letter, sometimes starting in the center and working out. She turns and shifts the blade, roughing the letter in at first, then finishing it, aiming for the perfect V-shape indentation that is the mark of a hand-carved inscription. (Inscriptions that are machine sandblasted through a stencil have a round center.) As in everything from squash to Frisbee, it's all in the wrist.

If the inscription is outside, the sun will provide the contrast necessary for the letters to be read. As the rays rake across the inscription, the shadows will lengthen, making the words pop. If the inscription is indoors, Hawkins paints the inside of the letters with a lacquer that's mixed with pigment, deepening the color of the stone.

Triangular Logic

If a walk around Washington's inscriptions is a classical education, a perambulation of Federal Triangle is the civics lesson. The limestone cliffs of the Triangle, stretching from their base at 15th Street down Pennsylvania and Constitution avenues, are inscribed with mottoes that immediately conjure up a nobler time.

The walls fairly sing with inscriptions, enjoining passersby to be eternally vigilant (it's *the price of liberty; Study the past,* says the National Archives), and to heed Thomas Jefferson and *Cultivate peace and commerce with all* (on the Commerce Building and an example of one of the tenets of good epigram selection: Try to work the name of the building into at least one inscription).

The Federal Triangle inscriptions also provide justification for the buildings that they decorate and government departments they praise. The inscription on the Internal Revenue Service headquarters on Constitution Avenue is not Dante's *Abandon all hope ye who enter here,* but Oliver Wendell Holmes's *Taxes are what we pay for a civilized society.* Just in case you were wondering what you were paying for every April 15.

Likewise, on the Justice Department we have:

Justice is the great interest of man on earth. Wherever her temple stands there is a foundation for social security, general happiness and the improvement and progress of our race.

While Justice certainly has its share of letters (including this bit of Latin: *Lege atque ordine omnia fiunt*—"By law and order all is accomplished"), the award for the most verbose structure must go to the Commerce Department Building. Stretched out along 14th Street, eight stories up and spread out over hundreds of feet, is this edifying ode:

The inspiration that guided our forefathers led them to secure above all things the unity of our country. We rest upon government by consent of the governed and the political order of the United States is the expression of a patriotic ideal which welds together all the elements of our national energy promoting the organization that fosters individual initiative. Within this edifice are established agencies that have been created to buttress the life of the people, to clarify their problems and co-ordinate their resources, seeking to lighten burdens without lessening the responsibility of the citizen. In serving one and all they are dedicated to the purpose of the founders and to the highest hopes of the future with their local administration given to the integrity and welfare of the nation.

It's a mouthful. But it's also redolent of a time that seems almost hopelessly naive now, a time when we could use words like "national energy" and "purpose of the founders" without smirking. This passage and two other long ones were created especially for the building, composed, it is believed, by Royal Cortissoz, for 50 years the influential art critic of the *New York Tribune* (and author of this much pithier epigram from the Lincoln Memorial: *In this temple as in the hearts of the people for whom he saved the union the memory of Abraham Lincoln is enshrined forever.*).

You can imagine Washingtonians in the 1930s watching as the inscriptions were going up in Federal Triangle, trying to guess what would be said, as if a huge game of hangman were being played. At least one Washingtonian wasn't thrilled with what he saw. In 1934, when the giant Commerce Department Building was in its final stages of construction, one Thomas Woodward wrote a letter to a friend in the Department of Justice, expressing his dismay. The letter was addressed to Charles W. Eliot II, son of the Harvard president who composed the Union Station and City Post Office epigrams. The younger Eliot forwarded the letter of complaint to Charles Moore, chairman of the Commission of Fine Arts, the body responsible—then as now—for reviewing the design of government building projects. Moore allowed as how his commission hadn't been consulted on the inscriptions. The younger Eliot followed up with a salvo of his own to Moore, stating that the inscriptions "seem to be thoroughly bromidic and uninteresting—a lost opportunity."

Eliot had a point. The Commerce Department inscriptions are lecturing rather than inspirational, long and sour rather than short and sweet. Moore must have forgotten that he once wrote: "Inscriptions are an art in themselves. They should be monumental and express in few words a great sentiment."

Still, there can be poetry in even the longest of inscriptions. Consider this moving sentiment, carved on the hemicycle of the Post Office Department building, facing 14th Street:

The Post Office Department, in its ceaseless labors, pervades every channel of commerce and every theatre of human enterprise, and while visiting as it does kindly, every fireside, mingles with the throbbings of almost every heart in the land. In the amplitude of its beneficence, it ministers to all climes, and creeds, and pursuits, with the same eager readiness and with equal fullness of fidelity. It is the delicate ear trump through which alike na-

tions and families and isolated individuals whisper their joys and their sorrows, their convictions and their sympathies to all who listen for their coming.

What is it about the Post Office that inspires the most poignant inscriptions? And to whom do we talk about getting "ear trump" back into common usage?

Oops . . .

What do you do if you're a stone carver and you make a mistake? After all, the expression "carved in stone" isn't much good if fixing a typo on a chunk of marble is as easy as depressing the backspace key. Ann Hawkins: "If I got a chip, there are epoxy resins I could apply. . . . It's very rare to make a mistake, unless you do something stupid."

On big projects, boo-boos can be lopped out entirely, the offending block of stone cut out and replaced with a "dutchman," a fresh piece that's inserted like a patch and—hopefully—carved correctly. There's no dutchman in what is perhaps the city's most obvious mistake. Inscribed in three sections on the north wall of the Lincoln Memorial is Abraham Lincoln's second Inaugural address. Twenty lines down in the first block of words is a phrase that concludes: "WITH HIGH HOPES FOR THE EUTURE." The poor stone carver added an extra stroke to the *F*, transforming it into an *E*. Because the inscription is inside—away from the sunshine and its shadows—it would be virtually unreadable if the insides of the letters weren't painted black. And so, the bottom stroke of the *E* was left unpainted, making the best of a bad situation.

Back to the Stone Age

The capital's official buildings, monuments, and memorials urge us in various ways to remember the past or strive toward a more perfect future. None of the blank verse, mottoes, or maxims, though, are as moving as what appears on a V-shape set of black granite panels set into the ground near the Lincoln Memorial. The inscription isn't made up of words at all, but it's as moving as any sonnet.

Etched into the stone of the Vietnam Veterans Memorial are the names of the more than 58,000 Americans killed in that war. The names weren't carved high atop a pediment out of reach but were sandblasted delicately into the wall. Washington's other inscriptions might be meant to provide edification from a distance, but this memorial is designed to be touched, its inscriptions traced with unsteady fingers. And behind the names we see ourselves, reflected in the stone as true as any mirror.

Which leads us to the state of stone carving in Washington today. Most newer buildings in Washington aren't graced with inscriptions. While a building named after a famous American might once have warranted an inscribed quotation from that person, today we have the James Forrestal Federal Building and the William McChesney Martin, Jr. Federal Reserve Board Building with nary a peep from either gentleman.

Gone, too, is the specially commissioned aphorism meant to enlighten or fire. Inscriptions like those on the Justice and Commerce department buildings—whether you consider them quaint optimism or naive bluster—are in short supply these days.

After all, the 1990s aren't like the 1930s, the period of Washington's big inscription boom. This is supposed to be the time of little, quiet government, not big, loud government. Why should government buildings assault the eyes of pedestrians and motorists with jingoistic slogans and propagandist mottoes? Shouldn't the feds just get out of our hair?

Perhaps, but somehow when we were willing to not only stand behind our words but carve them immutably into the living stone, it suggested we believed in them a little more, thought them worth remembering, no matter how self-evident or self-aggrandizing they seemed.

We don't seem to do much of that anymore. Maybe it's time to read the writing on the walls.

THE FEDERAL GOVERNMENT: HOW OUR SYSTEM WORKS

By Betty Ross

NEW YORK MAY BE the fashion capital of the United States and Los Angeles the center of entertainment, but government—and power—is the name of the game in Washington.

The federal government is a major employer, an important landlord, and a source of contracts, contacts, or conversation for Washingtonians. It is a patron of the arts and a provider for the needy. To some, pervasive government is what's wrong with Washington. To others, it's what's right.

The federal government occupies some of the choicest real estate in town, yet pays no taxes to the District of Columbia. On the other hand, although citizens of the District *do* pay taxes, they could not vote until some 20 years ago. This has changed; now they can help elect the president, but still they have only a nonvoting delegate in Congress.

In Washington, the "separation of powers" doctrine becomes more than just a phrase in the Constitution. A visit here gives you a chance to see the legislative, executive, and judicial branches of government in action; to see how the system of checks and balances works. As Boswell put it, you have an opportunity, "instead of thinking how things may be, to see them as they are."

The Legislative Branch

In Pierre L'Enfant's 18th-century plan for the city of Washington, the U.S. Capitol and the White House were just far enough away from each other on Pennsylvania Avenue to emphasize the separation of powers between the legislative and executive branches. L'Enfant chose Jenkins Hill as the site for the Capitol; it is the focal point of an area now called Capitol Hill.

Guided tours of the Capitol leave from the Rotunda almost continuously from 9 AM to 3:45 PM daily throughout the year. The Senate side of the Capitol faces Constitution Avenue, while the House side can be approached from Independence Avenue.

Drop by the office of your senator or representative to pick up passes to the Visitors Galleries. Without a pass, you are not permitted to watch the proceedings. There are two Senate office buildings at First and Constitution Avenue NE, named, respectively, for former senators Everett Dirksen and Richard Russell. A third, honoring Senator Philip A. Hart, opened in November 1982 at Second and Constitution NE.

The House office buildings, named for former Speakers Joseph Cannon, Nicholas Longworth, and Sam Rayburn, are located in that order along Independence Avenue between First Street SE, and First Street SW. It is generally agreed by residents and visitors alike that the Rayburn Building is the least attractive and, at $75 million, one of the most expensive structures in the city.

According to the Constitution, "the Congress shall assemble at least once in every year, and such meeting shall begin at noon on the 3rd day of January, unless they shall by law appoint a different day." In the years before air-conditioning, Congress usually recessed during the summer and reconvened in the fall. Today, however, with congressional calendars more crowded and air-conditioning commonplace, sessions frequently last much longer. It is not unusual for the House and/or Senate to sit through the summer and well into the fall.

Congressional sessions usually begin at noon; committee meetings are generally held in the morning. Check the *Washington Post's* "Today in Congress" listings to find out what is going on.

Don't be surprised to see only a handful of senators or members of Congress on the floor during a session. Much congressional business dealing with constituent problems is done in committees or in offices. When a vote is taken during a session, bells are rung to summon absent members to the floor.

To save time, many senators and members of Congress make the brief trip between their offices and the Capitol on the congressional subway. Visitors may ride, too. The Senate restaurant in the Capitol—famed for its bean soup—is open to the public at all times. Cafeterias in the Rayburn, Longworth, and Dirksen office buildings are also open to visitors. Watch the hours, however. From 11:30 AM to 1:15 PM, only members of Congress and their staffs are admitted.

There are two senators from each state, who are elected for six-year terms; the 435 members of the House serve for two years. Senate and House members receive an annual salary of $133,600.

How a Bill Becomes Law

Legislation is a complicated, time-consuming process. Here, briefly, is the usual legislative procedure in the House of Representatives.

• A bill is introduced by a member, who places it in the "hopper," a box on the clerk's desk. It is numbered (H.R. . . .), sent to the Government Printing Office, and made available the next morning in the House Document Room.

• It is referred to a committee.

• The committee reports on the bill, usually after holding a hearing, either before the full committee or before a subcommittee.

• The bill is placed on the House calendar.

• Any bill that involves the Treasury is considered by the House sitting as a Committee of the Whole. In that case, the Speaker appoints a chairman who presides, and there is a period of general debate, followed by a reading for amendment, with speeches limited to five minutes.

• A bill is given a second reading and consideration in the House. (Bills considered in Committee of the Whole, however, receive a second reading in committee.) Amendments may be added after the second reading.

• It is given a third reading, which is by title only. The Speaker puts the question to a vote, and it may be defeated at this stage by a negative vote.

• If it passes, however, it is sent to the Senate.

• The Senate considers the bill, usually after it has been referred to a committee and reported favorably by that committee.

• If the Senate rejects the House bill, it notifies the House. Otherwise, the bill is returned to the House from the Senate, with or without amendments.

• The House considers the Senate amendments.

• Differences between House and Senate versions of a bill are resolved by a joint House–Senate conference committee.

• The bill is printed in final form or "enrolled" on parchment paper.

• It is proofread by the enrolling clerk, who certifies its correctness.

• Once certified, the bill is signed, first by the Speaker of the House and then by the president of the Senate.

• It is sent to the president of the United States.

• The president approves or disapproves the bill, usually after referring it to the appropriate department for recommendations.

• If the president vetoes the bill, it is returned to the Congress. If it fails to pass by a two-thirds vote, no further action is taken.

• If the bill has either been approved by the president or passed over a veto, it is filed with the secretary of state and then becomes law.

Such a brief summary cannot possibly convey the intrigue, the drama, and the behind-the-scenes maneuvering by members, their staffs, and lobbyists involved in the legislative process. Often the stakes are high and the battles hard fought.

The Executive Branch

The White House is at 1600 Pennsylvania Avenue NW, the most prestigious address in the country. However, its first occupant, Abigail Adams, was disappointed in the damp, drafty "President's Palace." She complained that it had "not a single apartment finished" and "not the least fence, yard, or other convenience without." On the other hand, Thomas Jefferson found the house "big enough for two emperors, one Pope, and the grand lama"— and still unfinished.

When Franklin Delano Roosevelt became president in 1932, the entire White House staff consisted of fewer than 50 people. Today, approximately 1,800 people work for the executive office of the president. They are crammed into offices in the east and west wings of the White House and in the ornate Executive Office Building (formerly the State, War, and Navy Building), adjacent to the White House to the west on Pennsylvania Avenue.

The president's annual salary is $200,000; the vice president receives $160,600. They are elected for a four-year term. If the president dies or becomes incapacitated, the vice president is next in line of succession. He is followed, in order, by the Speaker of the House of Representatives, the president pro tempore of the Senate, the secretaries of state, treasury, and defense, the attorney general, the postmaster general, and the secretaries of the interior, agriculture, commerce, labor, health and human services, housing and urban development, transportation, energy, education, and veterans affairs.

The Judicial Branch

Traditionally, the opening session of the Supreme Court, on the first Monday in October, marks the beginning of Washington's social season, and the quadrennial inaugural festivities add to the excitement. The inaugural week in January usually includes a star-studded gala, as well as receptions honoring the new president, vice president, and their spouses.

The Supreme Court meets from October through June in a Corinthian-column white-marble building at First Street and Maryland Avenue NE. Until 1935, the justices used various rooms in the Capitol. For a while, in the 19th century, they met in taverns and boardinghouses. You can see the Old Supreme Court Chamber on the ground floor of the Capitol.

Approximately 5,000 cases are submitted for appeal each year, and the justices choose about 3%—roughly 160 cases in all—those which raise constitutional questions or affect the life or liberty of citizens.

Justice Felix Frankfurter said, "The words of the Constitution are so unrestricted by their intrinsic meaning or by their history or by tradition or by prior decisions that they leave the individual Justice free, if indeed they do not compel him, to gather meaning not from reading the Constitution but from reading life."

In the courtroom, the nine black-robed justices are seated in high-back black leather chairs in front of heavy red velvet draperies. Lawyers for each side present their oral arguments, with the justices often interjecting questions or comments. Generally, the court sits for two weeks and then recesses for two weeks to do research and write opinions.

They are on the bench Monday, Tuesday, and Wednesday from 10 AM to noon and from 1 to 3 PM from October through April and they usually hear about four cases a day. During this first part of the term, the justices meet privately every Wednesday afternoon and all day Friday to discuss the cases they have heard that week and to take a preliminary vote on decisions.

The chief justice assigns different members to write the opinions. If the chief justice is on the minority side in a particular case, however, the senior justice in the majority assigns the opinion. Any justice may write his or her own opinion, agreeing or disagreeing with the majority. During the remainder of the term, in May and June, the justices usually meet every Thursday to decide on releasing their opinions.

Monday is "Decision Day," probably the most interesting time to visit the Supreme Court. That is when the justices announce their decisions and read their opinions.

Throughout the year, in the courtroom, staff members give a brief lecture about the court Monday through Friday, every hour on the half-hour from 9:30 AM to 3:30 PM. Lectures are not given on holidays or when the justices are on the bench hearing cases.

Supreme Court justices are appointed by the president with the advice and consent of the Senate. They serve for life or, as the Constitution says, "during good behavior."

Associate justices receive $161,100 per year; the chief justice's salary is $171,500.

After 10 years of service, justices may resign or retire with full pay.

Lobbyists

Virtually every special-interest group in the country, as well as a sprinkling of foreign governments, is represented by someone who "lobbies" for its cause in Washington. Lobbyists frequently conduct their business over luncheons, cocktails, and dinners, as well as on the golf courses or tennis courts of suburban country clubs.

Lobbyists' backgrounds are as diverse as the causes they represent. They are usually lawyers, public relations executives, or former congressional staff members. Many were once members of Congress or high government officials from all over the United States who have developed "Potomac fever"; that is, they do not return home but find being a Washington representative the ideal way to continue to influence public policy.

Sometimes, it appears that every group is well represented here except the average citizen. Under those circumstances, if you have a pet project, discuss it with your senator or member of Congress—he or she is your lobbyist. In doing so—like Washington's highly skilled and well-paid lobbyists—you would simply be exercising your First Amendment rights to express your beliefs and influence your government.

MORE PORTRAITS

Classic Washington novels include *Democracy,* by Henry Adams, and Gore Vidal's *Washington, D.C.* Edward P. Jones's critically acclaimed *Lost in the City* is a collection of short stories about black Washingtonians. Margaret Leach's *Reveille in Washington* re-creates the city during the Civil War; E. J. Applewhite comments on the architecture of the city in *Washington Itself;* Louis A. Halle's *Springtime in Washington* is the definitive look at the flora and fauna of the capital; and in *Ear on Washington,* gossip columnist Diana McClellan recounts some of the town's juicier stories. *Literary Washington,* by David Cutler, explores past and contemporary writers who have lived in and written about the city. Sites and stories relating to the capital's African-American history are presented in *The Guide to Black Washington,* by Sandra Fitzpatrick and Maria R. Goodwin. Characters in Margaret Truman's mysteries have been found murdered everywhere from the Smithsonian to the Supreme Court.

For detailed, full-color maps of Washington, D.C., and its surroundings, pick up Fodor's *Flashmaps.* A more selective listing of attractions, dining, and lodging can be found in Fodor's slimmer, smaller, *Pocket Washington, D.C.*

For some reason, movies about Washington always seem to be about power and/or corruption. In the Frank Capra classic, *Mr. Smith Goes to Washington,* Jefferson Smith (Jimmy Stewart) is chosen to replace a recently deceased senator. He goes to Washington, naively thinking he is going there to work for the good of the people, but soon learns that those who appointed him have their own motives. The film version of *All the President's Men* (based on the book by the same title), starring Robert Redford and Dustin Hoffman, is the story of two *Washington Post* reporters, Bob Woodward and Carl Bernstein, whose investigation into the break-in at the Democratic National Committee's office in the Watergate Hotel led to the resignation of President Richard M. Nixon. When Henry Fonda is named Secretary of State, his Communist past threatens his confirmation in the film *Advise and Consent,* based on the book by Allen Drury. In *Seven Days in May,* a hawkish general (Burt Lancaster) plots to overthrow the president (Frederic March). One of the general's aides (Kirk Douglas) learns of the plot and saves both the day and democracy.

Born Yesterday was first made in 1950, with Broderick Crawford as a corrupt junk tycoon who comes to Washington with his unsophisticated girlfriend (a performance that won Judy Holliday the Academy Award) to create a scrap iron cartel. Reporter William Holden is hired to educate her. When she discovers that Crawford is using her, Holliday turns the tables. The film was remade in 1993 with John Goodman, Melanie Griffith, and Don Johnson.

Other recent movies set (at least partially) in Washington include: *No Way Out,* the story of a secretary of defense (Gene Hackman) who tries to shift the blame of a murder to an alleged Soviet spy (Kevin Costner); the comedy *Dave,* which stars Kevin Kline as a presidential look-alike who is asked to fill in for the president during social functions, but ends up taking on all his duties; *In the Line of Fire,* starring Clint Eastwood as a secret service agent assigned to protect the president against psycho stalker John Malkovich; and *Patriot Games,* with Harrison Ford as an upstanding intelligence officer who learns of an illicit war on drugs.

INDEX

NOTES

NOTES

NOTES

NOTES

NOTES

Escape to ancient cities and

journey to  *exotic islands with*

CNN *Travel Guide, a wealth of valuable advice. Host*

Valerie Voss will take you to

all of your favorite destinations,

including those off the beaten

path. Tune-in to your passport to the world.

CNN TRAVEL GUIDE
SATURDAY 12:30 PMet   SUNDAY 4:30 PMet

Your guide to a picture-perfect vacation

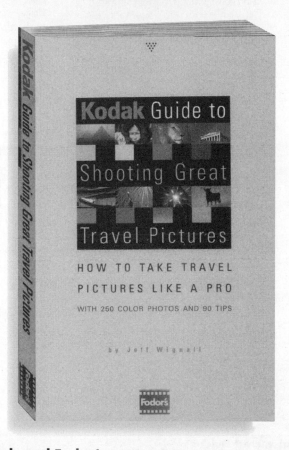

Kodak and Fodor's join together to create the guide that travelers everywhere have been asking for—one that covers the terms and techniques, the equipment and etiquette for taking first-rate travel photographs.

The most authoritative and up-to-date book of its kind, **The Kodak Guide to Shooting Great Travel Pictures** includes over 200 color photographs and spreads on 100 points of photography important to travelers, such as landscape basics, under sea shots, wildlife, city street, close-ups, photographing in museums and more.

$16.50 ($22.95 Canada)

At bookstores everywhere, or call 1-800-533-6478.

Fodor's. The name that means smart travel.™

Fodor's Travel Publications

Available at bookstores everywhere, or call 1–800–533–6478, 24 hours a day.

Gold Guides

U.S.

Alaska

Arizona

Boston

California

Cape Cod, Martha's
Vineyard, Nantucket

The Carolinas & the
Georgia Coast

Chicago

Colorado

Florida

Hawaii

Las Vegas, Reno,
Tahoe

Los Angeles

Maine, Vermont,
New Hampshire

Maui

Miami & the Keys

New England

New Orleans

New York City

Pacific North Coast

Philadelphia & the
Pennsylvania Dutch
Country

The Rockies

San Diego

San Francisco

Santa Fe, Taos,
Albuquerque

Seattle & Vancouver

The South

U.S. & British Virgin
Islands

USA

Virginia & Maryland

Waikiki

Washington, D.C.

Foreign

Australia &
New Zealand

Austria

The Bahamas

Bermuda

Budapest

Canada

Cancún, Cozumel,
Yucatán Peninsula

Caribbean

China

Costa Rica, Belize,
Guatemala

The Czech Republic
& Slovakia

Eastern Europe

Egypt

Europe

Florence, Tuscany
& Umbria

France

Germany

Great Britain

Greece

Hong Kong

India

Ireland

Israel

Italy

Japan

Kenya & Tanzania

Korea

London

Madrid & Barcelona

Mexico

Montréal &
Québec City

Moscow, St.
Petersburg, Kiev

The Netherlands,
Belgium &
Luxembourg

New Zealand

Norway

Nova Scotia, New
Brunswick, Prince
Edward Island

Paris

Portugal

Provence &
the Riviera

Scandinavia

Scotland

Singapore

South America

Southeast Asia

Spain

Sweden

Switzerland

Thailand

Tokyo

Toronto

Turkey

Vienna & the Danube

Fodor's Special-Interest Guides

Branson

Caribbean Ports
of Call

The Complete Guide
to America's
National Parks

Condé Nast Traveler
Caribbean Resort and
Cruise Ship Finder

Cruises and Ports
of Call

Fodor's London
Companion

France by Train

Halliday's New
England Food
Explorer

Healthy Escapes

Italy by Train

Kodak Guide to
Shooting Great
Travel Pictures

Shadow Traffic's
New York Shortcuts
and Traffic Tips

Sunday in New York

Sunday in
San Francisco

Walt Disney World,
Universal Studios
and Orlando

Walt Disney World
for Adults

Where Should We
Take the Kids?
California

Where Should We
Take the Kids?
Northeast

Special Series

Affordables
Caribbean
Europe
Florida
France
Germany
Great Britain
Italy
London
Paris

Fodor's Bed & Breakfasts and Country Inns
America's Best B&Bs
California's Best B&Bs
Canada's Great Country Inns
Cottages, B&Bs and Country Inns of England and Wales
The Mid-Atlantic's Best B&Bs
New England's Best B&Bs
The Pacific Northwest's Best B&Bs
The South's Best B&Bs
The Southwest's Best B&Bs
The Upper Great Lakes' Best B&Bs

The Berkeley Guides
California
Central America
Eastern Europe
Europe
France
Germany & Austria
Great Britain & Ireland
Italy
London
Mexico

Pacific Northwest & Alaska
Paris
San Francisco

Compass American Guides
Arizona
Chicago
Colorado
Hawaii
Hollywood
Las Vegas
Maine
Manhattan
Montana
New Mexico
New Orleans
Oregon
San Francisco
South Carolina
South Dakota
Texas
Utah
Virginia
Washington
Wine Country
Wisconsin
Wyoming

Fodor's Español
California
Caribe Occidental
Caribe Oriental
Gran Bretaña
Londres
Mexico
Nueva York
Paris

Fodor's Exploring Guides
Australia
Boston & New England
Britain

California
Caribbean
China
Florence & Tuscany
Florida
France
Germany
Ireland
Italy
London
Mexico
Moscow & St. Petersburg
New York City
Paris
Prague
Provence
Rome
San Francisco
Scotland
Singapore & Malaysia
Spain
Thailand
Turkey
Venice

Fodor's Flashmaps
Boston
New York
San Francisco
Washington, D.C.

Fodor's Pocket Guides
Acapulco
Atlanta
Barbados
Jamaica
London
New York City
Paris
Prague
Puerto Rico

Rome
San Francisco
Washington, D.C.

Rivages Guides
Bed and Breakfasts of Character and Charm in France
Hotels and Country Inns of Character and Charm in France
Hotels and Country Inns of Character and Charm in Italy

Short Escapes
Country Getaways in Britain
Country Getaways in France
Country Getaways Near New York City

Fodor's Sports
Golf Digest's Best Places to Play
Skiing USA
USA Today The Complete Four Sport Stadium Guide

Fodor's Vacation Planners
Great American Learning Vacations
Great American Sports & Adventure Vacations
Great American Vacations
National Parks and Seashores of the East
National Parks of the West

Before Catching Your Flight, Catch Up With Your World.

Fueled by the global resources of CNN and available in major airports across America, CNN Airport Network provides a live source  of current domestic and international news, sports, business, weather and lifestyle programming. Plus two daily Fodor's features for the facts you need: "Travel Fact," a useful and creative mix of travel trivia; and "What's Happening," a comprehensive round-up of upcoming events in major cities around the world.

With CNN Airport Network, you'll never be out of the loop.

HERE'S YOUR OWN PERSONAL VIEW OF THE WORLD.

Here's the easiest way to get up-to-the-minute, objective, personalized information about what's going on in the city you'll be visiting—before you leave on your trip! Unique information you could get only if you knew someone personally in each of 160 destinations around the world.

Everything from special places to dine to local events only a local would know about.

It's all yours—in your Travel Update from Worldview, the leading provider of time-sensitive destination information.

Review the following order form and fill it out by indicating your destination(s) and travel dates and by checking off up to eight interest categories. Then mail or fax your order form to us, or call your order in. (We're here to help you 24 hours a day.)

Within 48 hours of receiving your order, we'll mail your convenient, pocket-sized custom guide to you, packed with information to make your travel more fun and interesting. And if you're in a hurry, we can even fax it.

Have a great trip with your Fodor's Worldview Travel Update!

Fodor's WORLDVIEW TRAVEL UPDATE

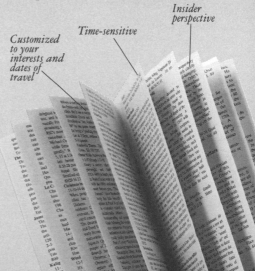

Insider perspective

Time-sensitive

Customized to your interests and dates of travel

DESTINATIONS

Worldview covers more than 160 destinations worldwide. Choose the destination(s) that match your itinerary from the list below:

Europe
Amsterdam
Athens
Barcelona
Berlin
Brussels
Budapest
Copenhagen
Dublin
Edinburgh
Florence
Frankfurt
French Riviera
Geneva
Glasgow
Lausanne
Lisbon
London
Madrid
Milan
Moscow
Munich
Oslo
Paris
Prague
Provence
Rome
Salzburg
Seville
St. Petersburg
Stockholm
Venice
Vienna
Zurich

United States (Mainland)
Albuquerque
Atlanta
Atlantic City
Baltimore
Boston
Branson, MO
Charleston, SC
Chicago
Cincinnati
Cleveland
Dallas/Ft. Worth
Denver
Detroit
Houston
Indianapolis
Kansas City
Las Vegas
Los Angeles
Memphis
Miami
Milwaukee
Minneapolis/St. Paul
Nashville
New Orleans
New York City
Orlando
Palm Springs
Philadelphia
Phoenix
Pittsburgh
Portland
Reno/Lake Tahoe
St. Louis
Salt Lake City
San Antonio
San Diego
San Francisco
Santa Fe
Seattle
Tampa
Washington, DC

Alaska
Alaskan Destinations

Hawaii
Honolulu
Island of Hawaii
Kauai
Maui

Canada
Quebec City
Montreal
Ottawa
Toronto
Vancouver

Bahamas
Abaco
Eleuthera/
  Harbour Island
Exuma
Freeport
Nassau &
  Paradise Island

Bermuda
Bermuda Countryside
Hamilton

British Leeward Islands
Anguilla
Antigua & Barbuda
St. Kitts & Nevis

British Virgin Islands
Tortola & Virgin
  Gorda

British Windward Islands
Barbados
Dominica
Grenada
St. Lucia
St. Vincent
Trinidad & Tobago

Cayman Islands
The Caymans

Dominican Republic
Santo Domingo

Dutch Leeward Islands
Aruba
Bonaire
Curacao

Dutch Windward Island
St. Maarten/St. Martin

French West Indies
Guadeloupe
Martinique
St. Barthelemy

Jamaica
Kingston
Montego Bay
Negril
Ocho Rios

Puerto Rico
Ponce
San Juan

Turks & Caicos
Grand Turk/
  Providenciales

U.S. Virgin Islands
St. Croix
St. John
St. Thomas

Mexico
Acapulco
Cancun & Isla Mujeres
Cozumel
Guadalajara
Ixtapa & Zihuatanejo
Los Cabos
Mazatlan
Mexico City
Monterrey
Oaxaca
Puerto Vallarta

South/Central America
Buenos Aires
Caracas
Rio de Janeiro
San Jose, Costa Rica
Sao Paulo

Middle East
Istanbul
Jerusalem

Australia & New Zealand
Auckland
Melbourne
South Island
Sydney

China
Beijing
Guangzhou
Shanghai

Japan
Kyoto
Nagoya
Osaka
Tokyo
Yokohama

Pacific Rim/Other
Bali
Bangkok
Hong Kong & Macau
Manila
Seoul
Singapore
Taipei

Name

Address

City	State	Country	ZIP

Tel # ( ) - Fax # ( ) -

Title of this Fodor's guide:

Store and location where guide was purchased:

INDICATE YOUR DESTINATIONS/DATES: You can order up to three (3) destinations from the previous page. Fill in your arrival and departure dates for each destination. **Your Travel Update itinerary (all destinations selected) cannot exceed 30 days from beginning to end.**

		Month	Day	Month	Day
(Sample)	**LONDON**	From: 6 / 21 To: 6 / 30
1		From: / To: /
2		From: / To: /
3		From: / To: /

CHOOSE YOUR INTERESTS: Select up to eight (8) categories from the list of interest categories shown on the previous page and circle the numbers below:

1 2 3 4 5 6 7 8 9 10 11 12 13 14 15 16 17 18 19 20 21

CHOOSE WHEN YOU WANT YOUR TRAVEL UPDATE DELIVERED (check one):
❑ Please send my Travel Update immediately.
❑ Please hold my order until a few weeks before my trip to include the most up-to-date information.
Completed orders will be sent within 48 hours. Allow 7–10 days for U.S. mail delivery.

ADD UP YOUR ORDER HERE. SPECIAL OFFER FOR FODOR'S PURCHASERS ONLY!

	Suggested Retail Price	Your Price	This Order
First destination ordered	$ 9.95	$ 7.95	$ 7.95
Second destination (if applicable)	$ 6.95	$ 4.95	+
Third destination (if applicable)	$ 6.95	$ 4.95	+

DELIVERY CHARGE (Check one and enter amount below)

	Within U.S. & Canada	Outside U.S. & Canada
First Class Mail	❑ $2.50	❑ $5.00
FAX	❑ $5.00	❑ $10.00
Priority Delivery	❑ $15.00	❑ $27.00

ENTER DELIVERY CHARGE FROM ABOVE: +

TOTAL: $

METHOD OF PAYMENT IN U.S. FUNDS ONLY (Check one):
❑ AmEx ❑ MC ❑ Visa ❑ Discover ❑ Personal Check (U.S. & Canada only)
❑ Money Order/International Money Order

Make check or money order payable to: Fodor's Worldview Travel Update

Credit Card ❑ / / / / / / / / / / / / / / / / Expiration Date: / /

Authorized Signature

SEND THIS COMPLETED FORM WITH PAYMENT TO:
Fodor's Worldview Travel Update, 114 Sansome Street, Suite 700,
San Francisco, CA 94104

OR CALL OR FAX US 24-HOURS A DAY
Telephone **1-800-799-9609** • Fax **1-800-799-9619** (From within the U.S. & Canada)
(Outside the U.S. & Canada: Telephone 415-616-9988 • Fax 415-616-9989)

(Please have this guide in front of you when you call so we can verify purchase.)

Code: FTG   Offer valid until 12/31/97

INTERESTS

For your personalized Travel Update, choose the eight (8) categories you're most interested in from the following list:

1.	**Business Services**	Fax & Overnight Mail, Computer Rentals, Protocol, Secretarial, Messenger, Translation Services

Dining

2.	**All-Day Dining**	Breakfast & Brunch, Cafes & Tea Rooms, Late-Night Dining
3.	**Local Cuisine**	Every Price Range—from Budget Restaurants to the Special Splurge
4.	**European Cuisine**	Continental, French, Italian
5.	**Asian Cuisine**	Chinese, Far Eastern, Japanese, Other
6.	**Americas Cuisine**	American, Mexican & Latin
7.	**Nightlife**	Bars, Dance Clubs, Casinos, Comedy Clubs, Ethnic, Pubs & Beer Halls
8.	**Entertainment**	Theater – Comedy, Drama, Musicals, Dance, Ticket Agencies
9.	**Music**	Classical, Opera, Traditional & Ethnic, Jazz & Blues, Pop, Rock
10.	**Children's Activities**	Events, Attractions
11.	**Tours**	Local Tours, Day Trips, Overnight Excursions
12.	**Exhibitions, Festivals & Shows**	Antiques & Flower, History & Cultural, Art Exhibitions, Fairs & Craft Shows, Music & Art Festivals
13.	**Shopping**	Districts & Malls, Markets, Regional Specialties
14.	**Fitness**	Bicycling, Health Clubs, Hiking, Jogging
15.	**Recreational Sports**	Boating/Sailing, Fishing, Golf, Skiing, Snorkeling/Scuba, Tennis/Racket
16.	**Spectator Sports**	Auto Racing, Baseball, Basketball, Golf, Football, Horse Racing, Ice Hockey, Soccer
17.	**Event Highlights**	The best of what's happening during the dates of your trip.
18.	**Sightseeing**	Sights, Buildings, Monuments
19.	**Museums**	Art, Cultural
20.	**Transportation**	Taxis, Car Rentals, Airports, Public Transportation
21.	**General Info**	Overview, Holidays, Currency, Tourist Info

Please note that content will vary by season, destination, and length of stay.